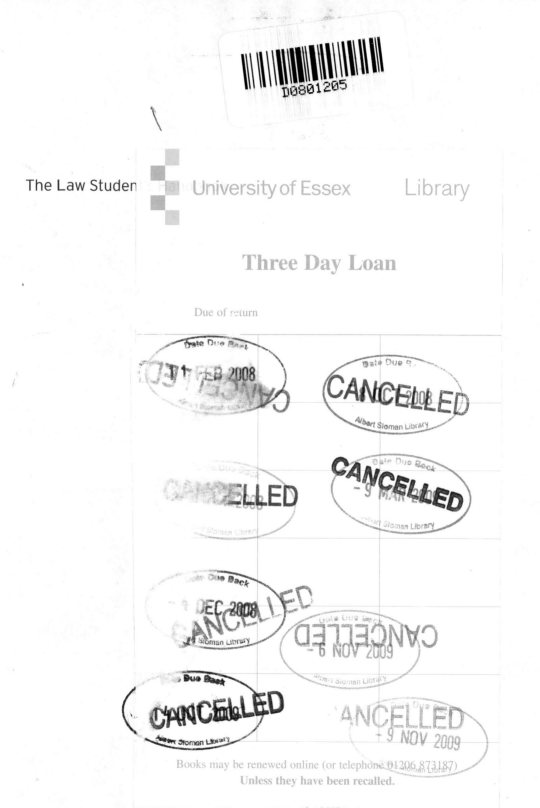

The Law Student's
Handbook

Steve Wilson and Phillip Kenny

OXFORD
UNIVERSITY PRESS

OXFORD

UNIVERSITY PRESS

Great Clarendon Street, Oxford OX2 6DP

Oxford University Press is a department of the University of Oxford.
It furthers the University's objective of excellence in research, scholarship,
and education by publishing worldwide in

Oxford New York

Auckland Cape Town Dar es Salaam Hong Kong Karachi
Kuala Lumpur Madrid Melbourne Mexico City Nairobi
New Delhi Shanghai Taipei Toronto

With offices in

Argentina Austria Brazil Chile Czech Republic France Greece
Guatemala Hungary Italy Japan Poland Portugal Singapore
South Korea Switzerland Thailand Turkey Ukraine Vietnam

Oxford is a registered trade mark of Oxford University Press
in the UK and in certain other countries

Published in the United States
by Oxford University Press Inc., New York

British Library Cataloguing in Publication Data

Data available

Library of Congress Cataloging in Publication Data

Data available

Typeset by Newgen Imaging Systems (P) Limited, Chennai, India
Printed in Great Britain
on acid-free paper by
Ashford Colour Press Limited, Gosport, Hampshire

ISBN 978-0-19-921271-2

10 9 8 7 6 5 4 3 2 1

Preface

In the last twenty years the teaching of law in England and Wales has been the subject of great change. In the 1980s, when the forerunner to this book was first published, law students were expected to spend a considerable amount of time in a law library. When new laws were made by Parliament or new cases reported it would be weeks before they appeared in the library. With the advent of the Internet less time is needed in the library, but correspondingly more time needs to be spent in front of a PC. Laws are easier to find in this virtual world and an Internet connection at home means that you have a law library at your fingertips. Laws may now become available within hours, sometimes minutes, of their making. For example, on the Parliament website it is indicated that the opinions of the Law Lords in a case before the House of Lords, domestically the highest court in the land, will be published on the afternoon that a judgment is given. The last two decades have also seen a move away from the traditional form of teaching law, that is an exposition of the law in a series of lectures followed by the development and exploration of ideas in seminars and tutorials. In today's law schools the teaching of specific legal skills, such as advocacy and drafting of documents, the use of role play and the development of clinical legal education, which allows students to experience advising on a 'live' case, are to be found. Another significant development for students is to be seen in the change to the methods of assessment. The three-hour unseen written examination paper, while still used in some subjects, has been replaced by many other forms of assessment, for example: supervised coursework and open book examinations, which permit the use of materials during the assessment; multiple choice questions; oral presentations; and videoed advocacy exercises. As the amount and type of assessment has developed so has the guidance as to what is expected of students.

To these changes may be added that the body of English law continues to grow at a pace that makes it impossible to be expert in more than a handful of areas of law. Indeed, at the time of writing in November 2006, Parliament has just passed the longest Act of Parliament, the Companies Act 2006 that runs to 1300 sections and additionally contains sixteen schedules. Alongside the amount of law, the complexity of the law has also increased, particularly in the light of the UK's membership of the European Union and the pervasive effect of the Human Rights Act 1998.

The above developments have had an impact not only on how law is to be accessed and used but also upon how lawyers are organised and in the future will work. The legal world is fast-changing and in many ways it is difficult to predict where the changes might lead. Students must be equipped to deal with change.

More is expected of the law student of today than ever before. Not only must the student be able to find their way around a physical law library, but they must also be able to navigate about a virtual law library. A range of skills must be developed, such as research, legal analysis, negotiation, drafting and advocacy among others. These skills must be supplemented by a range of other general skills, such as computer use.

There is a constant, however: that is in order to be lawyer there is a need to develop an ability to use legal source materials and to be able to express yourself effectively in oral and in written form. Above all there is a requirement to read. The methods of accessing law may have changed but this essential requirement remains the same.

The purpose of this book to introduce you to the key features of the law, the legal system, sources of law, finding law and careers in law. None of the chapters are exhaustive of the matters or issues raised. The intention behind the companion Online Resource Centre is to direct you to further sources of information. There is a second purpose to the Handbook, and that is to explore the study skills necessary for success in law. These relate primarily to the preparation and presentation of written work and factors to be taken into account in completing other assessment tasks. It does not purport to be a complete guide but it is an introduction to many of the matters that will concern you during the first year of your legal studies and beyond. The book also seeks to give an explanation and illustration of the mechanics of learning and assessment that a tutor might assume you already know.

In the preparation of this book we have benefited from the helpful comments and assistance of our colleagues, especially Andrea O'Cain, Philip Judd, Alan Davenport, Ralph Tiernan, Jan Cookson and Debbie Rook. We also found the remarks of the anonymous reviewers very useful and have acted upon these at the appropriate points; and thanks go to them. Finally, particular thanks go to Rachael Willis for her assistance but most of all for her patience, which, on occasions, must have been sorely tested during the preparation of the Handbook!

Steve Wilson
Phillip Kenny
November 2006

Contents

Detailed Contents

Acknowledgements

Appendix 1 is reproduced by permission of Reed Elsevier (UK) Limited trading as LexisNexis Butterworths. Crown Copyright material is reproduced with the permission of the Controller of HMSO and the Queen's Printer for Scotland.

Guide to the book

The *Law Student's Handbook* is a practical guide to the study of law and to the opportunities and issues which are particular to law students. It focuses on helping you to develop the skills required to study law, and to get the most out of your studies.

There are numerous features throughout the text which are designed to illustrate these skills, and to help reinforce your understanding and appreciation of what is involved in studying for a law degree.

---

w Reports,

rts of the
es, are as
nd Wales.
ant cases
ports are
es a year.
House of
a's Bench
w Reports
es in the
found in
red to be
the *Law*

> **HINT** →
> The *Law Reports* are the most authoritative versions of cases and should be used in preference to other versions of the cases.

Hint boxes

These are signposts to the most important pieces of advice that you need to consider when studying and planning for your future career, for example, answering examination questions, preparing coursework, or applying for a training contract.

---

learned
Hyde, a

> **KEY POINT** ●
> Mooting is a valuable experience in terms of developing your research and presentational skills. Again, involvement in such a practical activity will be an important feature of an application for employment.

Students
sound arg
worthwhi
oral prese
experienc
trying tho
searing e
Generatic
gained gr

Mock tr

Key point boxes

These boxes highlight the really essential points that you should consider very carefully, and ensure that you fully understand and appreciate before moving on to the next topic.

Examples

The examples provide illustrations of the advice given in the text. They will help to place the information and advice in a practical context, allowing you to apply the information effectively to your own studies.

Diagrams

It is often easier to process information in a visual way, rather than through a lengthy textual description. There are several diagrams throughout the text illustrating the structures or processes of the legal system and routes to qualification in a clear visual format.

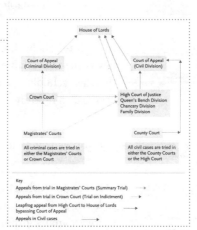

Checklists

Each chapter concludes with a checklist. These are designed to aid your understanding and revision by condensing practical information or considerations discussed in each chapter, and to highlight the key ideas to take away from each topic.

Guide to the Online Resource Centre

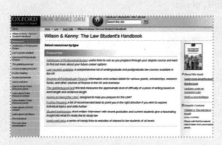

This book is accompanied by an Online Resource Centre, which can be found at www.oxfordtextbooks.co.uk/orc/wilson_kenny. The resources are all available completely free of charge, and the site provides additional information and advice to support the topics covered in the book, and will be a useful reference source throughout your law degree.

Law courses available

A comprehensive list of undergraduate and postgraduate law courses available in the UK, which includes links to the law schools on many university websites for easy access and reference.

The gobbledygook test

Many people think that to be a successful lawyer you have to learn to communicate in technical legal jargon. While there are many important legal terms that you will need to understand, a successful law student is one who has learnt to express complex ideas and concepts in a clear and straightforward way.

Reproduced from the Plain English Campaign material, this test measures the approximate level of difficulty of a piece of writing based on word length and sentence length. You can get an idea of how clear your writing is, as well as testing the clarity of your textbooks!

Addresses of professional bodies

This is a useful source of up-to-date contact details for the Bar Council, the Law Society, the Institute of legal Executives, and various chartered institutes. These will be useful links to use as you progress through your degree course and want to find out more about your future career options.

Sources of postgraduate finance

This list provides easy access to information and contact details for various grants, scholarships, research funds, and other sources of finance in the UK and overseas, if you are considering undertaking postgraduate legal studies.

Student testimonials

These short written 'interviews' with recent graduates and current students give a fascinating insight into what it's really like to study law. The students explain how they developed their skills, highlight areas of particular difficulty, and provide useful hints and tips for you as you progress through your own studies.

Advice on taking the National Admission Test for Law (LNAT)

As part of the admissions process, some law schools require applicants to complete the National Admissions Test for Law (LNAT). This test comprises a set of multiple-choice questions, plus a choice of essay questions. Here the authors offer tips and advice on how best to approach these different elements, to give you the best chance of securing a place in your chosen law school.

Further reading

This is a list of recommended texts to point you in the right direction if you wish to explore individual topics and skills further.

Useful web links

This is a series of handy links to websites of interest to law students of all levels.

Chapter 1

Choosing law

First steps

Law is one of the most popular subjects for undergraduate study. Law degree courses are very many times over-subscribed and the entry standard is quite high. Yet it is very commonly said by law teachers that students choose law with very little idea of the real nature of the years ahead. The whole of this book, although intended to be a companion for those embarked upon their career as law students, contains information, and opinions, which should help the would-be student. The bulk of students intend to qualify as solicitors and a much smaller proportion as barristers. In forming a judgement as to either of these options, the material which follows detailing the system of examinations, training and apprenticeship will be of some value. Perhaps there is some insight to be gained by reading books of a biographical or autobiographical nature about life in 'the profession'. It may be doubted if these often romanticised accounts are of much value for this purpose. Again, whereas the shelves of public libraries are well stocked with texts about successful members of the judiciary there is little to convey the real atmosphere of day-to-day life in solicitors' offices or even at the junior Bar.

There is no substitute for getting into an office or a set of chambers, 'getting stuck in' and seeing 'what is really going on'. There is a willingness both at the Bar and in solicitors' offices to take students on for a short period so that they can have a look at the kind of career in prospect. At the Bar this will be unpaid, and in a solicitors' office, little or no pay can be expected for a summer's placement of this kind. Indeed, it would be surprising if it were otherwise. In both cases, particularly in a solicitor's office, the student may be asked to undertake menial tasks such as making tea for his principal or delivering forms, briefs or correspondence or collecting forms from the law stationer. The prospective lawyer who shrinks from providing this kind of assistance will not make a good colleague. Solicitors, like God, love a cheerful volunteer. It should not be overlooked, either, that this vacation experience may assist greatly in the later obtaining of a training contract in a solicitor's office or pupillage in a barrister's chambers. The experience obtained merits inclusion in your curriculm vitae (cv) and a contact made and maintained may in itself lead to a training contract or pupillage.

As with employment at most levels in the legal profession, there is no clearly-established machinery for providing places for trainee solicitors and self-help is necessary in this area.

If you have family or social contacts in the profession, this will obviously help. But there is no reason why you should not approach firms of solicitors directly and ask if they have temporary vacation work available, explaining your reasons. You will meet with some rebuffs but if you persist you will eventually succeed and may obtain an entry to a firm which eventually leads to a training contract.

In a sense, though, the first thing you need to discover is what it is like to study law – not what it is like to practise law. Although there are no exact statistics, a reasonable guess might be that a quarter or even more of law graduates do not become law practitioners as such.

If you wish to gain some idea of the material which you will read on a law course at college, there are many preliminary works on legal topics which you will find helpful to read.

It is important in doing this to go further than material written at a very general level for laymen – you do wish after all to obtain an insight into the work involved in studying for and obtaining legal qualifications.

It is not easy to give examples of the kind of books which you could read which will both stimulate and test your enthusiasm for legal study. There are some modern introductory descriptive accounts which you will find interesting. Rivlin's *Understanding the Law* is published by the Oxford University Press. It does not set out to do more than give an introductory account of law, the English legal system and its main characters and some examples of cases demonstrating the impact of the law, but it is well written and accessible and worth reading. A book which gives an overview of the legal system of England and Wales, without going into too much detail, is Kate Malleson's *The Legal System*. It looks at themes and tensions and introduces the reader to the main features of the legal system. There is also *Invitation to Law* by AWB Simpson. This, like other works by Simpson, is brilliantly written, is intended to entice people on towards the study of law and is admirably suited to do so. It might lead you on to look at two other works by Simpson, *Cannibalism and English Law* and *A History of the Land Law*. Each of these is written on a very particular area but we think they are of interest to any reader. A more technical account of the basic substance of law is *Understanding the Law* written by Adams and Brownsword and published by Sweet and Maxwell.

Before embarking on the study of law it is helpful to look at one or two of the textbooks which you will be using and see how you find them. It is not suggested for a moment that you will find them an easy read but they should stimulate your interest, make you ask questions and, if

HINT ➡

Undertaking a placement with a lawyer is helpful in deciding whether law is the subject for you.

nothing else, they will give you an idea of the material you will be looking at in your legal studies. The first of these is *Principles of Land Law* by Martin Dixon (Cavendish). This is a very lucid account of a difficult legal subject. It will give you a good feel as to what the drier technical areas of law are like to study but hopefully will not put you off the idea. The other is Treitel *Law of Contract* (Sweet and Maxwell). This is a compendious work of authority on contract law written by one of the masters of analysis of English common law. It will give you some idea of the depth that is involved in study even if it is a first-year subject such as contract. Please do not attempt to read a book such as *Treitel* in its entirety but you might find it well worth dipping into to find one or two passages to get a grasp of what the detailed process of study will become.

By and large, wide preliminary reading is not advised before you embark upon a law course at college. The reading referred to is suggested to help you make up your mind whether you will enjoy the type of study involved in a law course, and not to lay any foundation for the course. Law teachers, whether teaching on a degree course or teaching law as part of another course, assume that the student has no particular knowledge at the start of the course. An uncluttered but critical mind is more important than any preconception as to the subject matter to be studied.

Many newspapers contain daily law reports. These are a little mysterious at first to the ordinary reader. However, familiarity will lead to understanding and enjoyment. As you will see, the stuff of English law is in great part the decisions of the law courts – and the daily law reports in the quality newspapers are often the harbingers of momentous legal developments. Similarly, important trials are reported in considerable detail and should be followed. The issues they deal with will often be raised at interviews at a law school. Current debates such as the legal position of persons on permanent medical life-support are not ones on which an interviewer would expect you to be familiar with the last word in legal philosophy. However, some understanding of current affairs with a legal content is important. A would-be lawyer will show an intelligent interest in such topics and be able to engage in healthy debate.

At one time law admissions tutors seemed to view 'A' level law with some suspicion. This is now not generally true. Indeed the benefit from doing this particular 'A' level is to allow the would-be law student an opportunity to test his enthusiasm and aptitude for the subject. To this, a warning should be given. Admission to a law degree does not require prior legal knowledge and so degree teaching starts from an assumption that all first year students possess no legal knowledge. In consequence, the subject matter of an 'A' level may overlap with some of the subjects studied in year 1 of a law degree course. Some students may be tempted to rest on their laurels, particularly in relation to familiar areas,

HINT →
Read generally about the law and legal systems. This will give you a flavour of the subject.

HINT →
Being aware of current legal developments is not only useful in deciding whether law is the right subject for you, but also of use when trying to impress at interview.

and thereby fail to appreciate the change in emphasis or the nuances of degree study.

It should be added that there are differences between what is expected of you at 'A' level and what is expected at first year degree level and also between the teaching you will experience at each level. On a degree you are expected to rely less upon your tutors and more upon your own efforts to find and interpret the primary sources of law – cases and legislation. The aim of degree education is to produce independent learners. In the main, study at 'A' level will be less reliant on consulting the primary sources of law and more so on the tutor and textbooks. The resources of colleges and schools may not stretch to providing a full law library so the opportunities for research will, in consequence, be limited.

Having said that, the material covered in an 'A' level syllabus may be the same, at least in part, as material in a degree level syllabus. For example, similar crimes may studied in a Crime syllabus both at 'A' and degree level. In terms of an experience what you might also discover is, as more time is available at 'A' level, that there is more teaching than self-study and greater opportunities exist for repetition and reinforcement than at degree level. The difference between the two levels of study does not reside necessarily in the material studied; this as has been seen could be the same, but in the expectation on a degree programme that students having been told what to do will be able to act on their own initiative in completing the task set. It is important to understand from the first weeks of your degree course what the expectations are of you. These expectations will inform your method of working and also give guidance as to the amount of work you will need to do.

Choosing a college

There are now around 100 universities and other colleges where students are able to take a first degree in law. Some of these degrees are called Bachelor of Laws (LLB) and some are called Bachelor of Arts (BA). No difference between the content or the quality of these degrees is indicated by the different title. In addition to the straight law degree there is now a wide range of opportunities to study law together with other subjects – social science, languages or business studies. It is not proposed to give any guidance on how to choose between individual colleges and their styles of degree. Opinions will differ and no one person's advice could suit the tastes of widely differing students. In terms of passing professional examinations later, there is probably some slight advantage in selecting a straight law degree. But, the opportunity of studying some other much-liked discipline perhaps for the only time in one's life should not be discarded lightly. The Online Resource Centre of this book lists the current providers of law degrees.

Readers should note in looking at this two things – first, that the list will of necessity in a short compass be incomplete as new courses are developed from time to time and, second, the contents and standing of individual courses will vary also.

Advice that can usefully be given is to take the process of selection seriously. In researching both courses and universities you should take into account the following advice:

(i) Obtain prospectuses – study them carefully – do they tell you anything about the quality of the educational experience you can expect? Additionally a wealth of material may be obtained via the Internet. University websites contain information on both courses and the university itself.

(ii) Compare syllabuses – are they developing? – are contemporary issues given reasonable but not undue prominence?

(iii) Take the opportunity to visit one or two colleges. Ask by letter for an appointment with a relevant member of staff – course leader, tutor, or whoever. Try to evaluate the reception you are given and work out how it reflects upon the institution. You may like to ask about teaching facilities and what support is available for students in their studies.

> **HINT** →
> If possible, visit your preferred universities.

(iv) With the introduction of student fees, universities must offer bursaries to students. The amount of the bursary may differ from course to course so it is important to approach individual universities to discover the level of award.

(v) Beyond the course, what is offered in terms of facilities and what would it be like to study and live in the city or town where the university is located?

In the last resort, as you will be aware, entry is very competitive and no student has an unrestricted choice. But, the more you inform yourself on this process of matching your aspirations to an available place, the more you will improve your chances of ultimate success.

The variety of law degrees available

Some students often choose their college for reasons unconnected with the content of the particular course in mind. Nevertheless, there are quite substantial differences between some of the main kinds of course on offer and a general description of them will be attempted. Do not, however, read this part of the text as a 'good course guide' – what is intended is a description of the styles of course available, and it is for the

> **KEY POINT** ●
> Consider the variety of degrees available and then decide which degree best suits your purposes.

student to choose between them if the opportunity to do so is available. At the time of writing in 2006, the UCAS website contained reference to 1,533 degree courses which have law in their title. Of the 1,533 courses listed, over 80 universities and colleges offered single honours law degrees.

Four-year law degrees

In England and Wales there are four four-year sandwich degrees in law. One is at Brunel University, two others at Nottingham Trent University and the University of Surrey, where there is also a three-year law degree of the traditional kind. The other is at Bournemouth in Dorset. Each of these degrees include periods where students are placed in some relevant area of legal practice.

The philosophy behind this development in legal education is self-evidently sound. The quality of understanding of law in the classroom is very likely to be much improved where it is complementary to involvement in law in action. The value of the experience is much dependent on the enormous effort which staff expend in finding suitable placements and also on the ungrudging effort students put into making their placements work and performing the tasks which they are given.

The overwhelming drawback of the four existing sandwich degrees is that they last for four years as opposed to the normal three years. The periods spent on placements during these degrees can, at most, be counted towards six months of the two-year training contract required for qualification as a solicitor. It cannot count towards the one-year pupillage required of barristers.

Students wishing to qualify as solicitors must decide whether the 'sandwich' element in the degree is sufficiently attractive to counter-balance the reduction in length of the two-year training contract to eighteen months. There are many solicitors' firms who are not willing to take trainee solicitors for a shorter period than the full two-year training contract.

Four-year 'exempting' law degrees

At the time of writing there is one four-year exempting LLB degree in existence. This is at the Northumbria University. An exempting law degree is one which completes the usual three-year LLB programme but also exempts the student from the requirement to take a Legal Practice Course in order to become a solicitor or where the student may alternatively pursue a programme which provides complete exemption from the Bar Vocational Course. This means that at the end of the degree the graduate is both a law graduate and has passed the vocational examination to become a solicitor or a barrister. Thus, a student completing the four-year LLB at the Northumbria University in

Newcastle has no further examinations to take before entering a training contract to qualify as a solicitor or being called as a barrister. Students at Northumbria University may alternatively choose to complete a traditional three-year degree.

The exempting degree is described further below. It combines the learning of academic law with the development of legal skills such as drafting and advocacy. It includes participation in work with real clients in a law office run as part of the Law School. Because this approach to law is so clearly advantageous many law schools are preparing to follow in Northumbria's footsteps when they are able to do so.

The traditional three-year law degree

Of the 80 or so single honours degrees in law available the preponderance are overwhelmingly *traditional* in style. It is not easy before your law studies commence to describe exactly what this means – although it will be quite clear to those who have experienced legal education.

The traditional pattern of a law degree involves studying law for all, or nearly all, of each of the three years. Subjects comprise 'proper' law subjects as opposed to complementary subjects such as economics, social science or philosophy. Even the most undiluted degrees will usually contain at least one subject which does not involve the analysis of legal rules. This is jurisprudence. Jurisprudence, as a subject, involves the study of law from the standpoint of other disciplines – for example, sociology or, more traditionally, philosophy, or perhaps from a historical or anthropological viewpoint. Questions are addressed such as: What is the definition of law? What is meant by a legal obligation? Is there any minimum content to a system of laws? Is civil disobedience ever justifiable? What is the relationship between law and morality?

The remainder of the degree will then consist of a number of subjects, each having as its content one area of law and studied from the standpoint of critical analysis of the pertinent legal rules. This is what most law teachers would describe as the study of law properly so-called.

The advantage of attending a law course following this model is that you learn a great deal of law and you have every opportunity to develop skills of legal analysis. On the whole, and this may strike you as a somewhat philistine approach, graduates from such courses are better equipped to, and do, perform better in professional examinations than their counterparts from the less traditional law schools. Nowadays, the breadth of subjects available to students and the opportunity for students to study complementary areas has grown in virtually all law schools.

For the very many students who have made up their minds irrevocably to join the profession, they will find congenial numbers of like-minded colleagues on the traditional law degree course and find its contents satisfactory for their purposes.

Non-traditional law degree courses

There are a number (rather small) of three-year law degree courses which have largely eschewed the traditional approach in favour of what is seen by them as a more intellectually stimulating framework of study. The hallmark of this approach is the phrase 'law in context'. An example may clarify. Contract law can be studied as a set of rules – for example: How are contracts made? What formal requirements are there for a valid contract? What are the legal remedies for breach of contract? It may also be studied in other ways, such as: How effective are the legal remedies theoretically available? How are contract disputes disposed of by negotiation and settlement? Yet another approach would be to ask what systems of political and economic thought are reflected in our contract law. How are the functions carried out by contract law in our state carried out in a Marxist economy?

The possibilities of broader approaches to legal study such as those indicated above are enticing. Examples may be found in the syllabuses of Warwick University and Kent University at Canterbury.

You will find it valuable to obtain prospectuses from the contrasting traditional and non-traditional law schools indicated. When you obtain prospectuses from many law schools you will note individual syllabuses with a gradual shift of emphasis towards the 'law in context' approach. Many law schools will now contain syllabuses preponderantly traditional in emphasis, but by no means exclusively so.

It can be said with certainty that the growing heterogeneity of legal study has enriched legal scholarship and helped to develop a much more questioning approach to the law. Most law schools have added new subject areas – welfare law and labour are now commonplace. Housing law, immigration law and the law of discrimination can also be found. In commercial areas, too, there is a healthier diversity of study – maritime law, international contract law, intellectual property law, eg copyright and patent, have each found their niche here and there.

The picture is now fairly diverse and the description of the *traditional and non-traditional* models is easily pilloried as crudely unfair. But it will help give your ideas some focus as your mind numbs following the perusal of many prospectuses. Do not be afraid when you attend for an interview or on an open day to ask searching questions. Is it more important for your undergraduate course to maximise your chances in subsequent professional examinations, or for you to seize the opportunity for more radical study of the legal system?

HINT →
Consider the range of optional subjects available on the various degree programmes. Does the law school specialise in areas of interest to you?

In talking to a very large number of students who are thinking of studying law it is evident how wide is the range of possibilities and how very little the would-be student knows about each. It is recommended that prospective students obtain and read the prospectuses of a large number of colleges before exercising choices. If time and opportunity permit it is worth attending several open-days, especially those where it is possible to meet existing students and chat about the reality of life as a law student.

Mixed degrees

There are very great opportunities now to study law as a part of a degree. If you wish to obtain exemption from the first stage of the solicitor's or barrister's professional qualifications, then it is necessary to study what are called the 'The Foundations of Legal Knowledge': tort; contract; equity and trusts; land law; constitutional and administrative law; European Union law; and criminal law. This, however, leaves potentially half your degree available for non-legal studies.

Even if you are taking a law degree as opposed to a mixed discipline degree, there is very often the opportunity to take one or more non-law options. This may be an important factor in selecting a course. Stimulating subjects for lawyers, such as criminology, sociology and economics, are frequently offered as a small part of a law degree and someone who will spend the remainder of his or her adult life in the practice of law has much to gain in the way of openness of mind from their study. A mixed degree gives an even greater opportunity for the systematic pursuit of some other discipline.

There is a range of colleges where law can be taken as part of a mixed degree. Some of those courses open the door to very interesting law-related careers. There are, for example, many opportunities in European government, and nowadays in private practice, for the lawyer-linguist.

A glance at the Online Resource Centre will show that there are many opportunities to study on mixed degree courses. Recent developments are in accountancy and business areas. Combining these areas with the study of law makes a great deal of sense for the future lawyer. It gives a background to the lawyer's understanding of the business world which should prove most useful.

Two-year law degrees

Buckingham University, which is privately financed, offers a two-year degree in law. The three-year pattern for a degree is not hallowed by reason but simply enshrined in tradition. It may be argued that there is a substantial loss to students in forgoing the steadier intellectual maturation process of a three-year degree. This is largely a matter of intuitive feeling and you can certainly gain a year by taking the two-year degree which is recognised by both the Law Society and the Council of Legal Education.

Other two-year law degrees are coming into existence, for example at Staffordshire University. Such a course may represent a cheaper and quicker method of obtaining a degree.

Completing UCAS applications

The system of allocating places is through the Universities and Colleges Admissions Service (UCAS). UCAS also offers through its website information on courses and universities and colleges. You may select up to six courses. No preferences are permitted. The first step is to ascertain the level of entry requirements for colleges in which you have an interest. There is a small book – *Degree Course Offers* by B Heap – which may be of help. Also of use is the *CRAC Degree Course Guides – Law and Accountancy*. You must have a realistic appreciation of your own abilities. Entry levels to law degree courses at universities are now very varied. Some require a number of grade As; other courses can be very much lower with mixed degrees reaching the level of a mixture of Cs and Ds or even lower. Can a sensible strategy be worked out to maximise your chances of ending up with an offer which you have matched with your own examination performance? It may, for example, make sense to include in your choices a mixed degree which will still enable you to qualify as a lawyer, but has a lower entrance requirement. You may hold two offers until after the examination results have been published in the summer. This is a great advantage to the candidate and the opportunity for security which it gives should not be thrown away. The number of applications for law places are such that in very many years no places will be available in the 'clearing' systems that operate after the 'A' level results for candidates who have failed to meet the grades of their offers. However, the more likely scenario is that there will be places available at some law schools. Rarely will it be sensible to turn down a place at university for the chance of improving your A levels. Work hard on your degree and do well and the whole world of law still lies before you.

Applicants give a very great deal of thought to the information to include about themselves in the application form. Statements explaining why law courses are chosen and showing strong career motivation may be helpful. Details of work experiences in legal areas should also be included. Beyond these rather obvious points the applicant should try to demonstrate a wide range of interesting occupations and achievements – to capture the readers' attention. Bear in mind in doing so that such matters may be subject to gentle probing at an interview. The simple truth though is that the main factor regarded by admissions tutors is examination performance and predicted grades. Nothing on your form tells so much as the achievement produced by sound consistent work.

Before submitting your UCAS form double check that the form is complete and contains no mistakes.

HINT →

Research in the published guides the entry requirements for your preferred universities.

Preparing for an interview

Some law schools invite applicants for interview and some do not. Among those who do use interviews for selection the interviewers' purpose will be very similar. The interviewer will be interested in establishing enthusiasm and commitment and also aptitude for legal study. The student should demonstrate that a definite choice has been made to study law and that this arises from a discovery of relevant information about law and legal careers. Some knowledge about the career(s) in mind and the routes to qualification should be demonstrated. As mentioned above, familiarity with current issues relevant to law in the newspapers should be shown. You will read about, for example, issues such as euthanasia, the operation of the criminal justice system and our constitutional position in Europe. If you are used to debating these topics vigorously with friends, parents and teachers then you will expect to do well in an interview at law school. The interviewer is interested in your general awareness of issues but will not expect detailed or technical knowledge. An ability to reason, to respond to critical argument and to reflect intelligently is what is required.

Some law schools may use a more specific aptitude test.

HINT →

In preparing for interview seek out information on current legal issues.

✖ EXAMPLE

Assume that English criminal law states the following rules:

1 'Murder is the intentional killing without lawful excuse of another person.

2 Manslaughter is the killing by culpable negligence of another person.'

Explain if the following fall within these rules:

(a) Adam shoots a gun at Bertram and misses Bertram but kills Cedric.

(b) Damion believes that God has ordered him to kill his wife Ethel and does so.

(c) Frederick parks his car on a hill and sets the hand-brake so that the car rolls forward while he is away and kills a child crossing the road.

(d) Gertrude who is pregnant is angry with her husband who neglects her. She throws herself downstairs and suffers a miscarriage.

Such a test may be given to you by way of questions in an interview or in writing as an addition to the interview. The first guidance is do not be flummoxed into rushing into a confession of stupidity or babbling incoherence. Take your time.

First, understand that the interviewer has limited goals. You are not expected to understand the law on murder or manslaughter. You are expected to be able to understand the rule which is stated and restate why the scenario posed is a problem and venture some solution. Eg: as to question (a) you might reply – Murder requires the guilty to intend to kill someone. The problem is do you have to intend to kill the person you actually kill. It seems equally criminal to me to kill one person while you are trying to kill another. *Or* as to question (d) – I do not know from the question whether Gertrude was trying to kill her unborn baby or not. If she had no such intention to kill it then I do still think that the issue of manslaughter has to be considered. What I do not know is whether the law regards the unborn baby as a 'person' for the purpose of manslaughter or murder. I think it might depend on how long she had been pregnant . . .

Here, of course, the interviewer would very much like to argue with you about the age when a foetus becomes a person. Again, no knowledge of the actual detailed law need be shown – but, you must be willing to take up a sensible position, defend it and argue rationally. Try this yourself with problems (b) and (c) – perhaps using a friend or parent as the 'interviewer'. Also in the interview you are bound to be asked if you have any questions to ask the interviewer. Asking questions which are clearly answered in the information that has already been sent to you may have a negative effect; neither need you strain to ask clever questions. If you really have no gaps in your required information you can say that you have found that the information supplied in the departmental brochure, prospectus or whatever has answered your questions.

Student life

Wherever you undertake to study law, there will be a broadly similar pattern to the course provided. There will be a certain number, four or five, of law subjects studied at one time or in one year. These nearly always form very separate items of study. There will be formal lectures in each subject – one hour, two hours more usually, and occasionally three hours in a week. Then, for each subject there will be small group classes – seminars, tutorials, problem classes – where you will discuss legal problems which have already been prepared by the student group. The proportion and frequency of these vary quite a lot from college to college and from year to year of a course. At any time, however, you will expect to have fewer than fifteen hours a week in the lecture or seminar room and very often ten hours or less in a week. The rest of your time is your own. This is the fact that above all invests the study of law with its distinctive character and discipline. Although the time is your own it needs to be employed usefully. A characteristic of degree level study, and particularly of law, is the requirement to read. During lectures and seminars you will be directed to much primary legal source material, with the expectation that you will find and read this material. The good student will take this opportunity and benefit not only by discovering relevant information but by eventually mastering legal technique. In the 'taught' part of the course you accumulate a somewhat shapeless mass of information – statements of law, opinions, and a large number of references. The study of law consists of the sum of your efforts to make order out of this apparent chaos. Much time must be spent in your study and in the law library or at a computer terminal aiming first at reducing the areas of law involved to a comprehensible pattern and then in following up references to critical materials – whether in decided case law or in the masses of secondary material produced by academics in journals, monographs and textbooks. This private study involves a disciplined use of time.

HINT
Ensure that you follow up and read the references given to you by your tutors.

The organisation of study time

The modern student most often comes to the study of law fairly directly from sixth form studies. The sixth form will have given the student a foretaste of private study. There is, nevertheless, a big divide to cross. Many students find the challenge of organising their time insuperable. At the beginning of the academic year June seems far away. There is much else to do other than study and, anyway, the course is three years long. These are tempting siren calls. In the authors' personal experience it is a workmanlike timetabling of one's efforts which is the most effective way of overcoming this. The proponent of the more free-and-easy approach to the academic life will decry this philistine attitude – and it is admitted that not all students will prosper under the same regime. But, it is strongly urged, the sensible student is one who knows for certain whether he is working or not working, who knows when work is finished and is ready for the other activities that student life offers.

HINT
Time management is an important skill to develop. At the beginning of your course of studies structure your working week.

KEY POINT
Degree level study is an exercise in self-managing your time. It is expected that you will find and read legal source material.

How hard to work

The work of a law student is creative. It involves a constructive reordering of material, considerable effort at comprehension and the development of highly-pronounced critical faculties. It is a dull student who thinks that work of this kind can be valuably pursued without break or recreation. Seven to eight hours of time *spent working* in a day means a very long working day. Certainly the sum of hours in a week *spent working* cannot usefully exceed fifty, at least for lengthy periods of time. For the student of good average ability not aiming for academic stardom a working week of forty hours will be more than adequate.

Two riders must be added to this dogmatic advice. First, the times suggested are inclusive of lectures and seminars. Secondly, the concept of *time spent working* is used very deliberately. What is important is not so much the exact quantification of time spent working as the realisation that there must be a clear division between work and recreation so as to maximise the effectiveness of the former.

It has always been a source of great puzzlement that some able students fail from the beginning of the course. All students selected for entry onto law degrees have the ability to pass. They have simply to decide how well they wish to do and work accordingly. Those who fail are very rarely the ones having the best time outside the lecture-room. The lesson is to enjoy both sides of university life – but not quite to the full.

■ CHECKLIST

■ CHOOSING LAW

▶ Before deciding that law is the subject that you wish to study read some introductory legal works and seek work experience with a lawyer.

▶ Read the quality daily newspapers to develop an awareness of current legal developments. This is not only useful in deciding whether law is the right subject for you, but also in trying to impress at interview.

▶ Research both courses and universities.

▶ Obtain and study prospectuses; compare the content of courses; take the opportunity to visit the universities that attract you; consider

the financial implications of your choice; give some thought
to what a university has to offer beyond the course; and finally,
consider the attractions of the city or town where the university
is located.

▶ You will have to decide what you want from a law course and then
choose the one that it most appropraite for your purposes.

▶ In completing a UCAS form the following should be considered:

  (i) consult the UCAS website;
  (ii) read the published guides to applying for a university course to
       discover entry requirements;
  (iii) an application should show your reasons for choosing law,
        including some evidence of your research into the subject;
  (iv) before submitting your UCAS form double check that the form
       is complete and contains no mistakes.

▶ In preparing for an interview consider the following points:

  (i) an interviewer will be looking for enthusiasm, commitment and
      also aptitude for legal study;
  (ii) a student should be able to articulate the reasons for
       choosing law;
  (iii) if you want to become a lawyer some knowledge of the routes to
        qualification should be demonstrated;
  (iv) an awareness of current legal issues discoverable in the news
       and an ability to explain and analyse will impress an interviewer.

▶ The hallmark of degree level study is an expectation that you will
take responsibility for your studies. In doing this you must follow the
guidance offered by tutors and read the texts and materials to which
you are directed.

▶ The ease of transition to degree level study will depend upon the
extent to which all of your 'A' levels or your pre-degree course
prepare you for independent learning.

▶ Time outside of the lecture and seminar rooms must be carefully
self-managed.

▶ While formal teaching sessions may account for ten to fifteen hours
of a week, a much greater amount of time must be spent in
research, reflection and preparation.

Chapter 2

English law and the English courts

English law and the English courts

English law consists of a very large body of case law and an enormous amount of statute law – the collective name for Acts of Parliament. In addition there is now a body of European Community law to consider, as well as the pervasive effect of the Human Rights Act 1998. The purpose of this chapter is to introduce the nature of English law and give an overview of the English court structure. Many other countries in the world have a system of law which is modelled on or derived from ours. What all these systems have in common is a system of law based upon precedent – this is the essential nature of the common law system.

Common law

The expression common law like many words used by lawyers has a number of different meanings. An unusual meaning nowadays refers to the time when England was not such a unified country as it is now. Common law in this context refers to the system of law applied by the King's courts throughout the whole country. As English law developed the common law came to be applied through a number of Royal Courts of Justice. Alongside this application of the common law in the courts the King still permitted suitors to apply to his Council for particular justice or relief from unfairness. This part of the royal prerogative came to be exercised by one of the King's principal servants, the Lord Chancellor, and the court in which it was exercised came to be known as the Court of Chancery. Common law in one usage, thus, means the rules applied in the common law courts as distinct from the more flexible rules applied in the courts of chancery (the latter being referred as the rules and principles of equity).

A hallmark of English common law is the role played by judges in developing case law, for example, the law of contract and of tort. Some law thus is 'made' by judges. Common law in this sense may be compared with civilian systems of law. A main feature of civil law systems, as seen in France and Germany, is that laws on a particular subject are codified, that is the law on each subject is to be found in a text created by the legislature. Under this system the role of the judiciary is more interpretative of the codfied law, rather than law-making.

As some law is judge-made, the common law courts developed the system of precedent which is such a feature of English law to regulate the growth of the law.

A system of precedent is one where the decision in one case can bind a court in another case. The doctrine of precedent is a very special feature of English law. It means that the study of law involves to a very great extent the study of case law. Nowadays the amount of statute law, that is law contained in Acts of Parliament, is also very great but the ability to deal with case law is still the hallmark of a good common lawyer. To understand how to deal with case law it is first necessary to understand the structure of the courts.

HINT ➡

The term common law has a variety of meanings, which are discernible from the context in which the term is used.

Court structure

This is explained in outline by the diagram below.

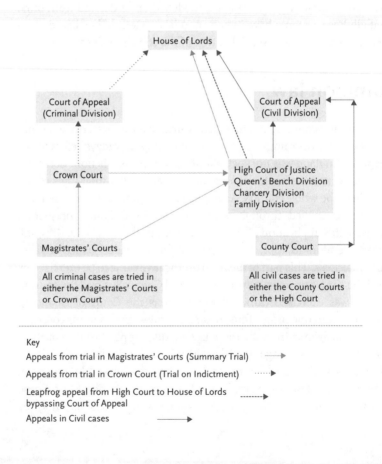

All criminal cases are tried in either the Magistrates' Courts or Crown Court

All civil cases are tried in either the County Courts or the High Court

Key

Appeals from trial in Magistrates' Courts (Summary Trial) ⟶

Appeals from trial in Crown Court (Trial on Indictment) ·····▶

Leapfrog appeal from High Court to House of Lords bypassing Court of Appeal -------▶

Appeals in Civil cases ⟶

One useful working division of cases in the courts is into civil and criminal cases. The diagram shows the different courts in which civil and criminal cases begin. The final appeal in each may be to the House of Lords. Although this had its origins in the role of Parliament as a court it is now in effect simply the ultimate court of appeal, its members being the Law Lords – the most senior judges appointed to that office. These are known as Lords of Appeal in Ordinary. There are presently twelve of these. It is to be noted that the Constitutional Reform Act 2005 will, when in force, replace the House of Lords with a Supreme Court of the United Kingdom. The newly created Supreme Court will have the appellate jurisdiction of the House of Lords and the devolution jurisdiction of the Judicial Committee of the Privy Council. The Law Lords title of Lords of Appeal in Ordinary will also change to 'Justices of the Supreme Court'.

Below this is the Court of Appeal. It has two divisions – the civil division and the criminal division. The President of the criminal division is the Lord Chief Justice; following the enactment of the Constitutional Reform Act 2005 the Lord Chief Justice is also head of the judiciary. The President of the civil division is the Master of the Rolls. This rather odd title has become the title of the most senior civil judge by historical accident. The 'Rolls' referred to are the rolls of parchment on which court records were formerly kept. The record of solicitors entitled to practise is also known as the roll and the Master of the Rolls has titular responsibility for this.

The Court of Appeal is a part of what is known as the Supreme Court of Judicature. The existing courts were reorganised by the Supreme Court of Judicature Acts 1873–75. The courts of first instance (that is, courts in which cases commence) became known as the High Court of Justice.

For convenience the High Court is divided into divisions which deal with different types of work and High Court judges in practice belong to one of these divisions. The present divisions are:

▶ Queen's Bench Division, which deals with general civil cases such as personal injury, medical negligence, libel and contract disputes;

▶ Chancery Division, which deals with company law cases, disputes involving trusts and trustees, bankruptcy and wills and probate;

▶ Family Division, which deals with marriage, divorce and children.

HINT →

A knowledge of the structure and hierarchy of the courts is essential to an understanding of the doctrine of precedent.

The previous divisions of the High Court since the Judicature Acts are as follows:

Divisions of the High Court since 1875

1875–1880	Chancery Division, Queen's Bench Division, Common Pleas Division/Exchequer Division,* Probate Division
1881–1971	Chancery Division, Queen's Bench Division, Probate, Divorce and Admiralty**
1972+	Chancery Division, Queen's Bench Division, Family Division

You will find this information of importance when searching for older cases in the *Law Reports* (see Chapter 6), which were and are organised to mirror the organisation of the courts.

The senior judge in the Queen's Bench Division is the President of the Queen's Bench Division and Head of Criminal Justice. The senior judge in the Chancery Division is the Chancellor of the High Court. The senior Family Division judge is the President of the Family Division. (More information on the judiciary may be found at www.judiciary.gov.uk.)

Precedent in the English courts

The rules of precedent mean that decisions of the House of Lords bind all the inferior courts. The House of Lords also regards itself as bound to follow its own previous decisions in most cases, but may depart from a previous decision 'when it appears right to do so'. The decisions of the Court of Appeal are binding upon itself, subject to exceptions, and upon inferior courts. Decisions of the High Court also have value as precedents. Beneath these are the inferior courts, the decisions of which rarely find their way into a law report and which are not formally binding upon any other courts. English judges do not give succinct judgments which announce 'the rule I am laying down in this case is . . .'. They give quite long judgments running for several pages. The lawyer has to determine from this what precise rule is laid down by the case. This rule is referred to as the *ratio decidendi* of a case. This expression is the Latin for *the reason for the decision*.

HINT →

Always note the name of the court giving a decision as from this you can establish if a principle of law from the case is binding on other courts.

---

* The work of these two courts was merged in the Queen's Bench Division.   ** Probate was transferred to the Chancery Divison and Admiralty to the Queen's Bench Division. + The present division of work derives from Schedule 1 to the Supreme Court Act 1981.

New laws are in fact made by the judges in laying down new precedents. This process is described as follows:

'It is to be observed, however, that many specific questions are perpetually occurring, in which the rule of the common law does not happen to be fixed by any known decision, and that these are disposed of by the judges in the manner that they think most comfortable to the received rule in other analogous cases; or if there be no such analogy to guide them, then according to the natural reason of the thing; though (in defence to the principle already referred to, that the opinion of the judge is not to make the law, but only ascertain it), their determination always purports to be declaratory of what the law *is* and not of what it *ought* to be . . . judicial decisions are the principal and most authoritative evidence, that can be given, of the existence of such a general custom as shall form a part of the common law. The judgment itself, and all the material, ie formal proceedings previous thereto, are carefully registered and preserved . . .

It has been uniformly considered to be the duty of those who administer the law, to conform to the precedents thus established. For the scale of justice is not intended to waver with every new judge's opinion (which would be productive of intolerable inconvenience), but when in any case the law has been solemnly declared and determined, what before was uncertain, and perhaps indifferent, is now become a permanent rule, which it is not in the breast of any subsequent judge to alter or vary from, according to his private sentiments; he being sworn to determine, not according to his own private judgments, but according to the known laws and customs of the land; not *delegated* to pronounce a new law but to maintain and expound the old one.'*

Often in giving judgment a judge will make a statement as to what the law would be in facts similar but not identical to the facts in the case before the court. This statement of law is an *obiter dictum*. This means it is said by the way – that is not strictly relevant to the case in hand. The rule which binds other courts is the *ratio decidendi* of the case. What is referred to as an *obiter dictum* (singular) or as *obiter dicta* (plural) does or do not bind other courts. An example may help you follow this: suppose a taxi driver called Clarke is kidnapped by a terrorist group and forced at gun-point to drive his car into the Royal enclosure car park at Ascot and leave it there to explode where it kills an innocent bystander. Clarke may be charged with murder and eventually an appeal in his case heard by the Court of Appeal. Then the Lord Chief Justice might say: 'it is no defence to murder for Mr Clarke to say he was under threat of his own

---

* These extracts are from *Blackstone's Laws of England*, one of the most influential law books ever written and first published in 1765.

life'. This could well be a version of the *ratio decidendi* of that case. The Lord Chief Justice might add 'nor would it be a defence if the threat was to Mr Clarke's wife or child'. That statement would be by the way and therefore an *obiter dictum* as clearly not necessary for the decision in Clarke's appeal (doubtless you will have your own strong views on these two alleged statements of law and when you study criminal law you will find whether either of these statements put in the mouth of the Lord Chief Justice is correct).

A great deal of the skill of a common lawyer is in identifying correctly the *ratio* of a case which tells you how one case will be applied in another. When a judge in a case does this he is said to *follow* the previous case. If a higher court wishes to depart from the rule (laid down in an earlier case) then it may *disapprove* it and *overrule* that decision. Overruling a case means that is it not law and indeed never has been the law; overruling is retrospective. Should a case go on appeal to a higher court, the decision may be *affirmed* or *reversed* by the higher court. If a court thinks a case lays down a rule which is not binding on the present facts then it may *distinguish* the previous case and refuse to apply the rule. If we return to the mythical case of *R v Clarke* then we may see how it could be applied in *R v Jones*. In this case Jones has killed a politician by shooting after being told that his wife Mrs Jones is held a hostage by a terrorist group and will be killed herself if he does not kill the politician. Here Mr Justice Wright says:

> 'I must consider the case of *R v Clarke* which says that a threat to the accused cannot be a defence to murder. I can *distinguish* that case because the threat here was not to Jones but to Mrs Jones. The Lord Chief Justice in *R v Clarke* said a threat to another cannot be a defence either. If that was a decision of a lower court I would *overrule* it as I find it repugnant to reason. However, it is not a part of the Court of Appeal's decision in *Clarke*, being an *obiter dictum*. Accordingly I am not bound to *follow* *R v Clarke* at this point. The view of the distinguished Lord Chief Justice is obviously of *persuasive* and not *compulsive* authority and therefore . . .'.

In reading this you should note that a view of a judge which is not binding is referred to as *persuasive*. If it is a view stated deliberately after thought and after the point is argued before the court it may be given appropriate weight. The law report will tell you whether the court gave its judgment on the day of the argument or after adjourning for some days or weeks to consider the point. A judgment given 'off the cuff' is referred to as *ex tempore* and one after a delay for thought as *reserved*. The report in such a case may indicate *cur. adv. vult*, which is short for *curia adversari vult*, which is Latin for 'the court wished to deliberate over the matter'.

KEY POINT ●

When reading a law report you need to find the principle of law upon which a case is decided, the *ratio decidendi*. Any principle of law which is not necessary for the decision in a case, an *obiter dictum*, is of less authority and is not binding.

HINT →

Early in your legal career learn the rules of precedent. These are important tools in using case law and will be of relevance throughout your course of study.

Legislation

The other major source of law is legislation. This encompasses laws made by Parliament and on behalf of Parliament in the form of delegated legislation. Laws made by Parliament are in the form of Acts of Parliament (see Appendix 2 for an example of an Act) and are referred to as primary legislation. Acts of Parliament may be contrasted with delegated legislation which is made under the authority of Parliament by, for example, government ministers and local authorities. This is termed secondary legislation and, in the main, takes the form of statutory instruments.

For a proposed piece of legislation, called a Bill, to become an Act of Parliament it must be passed by the House of Commons, the House of Lords and be given the Royal Assent by the monarch. Note that in certain circumstances a Bill may be presented to the monarch for Royal Assent without having been passed by the House of Lords. This process is governed by the Parliament Acts 1911–49.

Delegated or secondary legislation is normally made under the authority given to a person or body by an Act of Parliament. The Act, in this respect, is referred to as the 'parent Act'. (In Appendix 2 there are examples of sections giving authority for a minister to make regulations on behalf of Parliament in the form of a statutory instrument.) It may be noted that, whereas the validity of an Act of Parliament cannot be challenged in the courts, the validity of delegated legislation may be so challenged if, for example, a minister in making regulations exceeds the authority given by the parent Act. If a minister has exceeded his or her powers the court will say that the minister has acted *ultra vires* and the regulations will be void.

It is important to appreciate the relationship between Parliament and the courts as law-makers. Parliament is the supreme law-maker and should a conflict arise between law made by Parliament and law developed by the courts then the law of Parliament prevails. In other words, Parliament can change the law developed by the judges through cases, but case law cannot directly alter Parliamentary law. As with all general statements of legal principle, as you will discover, it is important to note any qualifications to the statement. While Parliament is supreme, its supremacy is curtailed in two important ways. First, as a member state of the European Union, Parliament has legislated that European Community law (the EC Treaty and Regulations) is directly applicable in the United Kingdom and overrides domestic law if there is a conflict. Second, by the passing of the Human Rights Act 1998, Parliament has, in part, incorporated into domestic law the European Convention on Human Rights; called in the Act 'the Convention rights'. In consequence, primary and secondary legislation 'must be read and given effect in a way which is compatible with the Convention rights', in so far as this is possible. Should an incompatibility between domestic law and

> **HINT** →
> It is necessary to learn a new vocabulary in order to interpret legal source materials. You will find that this develops more quickly by reading legal source materials.

> **HINT** →
> The term legislation encompasses both Acts of Parliament and delegated legislation.

Convention rights be found, a higher court may make a declaration of incompatibility. This does not mean that the legislation is invalid, but it does mean that Parliament will be expected to resolve the incompatibility by, for example, amending the offending legislation.

The divisions of law

There are many ways of dividing up the areas of English law and it is helpful for the student to know these at an early stage:

Public and private law

The expression public law covers the area of law involving the state. It may include conflicts between the individual and the state or the laws which govern government processes. The subjects which fall within public law in a law degree are public international law (concerning conflicts between states); constitutional law; judicial review (a very dynamic area of law concerning the circumstances when the courts will intervene to protect the citizen from improper exercise of power by or on behalf of the state) and criminal law.

Private law covers the areas of law which govern disputes and legal relationships between individuals. Typical subjects in the curriculum are contract, conveyancing, land law and the law of torts.

Criminal law and civil law

Law may also be divided into criminal law and civil law. It is to be noted that civil law means laws that are not part of the criminal law; it thus encompasses private law. The term civil law in this sense does not relate to civilian systems of law, as previously mentioned.

Common law and equity

The expression common law has been discussed above. Here we use it to mean the areas of law developed by the common law courts. The two most important of these for all students are contract and tort. The meaning of the first of these is quite obvious. Tort is the area of law concerned with remedies by one person against another in respect of injuries or loss wrongfully caused. Torts include such matters as libel, slander, nuisance, negligence and trespass. Tort and contract are together the two basic subjects in which students study the development of case law. Contract itself is the basis of many other legal subjects.

The expression equity refers to the system of rules and principles developed by the Court of Chancery. It includes wide remedial principles that allow the courts to protect individuals from strict common law rules. For example, a person may sign a contract when under unfair pressure from another. A child may give property to an overbearing relative. A pupil may be cheated in effect by a svengali-like teacher. To assist in such cases equity has developed a whole area of doctrine known as undue influence. As a concept it is protean and the courts have recognised that it is not easy to define. Lord Nicholls, in the leading case of *Royal Bank of Scotland plc v Etridge (No 2)* [2002] 2 AC 773, said of undue influence:

'If the intention [of a victim to enter into a transaction] was produced by an unacceptable means, the law will not permit the transaction to stand. The means used is regarded as an exercise of improper or "undue" influence, and hence unacceptable, whenever the consent thus procured ought not fairly to be treated as the expression of a person's free will. It is impossible to be more precise or definitive. The circumstances in which one person acquires influence over another, and the manner in which influence may be exercised, vary too widely to permit of any more specific criterion.'

✖ EXAMPLE

Its operation is powerfully illustrated by the case of *Lloyd's Bank v Bundy*. This case concerned a farmer who had mortgaged his farm to Lloyd's Bank in order to help out his son whose business had run into trouble. The case was introduced as follows by Lord Denning, the Master of the Rolls:

'Broadchalk is one of the most pleasing villages in England. Old Herbert Bundy was a farmer there. His home was at Yew Tree Farm. It went back for 300 years. His family had been there for generations. It was his only asset. But he did a very foolish thing. He mortgaged it to the bank. Up to the very hilt. Not to borrow money for himself, but for the sake of his son. Now the bank have come down on him. They have foreclosed. They want to get him out of Yew Tree Farm and to sell it. They have brought this action against him for possession. Going out means ruin for him.'

Then in coming towards a decision Lord Denning attempted to sum up the relevant rules of equity which could be applied and made this famous statement:

'Gathering all together, I would suggest that through this instance there runs a single thread. They rest on "inequality of bargaining power". By virtue of it, the English law gives relief to one who, without independent advice, enters into a contract on terms which are very unfair or transfers property for a consideration which is grossly inadequate, when his bargaining power is previously impaired by reason of his own needs or desires, or by his own ignorance or infirmity, coupled with undue influences or pressures brought to bear on him by or for the benefit of the other.'

Lord Denning sought to develop a wider principle of inequality of bargaining power by pulling together various principles of law such as undue influence, unconscionable bargains and duress. The majority of the Court of Appeal rested their decision, however, upon the equitable doctrine of undue influence. Note that while the three judges in the Court of Appeal came to the same decision they did so for differing reasons. This is a common feature of judicial decision-making and in reading a case you must exercise care to ensure that you have identified the correct basis of a decision. Applying the principles of equity the Court of Appeal was able to assist Mr Bundy and prevent Lloyd's Bank obtaining possession of his farm. Lord Denning's statement of principle concerning inequality of bargaining power was not the basis for the decision of the Court of Appeal and therefore was an *obiter dictum*. In a later case, *National Westminster Bank plc v Morgan*, the House of Lords cast doubt on the need for such a principle. This illustrates the changing nature of law and the need to consider a case in its context, particularly noting later judicial developments.

HINT ➡

In appellate cases there may be several judgments which reveal different ways to answer the same legal question. Do not read and rely on only one judgment.

Equity also includes the detailed law dealing with trust. The idea of a trust has been defined as follows:

'A trust . . . is the relationship which comes whenever a person called the trustee is compelled in Equity to hold property, whether real or personal, and whether by legal or equitable title, for the benefit of some persons (of whom he may be one and who are called *cestui que trust*) or for some object permitted by law, in such a way that the real benefit of the property accrues, not to the trustees, but to the beneficiaries or other objects of the trust.'

Keeton *Law of Trusts*.

Equity thus includes the detailed rules of law dealing with the management of trustees. However, as exemplified in *Lloyd's Bank v Bundy*, it has a wider function described as follows:

'Equity is not part of the law, but a moral virtue, which qualifies, moderates, and reforms the rigour, hardness, and edge of the law, and is a universal truth; it does also assist the law where it is defective and weak in the constitution (which is the life of the law) and defends the law from crafty evasions, delusions, and new subtleties, invented and contrived to evade and delude the common law, whereby such as have un- doubted right are made remediless; and this is the office of equity, to support and protect the common law from shifts and crafty contrivances against the justice of the law. Equity therefore does not destroy the law, nor create it, but assist it.'*

Criminal courts

In criminal cases there is a division between cases which are tried before a jury in the Crown Court and cases which are tried before a bench of magistrates in the magistrates' court. The former is called trial on indictment and the latter summary trial.

The indictment is the formal statement of the crimes of which the defendant is accused. The defendant is first brought before the magistrates who decide whether there is a case for him to answer. If there is the defendant is committed for trial to the Crown Court. There the accused is tried upon the indictment before a judge and jury. The parties in a criminal case are ordinarily the Crown Prosecutor and the accused and cases are entitled *R v Smith* (or whatever is the name of the accused). Sometimes the prosecution is taken over by the Director of Public Prosecutions in politically important, very grave or difficult cases. In this case the title of the case will be *DPP v Smith*.

A right to a trial before a jury of twelve lay persons is regarded as one of the great bastions of English freedom. The trial is in public. Any prospective law student would benefit from watching such a trial. If you go to your local Crown Court to do so there will be pinned up a list of the cases in each court. You should be able to find an usher (court servant)

---

* Per Sir Nathan Wright LK in *Lord Dudley and Ward v Lady Dudley* (1705) Prec Ch 241, 244.

who will tell you in a more helpful way what is 'on' in each court. You may be drawn to a notorious crime such as a rape or murder. These, however, often run to quite long trials. Ask the usher to direct you to a trial which will last only a half day or so, such as a shop-lifting case. Here, you will be able to watch the whole procedure of a trial and learn more than 10,000 words in a book could tell you. The trial is each time an absorbing drama conducted with a measured formality that heightens the excitement. From the time the jurors swear their oath 'I swear by Almighty God [alternatively, for those affirming, I do solemnly, sincerely and truly declare and affirm] that I will faithfully try the defendant and give a true verdict according to the evidence', until the foreman of the jury announces the verdict, there is an unfailing tension in the court.

A trial in the magistrates' court is considerably less of a drama. The ceremonial dress and procedure are absent. The magistrates try the case assisted by a legally qualified clerk who sits in front of and below them. Once more the proceedings are public and a session or two observing the process is worthwhile. You will readily be able to contrast in your own mind the strengths and weaknesses of each of the two trial systems.

Which is fairer to the accused? Which is more apt to discover (if such can ever be known) the real truth? What changes would you suggest to either of these ritual processes?

The civil trial

The two main courts are the High Court of Justice and the county courts. The High Court is situated in the Royal Courts of Justice in The Strand in London. It is open to the public and will inevitably be visited by the student of law. The High Court sits also 'on circuit' outside London. There are county courts in most important towns and they are also open to the public.

A civil trial is much harder to follow than a criminal trial. Much information is contained in the pleadings, now termed statements of case. These are the formal statements of the claimant's case and in the defendant's response to that claim. The aim of the statements of case is to define sharply the issues between the parties so that the trial itself can focus on these or possibly, as the issues become clear, lead the parties to settle the claim. A typical particulars of claim is reproduced on p 29 showing a claim for breach of contract. It is followed on p 30 by the defence which is filed in reply.

The civil trial is usually in front of a judge alone. The judge has the benefit of the formal pleadings prepared by the parties. There will be the statement of claim, a detailed defence to this and then further pleadings to narrow down the issues between the parties. There may also be agreed statements of evidence such as reports from expert witnesses.

IN THE OLDCASTLE COUNTY COURT   Claim No

BETWEEN

Fred String Esq,
(trading as Quikflo)   Claimant

and

Jerry and Co Limited   Defendant

PARTICULARS OF CLAIM

1   The Defendant is a building and civil engineering contractor carrying on business at
    27a, Marl Lane, Oldcastle.
2   By a contract in writing contained in correspondence between the Defendant and
    the Claimant dated July 12th 2006 and between the Claimant and the Defendant
    dated July 16th 2006 the Claimant agreed subject to the terms contained in the let-
    ter of July 16th 2006 to carry out certain works of plumbing and fitting at a new
    house under construction at Oldcastle.
3   The contract price for the said work was £320 plus VAT.
4   The said contract price was subsequently varied during the course of work because
    the Claimant had to carry out additional work as a result of the Defendant negligently
    and in breach of their specification hanging kitchen doors which opened inward
    instead of outward and the final contract price due to the Claimant is £400 plus VAT.
5   The Defendant has made payments to the sum of £200 only.
6   The sum of £260 remains owing to the Claimant AND THE CLAIMANT CLAIMS
    THE SUM OF £260 and interest on the same until payment or judgment.

Dated this day of   2006

I believe that the facts stated in this Particulars of Claim are true (signed by the
Claimant)

The Claimant's solicitors are Messrs Blank, Powder and Cartridge of Arsenal Buildings,
Oldcastle OC1 NE2, where they will accept service of proceedings on behalf of the
Claimant.

To the Defendant
To the Court Manager

IN THE OLDCASTLE COUNTY COURT   Claim No

BETWEEN
Fred String Esq

(trading as Quickflo)   Claimant

and

Jerry & Co Limited   Defendant

DEFENCE

1 Save that the Defendant admits that the Claimant was engaged to carry out works of plumbing and fitting at Oldcastle the Defendant denies the Claimant's claim and each and every part thereof.
2 The said contract in writing between the Plaintiff and the Claimant was contained in the letter of July 12th 2006 and not as alleged in paragraph 2 of the Particulars of Claim and the said Contract price was £280.
3 The Defendant denies that the additional work carried out in accordance with the Contract between the Claimant and the Defendant or as a result of the Defendant's lack of care or failure to comply with their specification.
4 Further and in the alternative the contract was a fixed price contract in the terms of the said letter of July 12th 2006 and no payment is due for unforeseen work undertaken by the Plaintiff.
5 Further and in the alternative the sum of £200 was paid to and accepted by the Claimant in satisfaction of all claims under the said contract.
6 Further and in the alternative the said sum of £200 was paid to and accepted by the Claimant in satisfaction of all the Claimant's said claims under the contract and in return for a waiver of all claims by the Defendant and Mrs Madge Lowrie as to the Claimant's defective performance of the said contract.

Delivered this day of   2006

I believe that the facts stated in this Defence are true

Signed

Fred Smith Director And I am authorised by the Defendant to make this statement.

The Claimant's solicitors are Tower Castle & Company of 14 High Street Oldcastle OC2 NE1 where they will accept service of Proceedings on behalf of the Defendant.

Wear, Old & Company
Solicitors
Oldcastle
To the Registrar
and the Claimant

The lawyers

The lawyers whom you will see when you visit these courts are divided into two groups – solicitors and barristers. The nature of the two professions and how you join them is the subject of Chapters 13 and 14. Solicitors deal more with work outside court and barristers in general with representation of the client in court. In court he is an advocate and when at his best fulfils this description of the role of an advocate given by the great criminal advocate Lord Birkett:

> The first quality beyond all others in the advocate, whatever his particular type of advocacy may be, is that he must be a man of character. The Court must be able to rely on the advocate's word, his word must indeed be his bond; and when he asserts to the Court those matters which are within his personal knowledge, the Court must know for a surety that those things are as represented. The advocate has a duty to his client, a duty to the Court, and a duty to the State; but he has above all a duty to himself that he shall be, as far as lies in his power, a man of integrity. No profession calls for higher standards of honour and uprightness, and no profession, perhaps, offers greater temptations to forsake them; but whatever gifts an advocate may possess, be they ever so dazzling, without the supreme qualification of an inner integrity he will fall short of the highest. In the conduct of any case, whether it be in the Magistrates' court or in the House of Lords, the advocate must have made himself master of all the facts; he must have a thorough understanding of the principles and rules of law which are applicable to the case and the ability to apply them on the instant; he must gauge with accuracy the atmosphere of the Court in which he pleads and adapt himself accordingly; he must be able to reason from the facts and the law to achieve the end he desires, and he must above all have mastered the art of expressing himself clearly and persuasively in acceptable English.

The two major legal professions have existed in their present form since the nineteenth century. Solicitors comprise by far the larger profession, consisting of over 96,000 practitioners. As of the end of 2005 there were nearly 12,000 practising barristers. Solicitors practise in offices which are in town and city centres and suburbs all over the country. These are similar to the offices of other professional and commercial persons. The majority of barristers practise in London in or around one of the four Inns of Court: Gray's Inn, Lincoln's Inn, Middle Temple and Inner Temple. Barristers do not practise from offices but from *chambers*. There are barristers' chambers in most major cities but not outside these.

Barristers are sometimes referred to as the senior profession. This is because they act in something like a consultant role to solicitors. Presently barristers appear more commonly than solicitors in the higher courts. The right to appear in a court on behalf of another person is called a right of audience. Barristers dress in a traditional way – men wear black jackets, striped trousers, a gown and a wig; women wear a dark suit, a gown and a wig. This form of dress dates from the eighteenth century and is long overdue for reform.

Two newer professions in the law should also be mentioned. The first is legal executives. This developed in the post-war period as a professional organisation for persons working in solicitors' firms who carry out work as assistants to the solicitors. The profession is run by the Institute of Legal Executives and has a very demanding system of examinations encouraging specialisation in a variety of aspects of solicitors' work. The second is that of licensed conveyancers. These came into being in 1986 as a result of the government's view that there should be more competition in conveyancing. The profession is run by a statutory body, the Council for Licensed Conveyancers. It also has a scheme for examining would-be entrants to the profession.

Useful legal terms

statute	may be used interchangeably with Act of Parliament.
legislation	term for Acts of Parliament and delegated legislation.
court of first instance	where a case commences; alternatively referred to a court of trial.
appellate court	a court of appeal.
claimant	a person who brings a claim. In older cases you will find the term plaintiff used instead of claimant.
ratio decidendi	the rule of law which is the basis upon which a court decides a case. Within the rules of binding precedent the *ratio decidendi* may bind later courts.
obiter dictum	a statement of law which is not necessary to the decision in a case. An *obiter dictum* is not binding on later courts but may have a persuasive effect.

persuasive	an authority which is not binding but may persuade a court to reach a particular decision.
follow	a court in a later case applies the *ratio decidendi* from a previous case.
overrule	a higher court overturns a principle of law stated in an earlier different case. The overturned case is no longer law.
reverse	where a higher court overturns the decision of a lower court on appeal in the same case.
affirm	where a higher court does not change the decision of a lower court in the same case.
distinguish	where the material facts of a previous case are sufficiently different to those of an instant case, so that the court in the instant case is not bound to apply the *ratio decidendi* from the previous case.
approve	where a higher court indicates that a principle of law stated in a different case before a lower court is correct.
disapprove	where a higher court indicates that a principle of law stated in case before a lower court is not to be followed.
consider	where a court looks at a case, but then does not use the case to determine the outcome of the instant case.
ex tempore	a judgment given 'off the cuff'.
reserved or *cur. adv. vult*	where a court takes time to consider a case before giving judgment.
trial on indictment	trial before judge and jury in the Crown Court.
summary trial	trial in a magistrates' court.
jurisdiction	the authority a court has to decide cases before it. Jurisdiction may be limited or unlimited.

■ CHECKLIST

■ ENGLISH LAW AND THE ENGLISH COURTS

▶ The sources of English law are case law and statute law.

▶ English law includes European Community law and is to be consistent with the European Convention on Human Rights.

▶ Common law has a number of meanings depending upon the context in which the term is used.

▶ English law falls within the family of Common law jurisdictions. The law is in part based upon law developed by judges within a system of judicial precedent.

▶ The English courts are based on a hierarchical system with the House of Lords, domestically, the highest court.

▶ The courts may exercise either civil or criminal jurisdiction, or in some case both. Some courts act solely as courts of trial or appeal and some courts have jurisdiction over both.

▶ A judge in reaching a decision will rely upon a principle of law, the *ratio decidendi*. Usually, this principle will not be stated explicitly. Other statements of law are referred to as *obiter dicta*. It is only the *ratio decidendi* of a case which is potentially binding on other courts.

▶ The law may be classified in a variety of ways. You need to be aware of the the ways in which the law is classified.

▶ Criminal and civil trials differ in a number of important repsects.

▶ The legal profession is made up of solicitors and barristers.

Chapter 3
Current issues in law

Access to the profession

To the lay person, both main branches of the legal profession of solicitors and barristers will seem conservative. Accordingly, persons who are not already associated in any way, through relatives and so on, with the profession might wonder how easy it is to enter the profession these days. There are certainly issues in this area. So far as the solicitors' profession is concerned, most firms who provide training to future solicitors have selection procedures which should eliminate discrimination on, for example, ethnic, class or gender grounds. Equally, the Bar Council has laid down a code of conduct for appointment of pupil barristers which should have the same effect. It is probably truer than ever that, at least formally, both branches of the profession are accessible to persons with the requisite talent. Nevertheless, if you read the more thoughtful newspapers, you will see that there is a constant interest in whether these formal access policies are actually working fairly and providing equality of opportunity. Wherever persons are in a position to select people to join their enterprise, there is a natural human tendency to select people who are 'like us'; but even the legal professions change very fast.

When the elder of the two authors was a trainee solicitor, he can remember clearly another articled clerk (as they were called then) being given a severe telling-off for walking around the office with his waistcoat buttons undone! Nowadays, in the large commercial firm where he is a consultant, the partners no longer dress in the formal attire of pinstriped suits and so on, but on a normal working day are dressed quite informally. The dress code in the barristers' profession still reflects an innately more conservative profession. To many it must seem a parody of suitable working dress for people still to be found in stiff collars, pinstriped trousers and black jackets, putting on an eighteenth century wig to address a judge. But, beneath these appearances, the currents of change, as in the whole of society, are very strong. Both solicitors' firms and barristers' chambers contain people of all types. It is probably fair to say that talent, aptitude and perseverance are the main ingredients of success. There will always be some who are there because they are well connected; but this does not mean that people who are not are excluded, and the extent to which there is openness of access to the professions has increased substantially in recent years and will doubtless continue to do so.

In the enormous pressures of commercial city practice and the hectic life of the Bar, there are particular life balance issues to address. Many firms have family friendly policies and encourage flexible working patterns and flexible working weeks. However, clients and the court calendar do not. The work is unrelenting, arduous and often inflexible. The choice for anyone facing a career in the hugely demanding atmosphere of a large city firm, where there are long hours in the office and occasional very late nights and overnight working sessions to complete big commercial deals, is a lifestyle choice and no-one is excluded from making this choice.

The cost of qualification

HINT ⇒
Calculate how much your legal education will cost and how you may finance it.

Although it is undeniably true that selection procedures to the professions have done much to create a level playing field, there is one important area in which access has gone backwards. That is the cost of qualification. In what now seem the much more relaxed days of the 1960s, the universities' grants system and the fact that there was no need to attend full time courses to take the vocational exams for barristers and solicitors made access to the professions much less expensive than it is now. In some ways, because of other factors, it may well have been a less even playing field but, so far as the financial cost is concerned, that was not so. There is now undoubtedly a very heavy cost to qualifying as a lawyer. There are university fees to pay. There is also the cost of maintenance at university. There are vocational course fees to pay and the cost of maintenance during this course. Whatever stance might be taken by politicians in justifying this situation, there can be no doubt that the financial burdens tell against equality of access, and it is very sad that education in this country should have developed in this way.

HINT ⇒
Consult the websites of the Law Society, Bar Council and law firms when deciding whether a career in the legal profession is for you.

It is particularly for this reason that it is advisable before embarking upon the lengthy and costly process of qualifying as a lawyer to find out as much about the profession and your suitability for it as possible before commencing upon this venture. The decision to do so is one to be taken after all the costs and consequences have been carefully considered and, if possible, when one has a rounded view of what life as a solicitor or barrister or other participant in the legal world is like. As already mentioned, work experience with a solicitor or barrister is valuable in deciding whether a legal career is one for you. In addition, the experiences you have may inform your legal studies by putting academic law into a practical context. A further advantage of such work experience, during the course of your legal studies, relates to future employment; it provides an opportunity to demonstrate your abilities, enthusiasm and personal qualities to a potential employer. As the cost of qualification is high this means that many will feel a justifiable need to recoup some of this cost as soon as possible after qualifying; more is said below and in the chapter on 'Becoming a solicitor', about the financial rewards in different parts of the profession.

KEY POINT ●
Work experience with a lawyer is valuable as it places your legal studies in a practical context and also may lead to future employment opportunities.

The changing face of the professions

It is also worthwhile to consider how the legal profession is developing and will continue to develop in the future. The current period is one of fast change. There is no doubt that any person entering the profession now will find that the process of change is even faster. Forty years ago, the kinds of organisations which are now law firms, with a thousand or more employees in large and luxurious city centre offices, did not exist as such. For those reading now, looking forward forty years into the future, there can be no doubt that they will also be able to say: 'When I started it was nothing like this'. What kinds of changes are ongoing and what consequence does this have for those choosing law as a career?

HINT →
Keeping abreast of developments in relation to the legal professions will inform any application you submit for legal employment and provides another subject upon which you can speak at interview.

Legal aid

Large corporations, public bodies and the wealthy in our society can afford to pay for the services of highly skilled lawyers. Most people cannot. For most of the second half of the twentieth century there was a very buoyant system of legal aid, which supported those who, through force of circumstances, had to engage in litigation such as for custody of their children, to recover damages for compensation due to industrial injury, and so on. The last decade has seen almost an abandonment of the principle of state legal aid for litigation. The inability of a civilised country in our stage of development to provide a proper system of legal aid must be a source of enormous regret. It has also produced great strains within the legal profession. Firms which depend upon this kind of work have found it difficult to cope financially and have become fewer in number. The future in this area looks extremely hazardous, thus the decision to take part in publicly funded work on behalf of the more disadvantaged in society is one that the future lawyer has to take very advisedly. How this will develop in future years cannot be predicted with certainty, but certainly at the time of writing there is a decline in the number of high flying new recruits to the profession who are willing to take part in such legally aided work as is available. It must be hoped that in future governments will have the courage to devote funds to this area of work. One particular movement has counteracted to a small extent the limited availability of legal aid. This is the 'pro bono' movement. The expression refers to lawyers carrying out work for nothing for those who cannot pay. The government, instead of funding legal aid properly, has encouraged this movement. Many of the larger and highly-skilled law firms contribute to 'pro bono' work; some, for example, by working with university law clinics – as happens at Northumbria University. This might be a consideration to have in mind when you are applying for work experience or training.

The provision of legal services

For many years certain areas of legal services have been the exclusive prerogative of lawyers and their position has been protected by legislation. There has been what is known as the protected areas of work, that is, conveyancing, probate services and litigation services. Solicitors and barristers have, because of their own professional rules, been forbidden from practising in partnership with non-lawyers, so these areas of work have remained the preserve of lawyers. Inroads have been made into this by permitting a new profession of licensed conveyancers, and that is discussed later on in this book. Presently, under a new Legal Services Act, further inroads are intended. The present Government policy is that organisations controlled by non-lawyers will be able to provide these areas of legal work subject to proper scrutiny by a regulatory authority. Thus, the Co-operative Group may provide litigation services. A supermarket, such as Tesco, may decide to provide property services including conveyancing services. A special interest group such as the RAC may provide legal services of an appropriate kind for its members. It can be argued that there is nothing undesirable in this development so long as the quality of the services is properly regulated in the public interest. Indeed it may produce a more satisfactory outcome for the consumer by enabling linked services such as estate agency, financial and conveyancing services to be provided under one roof. Nevertheless, however desirable this is in the public interest, it cannot be said that the prospect is welcomed by the profession. It is understandable that the legal profession, having a monopoly of supply of a particular service, would not welcome competition being opened up on a wide scale. This is, particularly so, with such healthy competitors as the very successful supermarket chains, who are clearly able to diversify their work effectively in many different areas. The impact of such competition on the legal profession could be profound. Let us suppose this development takes place, as it seems that it inevitably will, what does that mean for a career in law? It may well mean that in a future legal landscape there will be fewer lawyers employed in partnership in what are exclusively law firms than in the past. It does not however mean that there will be fewer lawyers employed. As the law becomes increasingly specialised, more voluminous and more technical, the need for properly qualified specialist lawyers will still be there. They will, however, not be lawyers in independent practice. For some this is appealing. Lawyers in independent practice have to run their own business, with all the stresses and risks which that involves. Employed lawyers in large corporations have the benefit of the security that such organisations offer, along with the financial regimes and associated benefits which such corporations are able to provide for their employees. There will be many who see the life of a highly skilled specialist working in a large corporation as preferable to that of the independent practitioner running a business in the high street. There will be others who do not. However, this change in the legal landscape will not drive people by force into one or the other. It will provide instead a wider range of opportunity and different kinds of careers. There will be undoubtedly lawyers who move from a purely specialist legal role into a managerial role within a corporation where they work or into a boardroom role in a similar corporation. There will be a richer range of career patterns and it is perfectly possible that this forthcoming change will be a benefit, not only to the consumer but also to very many lawyers. What it will do is sweep away some of the firmly cherished conceptions or misconceptions of the last hundred years. That is very much to be applauded.

The electronic revolution

As has happened throughout areas of commerce and public employment, the electronic revolution has had an enormous effect on the law and legal profession. Forty years ago, when an assistant lecturer, one of the authors can remember a physicist at the same university explaining about the invention of the silicon chip and what a revolution that it would cause in the workplace. It was decades before it was fully realised how true that was. Its effect upon legal work is even now only becoming fully apparent. This is dealt with further in the chapter on 'Alternative careers in law', but some explanation may be offered at this point.

First, a simple comparison: all readers will have noticed how much less banks rely upon in-house personnel to provide banking services, how all corporations seem to rely upon large numbers of persons in remote call centres to deal with the public. This is a process often described as 'de-skilling'. Electronic processes enable things which take the human mind a very long time to do to be achieved very quickly by a machine. This can be most easily seen in arithmetical calculation, where machines now do in nanoseconds what once took many man hours. This is also so in the production of legal documents and the completion of the form-filling that is so much part of legal practice. What does the ever increasing pace of the electronic revolution mean so far as the future of the lawyer is concerned? In general terms the answer is very simple. For the last hundred years or so, lawyers have been handsomely paid, often for very simple processing work. Much of the work in conveyancing and probate and even in litigation involves the processing of quite routine documentation. The extent to which lawyers in the future will rely upon transactional processing as their main source of income will be very small indeed. Increasingly, lawyers will become providers of expert legal advice and assistance. Although processing of documentation and forms has been revolutionised, the legal work itself has not been processed nor been made simpler. The law increases in both amount and complexity exponentially. Not only domestic law but European law and latterly the overlay of human rights law have created, even for those who have long experience in specialised areas of the law, almost overwhelming complexity. It is in this world that the future lawyer will operate and reap the rewards of very high expertise. The electronic revolution can be welcomed by making research in law more accessible and reducing the drudgery of processing documents. Just as the typewriter reduced the need for clerks to write out lengthy deeds in handwriting, so the PC has removed other elements of drudgery from the legal workplace and is to be welcomed. This revolution will also change the pattern of work – lawyers will be less tied to the office – and it is possible this may enable some of the contemporary treadmill of overly long hours in large corporate firms to disappear!

How the future affects barristers

HINT ➡

It is possible to specialise in advocacy as either a barrister or solicitor.

As you will see when you come to the parts of this book dealing with entry to the different professions in more detail, the barristers' profession is a small one. Barristers are specialists in advocacy and, although the majority are in and around the Inns of Court in Central London, many are found in sets of chambers in the major cities. The barristers' profession, until recently, enjoyed a monopoly on rights of audience in the higher courts; this meant that only barristers were able to act as advocates in the High Court, Court of Appeal and House of Lords. In recent years, solicitors have also been able to obtain such rights of audience and many solicitors' firms now choose to carry out some or all of their own clients' advocacy requirements. Barristers may be divided, for the purpose of seeing how the future will impact upon them, into two groups: those who are concerned largely with criminal work, and those who are concerned largely or exclusively with civil work. Outside London a very large proportion of practising barristers at the self-employed Bar are involved in criminal work. In every criminal trial there are two sides: the prosecution and the defence. In higher courts it has been customary for both sides to be represented by the independent Bar. Indeed, in a magistrates' court, where a large number of contested criminal trials take place, that was also quite often the case.

Some factors have encroached upon the volume of work available to the Bar, both in the magistrates' court and in Crown Court trials. The Crown Prosecution Service now carries out much more work through employed barristers. In more recent years, solicitors who specialise in advocacy have begun to encroach significantly on the work of the Bar. There is a growing feeling that a much more organised public defender service might be a more cost-effective way of providing representation in court for criminals. It is very likely in future that much of this representation will also be provided through employed lawyers rather than the self-employed Bar. This does not mean that there will be less work for advocates, as the same number of persons is required in each trial. It does, however, mean that it will be less the preserve of the self-employed Bar. The other factor, which has much exercised debate among barristers, is the way the government pays for the work done by criminal barristers. It is not possible to go into detail here, but, because of the volume of this work, it is essential in the public interest to control the fee levels. It may be that these have been controlled in a way that makes work at the Criminal Bar much less attractive than it has been in the past. Certainly this is the feeling of barristers. All these factors taken together make it unlikely that the self-employed Bar dealing exclusively with criminal work will grow greatly in the future. Quite the reverse may well be true.

So far as barristers dealing with civil work are concerned, it is even harder to give a clear picture. Among specialised lawyers with a high degree of expertise in a small area, barristers dealing in particular areas of civil work have been among the most highly regarded and highly rewarded. Recent decades have seen, however, an enormous growth of specialisation within solicitors' firms. As you will see when you begin to survey the legal scene yourself, many solicitors' firms are very, very large indeed. In a typical city, the largest firm will have more solicitors than all the barristers in that city put together. These solicitors are increasingly specialised and expert in particular areas within their firm. They have other specialist solicitors within the firm on whom they can call when there is a need. They thus often do not need to go outside to the Bar for specialised advice, as has been so in the past. Again the overall picture is that there will be an increasing need for highly specialised lawyers, as the law becomes more complex and its practice more demanding, but it does not necessarily mean that the most expert will be found in the specialised barristers' chambers. This picture is becoming very varied. Barristers, who for centuries offered their services only through solicitors, can now be employed directly by other professions, for example, patent agents and licensed conveyancers. On the other hand, some large firms of solicitors employ specialist barristers to give in-house advice to their clients. The writers' view is that the specialised Bar in England and Wales is so high in quality and so highly regarded for this quality that it will continue to thrive and, for the students seeking a career at the Bar which is both financially and intellectually rewarding, there is very much to be said for seeking out such an area of practice. In any event, the specialism they acquire will allow for a career outside the self-employed Bar.

What of the generalist practitioner?

KEY POINT ●

With the increase in the amount of law and also its growing complexity larger solicitors' firms have developed multiple specialisms in law. It is difficult for generalist practitioners to offer a full range of legal services.

We began this chapter by looking at access to the legal professions for students. Another side of the coin is access by members of the public to the legal services provided by the legal profession. In the last hundred years a feature of legal practice has been that every small town has its own 'high street practitioners'. These are small firms, maybe of two to six partners. They tend to be generalists. Some in the firm may do entirely litigious work, some entirely non-litigious, but within those areas there is a high degree of non-specialisation. In the debates that have raged about the future provision of legal services in England and Wales, much has been said about the importance of such firms in maintaining access to legal advice. This is closely linked with the topic that was discussed earlier in the chapter on the provision of public money through Legal Aid to pay for legal services. Many smaller firms have depended to a great extent on such funding.

Is there a future for the generalist practitioner and the small high street firm? It may well be that there are two sets of forces which will provide a negative answer to this question when taken together. First, there are the risks, complexities and uncertainties facing providers of legal services as the marketplace changes with such rapidity. Second, there is the difficulty of dependency on relatively small levels of routine work, such as conveyancing and probate, when large providers of such a service use electronic processing to provide packaged forms of such services which are in many respects more desirable to the consumer. This is the difficulty for the practitioner. Without such work they cannot be available on the high street to provide the legal advice and assistance that some members of the public will need. The volume providers of conveyancing and so on will not be interested in the giving of particular legal advice on issues such as boundary disputes, trespass, nuisance, neighbours and so on. Who will provide advice to the consumer who wishes to sue in respect of a package holiday where the accommodation services were far below that promised by the brochure? It is very hard for solicitors to provide a service in such an area unless the cost of doing so is subsidised by other areas of work such as conveyancing and probate. One answer, of course, might be to suggest that courts should be made more accessible to persons without legal advice and this does seem a very desirable reform, at least so far as claims for small financial amounts and limited complexity are concerned. Even with this, though, there will be a lamentable gap in the provision of legal services if it is not possible for the 'high street firms', accessible to and affordable by the generality of the public, to survive. As the new framework for regulation of legal services is developed, it is important that it develops in a way that encourages the continuance of these services. It is also important that it encourages their continuance with a quality of service that can compete with the large commercial firms; otherwise those using their services will be hugely disadvantaged.

> **KEY POINT** ●
> Access to justice is an important point for any legal system. How this is to be achieved is, and will continue to be, problematic.

Services provided by lawyers

As the legal marketplace changes and different kinds of commercial entities are allowed to provide legal services, solicitors will combat this sensibly by diversifying themselves. There are solicitors now who provide estate agency services, pension services, and a wide range of other financial services to their clients. This is important for them in both maximising their profit and in attracting and obtaining new business. It is mentioned here because it both pinpoints a development that will increase in the future and indicates an aspect of the life of many lawyers that is not much referred to by law schools – that lawyers are businessmen. The nature of their business will change. It involves, as all businesses do, the management of people and of human resources. It also involves understanding and taking commercial risks and adapting to the changing world around the business. Solicitors who are good at this will thrive.

> **■ CHECKLIST**
> **▓ CURRENT ISSUES IN LAW**
>
> ▶ The factors preventing ease of entry to the legal profession.
>
> ▶ The cost of qualifying as a lawyer.
>
> ▶ The funding of legal services – how is this to be achieved, particularly in relation to people of limited or modest means?

▶ The organisational changes faced by law firms in the next 10–20 years.

▶ Will the role of the barrister have to change, given the increasing specialisation in the larger solicitors' firms and the reduction in the level of state funding for legal services?

▶ The fate of the generalist practitioner.

▶ What needs to be done to ensure that members of the public have access to justice?

▶ The changing list of services provided by lawyers.

As your legal studies progress and your understanding of law deepens you may care to consider how the above list of issues has changed and what are now the main issues or challenges in law.

Chapter 4
The way law is taught

Lectures, seminars, and other methods of teaching

This chapter is concerned to describe law teaching. It should not lead you to forget that law is learnt more than it is taught. The most important part of the study of law is the effort and work that you make yourself and that you make largely on your own. But the lectures and seminars which you are given provide the essential framework for your study.

In many ways the format of lectures and the smaller group seminars and tutorials has remained unaltered for a century. Law teachers have been as conservative in their teaching method over the years as teachers of any other discipline.

There is always a danger that a method of delivering information, advice and explanation such as the lecture can become rather routine and dull. It is important that a continual effort is made to use the different forms of class lectures and seminars to the best advantage. Do not accept too readily a role as the passive recipient of instruction and allow the experience to flicker past your half-waking mind like a half-watched late-night film.

While lectures and seminars are still the principal teaching methods in law that is not to say that other forms of teaching are not used. The teaching of skills, such as advocacy and drafting, are found in some modules. Alternatively, legal skills may be used as a vehicle to illuminate a particular area of law. An example of this would be an instruction to draft a restraint of trade clause in order to demonstrate the constraints placed upon such a process by relevant case law. Other teaching methods include: transactional approaches to law, for example where students are placed in teams to simulate advising the buyer and the seller of property; other role-playing exercises; and clinical legal education, based upon advising 'live' clients. These other varieties of law teaching are considered in the next chapter.

Lectures

'Lecture means a teaching period occupied wholly or mainly with continuous exposition by the lecturer.' (Sir E Hale *Report of the Committee on University Teaching Methods*, London University Grants Committee).

'A means of transferring information from the notes of the lecturer to the notes of the student without passing through the minds of either.' (traditional definition of a lecture)

In most colleges, lectures are formal occasions. There are different types of lectures and exceptions to the rule but usually those attending are expected to listen and take their own notes without interrupting the speaker with questions at least until invited to do so, perhaps at the end of the lecture. However, some lecturers do encourage or allow questions and you will soon be familiar with the style of your lecturers, and whether they would prefer no interruptions at all, even to the extent of not asking them to repeat the name of a case you did not hear.

Why lectures?

You may wonder what is the value of a lecture. Lectures, as implied above, are usually monologues by the lecturer, generally twice a week for 50–60 minutes on any one subject. They are quite often a one-way process, your role being passive and your participation limited to attendance and note-taking. You may feel that attendance is not particularly beneficial, and that you could do as well reading a textbook or copying up somebody else's notes. Lecturing is sometimes portrayed as an unnecessary activity, a relic from the days when textbooks were rarer, and the lecture would have been an opportunity to communicate essential knowledge to a large number of people at one time. Lecturers obviously vary as much in style and quality as must do any other professional group – perhaps more so as the role encourages a certain independence, even eccentricity, of approach.

Looked at from the lecturer's viewpoint, it is not possible to satisfy everyone. The student's requirements themselves vary from those who prefer an accurate set of notes, which means the lecturer must speak mostly at dictation speed throughout, or make it clear what to write down, to those who would rather listen and make only outline notes, gathering the material and going through the sources for themselves. With the advent of blackboard and other virtual learning environments, you may find lecture notes or other materials on the subject site. You need to be aware of what the site contains and what use your lecturer makes of it. The provision of notes on such a site may influence your approach to lectures. What should the student expect to *achieve* from lectures?

A collection of notes

The second part of this chapter contains a lengthy discussion of note-taking. Many law students become a little obsessed with taking a verbatim record of their lecturer's golden words. Notes are important in lectures but not to the exclusion of intelligent thought. It might help to enumerate briefly what note-taking can achieve.

(i) It provides a body of material which can be used later to assist in seminar work and later still in preparing for examinations. All but the hopeless cases will expect to supplement their lecture material quite considerably for the latter purpose. A 'good set of notes' has a value in helping organisation of thoughts and in providing a psychological prop, but is not sufficient in itself for any but the barest of passes. Even with this aim in mind, a more valuable, useful record will be achieved if you concentrate on clear headings, sub-headings and brief simple points. Discovering the underlying structure of a topic should be one of your primary goals, as this gives you a good starting point for the exploration of a subject area. If a lecturer uses Powerpoint, a structure may become apparent from a slide show. Should the Powerpoint slides be made available on the virtual learning environment then there is no need for students to make a verbatim note of the slides. This leaves you more time to concentrate on what your lecturer is saying.

> **HINT** →
> In lectures look for the underlying structure of topics.

(ii) The record you keep of lectures provides a valuable indication of the real syllabus. Law syllabuses tend to be drawn in an indiscriminate way, including, in theory, the entire contents of very large areas of law. Lecturers will inevitably leave out parts of the given syllabus or place huge emphasis on some parts and little on others. It is wise to pay close regard to this.

(iii) The lecturer will provide frequent reference to decided cases, legislation, learned articles and other sources of valuable information and critical comment. Some lecturers give exact references, others give clues, for example 'there is an article on this worth reading by Professor Rogers in CLJ'. In either case the references are meant to be followed up; the different style reflects different degrees of belief in the amount of effort one can expect of students. If tempted into indolence, remember that lecturers refer you to articles that have stimulated

> **HINT** →
> Lectures provide signposts to further study and the weight to be placed on different parts of a syllabus.

their interest, and topics in which they have a keen interest frequently find their way into examination questions.

(iv) In the same vein, the lecturer will attempt to bridge the gap between the printed textbooks and the present state of knowledge. The law in nearly every field is developing rapidly. There is an ever-increasing deluge of decided cases, reforming statutes and law journals. The lecturer performs an invaluable role in making sense of all these indications of change. Sometimes, it may be felt academic lawyers place too much emphasis on 'the latest thing' in the way of case law. For the law students, however, the sieve provided by the lecturer between them and the welter of publications is essential.

(v) The lecturer will stimulate a student's interest, provide valuable background insight and impart to the student some of his or her own enthusiasm for the subject. This intangible set of benefits to be derived from lecturers is perhaps the most important. The lecturer will have strongly held, often controversial, views about the way the subject is and ought to be developing. These views expressed in a forceful and challenging way will assist the student in developing his or her own critical faculties.

> **KEY POINT** ●
>
> Lectures provide a focus for a subject, giving guidance as to where student effort should be concentrated.

Attendance

Apart from the reasons implicit in the above as to the benefit of attendance at lectures, it is quicker and easier to attend them yourself and make your own notes, than to copy by hand, or even, at some expense, photocopy other people's. Other people's lecture notes are seldom as useful to you as your own. The style will be different, making them harder to assimilate. They may have missed essential points. Finally, the mere fact of having listened and written them yourself helps to familiarise you with the material and eases the learning process.

Some lecturers teach by means of handouts containing all the information they consider necessary to be retained from a lecture. Is there any point in attending the lecture itself so long as you learn the handout? The answer would be 'yes' as hearing the area discussed, the explanations and the illustrations must cost less in effort for the same or better results than going through the work entirely alone. Also the handout approach allows more time for explanation and the development of themes.

Attendance at lectures and seminars is essential for a further reason that is hard to describe briefly. It lies in the nature of law. The law you study is a mass of statutes and case-law decisions. The essence of studying law is making shape and order out of this chaos. Things that are unclear can dramatically slide into focus when explained by someone who does already have a deep knowledge and profound understanding and above all is an enthusiast of the subject under discussion. The lecture is the place where systematic understanding can be greatly assisted and the enthusiasm of the student kindled.

It should not be forgotten also that while the lecturer has obligations as a full-time member of the faculty so does the student have obligations as a participant in the course. Education is a two-way process – and the giving and receiving are reciprocal. It is reasonable for lecturers to demand a high level of both attendance and participation. This, after all, is the purpose for which a place at college is accepted.

Equipment

You may think it too obvious to mention, but there are some students who use notebooks for taking lecture notes, whereas loose file paper is far more convenient. Your aim while gathering material from lectures or your own study should be to produce 'a package'. This consists of placing all the information relevant to any one point in the same place, and the basis of this package will be your lecture notes (unless you are on a course where the lectures are not intended to supply the basic information relating to a topic, in which case you will have to rely on your own notes to form the basis of this package). You can then supplement the lecture with cases, notes on articles and apposite quotations by interleaving them on additional sheets of paper, or perhaps even cards. Lecturers may place notes on the Internet that are downloadable. This makes your task easier when creating a package of materials. Such a package can then be used for coursework, and can be easily used for revision rather than having to remember that there is a note on an article somewhere else or trying to look at several files or books at once. A level of organisation and planning is required – not as a rigid strait-jacket – but as a precaution against the evaporation of time and the dissipation of effort.

Note-taking

Effective note-taking is essential to maximise the benefit to be gained from most law lectures. If you are attending a 'one-off' lecture by a visiting speaker, you may prefer to sit and listen, and make any notes, if at all, afterwards. Equally, with an 'ideas' lecture, it may be sufficient just to sit and listen and some people do find it easier to understand and recall without the distraction of note-taking. However, law lectures have a weighty factual content, and are both fact and concept intense. It has apparently been proved by research that the average number of items that a person can hold in his short-term memory is seven, plus or minus two, and a law lecture containing less than seven points worth remembering would be most unusual. Therefore note-taking is necessary.

For the notes to be an effective aide-memoire, you must read through them soon after the lecture, not only from the point of clarifying exactly what you have written down but also to begin consolidation of the information. It is important that you understand the material that has been presented to you. Any uncertainties should be explored and questions asked of the lecturer, either at the end of a lecture or later. If possible, you should go over your notes several other times before revision so that when revising you are able to read through them, as opposed to having to struggle through them painfully seeking comprehension.

In developing a system of note-taking these are helpful suggestions.

(i) You must develop your own system of abbreviations: particularly for the common terms on your courses. In this context, see the notes on the extract of the lecture and the comments on those notes later in the chapter.

(ii) You must find a way of setting out your notes on the page that highlights the main points, so that when you read through them, or are revising from them, the main points stand out in divisions of paragraphs and sub-paragraphs instead of just presenting a page uniformly covered with writing. Cases and legislation should be underlined. For an illustration of how notes are taken and can be set out, see the notes from the extract of the lecture.

(iii) You must be selective, and cultivate the ability to recognise information worth noting. Unless you are listening to a lecturer who makes it clear how much you should write down, the difficulty of what to note and what to leave out is a problem that totally defeats some students, even into their final year. It is certainly difficult to be selective when you are unfamiliar with a subject, its terminology, and in most cases the end result in the form of the examinations. The temptation is not to leave out anything in case it crops up again later. However, the endeavour to keep up with the lecturer and write down everything will in the long run lead to points being missed and critical gaps or mistakes in your notes.

The first step in being selective is to leave out repetitive material. Most lecturers repeat themselves, either directly or in slightly different words, to help make a point intelligible and emphasise it. If a lecturer has indicated that material, such as Powerpoint slides, is available electronically then there is little point to copy such material. Concentrate on what is being said.

Secondly, unless necessary to aid comprehension, many hypothetical examples and illustrations can be omitted. The same point can be illustrated by several different factual situations that are merely meant to strengthen an explanation, and are not necessary to the theme of the lecture. For example, while mentioning unreasonable behaviour in family law, the lecturer might give many examples of different types of behaviour, but not related to any particular case, which could amount to unreasonable behaviour. Rather than try to note them all, it would be better to listen and appreciate the sense of what is being said.

If, however, the example were a 'what if' factual variation to a case, introducing slightly new facts to the type of cases already discussed, it might be well worth noting. There is such a hypothetical example in the extract from a lecture below. It extends the factual situations already discussed and, once again, where it is referred to as a point of some importance, it is likely to arise again in later discussion or questions.

Below is an extract from a lecture on 'what amounts to an offer in contract'. What the lecturer actually said is set out in full, and this is then followed by a set of notes on that lecture, as an illustration of one possible way of taking down and setting out lecture notes. At the end of these notes you will find some comments on the notes themselves explaining why particular points were noted, and the further work that should be done in preparation of 'the package'.

✖ EXAMPLE

Extract from a lecture

After the somewhat brief introduction to the law of contract, I will start to look today at the ingredients of the basic idea I mentioned last – the phenomenon of agreement – and the premise that in English law this is judged objectively, an important point. The starting point is the offer – most contracts (later on I shall look in more detail at the extent of generality of this statement), most contracts in any event are formed by an act of one party clearly identifiable as an *offer* to enter into a contract followed by an *acceptance* by another party of that offer.

What is an offer?

Before coming to a definition of 'offer' – if such can be formulated – I am going to consider the nature of the problem of distinguishing an offer from other statements and acts before formation of a contract. The situation in question typically is: parties who might or might not end up in a contract 'chaffering', as the cases put it, about the terms of the bargain they might make. Only part of what is said will be 'an offer' and the rest will be characterised as an 'invitation to treat'.

The first question to discuss then is how to distinguish an offer from an invitation to treat. A major difficulty in commencing this discussion has been the reluctance of the courts to adopt a clear definition of an offer and then apply that to subsequent cases. I will start with a working definition. 'An offer is an expression of an intention to be bound contractually on certain terms.'

Taking this preliminary definition, let us look at an area where this invitation to treat/offer dichotomy has produced some debate – that is the situation of an 'offer' for sale of goods in a shop or an analogous situation.

Case law discussing the situation where a shop-keeper exhibits goods in a shop window with a price-tag seems consistent in holding that that is not an offer, but that the offer is made by a customer who offers to the shop-keeper or cashier the price of the goods which the shop-keeper is free to accept or not as he chooses. An example of this is seen in the theft case of *Dip Kaur v Chief Constable* [1981] 2 All ER 430, concerning the purchase of a pair of shoes intended to be sold for £5.99 but incorrectly marked with the tag £4.99. The suggested rule was certainly the assumption. See eg the Lord Chief Justice Lord Lane at p 432, referring to an offer made by the purchaser – *Dip Kaur*.

The *locus classicus* where this area was discussed is: *Pharmaceutical Society of Great Britain v Boots Cash Chemists Ltd* [1952] 2 QB 795; and this area has also given rise to a number of articles you might read eg Winfield in 55 LQR and on this point see pp 516–518, Unger in 16 MLR and also Kahn in 72 South African LJ 246.

The facts in the *Boots* case were as follows.

The shop was a self-service shop – drugs listed in the Pharmacy and Poisons Act 1933 were sold there. It was not lawful to sell these goods save under the supervision of a registered pharmacist (s 18(1)). Drugs were displayed and priced on a central island where customers would select them and place them in their basket. The customer then took them to a cashier's desk and paid for them and left the shop. The place where the money was paid was supervised but not the place where drugs were exhibited. The Court of Appeal accepted the decision and reasoning of the Lord Chief Justice Lord Goddard at first instance and he, [1952] 2 All ER at 456, stated quite clearly:

It is a well-established principle that the mere fact that a shop-keeper exposes goods which indicate to the public that he is willing to treat does not amount to an offer to sell. I do not think I ought to hold that there has been a complete reversal of that principle merely because a self-service scheme is in operation.

Before considering further the validity of this decision in the light
of a proposed definition of an offer, I will refer you to one or two
other relevant authorities:

Fisher v Bell [1960] 3 All ER 394, QBD concerned the interpretation of
the words 'offers for sale' in s 1 of the Restriction of Offensive Weapons
Act 1959. The question was: when a flick-knife was placed in a shop
window with a ticket with the words on 'Ejector knife – 4s.' had there
been an offer for sale? The Court said no. Lord Chief Justice Lord
Parker added, 'the display of an article with a price on it in a shop
window is merely an invitation to treat'.

A case in an analogous area is *Partridge v Crittenden* [1968] 2 All ER
421. The same kind of reasoning was applied to the same effect to an
advertisement in the magazine *Cage and Aviary Birds* which announced
'Bramblefinch cocks, Bramblefinch hens, 25s each'. (Again a criminal
case, this time for offering for sale a live bird contrary to the
Protection of Birds Act 1954.)

Before coming to the merits of these cases let us add to the plot a
hypothetical example given by Winfield in the article referred to
at p 518: 'even if the ticket on a clock in a jeweller's window were
"for sale for £1, cash down to first comer" we still think that it is
only an invitation to do business and that the first comer must be
one of whom the jeweller approves'.

If we recall the preliminary definition of an offer with which I
started – an expression of an intention to be bound contractually on
certain terms – let us with that in mind look at the merits of the
restrictive view of what is an offer shown by the cases and supported
so trenchantly by Winfield . . .

Notes on the lecture

Agreement[1]
(Objective standard?)[2]

A. The Offer[3]

Most contracts formed by one prty mking an offer, fllwd by an acceptance by ano. prty.

(i) Distinction from other statements and acts before contract.[4]
Prties chaffer about terms: which part is an offer & which invtns to
treat (ie preliminaries nt bng offers).
    – In distinguishing from invtn to treat crts are reluctant to give
    defn of an offer and apply it to other cases.

Poss deftn = an expressn of intn to be bnd contractually on certn terms. Distinction between invtn to treat & offer in sale of gds cases:

Dip v Kauer v Chief Constable for . . . . [1981] 2 All ER 430[5]

Theft case – prchse of pr of shoes. Price was 5.99 – one shoe wrongly labelled 4.99 Crt assumed offer was by customer, see esp. LCJ Lord Lane at 432, see also

Ph. Soc. of G. B. v Boots Cash Chemists Ltd [1952] 2 QB 795[6]

(also article in 55 LQR esp. pp 516–518 Unger 16 MLR Khan 72 So. Af. LJ) Self-service shop – listed drugs sold – unlawful to sell them except under supervision of reg. ph. Displayed on central island for cust to choose. Pd at cashier's desk – desk was supervd by reg. ph.
C. A. upheld 1st inst. judgment of LCJ Goddard & Fllwd his reasoning (Note [1952] 2 All ER 456).
Sd displaying gds is nt offer for sale. Particularly this rule wd nt be reversed for self-service scheme.
See: *Fisher v Bell* [1960] 3 All ER 731.[7]
Interptn of 'offer for sale' in s 1 Restctn of Off Weapons 1959. Flick-knife in shop window – ticket 'Ejector-knife 4s'.
Was this 'offer for sale' within 1959 Act?
Held Parker LCJ article in shp window with price on is merely invtn to treat. Same reasoning applied in:

Partridge v Crittenden [1968] 2 All ER 421[8]

Ad in mag – 'bramblefinch cocks, ditto hens 25s each' Poss offence to offer for sale a live bird (Protectn of Birds Act 1934). Winfield in 55 LQR at 518[9] says: 'For sale for £1 cash down to 1st comer' is still an invtn to treat. 1st comer must be one of whom jeweller approves.

How does this sq with hypothetical deftn?[10]

Comments on notes

The numbers in these comments correspond to the numbers in the lecture notes.

1   The heading 'agreement' is approximately in the centre of the page. The lesson from this astonishingly significant statement is this: the layout of your notes *is* important. You will be trying to learn from them and this process will be considerably assisted by an eye-catching reasonable layout.

2   'Objective standard' is followed by a question mark to remember to seek further elucidation about this point, probably in tutorials.

3 Sub-heading 'A'. 'The Offer', being the first element discussed in agreements (see comment 1 above).

4 (i) indicates that this is the first point discussed in relation to offers; the numbering serves to distinguish it from other points about offers. It seemed fundamental to note that offers must be distinguished from invitations to treat and that the courts are reluctant to give a definition of an offer. In the absence of a definition by the courts, it appeared worth noting the lecturer's definition, since, as is often the case with definitions, it was referred to again later in the lecture. Definitions tend to form a starting point and are frequently drawn into the lecture again later as a point of comparison. They are therefore worth noting.

5 Here the case name is misspelt. You should correct this, as it can give the impression that you have not bothered to look up the references or any relevant texts. Gap left in the name as it was impossible to get it all down, and this could be filled in later. Reference particularly was made to Lord Lane's judgment at p 432. The main points of this, or any apposite quotations, can be noted on a separate sheet/ postcard, and interleaved in the file in appropriate place.

   The case names should be indented and underlined to make them stand out. The references to cases are also taken down where possible. You obviously should not endeavour to learn them, but it expedites the work of preparing your 'package' (see above) if you have the references to hand.

6 The articles are noted as this is stated by the lecturer to be a *locus classicus*. These should be looked up, summaries made on a separate sheet/card of any points you wish to remember, together with any pertinent quotations. The quotations should be a matter of several phrases rather than lines long, as in this extract alone from one lecture there are six specific references and the task of memorising them all would be an intolerable burden. Therefore be selective, and paraphrase the arguments. The fact that so much material has been referred to, and such emphasis laid on the case means that it may well recur in tests/examinations/ assessment and is worth spending time on (see hidden curriculum, p 47 above). Incidentally, the annotator failed to notice that Winfield's article was written prior to the *Boots* case.

7 On reading through the notes again after the lecture, it would be apparent that *Fisher v Bell* did not merit much further time. The lecturer did not place the same emphasis on it as the *Boots* case,

and its main value would be illustrative. The greatest value that you would probably get out of it is in an examination where you are discussing this point and could say something along the lines: 'Another illustration is *Fisher v Bell* where the Court held that exhibiting a flick-knife in a shop window with a price tag does not amount to an offer for sale within the meaning of the relevant Act.' Therefore, do not waste time making a conscious effort to commit the details to memory. The reference in this was unclear and can be corrected.

8 Similarly, with *Partridge v Crittenden*. Further research and learning of the detail are unnecessary when you consider the possible use of the case. It is a later case than the *Boots* case and *Fisher v Bell*, but it seems from the lecturer's introduction not to make any new points.

9 A hypothetical example from Winfield, being a slight variation on the factual situations already discussed. Worth noting and reading later, and adding any important points in the article as part of 'the package'. (See above.)

10 This note, which in fact refers to the preliminary definition by the lecturer, is presumably going to be developed further in the next lecture. No indication is given on possible background reading before the lecture.

Throughout the lecture notes, abbreviations were used. Although there are formal shorthand systems, such as Pitman's or speedwriting, most students do not know these, and indeed using such a system as Pitman's it would probably be necessary to transcribe the notes. Therefore, abbreviations tend to be personalised, and those in the notes above were merely meant to be illustrative examples. As said before, you can adopt any system so long as you can read it back easily afterwards. Below are the full words for the abbreviations used in this text, together with some further suggestions:

prty, prties	party, parties
ano	another
fllwed	followed
invtns	invitations
nt	not
bng	being
crts	courts
reluctnt	reluctant

deftn	definition therefore
∴	therefore
∵	because
poss	possible
intn	intention
bnd	bound
certn	certain
gds	goods
prchse	purchase
pr	pair
Ph. Soc.	Pharmaceutical Society
supervsn	supervision
cust	customer
reg. ph.	registered pharmacist
inst	instance
pd	paid
sd	said
wd	would
interptn	interpretation
restctn	restriction
off	offensive
shp	shop
ad	advertisement
mag	magazine
protectn	protection
sq	square
CJ	Chief Justice
LCJ	Lord Chief Justice
HL	House of Lords
CA	Court of Appeal
HCt	High Court

CoCt	County Court
Mags	Magistrates' Court
PC	Privy Council
MR	mens rea
DMC	Donatio Mortis Causa
W	Will
cqv	cestui que vie
T	tenant
L	landlord
V	vendor
P	plaintiff or, conventionally Π
Cl	claimant
D	defendant or, conventionally Δ
eg	for example

The possible list is obviously immense, and with practice you will contrive your own shortforms and abbreviations.

■ CHECKLIST

■ TAKING NOTES

In taking notes consider the following:

▶ Structure

▶ Headings, sub-headings and points

▶ Cases, legislation and secondary sources, such as articles

▶ Abbreviations

▶ Examples

After the lecture:

▶ Check notes for accuracy

▶ Read around the subject-matter of your notes

▶ Follow up references given, such as, read cases

▶ Use the e-learning resources on the subject website

Making a fair copy of lecture notes

This is probably an unproductive use of time better allocated to understanding your notes, reading around them and supplementing them with further material, towards the end goal of establishing 'the package' (see above). You should be aiming to take sufficiently good and clear notes during lectures to make it unnecessary to spend further time merely in rewriting the same material again. You may find it necessary to add to your notes if you have had to leave a gap, or to correct small passages, but it should not be necessary to have to rearrange the whole fifty minutes' worth. There may be circumstances, however, in which you feel it is desirable to rewrite all or part of the lecture notes. Before doing so, the following are points worth considering.

(i) Rewriting the notes can help you assimilate the material but it is advisable to go through the lecture soon after anyhow, and this would probably have the same effect.

(ii) Was the lecturer's style unclear? Did they jump from point to point? Or speak quickly? With the result that it was impossible to take adequate notes? In this case it may be worth sorting out what you did manage to take down, adding your own material and rewriting the notes to form one comprehensible set. The criterion must be whether what you wrote down in the lecture was so bad it is a good use of your time to produce a fair copy, or whether you can make sense of what is left, even if somewhat messy, and simply add material of your own.

(iii) Was the lecture intended to supply essential core material for your course? In other words, will you have to rely on the information contained in the lecture notes at some later stage, or can you achieve equally good results without referring to them again? If so, again, there is little point in making a fair copy, however inadequate they are.

> **HINT →**
> Re-writing your notes is usually unnecessary and not the best use of your time.

Questions

There are several types of question you might want to ask during the course of a lecture:

(i) request for repetition of a misheard word;

(ii) an explanation of something you did not understand;

(iii) developing further a point made by the lecturer.

It is impossible to advise you how any one individual lecturer will react to questions. Attitudes vary as to whether any questions at all are permitted, and as to whether a request merely to repeat a case name or statute will meet with a chilling response. One of the authors recalls in an early contract lecture a student, asking for a point to be repeated, being told: 'I am not dictating a child's guide to the law of contract'. Students can expect a more helpful response from most people who have chosen to be law teachers! For the lecturer, questions interrupt the flow and thoughts, and with a large class this can be disruptive. You may find therefore that the atmosphere is quite formal, with questions only at the end, if then. On the other hand, some lecturers are quite willing to have a pause in the lecture, seeing the break as an opportunity to revive interest and attention.

Even where questions are allowed, you can consider whether the question is necessary. While appreciating the need for comprehensible notes, it can be irritating for the lecturer to have repeated requests for spellings of case names or of parties involved in a case. This is something that can easily be checked up later, if in doubt. Therefore, even where questions are permitted you should ask yourself whether it is something to which you can easily provide the answer yourself afterwards.

Seminars, tutorials, problem classes

The style, frequency and content of these classes is by no means constant. Typically, before each class a student is set a problem or an essay title and is required to either prepare the same for discussion or to submit a written answer. Some suggestions as to preparing written work are made below.

A crucial question for students is the amount of time to spend on seminar preparation.

Let us consider two simple examples of seminar topics.

(i) From contract law: 'The doctrine of promissory estoppel has driven a cart and horses through traditional contract theory.'

(ii) From constitutional law: 'A government with a large majority in the Commons faces defeat in the House of Lords over a proposal to abolish the constitutional role of the monarchy'
Discuss the various implications of this proposal.

Each of these topics has in its way enough dimensions to form the subject-matter of a separate book. Yet each might also form a question on a subsequent examination paper where the candidate has to answer four or five questions in three hours. It is helpful for the student to regard the seminar as both an educational experience in its own right and as part of a specific programme of preparation for the examinations. Given these twin aims it might be suggested that there is little point in a preparation for seminars in such a depth and quality as cannot be utilised in the examination. Certainly so far as the preparation of written work for seminars is concerned this is true, although wide-ranging reading is to be encouraged, the accumulation of notes made on obscure articles is not likely to be helpful.

Making the most of seminars

The importance of seminars cannot be overstated. The seminar provides an opportunity to test your understanding of an area and to develop your lawyerly skills, particularly in relation to the correct handling of authorities. Careful preparation should be undertaken to ensure you maximise the experience; mere attendance is not sufficient. You need to ensure that you are able to contribute to the seminar discussions. Some students fail to take advantage of the opportunity seminars provide.

HINT →
Attend seminars well-prepared, to maximise a valuable learning opportunity.

Consider the following as a guide.

(i) *Preparation.* It is very annoying to lecturers when students 'do not bother' and attend seminars unprepared. No-one expects days of preparation to precede each seminar. For a typical seminar discussion of the kind mentioned above, four or five hours' preparation might be a norm. References given, in a lecture or as reading on the seminar sheet, should be followed up, read, understood and the main points noted. If the seminar is to take the form of an oral discussion, the main points should be set out, gathering arguments and references under suitable headings.

  The students who prepare for a seminar by perusing lecture notes and then turning to them whenever they are asked to contribute are wasting their own and the lecturer's time. Everyone knows already the arguments and materials rehearsed in the lecture.

(ii) *Contribution.* It cannot be overstated how important it is for students to make every effort to become involved in seminar discussion. During the seminar you have the opportunity to develop your nascent skills in oral argument. Putting forward an argument, you will be rebutted by lecturer or fellow-student and have the opportunity of rejoinder. Never sink into apathy. You can expect early on to find that your reasoning does not convince all your colleagues. Unfortunately there are a few lecturers, but you may well meet one, who revel in the demonstration of effortless intellectual superiority over their

HINT →
Seminars allow you to test your understanding of an area.

students. It is very important not to let the situation overcome you, in life as a lawyer you will often have to argue with people who appear to have greater forensic fire-power and from time to time with those who assume an intellectual strength because of their position instead of because of their argument. Argue tenaciously and forcefully when you have a good point to make; accept correction gracefully if your argument is shown to be false. A mistake made is also an important learning experience if you then appreciate the source of the error and the correct approach to be used.

HINT ⇨

Seminars help you to appreciate how to use and apply law.

(iii) *Applying law.* A seminar will give you an opportunity to understand how the law may apply to various factual scenarios. In your early days as a law student you will find that understanding the method and content of the law challenging, but in addition applying the law presents its own challenges. Seminars help to make clear not only what the law is but also how the law is to be applied.

(iv) *Assessment process.* Seminars are also important for an appreciation of how to tackle examinations. Guidance will be given as to the techiniques to employ in answering law questions, both problems and essays. As your tutor will also most likely mark your work it is worth paying particular attention to any advice given. To benefit fully it is advisable to submit written answers to some seminars at least to get specific feedback on your understanding and style.

(v) *Make use of the tutor.* Careful preparation and seminar attendance may alert you to problems over comprehension and deficiencies in your approach. The tutor in the seminar as elsewhere is the provider of a service. If you cannot understand something, if an explanation is confusing to you, if you would like to go over some ground again – ask the tutor. If you require further elucidation, ask to see the lecturer at some other time or at the end of the seminar. You will find the overwhelming preponderance of lecturers and tutors welcome the chance to give further assistance.

■ **CHECKLIST**

■ **THE WAY LAW IS TAUGHT**

▶ Lectures are a good method of giving general guidance on, and an explanation of, an area of law.

▶ In lectures look for the underlying structure of topics.

▶ Lectures provide signposts to further study and the weight to be placed on different parts of a syllabus.

▶ Lectures provide a focus for a subject, giving guidance as to where student effort should be concentrated.

▶ You must develop an effective system of note-taking to maximise the benefit to be gained from lectures.

▶ Notes should be organised using headings and sub-headings to help highlight the main points.

▶ Read through your notes soon after the lecture to ensure that you understand.

▶ Be selective; concentrate on recognising the information worth noting.

▶ Re-writing your notes is usually unnecessary and not the best use of your time.

▶ Be prepared to ask questions if you do not understand, but do so appropriately.

▶ The importance of seminars cannot be overstated; attend all seminars.

▶ Attend seminars well-prepared, to maximise a valuable learning opportunity.

▶ Make every effort to contribute to the discussions in a seminar.

▶ Seminars allow you to test your understanding of an area.

▶ Seminars help you to appreciate how to use and apply the law.

▶ Get into the habit of writing answers to seminar questions and submitting them for feedback from your tutors.

Chapter 5
Varieties of law teaching

Other methods of teaching and learning law

The previous chapter has described what may be termed the 'traditional' style of law teaching. There are other approaches, each of which has possible advantages and possible difficulties. The purpose of this chapter is to describe the range of varieties of law teaching and give some idea of what the law student may expect to derive from each. No assertion is made that each law degree should contain such methods of teaching. The authors' own preferences are strongly in favour of change and innovation particularly as stimulating student interest. Law teachers are refreshingly individualistic and have widely differing views on this issue especially.

The case method

For very many years the dominant approach to law teaching in the United States of America, the case method, has had a small but persistent role in this country. In its classic form, the students use a set text consisting of extracts from a number of cases and perhaps other materials such as government reports, socio-legal studies and so on. This text will have been prepared with a view to its use in teaching through the case method. The best, and perhaps the only, example in this jurisdiction of a text that is especially designed to fulfil this requirement is Smith and Thomas *A Casebook on Contract*. There are casebooks in other subject areas but not such carefully structured programmed texts. Armed with their casebooks the students are set a number of pages to digest *before* each lecture. Instructions in the lecture then takes the form of the lecturer posing questions – very frequently to a named student – and the development of this question and answer process, which in American jargon is called 'Socratic dialogue'. The strength of this method is in displaying to the student the processes of legal reasoning in a case-law subject. The students are forced into the considerable effort of finding the reasoning upon which discussions are based, applying cases to hypothetical facts, distinguishing one case from another and seeing the development of doctrine in particular areas of the law unfold. The weakness of the method is that it is an inefficient way of teaching students the set of rules which make up a particular area of law. A student exposed to the case method will find it essential to follow the syllabus in a more traditional narrative textbook and perhaps to make his own notes or synopses of each area covered. Where the case method is used, the class can easily become dominated by a small number of eager students. As always the student is urged to make strenuous efforts at participation and avoid any temptation to linger in the background.

In American law schools the method is used in teaching very large groups of students, sometimes in excess of 200. Also in American law schools, there are very often no seminars or other small group classes, so presumably the method can be used to good effect. Experience has shown that it is very hard to prevent the emergence within a class of a group of 'strenuous non-participators'. If you find yourself in a class which is exposed to the case method then if you are not a naturally extrovert speaker, the vital effort must be made right at the beginning before there is any danger of your falling into the overlooked group.

It is equally important, since you will have no systematic exposition of the subject from your lecturer, to follow the course in a clearly written textbook. You cannot, if the course ends in an unseen written examination, rely on notes taken from case method classes to provide the backbone of your revision. You will need to make your own full notes and to do this right from the beginning of the course. You will probably derive most benefit from case-method teaching if you are able to anticipate the lecturer by a substantial margin and read before each lecture not only the case material set, but also further textbook and journal material and prepare your notes on that part of the syllabus before the classroom discussion. Do not despair if at the beginning a part of the course taught by this method appears unproductive and confusing. It is undoubtedly a very much slower method of covering the syllabus than the traditional method of lectures and seminars, and you will need to persist in your programme of preliminary reading and vigorous participation in class in order to achieve rewards.

HINT →

While the case method may not be used on your degree programme it is still important to consider the process of legal reasoning in cases.

What is clinical legal education?

First of all, before examining legal education, consider the following quotation. This is from an old text by a barrister called Dr Bateman Napier[1]. There he wrote:

'I would earnestly impress upon those who intend to spend their life's energy in the legal profession, to cast away once and for all that stupid and pernicious notion, that all that is wanted to become a good lawyer is practice and experience, and that the man of study and of theory is of little or no use in the business of daily life. Doubtless men do become fair – perhaps even good – lawyers by long practice and the teachings of experience, but they acquire their professional skill at an enormous and unnecessary price, and probably no small share of the expense of their education falls upon the shoulders of their early clients or employers. Let a student come to the daily practice of an office armed with, I do not say a deep or wide, but a respectable knowledge of the theory and principles of law, and he will progress with a rapidity unknown to the man who is content to learn all things from practice. Let a student learn such part of the law relating to real property as he may gather from Mr Joshua Williams' or Mr Elphinstone's works, before he begins to spoil stationery by drawing impossible deeds. Let him master the principles of common law as he will find them in the works of Mr Broome, Sir William Anson, or Mr Underhill, before he attempts to talk nonsense on a summons at Chambers under Order xiv. I do not suggest that early in his career a student should be crammed with the details of common law or conveyancing; but I do desire most emphatically to place on record my conviction that, under the present system of legal education, the time of students is wasted, and the best days of their education are squandered in the comparatively futile attempt to teach them the practice of the law before they have any reasonable grasp of its theory.'

This sets forward, in the confident language of the Victorian era a very clear view of legal education and one which encapsulates many of the debates which are still current. What is the proper relationship between learning the words of the law (the theory) and learning how to apply the law in practice in the drawing of court documents, the preparation of deeds and the carrying out of transactions on behalf of clients? By now

---

1 T Bateman Napier LLD *A Modern Digest of the Law Necessary to be Known for the Final Examination of the Incorporated Law Society* Maxwell & Son, 1887.

you will have realised that in legal education in England and Wales there has been something of a dichotomy between the learning of theory, the so-called academic stage, and the learning of practice, the so-called vocational stage. When you read the words of Dr Bateman, you will realise that he appreciates that there must be a strong symbiosis between the two stages. It is with this thought in mind that we come to discuss what is meant by clinical education and what role it might have in the education of lawyers.

Clinical Legal Education – the general background

Many law teachers have thought that legal education would be improved by the involvement of students in some form or other of legal practice. After all, this is a principal method of educating doctors, the argument runs, so why should it not have its place in educating lawyers?

In the development of legal education this century in England and Wales, there has certainly been an undesirably large gap between those involved in the academic side of legal education and the practitioners. Neither has there been the tradition of senior members of the practising profession holding academic posts that is so important a feature of the medical profession. Nevertheless, in various ways, clinical legal education of one kind or another has become a feature, albeit a small one, of the overall scene.

One model which clinical teaching takes is the involvement of students in live cases. Several colleges have set up law clinics or law centres which clients are encouraged to attend in order to receive advice and possibly other legal assistance. Occasionally the performance of student advisers at such a clinic becomes an assessed part of their course.

In other courses, some form of simulation of 'real' legal problems may be used – varying from the examination of some legal document, to the re-creation of extensive examples involving lengthy sets of materials and complex scenarios.

There are dangers involved in an enthusiastic espousal of clinical legal education. Cases that arrive willy-nilly at a law clinic have no particular ordered relationship to the fields of legal doctrine with which a degree student must become familiar. There is also the very prevalent risk of students becoming swept whole-heartedly into this work because it is such an exciting challenge. It is easy then to lose sight of the all-round academic goals which legal education must pursue. A final danger, and a much more controversial one, is the difficulty that can be caused by the desire of students or staff to use the law clinic experience to put the world to rights. Conflicts of interest can be generated between students and their colleges; issues such as student grants, immigration and housing can become items of impassioned debate and the focus moves from the legal into the political arena.

HINT →

Some universities as part of their degree programme offer involvement in live cases. This is an aspect of legal education which is worth considering in determining to which universities to apply.

In their professional work, lawyers are constrained by professional rules – a code of ethics. There is a strict discipline dealing with confidentiality, duties to their clients and conflicts of interest. This is not necessarily present in students' law clinic work – though it seems to the writers, at least, much more satisfactory that it should be. It is equally important for students to accept other forms of professional discipline. Proper files should be kept, telephone calls and interviews properly noted, appointments made and kept and the adviser's duties to his client fully recognised.

If the work takes place in this kind of background, then, within limits, it can be valuable. The student cannot in a 'live' clinic learn much law – the collection of cases is so haphazard and the range of legal issues addressed in a law degree so great. Much, though, is to be learned about the relationship between legal rules and their practical context. The student can gain valuable, supervised experience of the discovery of legal issues in a client's jumbled case history, and of the skills involved in giving clear and helpful legal advice. Hopefully, the student will also become aware of the responsibilities involved in putting oneself in the position of another's legal adviser. It may be seen from this that it is the authors' view that experience of clinical work is a valuable complement to a student's proper academic work rather than a substitute. It is one of the many experiences that can be used to enrich the academic stage of a lawyer's education and make the essential learning that takes place in the library and lecture room more valuable and memorable.

Whether the clinical programme you are offered includes live cases or sets of simulated case studies in the form of documents and so on, you will find it much harder and much more time-consuming than instruction through the familiar pattern of lectures and tutorials. If we consider one area where the simulated case-study method might be used you will see the added dimension.

When you learn basic property law, you will find the topic of registered land, and the topic of co-ownership of land both quite hard to grasp in the classroom. The problem areas which you are dealing with can be recreated using registered land documents, conveyances and other documents. Recreating the academic problems involved through documents such as these requires the production of quite complicated material. In order to understand it, the student has to make some considerable effort but, having done so, instead of learning a set of legal rules in the abstract, has seen how they operate in the practical setting in which they appear to lawyers. The student is able to see the rules working in their real context instead of a set of abstract referenceless rules. For the student, the drawback of this method is that another set of material has to be mastered. The reward is eventually a more all-round understanding of the subject in question.

In the 'live-case' law clinic, it is even harder to see any relation between the learning experience offered and the traditional course of lectures and seminars. Real life refuses to follow the orderly pattern of a

HINT →

An advantage of 'live' client work is that students will be involved in the practical application of legal rules and introduces the idea of managing a case.

KEY POINT ●

Considering law in its practical context and using skills, such as drafting and advocacy, may lead to a deeper understanding of the operation of legal rules.

textbook or lecture course. Cases involve unexpected or confused legal issues or issues purely of fact or credibility. Consequently, this kind of experience is better seen as a complement to the academic programme. It will increase a student's awareness of how his or her knowledge may be later developed and provide an introduction to the acquisition of professional skills but it will not actually form a large part in completing the academic foundations of a legal education.

If you are envisaging embarking on 'live' clinic work in your course or as a voluntary extra, try to see this as preparation for practice in a real sense. Law clinics at colleges in the past have run into difficulties where students (and teachers) have had no sensible idea of professional practice and seen the clinic as a campaigning vehicle. Campaigning for social and political change is something in which you may very well become involved – the lawyer has much to contribute in this area. It is, though, a different thing from representing and advising individual clients and should be kept apart.

You will require an ethical framework in which to work. You will not yet be in a profession so you will not be bound by its traditions and rules. Your teachers or supervisors probably will and can be expected to give you careful guidance. You might like to read *A Guide to the Professional Conduct of Solicitors* published by the Law Society. It should give you much to reflect on when you consider individual ethical problems in your clinical work. Perhaps your law clinic will have clear rules and cover issues such as the following:

(i) Can you deal with cases in which you have a potential conflict of interest, eg where 'the other party' is your college or university?

(ii) With whom is it permissible for you to discuss a client's affairs? How wide is the circle of confidentiality? Does it extend to fellow students or only some of them, law faculty staff or only some of them? Who has access to an individual client's files?

(iii) How should you conduct yourself if you have correspondence with other professional advisers? Have you any duties of truthfulness or fair dealing to them or does 'anything go'?

You also need something in the way of office procedures. Files must be maintained and kept properly secure. You must have some means of making yourself available to your client. It is probably much better if you cover some of these practical matters by written guidelines. This may be especially important in a student law clinic where the same person does not deal with an entire file from beginning to end and it is essential that your work so far be comprehensible to others.

You may find in your own college that there is no existing law clinic run on an official basis. There may be one run by students or you may feel students should fill a gap and commence one. This will, indeed, be a potentially valuable experience – there is no substitute for real experience, although the lessons it gives may be hard-earned. If you are involved in a student-run clinic, I think the above strictures as to ethical standards and having an established office routine are even more important. You will learn most of value if professionally qualified and experienced staff are willing to be involved.

Clinical Education – examples

The first example that we will describe, because it is the one most familiar to the authors, is the model of clinical education at Northumbria University. Here, all the students in the fourth year of the degree are divided into 'firms'. Each firm is supervised by a practising solicitor who is a full-time lecturer in the law school. Each firm is allocated clients in different areas of law. There are firms which specialise in, for example, housing law, in employment law, in property law, in criminal law, family law and education law. The work done in these firms then represents a very substantial part of the assessed work on the fourth year of the law degree. In order to prepare for this, students have modules in the third year of the degree, which lay the foundation for the work they have to do in the student law office and introduces them to the skills of interviewing clients, corresponding with clients, maintaining clients' files, advocacy on behalf of clients, drafting legal documents and so on. Earlier on in the law degree, the students have been further prepared by being taught civil and criminal procedure, for example as an integrated part of their learning of common law subjects. Each firm has a number of firm meetings, where the progress on different cases is discussed and decisions taken on how to proceed. Letters and other drafts by students are looked at and appropriate feedback given. The students are videoed interviewing their real clients and this enables the law office tutors to keep abreast of developments in each case. As the cases proceed, the students represent clients in tribunals such as the Employment Tribunal or before a District Judge in the county court. At the end, students are assessed for this part of their law degree on a portfolio of the work they have completed in the student law office and reflective commentaries they have written on it.

Another example is called Street Law. This is not exactly legal practice. It involves students meeting with local interest groups, say a tenants' group in rented accommodation, and discovering from them which areas of law they would find it valuable to have explained. Under supervision from their tutor, the students then prepare presentations on these areas and meet the local interest groups again to give the presentations. This provides valuable experience of research and development of skills in explaining, for example, land law to real people.

HINT →

When seeking a training contract involvement in 'live' client work can be an important feature of your application.

Developments in skills teaching

Legal education has historically been quite rigidly divided into academic legal education and vocational education. The former concentrates on a systematic and critical understanding of the main areas of law. The latter concentrates on things more directly concerned with practice. In both stages of legal education concentration has been much greater on learning law than on learning lawyer's skills. However, in recent years there has been a heated and productive debate about the proper role of skills teaching in legal education. More will be said about this in Chapters 13 and 14, which deal with the schemes of training for barristers and solicitors. Some discussion of the place of skills training at the law degree stage is also desirable. It is helpful to ask the question – what lawyerly skills should be developed in the academic stage of a lawyer's education? The answer first and foremost is skills of legal research. By this is not meant esoteric historical analysis, but the ability to find, use and apply legal source material; the ability to read cases and statutes and apply them to new or complex situations. This set of skills is developed throughout the course by students who read widely and learn to use properly the materials available in their law library and on the Internet. The bare pass student who relies almost entirely on lecture notes and introductory textbooks will fail to develop these very important abilities. As you will see when you begin the formal study of law, change in the laws and in the legal system is now an endemic process. The good lawyer is one who can comprehend these changes and make use of them in practice. There is now more need than ever to develop basic research skills while reading for one's law degree.

There are also other skills which should be developed by lawyers and it may be of interest to list these and examine their relevance to law degree studies.

▶ Skill in presenting legal argument in writing

▶ Skill in presenting legal argument orally

▶ Advocacy

▶ Counselling

▶ Interviewing

▶ Drafting of legal documents

▶ Negotiating

▶ Business skills

▶ Computer literacy

The first two items in this list are matters which should be at the core of your legal education. They are closely related to the research skills. Your law degree should provide ample opportunity for developing your muscles in these areas.

The remaining 'skills' on the list are more controversial. There are many academics who believe that their development belongs more properly to the vocational stage of a lawyer's education. It is suggested, however, that using legal materials to perform 'tasks' in these 'skills' areas is something that will not only produce better ('more skilled') lawyers but will also improve the quality of the academic experience as such. There is room on a good law degree programme for students to have experience of lawyers' activities such as drafting, negotiating and counselling. There should also be opportunity for students to examine related business areas and appreciate the relevance of computers and modern business information technology. None of this should in any way diminish the importance of the systematic analysis and criticism of the law. On the contrary, it will assist understanding – because practical use and application must do so. It will improve appreciation of the real role of law in society by bringing the classroom experience nearer to the real world. Many law schools are now embracing whole-heartedly the importance of 'skills' in legal education. In choosing a law school for your studies this should be a relevant factor. The world in which the future lawyer will operate will be an even more challenging one. A high level of skills will be at a premium. Developing these will in future come to be a continuing process throughout a lawyer's education.

One example of the kind of exercise that you should expect to perform will show how drafting documents could become an important part of your education. You will learn in looking at property law the important difference between a licence and a lease. A licence can be a permission to occupy another person's property. A lease is a similar arrangement but in English law has the status of being an interest in land. The difference between such a licence and a lease may be of great practical importance. The tenant may have his continued occupation guaranteed by an Act of Parliament. The licensee may not. A typical drafting exercise could be: 'A client wishes to grant a licence of a shop on Oxford High Street for the next year to the Liberal Democratic Party as its campaign headquarters. Draft a suitable document'. This exercise requires the bringing together of substantial knowledge of case and statute law before a successful – albeit simple – draft document can be produced.

Such an exercise can then be taken a stage further by introducing other important skills. For example, a student can be asked to draft a letter to a client explaining, in terms the client will understand, the nature of the legal arrangement. The same exercise can be transformed into a negotiating session. One side is briefed to represent the 'tenant'

HINT →
A consideration of the practical application of law can give a deeper understanding of the concepts and principles of the law itself.

and as to the desired outcome from that point of view, and the other briefed to represent the 'landlord' clearly with a different desired outcome as to the terms and effect of the agreed document. This form of negotiation requires a sound understanding of the difficult legal issues coupled with the ability to deploy this knowledge to good effect. It is an excellent way of reinforcing the understanding of legal rules.

Interviewing and negotiation

The introduction of exercises of interviewing and negotiation into an academic law course is quite controversial. Many law courses are coming to involve such tasks. As you will see later in this book the professional courses for solicitors and barristers involve assessment of such skills. It may be doubted whether there is much place for the formal teaching of these skills. Practice at interviewing and negotiation has a small but useful part to play in a lawyer's education – the rest is learned in the rough and tumble of practice.

However, as with other skills, simulations of useful settings can be devised in which to puzzle out legal problems, to analyse and apply legal concepts.

The most important lesson such exercises should instill is that the foundation of all practical lawyering is sound research, understanding and knowledge of law. If thoroughly based on this foundation then practice of negotiating and interviewing is of value. If it is an exercise in negotiating or interviewing divorced from research and deployment of legal information then it is little more than an amusing game.

Mooting, mock trials, and role playing

These exercises have a marked similarity to clinical legal education but can be discussed separately as having a separate tradition and identity.

Mooting

A moot is an oral argument on some contentious point of law. A moot is set as if it were in a court of law. Some person, usually a member of the teaching staff or a visiting lawyer, takes on the role of a judge either of the Court of Appeal, or the House of Lords. Those appearing in the moot are divided into two teams of two – leading and junior counsel for the appellant and leading and junior counsel for the respondent. The moot problem prepared by one of the lecturers will be carefully constructed so that there are two interlocking points – one to be taken by leading counsel and one to be taken by junior counsel. It is conventional for both counsel for the appellant to address the court, followed by both counsel for the respondent. The presiding judge is at liberty to vary this convention. When the time comes for you to participate in a moot, your lecturers will doubtless provide detailed guidance on what is expected from you. The following may be of some assistance, nonetheless:

(i)   Do not present a welter of authorities. Students frequently feel impelled to show the judge that they are aware of every last case on a subject. In the brief time allowed in a moot to each partici-pant, usually no more than fifteen minutes, this will not impress. As you will know from attending lectures, following complex oral arguments is quite difficult. The number of cases should be kept small. What is demanded is clarity of argument, the demonstration of analytical powers, and the ability to make oneself understood. The good moot speech is surprisingly simple and uncluttered.

(ii) Do not write out the whole of your speech to the court even in order to rehearse it. It is a convention that counsel must not read their argument to the court. It is in any event extremely tedious for a judge to be subjected to somebody's written prose read out verbatim.

(iii) An important test of the good mooter is the ability to deal with interjections from the judge. These will sometimes be extremely penetrating and demand a considered reply. Consequently you will be expected to pause briefly before replying. If, indeed, it is more convenient for you to deal with the point at some later stage then say so. On no account then omit to answer the ques-tion at the appropriate point. If possible deal with the question as it arrives – try to meet it with pertinent authority and reasoned argument, not mere rebuttal. From time to time you will moot in front of a judge – perhaps a visiting lawyer – who has slightly misunderstood the facts or the legal points you are making. It will have been a long day in court, the sherry before-hand was plentiful and the room is warm – his concentration has lapsed or he has, as one of the writers once witnessed, irre-deemably confused your case with your opponent's. As counsel, you must firmly but politely correct the judge and put him on the path of magisterial rectitude. Bluntness in this situation is not recommended – but no lawyer worth his salt will judge your arguments the less favourably because you have rightly stood your ground and he is found to have erred.

(iv) It has been the custom in the past for dress in moots to be formal, at least to the extent of dark suits for mooters of either sex. You will certainly be told in your college if that is required. Even if there is no explicit instruction, you should be prepared to dress in a way appropriate to the setting. An appeal court demands some sobriety both of dress and demeanour. In the same way the audience, if any, should try to approximate their behaviour to that which may be expected by the visiting public in a court of law.

(v) In citing authorities it is expected that you will be able to refer the court to the exact reference. You should be able in the middle of your speech to turn to the correct volume of the law reports, cite the exact reference and read the relevant brief passage from the law report itself. In citing from books and learned articles the convention has been that authors are treated as authorities only after their death. This led to the curious custom that if the author were alive, counsel would adopt his or her words as part of counsel's argument. The custom is no longer rigidly followed; but it is still wise to use references to such material sparingly, and especially to avoid reference to textbooks to support trivial propositions.

(vi) You will still be expected to address fellow counsel and the court formally – fellow counsel as 'my learned friend Miss Smith', the judge as 'My Lord' or 'Your Lordship'. The first counsel to address the court will go through the ritual known as 'making one's appearances'. An example of this would run as follows:

'My Lord, in this case I appear for the appellant, Sugden, together with my learned friend Miss Smith, and my learned friends, Miss Jones and Mr Hyde, appear for the respondent, Challis.'

KEY POINT

Mooting is a valuable experience in terms of developing your research and presentational skills. Again, involvement in such a practical activity will be an important feature of an application for employment.

Students are quite often reluctant to participate in mooting. Making a sound argument in a moot involves a great deal of time and effort. It *is* worthwhile. The experience of research is valuable. The experience of oral presentation of complex legal argument is invaluable training. The experience of being put to the question by an incisive presiding judge, trying though it is at the time, will stand you in good stead for later more searing encounters. It is unwise to turn your back on a challenge. Generations of students have enjoyed the experience of mooting and gained greatly from it.

Mock trials

These are more cumbersome than moots. Students take the roles of all the participants in a jury trial including witnesses, defendant and jury.

The part of the judge is very often taken by a more senior person. Nevertheless, the mock trial is essentially a more light-hearted event. Characters frequently dress the part, assume quaint accents or amusing mannerisms. Sometimes this all degenerates into knockabout comedy. While not too serious a part of the education experience, there is no doubt that participating in such an entertainment can be good fun and may point the odd valuable lesson as to courtroom procedure, forensic skill or rules of evidence.

Role playing

Other less structured forms of role playing may be encountered, especially in seminars. Participants may take the role of a pressure-group arguing for reform of the law, of proponents of a particular legal philosophy or even of the claimant or defendant in litigation. For example, the seminar might be on the issue of whether the criminal law should be based on an equation between punishment and responsibility, or between deviance from normal behaviour and the need for treatment. Students could then adopt the position respectively of a proponent of the traditional view of punishment as retribution and an advocate of treatment of offenders in place of punishment. Exercises such as this in the form of game-playing undoubtedly enliven proceedings. It is, moreover, not unlike the real-life role of a lawyer, to have to argue a given brief, not the one in which you happen to have faith.

Teaching through computers

You may also expect to be exposed to computer-assisted learning. A lecturer will have written a problem or series of problems in such a way that it can be used as a teaching exercise through your college computer or a personal computer. The computer, or a tutorial sheet, will reveal the problem. The visual display on your computer will then ask a series of questions. You will provide answers or choose from a menu of possible answers. The computer will provide comment on your answers and lead you on to further questions. This kind of computer-tutorial is quite difficult and time-consuming for the lecturer to prepare. Nevertheless, such an exercise has two functions. It can be a useful stimulus to student interest in difficult areas and assist in the clarification of a complete set of rules. It also provides an introduction in the form of 'hands-on' experience to the use of computers in a legal context.

Alternatives to lectures

It would not be right to leave the subject of innovation in law teaching without a glance at the possibility of dispensing with lecturers and employing more student-based course structures. At its simplest this may mean a small group meeting more or less regularly for seminar-type discussions on the subject in question. At a more organised level, students may be provided with 'custom-built' learning packages or materials and be expected to pace their own progress through a part of the course studying the material in prescribed sections and meeting singly or in groups to review progress and discuss difficult topics. This approach is dignified by the name 'self-paced learning'. Law schools have adhered fairly strongly to the traditional methods of instruction and you are more likely to find this kind of 'lecture-less' approach, if at all, on the final stages of a degree course. Very commonly when used it is associated with some form of continuous assessment. Whether this is so or not the absence of the routine discipline of a steady lecture programme throws a much greater onus for self-discipline on the student. It requires a much more conscious effort from students to map out their work programme and organise their own time. The process of self-discovery of the subject is doubtless an invigorating alternative for the student to the more passive role often encouraged by the lecture/seminar programme. Like other forms of radical innovation it is much to be welcomed – in strict moderation.

Distance learning and part-time degrees

Some universities have for many years provided evening degree courses in law. The University of London has a long-standing external degree for which tuition is available in some centres. Recently universities began to look at the possibility of providing 'distance learning' modes for courses. In respect of each of these possibilities the sensible advice has to be that it is harder to complete a degree in any of these ways than by the 'traditional' full-time routes. A part-time law degree might involve attendance on two evenings for tuition from, say, 6 pm to 9 pm. On top of this the student will have to find very many hours for private study and should be able to make some time available for study in the law library. The advent of the Internet means, however, that students with access at home will be able to read primary legal source materials without having to travel to a law library (see further Chapter 6).

Our experience is that many students fail in the early years of a part-time degree course because they simply have not calculated the huge commitment of time and energy involved. The whole degree will take, on average, four to five years and the impact of this will be considerable on any successful student's life. Every year from a long-standing part-time law degree course such as ours, students graduate with great credit and a number progress to their professional examinations. At the other end of the scale, a large number always fall by the wayside because the demands of part-time study are so great and in the end beyond them.

Given the expense of full-time study in terms of fees and maintenance, study on part-time and distance learning programmes offers clear financial advantages. The course fees are lower than for full-time study and it is possible to have full-time employment at the same time as pursuing your legal education. It is worth calculating the relative costs of full-time and part-time or distance learning study.

The present picture is now very diverse. There are many universities offering distance learning programmes and many offering part-time evening courses. For nearly all students a course with the opportunity for some attendance and ready contact with other students and lecturers is the preferred choice.

■ CHECKLIST

■ VARIETIES OF LAW TEACHING

▶ Law may be taught in a variety of ways. On any degree programme you may find various teaching methods are employed.

▶ A consideration of the practical application of law can give a deeper understanding of the concepts and principles of the law itself. In choosing a degree programme or optional degree subject a practical approach in teaching may be a factor to influence your decision.

▶ Involvement in clinical legal education will be an important feature of your application for a training contract.

▶ For would-be advocates mooting is an essential opportunity which must be taken. For all law students it is invaluable experience, drawing together a number of aspects of the study and practice of law. Additionally, the experience is always part of further relevant information to include in an application for legal employment.

▶ Modes of legal education other than full-time attendance are available. Part-time and distance learning provision is well developed and offer potential financial advantages to students. It is important to consider the financial implications of any choice you make.

Chapter 6

The law library and the Internet

Finding legal source materials

An essential aspect of the work of a lawyer is to be able to locate legal source materials. Finding relevant law reports and statutes is a necessary prerequisite to preparing any legal advice. To achieve this you must be able to find your way around a law library and now, in the electronic information age, be able to navigate legal databases on the Internet. You will find that there is an overlap between materials available in a law library and on the Internet, but in 2006 not all material, particularly older sources and journal articles, is accessible in an electronic form. In consequence, it is important to appreciate how to use both a physical law library and electronic sources.

The law student will spend a great deal of his time searching for legal source materials. Even the most rugged of practising lawyers will have regular recourse to a library, if he is carrying out his work at all properly. It is common these days on law courses to ensure that students receive a systematic introduction to the law library and electronic sources. Even so, you will find that ability to search for law efficiently and enjoyably is a facility that develops slowly. The variety of materials in the law library is large and you will take some months to become familiar with their different uses. Law books tend to be written in a somewhat forbidding style, perhaps an inevitable by-product of their complex subject-matter. You will need to persevere when you are frustrated and confused. You will need to read sometimes without being at all sure of what is the useful product of your reading. If you persist until the style and format become familiar you will develop, unconsciously, skills of reading legal material that will provide both pleasure and profit throughout your professional life.

HINT →

Familiarise yourself with the layout and content of the law library.

The law library

Material in the law library is contained in four main sections: the law reports and statutes, containing the primary sources of law; the academic journals and periodicals; the textbooks and monographs; and, finally, the bibliographic works and encyclopaedias. The geography of each library is obviously different and the first stage of learning law for any serious student is to become thoroughly familiar with that in his or her university. In your first week or so at university you will, as mentioned, have some guidance from your lecturers in this, usually coupled with a 'library tour' and some carefully structured 'library exercises' to introduce you to various species of legal text. Enter into this part of the programme whole-heartedly. Even if the 'search exercises' in the library do not excite your imagination, remember that they help to lay the foundation for the whole of your legal studies.

The amount of detailed information given to you on an introductory library tour is usually such that it cannot all be remembered, let alone fully digested. It will take you some months to feel at home in the library; to know where to turn for a particular reference, and so on. The use of a library is a skill that is learned not taught. You will obviously listen carefully to your own university's talks on the subject; read thoroughly the material they give you and perform these 'library' exercises. At the end of this you will probably still not feel entirely at home in the library.

In the following weeks you will find yourself deluged with references on reading lists, in lectures and in seminar material. It is at this stage of following up and reading references that your training as a law library user starts in earnest. The process is frustrating. Each reference takes a while to locate. Some seem unobtainable. Where on earth will I find (1789) 3 TR 148 or 72 SALJ 246? When you do unravel the reference and locate the series, a more resourceful student has arrived there first and you must mark time, or proceed to the next reference, until the volume becomes available. Quite often you will be able to find the same case or statute in another series of law reports or statutes. Additionally, the same information may also be available via the Internet.

The weak student will withdraw from this process only too easily, taking comfort in his lecture notes and the textbook or some condensed version thereof. The good student will soldier on until his familiarity with the layout and the abbreviations grows, and retrieving the correct report from its place becomes second nature, a matter of only a few seconds. Nothing can be written to replace this trial and error process of growing acclimatisation to the library and if it is shirked in the early days of your legal study, it can be replaced only with the greatest difficulty. The temptation to leave things until later or to cut corners at this stage will very much reduce the quality of your later studies and prevent you acquiring the 'feel' for legal material that is the hallmark of a well-trained lawyer.

Finding and using law reports

It is not the purpose of this book to provide a bland catalogue of the variety of law reports. Those available in your library will be listed in some prominent place in the body of the library. You will quickly locate this list and use it to acquaint yourself with the series available in your library.

There is an extremely useful text containing detailed guidance on how to use the contents of a law library. This is *Effective Legal Research* by Knowles and Thomas. You will find this book a valuable companion to your studies – it probably cannot be usefully read as a whole – but more fruitfully kept by you for occasional reference and explanation.

The law reports described

The series of reports that are used most by students are the *Law Reports*, the *All England Law Reports* and the *Weekly Law Reports*.

The *Law Reports* or, as they are properly called, the Law Reports of the Incorporated Council of Law Reporting of England and Wales, are as near to an official series of law reports as exists in England and Wales. These contain the overwhelming preponderance of important cases decided since their first publication in 1865. The *Law Reports* are presently published in four series, each of one or more volumes a year. They are: Appeal Cases (AC) consisting of cases decided in the House of Lords and the Privy Council; Chancery Division (Ch); Queen's Bench Division (QB); and Family Division (Fam). The series of *Law Reports* published have varied from time to time, reflecting changes in the division of work in the High Court. A table of these changes is found in Knowles and Thomas at p 32. The *Law Reports* are considered to be the most authoritative reports. If a case is reported both in the *Law Reports* and in other sets of reports, then the report contained in the *Law Reports* is to be preferred. The reason for this is that this version of a report has been checked by the judge or judges who have delivered judgment.

> **HINT** →
> The *Law Reports* are the most authoritative versions of cases and should be used in preference to other versions of the cases.

Earlier law reports

Before 1865 when the Incorporated Council of Law Reporting commenced its work, the system of publishing decided cases was quite chaotic.

From the reign of Edward II to Henry VIII there were published series of reports of cases known as Year Books. Probably these originated in longhand notes of cases taken by trainee lawyers. The language used is not modern English and, as they are of extremely limited value to the student of contemporary law, you are most unlikely to be called upon to read them. Various volumes have been published by the Selden Society. If your law library is housed in a general library, this part of the collection will probably be in the history section of the general library.

The law reports to 1865

Until the reforms of the court system in the second half of the nineteenth century, both the court system and law reporting were something of a jumble. Law reports were published privately and in individual series which lasted sometimes only a year or two and sometimes many years. It was common for each series to be called after the name of the law reporter who collected the cases. These reports are accordingly known as the 'nominate' reports, and your library will probably have some volumes of reports published by a variety of these named reporters. They are in fact little used today because almost all the important series of private reports are collected in the *English Reports* or the *Revised Reports*. It should be noted that the vast majority of these are to be found in the *English Reports*. Any case to which you are referred before 1865 will be reported in one of these two series or, if it is not, your lecturer will explain whether or not he expects you to discover the case in your college's library.

Although you will find the nomenclature of individual nominate reports confusing, it is simplicity itself to look up a case in the *English Reports*. The final two volumes (177–178) consist of an alphabetical list of the cases to be found in the main volumes. Additionally the *English Reports* are now available electronically on the Justis database. There are still very many cases referred to in basic law subjects which are reported in the *English Reports*. This is especially so in contract law. Nevertheless, as general advice, you will find your time more profitably spent reading the leading cases of the last twenty years in common law subjects than ferreting around among the faded relics of another century's ideas. Cases in the old reports are frequently badly reported, the judgments confusingly expressed and, on the whole, not so fully reasoned as in the contemporary period. Our present judges are, taken as a whole, a better educated group than at any previous period.

When you are given references to these reports you should not shirk the undoubted effort involved in making sense both of the reference and the eventually discovered report. The occasional foray into the *English Reports* is a part of the good student's all-round training.

HINT →
Pre-1865 cases may be found in the *English Reports*.

Contemporary law reports

The two series in your library that you will find most useful in your day-to-day study of law are the *Weekly Law Reports* and the *All England Reports*. The former is published by the Incorporated Council of Law Reporting of England and Wales and the latter by LexisNexis Butterworths.

The Weekly Law Reports

This series is published in three annual volumes. The first volume contains those cases which are not intended to be included in the *Law Reports*. In the national hierarchy of law reporting this series stands next below the *Law Reports*. It aims to provide a comprehensive coverage of all the Supreme Court, House of Lords and Privy Council cases worthy of reporting. (Note the 'Supreme Court' presently includes the various divisions of the High Court and the Court of Appeal.)

The All England Reports

This is the most important contemporary private series of reports and in terms of its acceptability for citation in court is accorded considerable status scarcely inferior to the *Weekly Law Reports*. Again the series aims at comprehensive general coverage and is now published in four annual volumes, the volumes being published in consecutive weekly parts. The weekly issue of each series will contain cases relevant to your course and other cases of political or social significance. If you make a point of leafing through each weekly issue and reading through important or interesting cases, you will do a great deal to make yourself a better informed lawyer and to understand the role seemingly dry legal doctrines play in the social and political ebb and flow of the country. Also from a practical point of view, lecturers are prone to set questions on striking current developments in case law.

> **HINT** ⇒
> It is a good discipline to set aside time each week to look at current legal developments.

Other series of law reports

There are many other series of law reports from English and other jurisdictions which you will find in your library. Mysterious references to law reports and journals can be checked in a number of volumes (notably: *Osborn's Concise Law Dictionary*, which includes a good section on abbreviations; and the front page of any volume of *Current Law Yearbook*). Some of these that might otherwise be overlooked are worth mentioning.

Estates Gazette

The *Estates Gazette* is a magazine which students of law will not customarily read. It is published for surveyors and estate agents. Yet it contains almost all the important cases on real property law, landlord and tenant and other matters of interest to the landed professions, such as the law of tort. The judgments are printed in full and the reports quite often cited in court and very often in learned articles. You will often find in this magazine reports of cases of current interest in the property area which you do not find easily or at all elsewhere.

In addition to the law reports the magazine often carries notes of interest to students of law – often written especially for students. These can be read with value by law students especially if they concern some complex area of law which the student finds for the first time explained clearly in this 'layman's' magazine.

Property and Compensation Reports

This is a valuable series of reports published privately. It contains reports of property law cases that you will not find or not find readily elsewhere.

Abbreviated Law Reports

The weekly journals (see later) – the *New Law Journal*, the *Solicitors' Journal* and the *Gazette* – each contains brief reports of recently decided cases. These are the first reports you will come across of some important newly decided case. The regular reading of one of these magazines, including its case reports, will be an important part of your metamorphosis into a fully fledged lawyer. There is a plethora of other reports (English and overseas) which you will find in your library. Not all are really useful: there is a strong element of commercial opportunism in some recent ventures into this area. You will gradually, as your use of the library develops, become fully aware of the range of material on offer and its varying value. The important watchword is not to shrink from the little effort involved in chasing up puzzling references: there may not be gold at the end of every trail but if you do not set out on the search there will be none at all.

Citation of law reports

One of the first problems you will encounter in seeking law reports is the almost hieroglyphic nature of case citation. The following examples serve to illustrate the point:

DPP v Camplin	[1978] AC 705
	[1978] 2 WLR 679
	(1978) 67 Cr App R 14
Chaudhry v Prabhakar	[1988] 3 All ER 718

(Note the multiple references to *Camplin*, indicating that the case is reported in several series of reports.)

The citations to cases can appear daunting, but as with many esoteric points once you have learned the significance of the parts of the citation the mystery dissolves.

DPP v Camplin	[1978]	2	WLR	679
Name of case	Year	Volume	Series of reports	Page number

The key to understanding the citation is the abbreviation, which refers to the series of reports. The abbreviation may be 'deciphered' by use of, for example, *Osborn's Concise Law Dictionary*.

✖ EXAMPLE

In *R v Camplin*, the abbreviations AC, WLR and Cr App R refer to series of reports. They are respectively: *Appeal Cases* (part of the *Law Reports*); *Weekly Law Reports*; and *Criminal Appeal Reports*. In *Chaudhry v Prabhakar*, the abbreviation All ER refers to the *All England Law Reports*.

Once you know where the various series of reports are kept in the library it is a simple task to find a case. Where square brackets [. . .] are used the year is an essential part of the citation, which you need to locate the case; round brackets (. . .) indicate that the year is not an essential part of the citation, but the volume number is essential as in *DPP v Camplin* (1978) 67 Cr App R 14. Note *Camplin* is to be found in volume 67 of the *Criminal Appeal Reports*.

Finding and using legislation

Legislation falls into two categories: primary legislation, that is the law made by Parliament; and secondary or delegated legislation, that is law made by another person or body under powers delegated by Parliament. As has been seen, primary legislation is made in the form of Acts of Parliament, also referred to as statutes, and secondary legislation is found most usually in the form of statutory instruments.

Primary legislation

During the course of a year many new Acts will be added to the statute book. In 2006 more than fifty new Acts were passed. On the shelves of any law library you will find several sets of Acts of Parliament. The main sets are: *Halsbury's Statutes of England*; *Public General Acts and Measures*; and *Current Law Statutes Annotated*.

Halsbury's Statutes of England

This is a major reference work, running to fifty main volumes, which arranges statutes according to subject area. The text of a statute is reproduced in an up-dated form to the time of publication of the volume. Each Act has annotations indicating amendments, repeals, commencement dates and references to cases interpreting the particular provision. The service is updated by:

▶ the Current Statutes Service binders, which contain all Acts passed since publication of the main volumes;

▶ an Annual Cumulative Supplement, containing information on the effect of new legislation and cases on the Acts in the volumes and binders; and

▶ a Noter-Up Service, produced monthly detailing current developments.

There is a useful volume also produced entitled '*Is It In Force*', which indicates the dates on which Acts of Parliament have come into force over the last twenty-five years. Also of use for locating Acts is *Halsbury's Statutes Citator*. This is arranged in two parts:

▶ Part 1 alphabetically lists statutes: and

▶ Part 2 contains the names of statutes, arranged chronologically, together with information on amendments and relevant case law.

Halsbury's Statutes of England has the following uses:

(i) finding *Acts of Parliament* on a particular subject;

(ii) discovering how an *Act of Parliament* has been amended;

(iii) if an Act or section of an Act is *currently in force*;

(iv) if you only have partial information concerning a statute eg know the name of the Act but have no date or have a date but do not know the exact name of the Act then *Halsbury's Statute Citator* provides alphabetical and chronological lists which will give you the information you need.

Public General Acts and Measures

The official version of Acts of Parliament is the Queen's Printer's copy. New Acts of Parliament are produced online and in hard copy shortly after the date of Royal Assent. At the end of a year the individual Acts are collected into a volume which forms part of Public General Acts and Measures.

A major drawback of this set of statutes is that they are not updated (not even online) and so must be treated with caution.

Since 1999 explanatory notes accompany new Acts which result from Bills introduced by a Government minister (see Appendix 2 for an example of such notes). The notes seek to explain the impact of the legislation in layman's terms, helpfully giving a summary, background information, a clause-by-clause commentary and a table of Hansard references, chronologically outlining the passage of the Bill through the Houses of Parliament. The notes are not part of the Act, nor have they been endorsed by Parliament. Nonetheless the House of Lords has indicated 'in so far as they cast light on the setting of a statute, and the mischief at which it is aimed' the notes may be used as an aid to interpretation of the statute.

Current Law Statutes Annotated

In this series the full text of Acts of Parliament passed since 1948 is reproduced together with a commentary. The commentary is particularly useful as it gives background to the Act, its passage through Parliament and the likely effect of the legislation. It is also a useful source of reference material. However, there is no updating done in relation to this series.

Textbooks in the law library

These are arranged in the same way as other non-fiction books in a general library, that is, according to a conventional subject classification. You will quickly be able to sort out which subject groups appear where in the collection of texts. There will usually be a separate 'short loan' collection of textbooks which are loaned to students only for short periods for use in the library; the books in this collection being those, generally, which it is hoped students will acquire for themselves.

A law library is not really a lending library; many of the textbooks will have their use restricted to 'reference only'. It would probably be a good thing if borrowing from the library was proscribed altogether and students encouraged to read the necessary text then and there. You should especially avoid the modern danger of photocopying part of a book or article, filing your copy and then letting it slide from your mind, in the belief that reproduction is as good as perusal.

Journals and periodicals

Particular attention to the use that can be made of these is given in the following chapter. Within the library, bound law journals and periodicals will be collected together on the shelves in alphabetical order according to the title of the journal. Usually there will be found on a separate display rack the current issue or recent issues of each journal subscribed to by the library. You will probably develop the habit of glancing at new issues from time to time as you enter the library so that you can read those pertinent to your present studies. Some regular features in journals will have great current interest; you will find, for example, the weekly editorial in the *Solicitors' Journal* has a valuable commentary on current legal topics. Similar columns, more conservative in the *Gazette*, more radical in the *New Law Journal*, will also come to attract your regular attention. This is a specialised branch of journalism. At first much of the debate in these columns will perplex you; but persist, and you will come to be a well-informed lawyer. The legal profession and legal system are under stronger pressure for change at present than perhaps at any time since the Judicature Acts of the 1870s. Much of the debate is found in the regular correspondence and columns of the weekly journals. If you browse through these throughout your time as a student, you will all the sooner be able to play an active part yourself in the great discussions which are shaping the future provision of legal services.

Bibliographic sources and similar works

A very important series of books in the law library will be found gathered together at some convenient place usually near the entrance to the law section of the library. These are the encyclopaedic works of reference or bibliography which play such an important part in legal research – particularly so far as the busy practitioner is concerned.

At the beginning of your career as a law student you will not find these works of enormous value. You will rely mainly (and quite sensibly) on references provided in your lectures and in your main textbooks. Later on you will need to prepare lengthier essays or other pieces of work or perhaps participate in some clinical legal education programme. You will then need to be able to discover for yourself references in a particular area of law.

Quick reference works

One of the simplest levels of reference is the law dictionary. *Jowitt's Dictionary of English Law*, in two volumes, is quite detailed and because of its articles on long forgotten legal persons, incidents and maxims an amusing read in itself. Another comprehensive dictionary is *Stroud's Judicial Dictionary*. Given that these will certainly be on your reference shelves, there seems little point in a more concise dictionary – though students sometimes buy and find a valuable use for *Osborn's Concise Law Dictionary*. (On the subject of dictionaries all students should possess a good English dictionary. *Chamber's Twentieth Century Dictionary* or the *Concise Oxford* are good enough. The *Shorter Oxford* is well worth the extra investment and can often be purchased at a discount through book clubs.) Also in the quick reference category are the manuals of legal reference referred to above.

The encyclopaedic works

These particular works are much used in the lawyer's office but worthy of some description especially as it is felt that the law student too often passes them by unused.

Halsbury's Laws of England

It is hard to describe the flavour of this work that sets out to gather under subject heads an encyclopaedic account of every contemporary legal subject. Knowles and Thomas (in *Effective Legal Research*) say:

> '*Halsbury's Laws* covers all areas of English law and is a useful starting point for research on any legal topic. Because it is kept up to date, it has the advantage over textbooks of including recent information . . . *Halsbury's Laws* provides an effective statement of the whole of the law of England and Wales.'

Its most useful function is not as a source of law but as a source of reference.

However, *Halsbury's Laws* is encyclopaedic in its coverage. It contains the vast bulk of the references on any area of law with which you are likely to be concerned. It is from time to time cited in court and some sections contain detailed and authoritative accounts of the law. Material in the encyclopaedia is contained under alphabetical subject headings and the headings within each volume are printed on the spine. There are two general index volumes and although the size of the work is formidable, its use presents no difficulty.

A work which is similar in scope to *Halsbury's Laws* is The *Digest* (*formerly The English and Empire Digest*). This is arranged in similar fashion – by volumes alphabetically according to subject matter. The work is probably not nearly so widely used nowadays as *Halsbury's Laws* and it consists of summaries of decided cases and not of authoritative statements of law. It does quite often contain references to further reports of particular cases or references to cases not cited in *Halsbury's Laws*, and for that reason should not be overlooked.

HINT

Halsbury's Laws of England is a good place to commence research into a particular legal subject area.

Encyclopaedia of Forms and Precedents

Two specialist practitioners' encyclopaedias may also be mentioned. *The Encyclopaedia of Forms and Precedents* is an invaluable work for practising solicitors. It is published in volumes arranged under alphabetical headings and is available electronically via LexisNexis Butterworths. Law teaching at undergraduate level has for many years been rather divorced from the different requirements of legal practice. Opinions differ as to the validity of what remains a clear distinction between the 'academic' stage and the 'vocational' stage of training lawyers. For one reason or another, law degree teaching has refrained from the use in any systematic or widespread way of materials such as contracts or deeds culled directly from legal practice. So, you will not during your undergraduate legal career have much direct recourse to the strictly practitioner texts.

The Encyclopaedia of Forms and Precedents is by far the best example of a 'precedent book' published in our jurisdiction. It aims for comprehensiveness and on the whole succeeds, except in the areas where the pace of change is quickest. You will find it useful to look at specimen documents and the notes thereon in very many areas – the introductory material is often very helpful indeed in assisting the reader to grasp difficult areas of law or procedure. This encyclopaedia is undoubtedly the work most used by practising solicitors and its occasional perusal will assist your growing understanding of the relationship between the law you are being taught and the work of a practitioner.

Atkins Court Forms

Atkin's Court Forms is an encyclopaedia of court forms and related documents. It is the bible of the practising barrister. This publication is also arranged in volumes under alphabetically ordered headings and is also available electronically via LexisNexis Butterworths. It can provide stimulating background material to even the most tedious part of a course. For example, in constitutional law: how would you obtain a writ of habeas corpus; what steps would you take; and what would the court order you obtain actually say? Despite the simplification of many areas of legal practice the drafting of statements of case, that is the formal documents in a law suit setting out a party's claim, defence, counterclaim, defence to a counterclaim and so on, remains an important part of the lawyer's art and you will derive much instructive amusement from this work.

Current Law

This is a unique work. The full publication consists of the following.

(i) *Monthly Digest*. Published throughout the year this has brief references to decided cases, learned articles and the progress of legislation. The subject matter is arranged under alphabetically ordered headings. This claims to contain 'all the law from all the sources'. It does not: there are inevitable omissions and occasional indexical slips. But, for the serious researcher it is an essential tool. When you are preparing a long essay or project, you will find it useful if you are to ensure that you deal with all the latest references.

(ii) *Current Law Yearbook*. The material in the monthly issues is collected each year into one volume and this is again a most useful source of further references in any area.

(iii) *Current Law Statutes*. New legislation is issued throughout the year and collected in annual volumes. The important Acts of Parliament are annotated by practitioners or academics. These annotations are often a valuable source of insight into the effect of a statutory provision which has not yet been dissected in the textbooks.

(iv) *Current Law Week*. This consists of a weekly newsheet of cases together with a focus on a particular area by an expert contributor.

There are now also many other specialist 'subject' encyclopaedias which you will find useful. These, however, will be found in the textbook section of the library.

Ensuring that your law is up to date
Having found primary legal sources of interest you will need to ensure that these are up to date. The law is dynamic in that it changes and

expands on an almost daily basis. Legislation may change. It may be amended by later legislation, or parts may be substituted or it may be repealed in part or in its entirety. Equally, in cases principles of law may be modified, clarified by later cases or indeed overruled by a higher court. The important point is to avoid falling into error you must be able to state the current law and to do so you must be familiar with the tools available for updating purposes.

There are several ways to update law but to explain all methods goes beyond the scope of this book. The use of *Current Law* is explained below by way of illustration. For a comprehensive explanation see Guy Holborn *Butterworths Legal Research Guide*.

Current Law Legislation Citators

The *Legislation Citators* are contained in several volumes 1947–71, 1972–88, 1988–95, 1996–99, 2000–01, 2002–04 and 2005. This service is to be used in conjunction with *Current Law Monthly Digest* to bring information on legislation up-to-date.

Information is provided on Acts of any date which have been **repealed**, **amended** or otherwise **modified** since 1947 and any **cases decided on Acts** of any date since 1947.

The *Citators* also deal with statutory instruments (a form of delegated legislation) and their amendment and revocation.

Current Law Case Citator

When seeking information on case law the *Current Law Case Citator* is invaluable. Time spent appreciating what this resource does is time well spent. The *Citator* is arranged in parts: 1947–76, 1977–97, 1998 – 2001, 2002–04, and 2005. It contains an **alphabetical list of cases** decided between 1947 and the present day, providing a variety of references to such eg WLR, All ER, QB etc. The *Citator* also gives information concerning what has happened to a case since it was decided eg has the case been overruled, applied, reversed, distinguished etc. This information extends to the history of any case, of whatever date, which has been considered in a case decided between 1947 and the date of the most recently published volume.

The *Case Citator* also contains information on articles written about cases and legislation affecting case law.

The *Case Citator* is useful if you know the name of a case but do not have the reference. Usually (unless the case name appears several times eg R v Smith!) you will be able to find the reference to the case in the *Case Citator*. Should you be unable to find the case this may indicate that it pre-dates 1947 and has not been referred to in a case since 1947. You should then consult *The Digest* mentioned above. Alternatively it may be

HINT ⇒

As the law changes daily it is important that you know how to check what the law is currently.

HINT ⇒

The *Current Law Legislation Citators* are particularly useful for updating statutes and discovering any cases decided, on an Act of any date, since 1947.

a very recent case and you will have to consult *Current Law Monthly Digest*, which gives information on the latest case law. The *Case Citator*, as noted above, has another important use; if you wish to trace the subsequent judicial history of a case this information is contained in the *Case Citator*. Remember when tracing the history of a case it is important to work through all of the volumes to ensure a later case has not had a significant impact on the previous case.

HINT →
The *Current Law Case Citator* is useful for finding the reference for a case when only the case name is known and for tracing the subsequent judicial history of a case.

Electronic sources

Many of the legal sources outlined above are now also available electronically online. Universities subscribe to electronic services supplied by commercial providers. These may be accessed via Athens, which allows users by entering a password to use multiple databases. The scale of online legal sources is enormous and with an Internet connection at home much legal research may be performed without recourse to a library. Two main providers of electronic sources are Westlaw and LexisNexis. The following explanation only refers to Westlaw.

The key features of Westlaw are contained on the welcome screen and consist of facilities to locate cases, legislation and references to articles in legal journals. There is also a list of shortcuts to other sources, such as European Union materials.

Case Locator

On the welcome screen, the Case Locator allows you search for a case by:

▶ party name;

▶ citation; or

▶ term(s).

The functions performed by the *Current Law Case Citator*, for example finding the citation for a case where only the name is known, are similarly performed by the Case Locator. However, the Case Locator may then link to a full text of the case sought and further links to the texts of cases or legislation cited in the case and to journal articles dealing with the case.

On finding a case you will see in the top left-hand section of the frame an icon in blue labelled 'History'; click on this and information concerning the direct history of the case, for example has it been reversed on appeal or affirmed, and any subsequent consideration of the case by later courts. This is a very helpful method

of discovering quickly what has become of a case and ensuring you
are up to date.

Legislation

The legislation search facility, found on the welcome screen, allows you
to access legislation (both Acts of Parliament and statutory instruments)
by name and by provision (for example, section number). Additionally,
under the Quick Search menu, in the left-hand frame of the screen, it is
possible to search for legislation by terms (click UK legislation to access
the search). Also, in the left-hand frame of the screen, you will find a
table of contents which allows you to view an alphabetically arranged
list of Acts of Parliament (and statutory instruments). This enables you
to select a specific Act, go to a specific section and then read the full text
of the section. The full text legislation is presented as in force and as
amended.

A useful feature in the Quick Search menu is the UK Legislation
Locator. By clicking on this and entering the name and section of the
Act of Parliament you are researching, the following information is
given:

▶ whether the law is currently in force;

▶ when the law commenced in force;

▶ 'read with', this indicates links to other legislation;

▶ cases citing the legislation;

▶ secondary sources, such as journal articles;

▶ general legislative materials, which relate to the whole of
   the legislation.

The advantage is that legislation is updated and materials relevant to
the legislation are collected together. This greatly aids the research
process.

Legal Journals Index

On the welcome screen, at the bottom of the right-hand frame,
articles may be searched for by term(s). Entering key terms may find
a list of articles. For each article a citation and an abstract of the
contents, together with links to relevant cases and legislation, will be
provided. If the journal, in which the article appears, is available on
Westlaw there will be a link to it. At present only a few journals are
available online.

Using the library and legal databases for research

A real test of your familiarity with the law library will come when you have to prepare an original piece of coursework, project or dissertation. It is true, sadly, that once this challenge arrives later rather than sooner in a student's course, many are found wanting in the basic research skills.

The following illustration demonstrates how a list of sources may be built up incrementally, as new sources provide further avenues to explore.

✖ EXAMPLE

Suppose you are asked to write an essay on whether a publican might be liable to a drunken customer if he fails to warn him that one apparent road from the pub leads to a 200-foot drop into a quarry, or if he in fact misdirects him onto this fatal road. The first problem as with all new legal tasks is one of classification. The lawyer who can rephrase the question to point him towards the right legal sources will be half-way home. In this problem there are three possible areas to search. The first is contract. Contract law is concerned with enforceable promises between persons. The customer is a paying customer and clearly he has a contract with 'mine host' – does this entitle him to correct directions?

The second area is tort law – this is the area of the common law which imposes upon one person a duty to another. Does it impose upon a landlord of a public house an obligation to take care of drunken customers or at least not to misdirect a customer? The third area that may be relevant is statute law. It is well known that licensed premises are very much controlled by Acts of Parliament. Is there any Act which is relevant to the landlord/customer problems?

A search for an answer will begin in a relevant textbook. Will a straightforward search enable you to tell that contract law and the licensing statutes can be discounted? Is the problem in a tort textbook to be found under drunkenness, landlords, misdirection, personal injury, or where? Suppose you decide that the correct questions are:

(a) Does the landlord owe a duty to volunteer instructions – that is, not to omit to see to the safety of his drunken customer?

(b) Does the landlord owe a duty not to give inaccurate instructions?

(c) Does the drunkenness of the customer – which may contribute to his downfall – provide any kind of defence to the landlord?

Examining these three questions in a tort textbook such as *Winfield and Jolowicz on Tort* will lead you towards the relevant case law. Some of these cases will require reading. You will then wish – having determined which are the relevant cases – to check that no further case law not mentioned in the textbook since Professor Rogers last updated the text is relevant to your problem. To do this you may use Westlaw or Current Law Yearbook discussed above. Whichever updating source you use you will here again have to be sure that you are classifying the question correctly. The end result of your search will involve clear statements from textbooks, examination of leading cases, and reference to any further cases not mentioned in the textbooks. In the course of your research you would eventually discover the interesting case of *Munro v Porthkerry Holiday Estates* (1984) 81 LSG 2450. In this case a father sued the occupiers of a leisure centre on behalf of his deceased son's estate. The leisure centre was on a cliff-top. The son, after having consumed some alcohol, climbed over a fence and fell down the cliff and died. Should the court hold the licensee liable and, in coming to its decision, what test should it apply? Is discovering this case with very similar facts the end of your quest or does it leave questions unanswered?

If you go to *Munro v Porthkerry Holiday Estates* on Westlaw and click on the History button you will discover that this case was later considered in a Northern Ireland case *Joy v Newell (t/a Copper Room)* [2000] NI 91.

You may also be directed to relevant articles which may illuminate the subject and provide interesting routes of enquiry. For example, a search on the Cambridge Law Journal website directs you to an article entitled 'Liability in Respect of the Intoxicated' by C McIvor (2001) 60 CLJ 109. The article in turn directs you to cases you may not have discovered so far, including case law from Commonwealth countries.

Using the Internet as your library

You will expect to do a considerable amount of your research via the Internet. There are now a huge number of resources available. Indeed in choosing a law school, you might find it an interesting question to ask: 'which computerised legal databases your law school makes available to its students?' The range of information available on the Internet is enormous. Public sites such as the Office of Public Sector Information, the Charities Commission, Companies House, the Inland Revenue, Customs and Excise, the Land Registry and indeed all government departments are of great value to students in preparing work and obtaining downloads of useful background and technical information.

Many sites may be accessed free of charge. Below is a list of websites that are of use to law students.

Law sites

▶ *www.opsi.gov.uk/acts.htm* The website of the Office of Public Sector Information provides links to all Public General Acts in full text form from 1988. Explanatory notes, published alongside Acts since 1999, may also be accessed. Links are also provided to the legislation of Northern Ireland, Scotland and Wales.

▶ *www.opsi.gov.uk/stat.htm* This site contains full text versions of statutory instruments published since the first printed statutory instrument of 1987.

▶ *www.direct.gov.uk* This site provides links to the websites of central government departments, executive agencies, non-departmental public bodies and local authorities.

▶ *www.dca.gov.uk/index.htm* The website of the Department of Constitutional Affairs contains information, amongst other things, on the following areas: the constitution; the legal system; judges; magistrates; and freedom of information. To get an overview of the material available on this site go to www.dca.gov.uk/sitemap.htm

▶ *www.parliament.uk/index.cfm* The website of Parliament has links to Hansard, Bills currently before Parliament, judicial work (detailing the work of the House of Lords as a court of appeal and includes useful related links) and Parliamentary publications and archives.

▶ *www.publications.parliament.uk/pa/ld/ldjudgmt.htm* This website links to full text versions of all House of Lords judgments since 14 November 1996.

▶ *www.lawcom.gov.uk/* The Law Commission is a statutory independent body reviewing and recommending reform of the law. Its website contains information about the Law Commission, its publications, projects and the law currently being reviewed.

▶ *www.legalservices.gov.uk/* The website of the Legal Services Commission provides information on the legal aid system in England and Wales, the Community Legal Service and the Criminal Defence Service.

▶ *www.bailii.org* The British and Irish Legal Information Institute's website contains numerous databases providing the following: full text versions of United Kingdom statutes since 1988; statutory instruments of England, Scotland and Wales; full text case reports of the House of Lords, Privy Council, Court of Appeal, High Court and various tribunals (the databases have various start dates with none before 1996); Law Commission publications; and Court of Justice of the European Communities decisions, since 1954, and Court of First Instance decisions.

▶ *www.echr.coe.int/echr* This is the main access point for the European Court of Human Rights and records its decisions.

▶ *www.lawsociety.org.uk/home.law* This website contains useful information on the Law Society and Solicitors. There is information on becoming a solicitor and alternative careers in law.

▶ *www.barcouncil.org.uk/*Information about the Bar Council and barristers is to be found on this website.

▶ *www.timesonline.co.uk/uk/* This is the website for *The Times* newspaper. Articles and items on law are to be found at www.timesonline.co.uk/law.

■ CHECKLIST

■ THE LAW LIBRARY AND THE INTERNET

What you should know about the Law library and Internet

▶ Can you name the primary and secondary legal source materials?

▶ What is the use of *Halsbury's Laws of England*?

▶ Do you know where these sources are located in the law library?

▶ How can you find a case when you only know the name of the case?

▶ What aid can you use to find the meaning of an abbreviation in a case citation?

▶ How can you find out if a case still represents the current law?

▶ Can you identify when an Act of Parliament comes into force?

▶ Where can you find information on the amendment, repeal etc of a particular Act of Parliament?

▶ How can you discover articles on a particular legal area or point?

▶ By using the Internet can you ensure that a case still represents current law or that an Act of Parliament is up to date?

Chapter 7

The sources of legal study

Choosing legal source materials

The study of law is the preserve of the literate. It requires a good command of the English language and the successful study of law will prove difficult for students who do not enjoy reading and writing or who find these activities burdensome. The practical problem for a law student is one of selection – which materials should be read and which, for omission is inevitable, should be left unread; what should be written down in the form of detailed notes, which material should be browsed, read carefully, or systematically annotated? From the time a student commences a law course, these questions will very often present themselves to his or her mind and too often a clear answer, producing a clear pattern of work, will never emerge. But the student will muddle through, picking up some references, missing others, noting some trivial or inconsequential areas in enormous detail and omitting others. How is the problem of the disorganised, amorphous and massive nature of the legal literature available to the student to be surmounted?

We have already seen that the subject matter of each law course stated explicitly in the syllabus contains an implicit assumption that the taught and examined syllabus will be different and smaller, ie the 'hidden' curriculum. Accordingly, the scope of the course as defined by the syllabus that is in fact taught will provide the first and crucial source of guidance to the student on what and how to study.

But even when you have elucidated from the lecturer in lectures the subject matter to which he or she is giving some or particular attention, there remains a major problem of selection. Lecture notes often appear like sections from a stream of consciousness novel but with a heavy legal bias. There is case name after case name, references to numerous books, still more numerous articles bound closely together with the lecturer's own comments on the topic under review. Which of all these references will be read and how?

Should the student read the law itself or things about the law? There are primary sources – the reported cases and Acts of Parliament and there are

HINT →

Be aware of the syllabus for each subject, but pay particular attention to the emphasis placed upon individual areas in the syllabus by your lecturer.

HINT →

In the first instance, read those sources to which you are directed by your tutor.

even more numerous accounts of the primary sources – practitioner's tomes, textbooks, nutshells, articles, annotations, case notes and monographs. What will be suggested here is that it is essential to use primary and secondary sources together for different purposes and as a complement to each other. Primary and secondary sources will be considered in turn to see how best each can be used to satisfy the various aims of legal study.

Primary sources

Reading law reports

It has already been noted that there are two primary sources of law in England and Wales – the reported decisions of the higher courts and legislation. To this must, of course, be added the mountains of law generated by the institutions of the European Community. The study of law, particularly in the early years of a degree course, is still overwhelmingly concerned with the first of these – the arrangement and analysis of case law. Students invariably have problems coming to grips with case law. How many cases should they read? Should the whole of the case be read, or only some particular identifiable part of it?

The parts of a law report

HINT →

From the outset of your legal studies make it a habit to read cases.

In Appendix 1 you will find a copy of a law report. This has been annotated to give a description of the various parts of a law report and their functions. In reading the case you will discover that the first two pages contains information to help you find your way around the case while the remainder, and most important part, contains the judgments of the members of the court. The judgments should be read in their entirety not only to discover what the court has decided but also why the court has reached the decision that it has.

The nature of the problem

A law case commences as a 'matter' on 'file' in a solicitor's office when a client, Mr Brown, calls on his solicitor for advice. The solicitor records this interview and the record is an 'attendance note'. Soon the potential defendant, Mr Black, will see his own solicitor. A correspondence, often protracted over many months, will follow. A claim will be issued; a defence filed; further information requested; and details given. In the course of time there will be a trial; witnesses will give evidence for many days; there is a difficult point of law; the learned judge reserves judgment; and the parties return to court some days later to hear the court pronounce judgment. The claimant loses and his lawyers feel he has a grievance. They appeal to the Court of Appeal. Opinion of learned counsel is sought and given, conferences and interviews follow. The parties assemble at the Court of Appeal in The Strand. There is a two-day argument and the court reserves judgment. They return, and the three members of the court give a unanimous decision in favour of the claimant (or appellant as he has become) through the voice of Lord Justice Wright. The point of law is interesting, and the case is now reported as *Brown v Black* in the law reports.

The law report, however, contains only a fraction of all the papers, documents, notes and speeches that have culminated in Mr Brown's triumphant victory.

In order to examine this, it will be useful to look at one case between a number of parties and see how it was reported.

✖ EXAMPLE

Hardwick v Johnson [1978] 1 WLR 683

This is a case you will look at both in contract law and in an introductory land law course, because it raises fundamental issues in both areas. Mrs Hardwick had a son called Robert. He was divorced. When her son decided to remarry for a second time, a girl called Janet, Mrs Hardwick decided to buy a house for them to live in. She paid £12,000 for the house; in 1972 this was quite a substantial price. The couple agreed to pay her £7 per week. Only £88 was paid and that in the first year of their occupation. They had moved in during 1973 and by 1975, although Janet was pregnant, the marriage had broken down. Robert deserted her. Mrs Hardwick brought an action in the county court to regain possession of her house. In the county court, Mrs Hardwick lost, and she appealed to the Court of Appeal. The hearing was on 5 and 6 December 1977 and the Court was able to pronounce judgment the same day. The mother lost again. Janet and her child could stay in the home indefinitely. When you read this case you will see that Lord Denning MR says: 'The correspondence and the pleadings show that the parties canvassed all sorts of legal relation-ships.' They are not, however, reproduced. You will have to read between the lines to see how the protracted legal struggle developed. The law report begins with the title of the case. This is followed by a series of jottings called the 'catchwords' which are of little value, though perhaps useful in catching the eye of a lawyer in a hurry. There follows a potted account of the facts and findings, the cases referred to and the history of the case. This is called the 'headnote' – for the beginner in law especially, this is worth reading as a prelude to reading the opinions of the judges. It is quite hard often to pick up 'the story' from a judgment and the headnote writer has already performed the task of doing so and making a précis of the most important aspects of the case. Having rushed through the headnote, for there is no point in dwelling on it, you come to the judgment of the court. In this particular case, all three judges gave a judgment, that of Lord Denning being the principal one, and containing a very full statement of the facts of the case as seen by him. In all there are five pages of judgment.

HINT ➡
The catchwords and headnote are not authoritative parts of a case; you must read the judgments.

Reading the judgment

It is not important to settle in your mind exactly how much of each of these judgments to read. What is important is to settle the purpose for which you have read what you read. No one can have a good intellectual understanding of English law and the way it works until they have read a large number of cases in full. You can certainly become a lawyer without doing so. You can learn a lot of law, probably all that a working lawyer needs to know, from commentaries, guides, workbooks and textbooks. But it may be that you wish for something more. You want to be able to understand the way the judicial mind works, to see how new rules creep into the great body of case law, and form some *critical* appreciation of the areas of law you are studying. In order to do this, you need to take cases in 'growing areas' of the law like the case under discussion and read them thoroughly and thoughtfully. However, you will also have, in looking at a case such as *Hardwick v Johnson*, a more direct objective – preparation for an examination in which the area covered by the case will be a part. These two purposes each demand a different approach to the material.

HINT ➡
To understand how case law operates as a source of law, there is no substitute for reading cases.

Reading for education

In order to develop the widest possible understanding of the common law and to develop your analytical ability as a lawyer, it is essential to read cases as fully and carefully as possible. You will find that the form in which judgments are written (or spoken) will become familiar and reading them less of a challenge. The first judgment in *Hardwick v Johnson*, that of Lord Denning, displays a familiar pattern. His opening paragraph gives a very helpful and typically clear summary of the problems that arise in the case. The following page consists of a review of the facts and previous history of the case – if you have read the headnote, or been given a fullish lecture on the case, you will be able to skim through this although to do so means depriving oneself of the pleasure of reading Lord Denning's distinctive narrative style. Then Lord Denning turns to the relevant case law: 'So we have to consider once more the law about family arrangements . . .' (p 688A). He proceeds to apply the law as he sees it to the facts, and comes to a conclusion about the nature of the relationship between the parties (p 688C). Having come to this legal conclusion, that the son and daughter-in-law have a licence (this is a legal term essentially meaning *a personal permission*) to occupy the house in return for £7 a week, he now examines the nature of that type of relationship to see if it permits the mother to have the result she desires – the eviction of her 'tenant'. When you proceed to the concurring judgment of Roskill LJ, you will see that it is briefer but different in emphasis. He says: 'It is . . . plain in my judgment, that there was here a licence' (p 690F); he then deals briefly with whether the licence could be brought to an end by Mrs Hardwick. Browne LJ comes to the same decision and agrees with Roskill LJ as to the species of licence which the daughter-in-law and son had been granted. Having read this case, consider the following questions:

▶ What does it tell you about the enforceability of family arrangements?

▶ How does the court 'fill in' the terms of an agreement when the parties have left them unspecified?

▶ How did the judges decide that this arrangement was a licence and not a tenancy or a trust or a gift?

Having considered these questions, are you able to write in a sentence or two: 'the reasons given by the Court of Appeal for its judgment are . . .'? Can you use your statement of the reasons given in this case to predict how the court would decide a similar case? Does it add anything to your understanding of what kind of 'thing' a licence is? When you study the case you will find the judges differ as to the type of licence concerned – two say it is a 'contractual licence' and one says it is an 'equitable licence' (see pp 688H, 690F, 691G) – the nature of this distinction, and how the judges arrive at making it, you will find rather troublesome – is the distinction significant?

> ✖ EXAMPLE
>
> *An example in full*
>
> Appendix 1 sets out a law report in full as an example for you to read. It is a report of the Court of Appeal in *Mullin v Richards* [1998] 1 All ER 920. The case involves facts with which every reader will be familiar. Two persons at school are fighting with plastic rulers and one of them is blinded accidentally in their right eye. The case concerns the law of negligence – were either the school or the other child, Heidi Richards, liable to Teresa Jane Mullin for her loss of sight? The case is a good example of judges making new law. When you read it you may be puzzled that such a common event as one school child injuring another accidentally should give rise in 1998 to new law. For there to be liability in negligence the court must find that there has actually been actionable failure to take proper care. What made the court decide there was no liability in this case? In what circumstances would the school have been liable? Are there any circumstances in which Heidi would have been liable for the accident? You need to be able to answer these questions to use this case in order to advise whether legal proceedings should be taken in similar cases.

Reading cases for examination purposes

It may have occurred to you as you read the above account of *Hardwick v Johnson* that it would be impossible to remember such a lengthy account of every case read, and even if it were possible it would not be usable in an examination in that form. In discussing lectures and lecture notes (see Chapter 4) the point was made at length that accumulating in a digestible form the body of material that you will attempt to learn and, having learned, utilise in examinations is an important and ever-present goal of study. How can a reflective academic perusal of a case such as *Hardwick v Johnson* be absorbed into the *corpus* of your notes and brought forth to do battle in the examination hall?

An examination is an unusual form of exercise and like any other requires special preparation. Law students at the start of their career must find the relationship between the hours and weeks in the library and seminar room and the hasty scribble in the examination hall particularly difficult to comprehend. Law examinations and how to answer them are discussed more fully in Chapters 11 and 12 but here a specific issue is addressed – how is the wealth of case material more or less digested during the year to be used in such exercises?

It is important to develop some feeling for the types and pattern of examination question that are likely to occur in the areas you are studying. Armed with this insight you will be better able to visualise how to utilise material from the case law you are reading. Let us take a particular example, in what kind of areas might *Hardwick v Johnson* occur? If the relevant course is contract law, there is only one area, that of intention to create legal relations. Experience of studying past examination papers will inform the student that there is a relatively small range of questions in which this appears.

If the relevant course is an introductory land law or introduction to property course, there is a wider range of potential questions. There will be both essays and problems which raise pertinent questions concerning the nature of licences, the distinction between licences and tenancies and the questionable existence of some interest known as an 'equitable licence'.

An answer by a good student to a law examination question in the typical unseen written format of a three-hour paper with four questions will not exceed 800 words. The average of all pass papers (although this is only a 'guesstimate') is probably no more than 500 words per question. It will not escape your attention that there are a large number of cases on 'intention to create legal relations' and cases considering the 'nature of a licence' are prolific. In either area, reference will have to be made to a number of cases and a number of viewpoints.

✖ EXAMPLE

A question which might occur where *Hardwick v Johnson* is much in point would be, 'Does the developing law of licences provide an example of "an interest which can cross the chasm which lies between contract and property"?' (Professor H W R Wade). The question calls for a searching review of case law in this area and for a particular look at the question of terminability of licences (where *Hardwick v Johnson* is vague in the extreme) and whether licences can bind third parties (where *Hardwick* is irrelevant). In such an essay, you will begin with a statement of the traditional view of the nature of a licence – you might couple this with an examination of how the court in *National Provincial Bank Ltd v Hastings Car Mart Ltd* [1965] AC 1175, a case you will inevitably read thoroughly – defined, or at least grappled with, the distinction between rights which are 'property' and rights which are not. Then the central part of your essay will be taken up with an examination of some of the plethora of cases of which Hardwick is one. In this essay you may dispose of that case in a passage such as:

Hardwick v Johnson was a case where the Court of Appeal had to consider the nature of an agreement whereby a mother allowed her newly-married son and daughter-in-law to occupy, for a weekly sum, a house she had purchased for their connubial bliss. When she sought possession against the deserted wife the Court of Appeal had to analyse this agreement. Denning MR thought it was 'in the nature of an equitable licence'. The other judges both thought it to be a 'contractual licence'. All three judges agreed the mother could not terminate the licence but agreed it could be terminable in unspecified circumstances. They did not think, or at least articulate their judgments, in terms of property law theory of rights, 'in rem' or 'in personam', but gave a pragmatic answer to the particular case at issue.

You will see that time will not allow more on this case. Perhaps a briefer treatment might be preferred but even this use of the case utilises only a brief statement of the facts, a snippet from Lord Denning's judgment and a reference to the views of his two fellow judges. To have annotated the case at greater length in your own notes and attempted to memorise for the examination a far bulkier account of it would be to provide your memory with a needless and unprofitable encumbrance.

> **HINT** ⇒
>
> Cases are to be read widely and mulled over thoroughly but annotated concisely.

Thus, cases are to be read widely and mulled over thoroughly but annotated concisely.

The use of statutory material

A statute is an Act of Parliament. In many areas of law now, Acts of Parliament are paramount. Early on in your studies you will learn the importance of the '1925 legislation'.* Early on in contract law, you will see the very profound inroads that have been made by Parliament into traditional areas of judge-made law. An example of this is seen in relation to exemption clauses with the introduction of the Unfair Contract Terms Act 1977. Students find statutory material very hard going. In the later stages of a degree course where huge areas of study are very largely statute-based (family law, company law, tax law, welfare law, industrial law, etc) the need for a sound technique in dealing with Acts of Parliament becomes even greater.

The parts of a statute

> **HINT** ⇒
>
> Familiarise yourself with the layout of Acts of Parliament.

In Appendix 2 you will find an Act of Parliament. The Act has been annotated to indicate the various parts of an Act and their functions.

---

* The Settled Land Act, Trustee Act, Law of Property Act, Land Registration Act, Administration of Estates Act.

Familiarise yourself with the layout and the parts of an Act before you attempt to read the text of an Act of Parliament.

Reading an Act of Parliament

The problem of student difficulties in tackling the statute-based areas of law has a simple solution and one that is told to students by all their lecturers. It is essential to become familiar with the words themselves of those Acts of Parliament that form the backbone of any particular part of your course. It is not sufficient to follow somebody else's paraphrase or synopsis of the important sections. You must master them yourself.

As was seen in the last chapter, since 1999 explanatory notes accompany new Acts which result from Bills introduced by a Government minister. Explanatory notes seek to explain the impact of the legislation in layman's terms and may be used as an aid to construction of the statute. See *R (on the application of S) v Chief Constable of South Yorkshire* [2004] 1 WLR 2196. The notes thus give the context of an Act and an indication of what the Act is intended to achieve. They are helpful, but again are not a substitute for reading the Act itself.

It is, thus, vital to equip yourself with your own copies of the relevant statutes. Many groups of statutes have been collected by publishers in sets of material intended primarily for student use. We can take one example. On your foundation course in property law, you will be referred time and time again to the 'LPA' (Law of Property Act 1925). Many of the provisions of this Act have to be known very well if you are to have any real competence as a property lawyer. On the same course you will be referred to many other 'property statutes'. There are a number of very good collections of this material, including *Blackstone's Statutes on Property Law*.

When you commence your study of property law, you will need to buy one of these collections of statutory material. You will need to take the volume you purchase to tutorials and to consult it frequently. In a property law examination, and in the practice of property law, you need to be familiar with and understand the precise words of important sections of the legislation. This is not achieved by last-minute memorising of some condensed version of the relevant rules. It is best achieved by using the Act itself as you pursue the course; using it to prepare your essays and seminar questions and referring to it during the discussions that take place in your seminars.

Statutory language is forbidding. It will take you much intellectual effort to become at ease with the important Acts of Parliament in each subject. The task will be both eased and made more rewarding if

HINT →

You must develop a capacity to understand Acts of Parliament; again there is no substitute for reading the actual words of an Act.

approached not as one of comprehension and memorising but in a wider critical framework. Take the simplest of examples:

'37 Rights of husband and wife

A husband and wife shall, for all purposes of acquisition of any interest in property, under a disposition made or coming into operation after the commencement of this Act, be treated as two persons.'

[Law of Property Act 1925, s 37.]

This has behind its simple and, in the new millenium, rather unremarkable pronouncement an enormous wealth of social history, a long struggle for the individual property rights of women and also a place in the highly technical doctrines of English land law. More than fifty years later, we find another Act passed concerned with the protection of one spouse's right to live in the matrimonial home owned by the other spouse.* In the years of the twentieth century, the matrimonial home was the scene of enormous and exciting legal developments reflecting periods of the profoundest change. The effect of these social forces is found in the case law and more importantly in the cold words of intricately wrought Acts of Parliament.

As issues like those touched on above come to feature in your course you will become involved in much more than the mere comprehension of difficult draftsman's phraseology. You will try to understand how Acts were used to amend technical areas of doctrine inextricably muddled by the judges; how Acts are used to implement desired social changes and how these reforming measures are formulated and moulded by the forces of different individuals and groupings.

In using statute law, the first great difficulty is in mastering the language and format. This skill is learned slowly, painstakingly, by thought and application. A real pleasure will be derived eventually from the ability to handle these strange forms for communicating the written word. It should not be forgotten, however, that the analysis of the printed word of an Act of Parliament is not in itself sufficient. Each small part of an Act is designed to carry out some important effect upon society – to remedy or prevent some undesired state of affairs, to confer or reduce the exercise of power, to punish or protect. The movements in society that produce legislative change and the effect which new measures produce will always be in your mind as you pore over some otherwise unexciting product of the parliamentary draftsman's skill.

---

* Now found in the Family Law Act 1996.

Dealing with new statutes

The modern law is concerned as much with statutes as with cases. Under the increasing pressure of work, Acts of Parliament seem to have become less clearly drafted than in the past. They are not 'a good read'. But, for the accomplished lawyer, a confident ability in the reading of a new Act is an essential skill.

How is this to be acquired? We can look briefly at two examples – the Law of Property (Miscellaneous Provisions) Act 1989 and the Football Spectators Act 1989.

Law of Property (Miscellaneous Provisions) Act 1989

The first of these has only six sections, but before you become a qualified lawyer you will come to know part of it verbatim. Let us take a small part:

'Section 2(1)

A contract for the sale or other disposition of an interest in land can only be made in writing and only by incorporating all the terms which the parties have expressly agreed in one document or, where contracts are exchanged, in each.'

This subsection is now one of the most important in English law. To read it you first need to read the remainder of the Act to ensure that you have understood any *definitions* or *qualifications* elsewhere in the Act which will affect your reading of these words. You will see that 'disposition' and 'interest in land' are both explained further in s 2(6). Section 5 tells you when the part with which we are concerned actually came into force.

Now suppose you are faced with the very interesting question as to whether words held on one computer terminal and transmitted over the public network can satisfy the requirement of being a *document* in *writing*. You will readily discover that these two expressions are not defined within the Act. A useful next step with a law reform Act such as this is to look at the Law Commission papers, its working papers and reports which lead to the Act being introduced. The Law Commission is a body set up to keep statute law under review and introduce law reform and codification. Before any reform is made it will have published consultation or working papers and reports. These are all kept in every college law library and are also available on the Internet. They are invaluable for the student of statute law. They frequently contain refreshingly clear re-statements of the law as it was before the intended reform and of the intended effect.

HINT →

Preparatory legislative materials often give guidance as to what the legislation is intended to achieve.

A second further source of enlightenment may be commentaries written on the Act by academics. These are, with important Acts, often written in some detail and a number will be available. For Acts such as these there will be an annotation in *Current Law*, articles in the journals such as the Law Society's *Gazette* and *New Law Journal*. Commentaries written at the time an Act is passed can often provide the vital clue you need. For example, one of the authors has a collection of commentaries written on the hugely important 1925 property legislation during the period of the legislation which are used very frequently. Nearly every important Act you look at as a student will have attracted the attention of academic writers at the time of its passing and these can often be used to good effect many years later.

HINT →

Use of annotated Acts of Parliament may shed light on the intended meaning of an Act.

As to the particular problem of what is 'writing' under the Law of Property (Miscellaneous Provisions) Act 1989 you may need to look much further to find an answer. In fact, on this precise point you would find there is no clear answer and you are left with no alternative except to argue by 'analogy'; to look at other cases where the law has been concerned with 'what is writing' and see if those areas will help you come to an answer.

Football Spectators Act 1989

Let us look briefly at the other statute, the Football Spectators Act 1989. In many ways this Act is typical of the way legislation may have to be dealt with by a solicitor. Suppose a Premier League football club was an important client of yours. You might be asked to brief the directors on the important consequences of this Act. This is very similar to the kind of work that is often attempted as a student project, giving it a suitable academic title such as 'The importance of the Football Spectators Act 1989 in the control of public disorder'.

Not surprisingly, the lawyer and the would-be lawyer might approach this task in a very similar fashion. The first step is to read the Act for that is the law. You will find that often in reading an Act much still remains opaque. The Act (s 8) creates a new corporate body – nearly every modern Act seems to create such bodies. This body is the Football Licensing Authority. What will it do? How will it operate? Unlike a law reform statute such as the Law of Property (Miscellaneous Provisions) Act 1989 there may be little in the legal academic press about such an Act as the Football Spectators Act. But, both to impress an important client and to record a first-class mark on our statute law project some further groundwork must be undertaken. Much of interest about the background of Acts of Parliament can be found from Parliamentary Debates (as noted in the last chapter the record of Parliamentary debates, Hansard, is available on the Internet at www.parliament.uk). The principles of a Bill are discussed in the Second Reading debate. It is discussed clause by clause in the Committee Stage. These are the two parts of the procedure that are likely to provide interesting reading and penetrating insight into the way the thing will work. The Bill will also be preceded by reports or enquiries, in this case the enquiries into football disasters, these may not provide the nice legal analysis of the Law Commission Report but will provide important background facts and give some indication of what the proposed law is intended to achieve.

Finally, with areas such as these there is often no substitute for personal enquiry. If you were a student doing such a project you would gain much from discussing the issues with your city's club and from direct contact with the relevant police force and, of course, the Football Licensing Authority. It is a good idea to let your enthusiasm carry you away. This will show in the finished piece of work or advice to your client.

HINT →

Reading Parliamentary debates can aid your understanding of an Act.

Secondary sources

Textbooks

In your first and every other year of legal study you will gather at least one and possibly two or more textbooks for each course of study. The names will be repeated by lecturer and student alike as hallowed talismans: *Cheshire, Fifoot and Furmston on Contract*; *Winfield on Tort*; *Smith and Hogan on Criminal Law*; *Megarry on Land Law*. The purchase of these textbooks represents a significant investment for the law student; what return is to be expected?

The first advice to give all eager purchasers of legal textbooks is that they cannot be read as other books are read. A legal textbook takes an area of law and describes it from end to end with frequent excursions and prevarications and an indigestible wealth of detail and footnotes on the way. The book is not meant to be and cannot usefully be read from cover to cover. It may profitably be used as follows. It is to be expected that the lecturer in each part of the syllabus will plan his programme so that you are aware of what is coming next. It may help to look over the relevant few pages in the textbook for a day or two before a forthcoming lecture. Detailed reading or intensive preparatory study are not worthwhile. You may delve deeply into things that your lecturer ignores, you may waste hours unravelling perceived mysteries which he disposes of with cogent simplicity. A light reading to grasp the framework and essential drift of a topic *may*, however, make lectures a more profitable experience.

Once your study of a particular topic is under way the textbook will be used to help in comprehension of difficult points and perhaps to amplify your lecturer's notes. Further than that it will be an important source of reference to supplementary reading of both cases and articles. In all these ways the textbook should be used as a signpost not as a prop. It is like an anthology of poems but with all the poems described briefly or tersely summarised – it would be a curious approach to literature to try to understand or acquire a feel for a poem by relying on such a work.

Case books

Before leaving the subject of student books, the other forms in which material is presented peculiarly for the use of law students may be mentioned. The first of these is case books.

Case books are collections of extracts from cases. They now exist in many areas of law. The idea that law may be studied almost exclusively through a programmed set of case reports or extracts from cases is discussed in Chapter 5. If your lecturer is adopting such a course of instruction, then you will be coerced into the use of a case book. Otherwise, it is suggested that the case book be approached with caution. One advantage of a case book is that the author acts like a filter, extracting the relevant parts of a case for you and highlighting important sections. But this in turn may be viewed as a disadvantage in that part of the skill of the lawyer is an ability when reading a case to sort the 'wheat from the chaff' and habitual use of a case book will never allow you to develop this particular skill. Also, generally, a case book will have space for only the cases of central importance. Many of these you should in any event make the effort to read in full. Case books do have uses which make it sensible, while not relying on one for your knowledge of case reports, to possess one for each area of the course, where available. You will find it valuable to read the selected extracts from cases you are, regrettably, too occupied to read in the library. In many, look for example at *Smith and Thomas on Contract* and *Weir on Tort*, you will find probing questions, suggestions and illustrations, some amusing in the extreme. Indeed these are frequently the most valuable part of a case book. Lastly, you will find it an aid to have the case book by you to refresh your recollection of cases long since read and fast becoming a blurred memory.

Study aids

Students will quite early in their career come across fellow students supplementing (or replacing) the traditional sources of legal study with a variety of handbooks, nutshells, companions and so on. It is customary for law teachers (who presumably write these) to be dismissive of their value. It can certainly be said that they are no substitute for a full study of the range of materials available in the law library.

However, there is equally no doubt that many students can benefit greatly, not only in time-saving, from making use of the careful guides by which other pilgrims have described the stony path to legal understanding. If you substitute these 'potted versions' for a comprehensive study you will inevitably not perform in the first or perhaps even the second flight of law students. In areas you find difficult, however, it is no confession of weakness to take advantage of the distillation of another's efforts and build on that.

HINT →
There are advantages to case books, but they should not be used in preference to reading cases in full.

HINT →
While not an alternative to the use of primary legal materials or the consideration of longer texts, study guides may provide a basic understanding upon which to base further legal study.

One final word of caution. Obviously many areas of law are difficult to understand. It is possible that the confines of a brief commentary may make comprehension even harder – very often it will aid understanding to read a more detailed rather than a less detailed account.

Legal journals

For the purpose of discussion, an arbitrary division may be made between academic journals, professional journals, journalistic publications and student publications; the distinction is made purely for the purpose of illustrating the type of reading matter available. It is the writers' experience that students do not *browse* widely enough in journals of all kinds – even the lighter-hearted range of articles about historical quirks, humorous incidents in practice and so on can be very valuable in bringing the legal world into a sharper focus and adding to the law student's perception of the place of his profession in the world outside.

But the starting point in looking at journals will be the academic journal, because it is to these that lecturers will most commonly refer the student. Among these the *Law Quarterly Review* (LQR), the *Modern Law Review* (MLR), the *Cambridge Law Journal* (CLJ) and the *Oxford Journal of Legal Studies* (OJLS) are the main generalist academic journals accepting articles and other pieces on the whole spectrum of legal study. There are also specialist journals such as the *Criminal Law Review* (Crim LR), *Conveyancer and Property Lawyer* (Conv) and *Industrial Law Journal* (ILJ): the scope of the first two journals is self-evident, the third deals with issues arising out of the employment relationship. It may be of assistance to examine the typical format of an academic journal to see what the student can expect.

Editorial notes/case notes

Each of these journals will begin with or end with or both begin and end with small pieces sometimes written mainly by the editor, sometimes unsigned commentary on developments and especially recent cases of particular interest. In this section the part most valuable to the student will be the *case notes* ranging from a paragraph or two to a short 'article' on a number of the most important recent cases. The usefulness of these case notes is often missed by students. They usually unravel the facts of cases clearly and explain the salient legal arguments which the judges have deployed. This exposition is then followed by comments explaining how the case fits in with existing case law, whether it is a desirable development, what awful consequences follow if the case should ever be applied and so on. Especially when dealing with controversial and 'key' cases the student will find a number of these notes. It should not be overlooked that cases the student finds difficult can be explained by reference to the case note in an ancient volume of one of these journals, and the case notes very often no longer cited in textbooks can be found simply by reference to the index to the volume for the year in question – think also what a pleasant surprise for your lecturer to find in coursework or an examination a reference to a case note which neither he in his lecture, nor the textbook in its footnotes, has referred to.

The academic article

Articles are the staple of academic journals. For the student, they are of very varying and often limited value. Each published article aims to be an original contribution to legal scholarship and it will not be surprising if the student still laying the foundation of his legal understanding has difficulties of comprehension. Particular uses which a student will find for such articles are as follows:

(i)   Some will contain vital arguments pursued by a lecturer or tutor and such articles specifically emphasised in lecture or seminar must be read. Such references afford very useful indications to the student as to the drift of the lecture course and final examination.

(ii) Many articles contain useful reviews of areas which have an abundance of case law and are ill dealt with, perhaps, in existing editions of textbooks. Where an area of the course is causing a special headache, this type of review article should be sought. At first in reading such a piece a student will very often feel that the business of its perpetrator has been to obfuscate rather than clarify. This is perhaps due to the inevitable tendency of academic writers to concentrate on 'the difficult bits'. A high degree of perseverance is obviously necessary if a student is to derive a positive gain from such reading. Perseverance in reading tortuous intellectual arguments is not in itself enough. What is needed is purposeful reading. You should have clearly in mind the gains you expect in reading an article – will it fill in gaps in my knowledge? Will it assist my understanding of this or that point? Will it give coherence or shape to a difficult area of case law? Will it provide a telling quotation which I can note for use in the coming examinations?

Another important use of the academic article is to comment on significant changes in the law. The student will obviously find it essential to read commentaries on reforms contemporaneous with his studies. What is easily overlooked is that in considering previous legislation that

HINT →

Reading a case note in a legal journal may assist you in understanding a case or in seeing its wider significance.

HINT →

Should you be referred to an article by your lecturer ensure that you read it.

HINT →

Articles in legal journals are an important source of information and may be used to aid understanding and also to good effect in preparing written work.

is no longer a novelty to the lecturer but of course is to the student, the commentaries written at the time of its passage may often be of value in allowing the student to see what the Act was attempting to achieve and how its effect was perceived before it was glossed by layers of case law.

The weeklies and professional journals

Reading one or other of the weekly journals or professional magazines is a very good way for the student to develop a general understanding of the modern legal world and a feel for the law. As an indication of how journals such as these may be used there follows a description of a few of these. The *New Law Journal* is a commercial publication primarily intended for practising lawyers but very widely read (and contributed to) by academics. The *Solicitors' Journal* is a commercial publication of very long standing intended evidently for the solicitor but widely read and contributed to by academics. The *Gazette* is published by the Law Society and together with its companion, the *Guardian Gazette* (which is the name for the last issue of each month), is easily the most widely read legal periodical. In his or her student career the student should ensure that opportunity is taken to read these journals from time to time. They will convey a great deal about the legal world of which the student is becoming a part. The *New Law Journal* is frequently critical and probing into the legal establishment and carries articles of a fairly polemical character. The *Solicitors' Journal* is again often critical of aspects of the solicitor's role and professional organisation but the nuances of its commentary are more finely tuned and being written by practising lawyers for practising lawyers may be less meaningful to the student.

The *Gazette* produced by the Law Society is essential reading for any would-be solicitor. The *Guardian Gazette* contains material directed also towards the barrister's profession and is essential reading for aspirant barristers. As do the other periodicals, the *Gazette* carries signed pieces by independent contributors. It also carries the official statements of the Law Society – about examinations, training regulations, conferences and so on. It has a regular column written by trainee solicitors for trainee solicitors. Once you are enrolled as a student member of the Law Society you will look forward to weekly sight of the *Gazette*. Read it regularly, since the regular columns and the debates carried on through the letter columns are not only informative and occasionally amusing but will gradually give you a very good insight into the preoccupations of solicitors and the nature of the profession and may help you considerably in deciding whether and in what type of firm you wish to practise. The *Gazette* will arrive weekly in its cellophane wrapper; if you find you are leaving these to pile up unopened or unread, ask yourself seriously whether you are enrolled as a student member of the right profession!

HINT →

Make it a habit to read the weekly legal journals to keep abreast of current legal developments.

All students will find it of inestimable value to read one of these three weeklies punctiliously. Each makes a point of providing a comprehensive updating service which will keep you informed of the new cases, progress of Bills, other developments. Not all the articles will be worthwhile reading for students. Each has many very specialist articles – the Gazette particularly on property, taxation and professional practice. But where there are practically-orientated articles which relate to your degree course you should make the effort to read them and gradually acquire some comprehension of the manifold links between the world of study and the world of practice.

It will not take the student long to realise that there are too many journals published for it to be possible to become familiar with them all. It is admittedly invidious to pick out a small number of these for comment but it is probably helpful to select one that might otherwise be overlooked and explain the use to which they might be put.

Legal Action   This is the monthly publication of the Legal Action Group, a society whose aim is the improvement of legal services. It is essential reading for the thoughtful lawyer. Its views are trenchant, sometimes intemperate, but it has gradually become the journal of a respected and influential radical movement. It asks serious questions which concern all aspirant lawyers – are equal opportunities provided for women lawyers? How can access to justice be achieved?

Before leaving this wide subject of general reading, a word should be said about newspapers. Lawyers and law students require to be well informed about current affairs. The newspapers are full of interesting topics of a 'legal nature' – from questions of international law in the perennial danger zones of the world to the detail of murder trials painstakingly reported in the press. The sophisticated student of today will be aware of the political persuasions of the major newspapers and perhaps be discouraged by that. Whatever other reason might, however, direct a choice of newspaper the serious law student will read *The Times*. It has been for many years the only newspaper to regularly publish a proper law report. This daily law report service is much overrated by academic lawyers. It concentrates too much on the trivial and the sensational. It is, however, a vital way of noting contemporary developments in areas of law being studied. The *Financial Times* is recommended as having regular stimulating articles on legal topics. *The Times* and the *Guardian* even more so have from time to time valuable and usually critical articles on aspects of the legal professions, the law in action and the judicial system. An interest and even excitement in these areas will develop as regular reading provides a knowledge of the issues, characters and dramas involved. Does the backbencher make an effective contribution to legislation? Should lawyers have a monopoly of particular areas of legal work? Are our judiciary able to respond to the exponential rate of social change? Is it divorced husbands or divorced wives who are dealt with harshly by our family law? In the classroom even such issues as these can seem dry – if you develop a sense of the forces at work in society that give rise to the need to answer such questions, you will also begin to develop an appreciation of the value to yourselves, and the future of the legal profession and the society in which it works, that will derive from the critical study of law.

The Internet as a source

Very rapidly the Internet has become an invaluable source of information about the law, as has been seen in Chapter 6. There are now sites which contain in whole text form some of the information which law students should be reading. Organisations of interest which can be contacted on the Internet are listed at the end of the previous chapter. No comprehensive listing of such sources will ever be possible. Different sites contain whole texts of cases, Acts of Parliament, guidance on practice, the views of sensible and extreme pressure groups, and so on. For students and lawyers alike 'literacy' on the Internet is essential and will come only with hours of practice. An important warning should be given – ideas from the Internet may inform your work – however they must be properly referenced just as ideas culled from other people's written work. It is just as much plagiarism to copy work from the Internet as from a library text. You should also be aware of the problem of authenticity of the sources on the Internet; remember, anyone may place material on a website. The advantages and disadvantages of the Internet as a source of information are considered in Chapter 10.

General approach

We hope enough has been said to encourage the student to adopt an eclectic, wide-ranging approach to reading law. If you read, as few students now ever will, the preface to *Coke's Littleton* (a property law textbook revised in the seventeenth century) you will find the great judge saying:

> 'Our hope, is that the young student, who heretobefore meeting at the first, and wrestlying with as difficult terms and matter, as in many years after, was at the first discouraged as many have been, may, by reading these Institutes, have the difficulty and darkness both of the matter, and of the terms and words of art in the beginning of his study, facilitated and explained unto him, to the end he proceed in his study cheerfully and with delight.'

And how did Coke propose that this cheerful understanding be achieved?

> 'Mine advice to the student is, that before he read any part of our commentaries upon any Section, that first he read again and again our author himself in that section, and do his best endeavours, first of himself, and then by conference with others, (which is the life of study) to understand it, and then to read our commentary thereupon, and no more at any one time then he is able with a delight to bear away, and after to meditate thereon, which is the life of reading.'

We hope you have gathered enough to know that Coke's approach is very wrong in part. He is quite right that discussion with others must be of great help with understanding. He is wrong to adopt the 'textbook-hugging' approach. Too many students mull over the same words in the same textbook or in the lecture notes over and over again. This concentration on one digested source of law dulls the mind and the understanding and is the antithesis of good practice in studying law. The syndrome of concentration on a single textbook has long been an unwelcome feature in legal education. Contrasting views, different perspectives and different sources are the necessary ingredients for producing the well-informed lawyer who has a sound grasp of the common-lawyer. The advantages of reading in a variety of sources is emphasised in these brief sentences from Edward de Bono (*The Use of Lateral Thinking* 1967):

> 'It is not easy to get outside a particular way of looking at things in order to find a new way. Very often all the basic ingredients of a new idea are already to hand and all that is required is a particular way of assembling them . . . This encourages much greater flexibility of mind, for the pupil is actively encouraged to consider a problem from many different points of view, and to appreciate there may be several ways of reaching a correct conclusion.'

■ CHECKLIST

■ THE SOURCES OF LEGAL STUDY

▶ The primary sources of English law are cases and legislation. Additionally you need to be aware of the sources of European Community law and the impact of the Human Rights Act 1998.

▶ For each subject you study, be aware of the syllabus and pay particular attention to the emphasis placed upon individual areas in the syllabus by your lecturer.

▶ You are expected to read those sources to which you are directed by your tutor.

▶ From the outset of your legal studies make it a habit to read the primary sources of law, ie cases and legislation.

▶ It is important to understand the structure of a law report before you start reading cases.

▶ Familiarise yourself with the layout of Acts of Parliament. Such an understanding helps in the task of determining how to interpret the intention of Parliament.

▶ Various practical aids can be used to assist in an understanding of an Act of Parliament. Consider preparatory reports, with newer Acts explanatory notes, and academic commentaries.

▶ Secondary sources of law are valuable but should be used appropriately; they are not a substitute for reading the primary sources.

▶ Articles in legal journals are an important source of information and should be consulted. Articles may be used to aid understanding of an area of law and also to good effect in preparing written work.

▶ Make it a habit to read the weekly legal journals to keep abreast of current legal developments. The quality daily newspapers are also an important source of information.

▶ Some material on the Internet must be treated with caution; use of material from the Internet must be appropriately acknowledged.

Chapter 8
Preparing written work

Preparing essays and projects

Writing legal opinions and advice, complex letters and documents is a large part of the lawyer's business. Curiously legal education has more recently seemed to place little direct emphasis upon the teaching of these skills. From an early age we are educated in an atmosphere of scribbled lecture notes and even more hastily scribbled examination papers. Later on in the lawyer's office we find that modern lawyers do not in fact write but instead dictate into machines. This practice, fed by the deplorable standards of English now prevalent, has done a great deal to increase the sloppiness and unintelligibility of lawyers' written communications. Letters which seem to have no structure of sentences and paragraphs are commonplace. The public seems to think that the main skill of the lawyer lies in the unintelligibility of his written products!

It is to be assumed that the law student possesses a healthy competence in both spoken and written English. Sadly this is not always the case. It is only too apparent that schools these days place little emphasis upon spelling (perhaps not so very important!) or syntax and sentence construction (essentials of clear direct communication). Much of your experience on a law course will not be conducive to improving written English; it is very difficult in law lectures to make notes in any but the most rudimentary English. Where problem-classes take the form of a discussion it is easy to rely simply on hastily written notes, and in unseen written examinations, speed of delivery seems more of the essence than the well-rounded phrase and skilfully constructed sentence. Nevertheless, you will, hopefully, be given plenty of opportunity to prepare written work for correction whether in the form of short essays or more ambitious pieces of work entitled thesis, project, long essay or whatever. Where essays do not 'count' towards examination assessment there is an obvious human tendency to treat them with less regard. They are, despite this, invaluable. Marshalling your thoughts and the muddled information from textbooks, articles and lectures into an ordered coherent essay is in itself worthwhile training for a lawyer.

> **HINT →**
> The invitation to submit practice or diagnostic essays ought to be taken; this is an important learning opportunity.

Given the nature of legal source material, its prolixity and inherent ambiguity, it is a skill which comes naturally to no person. It is the case that time spent in preparing essays will be reflected in improved examination performance. Essay writing will have clarified your understanding of difficult areas and over a reasonable period improve your qualities of expression.

Answering law questions

HINT ➡

Consider what a marker is looking for in an answer.

In preparing an answer to a question as coursework or in an examination you need to consider what it is that you are expected to achieve. This goal may be reformulated as a question: What is a marker looking for in your answer? Some reflection on this question will lead to a deeper understanding of the assessment process. Simply stated, the overall aim of your answer is to demonstrate to a marker that you *understand* an area, or areas, of law. There are a number of features that your answer must include to allow an examiner to reach the conclusion that you do indeed understand.

Features of an answer

KEY POINT ●

A marker can only assess the understanding you express in your written answer.

A marker may be looking for the following features in your answer:

▶ analysis of the issues raised by a question;

▶ statements of relevant legal principle;

▶ an awareness of sources;

▶ the application of law to an issue;

▶ accuracy;

▶ logical organisation of material;

▶ appropriate citation of authorities, use of footnotes and inclusion of a bibliography.

HINT ➡

Your answer should be understandable to a reasonably intelligent layperson.

Before you start writing your answer it is important to identify the audience for whom you are writing. Clearly, if you are writing for a lawyer you may assume certain knowledge in the reader. However, in formulating a law answer at undergraduate level you are not writing for a lawyer but for a *reasonably intelligent lay person*. Therefore, you must explain technical terms and concepts. It is important not to assume knowledge on the part of an examiner; remember it is your understanding that is being assessed, not that of the examiner.

When reading a question you should be noting both the general area of law raised and the sub-issues raised within this area. In order to identify pertinent issues you must have a full knowledge and understanding of the relevant law. It is not enough to know the law; you must be able to apply it in a number of situations. In appreciating how the law may be applied it is essential to be able to refer, for example, to decided cases as illustrations. Your research should encompass how and why courts decide cases. Careful preparation is a prerequisite to success in written work and examinations.

Having identified the issues you must then set about analysing them. What is the difficulty or problem raised? Choose the legal principles relevant to the problem identified. Precise analysis will allow you to deal solely with that problem; you must not fall into the temptation of writing all you know about the law in a particular area. Many students cannot decide what is *relevant* or irrelevant and therefore 'play safe' by writing at length about a particular area of law in the hope that something is right. Such is known as the 'kitchen sink approach', everything goes in, but it does not demonstrate that you understand. It is really a request to an examiner to do the work for you. Few marks can be awarded on this basis as relevant material is lost among material which is irrelevant. *The issue of relevance is determined by the issues raised by a question.* Only consider those areas of law that relate to the issues you have identified.

✖ EXAMPLE

If a contract question only raises the issue of termination of offer by revocation, consider only the law relating to revocation. Do not discuss the law relating to other methods of termination of offer such as rejection, lapse of time and so on: the inclusion of such only clouds an examiner's appreciation of your understanding.

HINT →
Relevance is determined by the issues raised by a question.

You have started the process of analysis, but what should you be committing to paper? In general, description is to be avoided. For example, do not merely recount the facts of a problem. This is a waste of time as it does not help the marker assess your understanding. Indicate the issue raised by the facts and *then explain the law directly relevant to the issue*, stating the source of the law, for example cases or legislation. Having done this you must seek to *demonstrate how the law applies to the facts of the question*. Some assistance may be gained from decided cases.

HINT →

Avoid description in your answer; the expectation is that you will analyse the question.

> ### ✖ EXAMPLE
>
> In the law of contract cases seem to indicate that, if an agreement is purported to be uncertain, the courts may be influenced in reaching the conclusion that the agreement is certain by the fact that some perform-ance under the 'agreement' has taken place. The presence or absence of such performance in the facts of a question is worthy of comment, in the light of the case law. It is obvious that a thorough understanding of the law is essential in the above process.

Another indicator of understanding is *organisation* of material. Do not relate page upon page of law before attempting an application of the law to the facts of a problem. Often the chronology of events in a problem gives a framework for discussion. Also be aware of the logic of the law.

HINT →

Your answer should have a clear and logical structure.

> ### ✖ EXAMPLE
>
> Unless it is clear that liability is assumed in the question, it is not logical to discuss a defence before liability has been proved. In criminal law you should not discuss the defences to murder if it has not been established that murder has been committed (unless, of course, the question makes clear that a murder has taken place and that the student should only concentrate on discussion of defences). Equally, given that for a promise varying a contract to be contractually binding there is a need for consideration and that the doctrine of estoppel, while giving some protection, is not as good as consideration, it is necessary to seek to find consideration before determining whether, as an alternative, an estoppel has arisen.

In structuring your answer there should be an introduction, a middle section, developing the issues raised in the introduction and a conclu-sion, summarising and evaluating your discussion.

Law answers must *contain authorities* handled appropriately. So for each principle of law stated there should be a case or legislative provi-sion cited as authority. It is not always necessary to cite the facts of a case. As a rule of thumb, in answering problem questions, only use the facts of a case if you are seeking to show similarities or differences between the facts of the question and the decided case for the purposes of illustrating how law may be applied. Ideally, upon stating a legal prin-ciple you should then provide an authority for the principle. In citing cases you should give the name of the case; for example, civil cases

HINT →

When stating a principle of law, always cite authority.

should be referred to by their full title *Hedley Byrne v Heller*, while criminal cases may be referred to as *Howe* (instead of *R v Howe*).

Sometimes a question may require a more in depth analysis of a case or cases. See the example given in Chapter 7 concerning the use of *Hardwick v Johnson* in answering a question; in this instance an explanation of the basis of the decision in the case was needed.

Depending upon the question asked there may be opportunities to *discuss problem areas of law*. If the law is unclear, or there are conflicting authorities, or the case law is not consistent in approach, then you will be expected to discuss the issue and to indicate the problems in advising a client as to the application of the law. A good answer will consider these difficulties, also showing an understanding of judicial precedent; was a statement of law the ratio decidendi of a case or merely an obiter dictum? Was a case decided by the House of Lords and therefore binding on the courts lower in the hierarchy or was it decided by a court lower in the hierarchy and therefore merely persuasive? Such information will be important in supporting an argument or in challenging an argument presented to the contrary.

HINT ➡

If relevant, use the doctrine of judicial precedent in presenting arguments based on case law.

It is sometimes necessary to explain *why a rule of law does not apply on the facts of a problem*.

✖ EXAMPLE

If a question states that parties agree that one of them should only pay part of an existing debt in full and final settlement, then the law provides that such payment is no discharge of the full debt. The balance remains payable. The legal reason for this is that there is an absence of consideration for the promise to forgo the remainder. However, the law seems to have moved to a more flexible approach as to what constitutes consideration, as seen in *Williams v Roffey Brothers*. Does this approach apply to part-payment of a debt? The answer, given in *Re Selectmove*, was no. Thus, a negative point is explained as to why a particular rule does not apply.

One aspect of your answer that depends very much on your previous experience of writing answers is *clarity of explanation*. This is a matter of prose style. Long and convoluted sentences are to be avoided and, perhaps, short sentences should be employed. Read a Lord Denning judgment for an example of the use of short sentences.

Your *answer must be reasoned and not rely merely upon assertions*. Students quite often will understand how a principle of law applies, but rather than explain this they merely assert that the rule applies. The two examples below illustrate this point.

✖ EXAMPLE 1

Under the Unfair Contract Terms Act 1977 an exclusion clause may be subject to a test of reasonableness. A good answer will indicate not only that the test applies, but also indicate the circumstances that need to exist in order for the test to apply: there must be an exclusion clause, s 13; the contract must not fall within the category of contracts to which the Act does not extend, Sch 1; there must be 'business liability', s 1(3); the type of liability that is sought to be excluded must be identified, ie strict liability or negligence and so on. All of these points must be explained by reference to the relevant provisions of the Act and any case law.

HINT →
You must explain the reasoning for your answer and not rely upon assertions.

✖ EXAMPLE 2

When seeking to establish vicarious liability in the law of tort it is necessary to ascertain that the person committing a tort is an employee. A poor answer would raise this issue, but then fail to explore it, merely stating that the tortfeasor (the person committing the tort) is an employee. Whereas a good answer would consider the tests the courts use in determining whether a person is an employee or an independent contractor and then show how these might apply.

HINT →
Never commence your answer with a conclusion.

It is the explanation of the reasoning process that attracts full marks.

Allied to the previous point is the correct use of a conclusion. A common failing among first year students is to start an answer with an assertion as to the outcome of a legal problem, for example 'X is liable for a breach of contract'. Your answer should explore the issues raised by the question and then progress towards a conclusion.

You must ensure *accuracy* at all times. Again, careful preparation will ensure that you achieve this. After a lecture or seminar you must check your material. All too often some students will record, in their notes, the name of a case spelt phonetically, but never bother to check for accuracy. This misspelt case will then appear in an answer, thus revealing that the student has not read around the subject area and is relying merely upon notes taken during lecture or seminar sessions.

HINT →
Ensure that you answer the question asked, not the question you would like to have been asked.

Finally, remember to *adhere to the parameters of the assessment*. If there is a word limit ensure that this is not exceeded or if there is a time limit ensure that you deal with the issues raised by the question within the time permitted. This latter task requires the exercise of judgement as to what is essential to an answer and what is merely peripheral or, indeed, irrelevant.

Preparing written work

There is no value in hurrying through a set task merely for the sake of completion. In preparing, particularly in law, for any piece of scholarship the first task is researching the relevant material. It is of no profit to you whatsoever simply to repeat in your own more polished and elegant words the profound insights of your lecturer. In terms of developing skill as a lawyer, it is of little more value to cull your ideas secondhand from a textbook and rearrange them into the routine paragraphs of your essay.

Preparation for writing an essay in law begins with the primary sources of law. The task must be kept in reasonable proportions. Each student essay cannot be a definitive work and the amount of time must be allocated carefully. Given that, you will not produce an interesting piece of work, saying something moderately novel about the subject on which you are asked to comment, unless you read the relevant source material and make an effort to find in it that which is especially relevant for or against the theme of your argument.

✱ EXAMPLE

Let us take a simple essay title that could be set as a first essay in a first year tort* course: 'Discuss the requirements that a court must consider in establishing a duty of care in the tort of negligence.' A straightforward, and most likely descriptive, answer to this can be cobbled together straight out of a chapter on 'duty of care' in a tort textbook . The good student, however, will already have read the great cases of the last four decades, in which the House of Lords examined the approach of the courts to the issue of establishing a duty of care, noting particularly the policy arguments concerning restriction of potential liability. In these cases will be found ideas and sometimes quotations to enliven passages in an essay. Proceeding from the textbook and cases to read some of the many instructive journal articles to which case law in this area has given rise will prove fruitful. The good student will find articles in this area which are both interesting and useful such as Tony Weir 'Fixing the Foundations' (1991) 50 CLJ 24.

---

* You will find it easier to return to this example when you begin your tort course if you have not already.

Before setting pen to paper in earnest, the diligent student will have read a much greater range of material than he can hope to digest in his essay. The watchword in legal research is to read widely but note only briefly. To understand a topic like that under review, many cases must be read and conflicting, perhaps ill-structured, judicial views pondered. Legal journal articles equally are often prolix and rarely wholly digestible at first sitting. When you read a lot you will begin to understand the shapes and patterns of rules and concepts which form a developing area of law. But, it is not profitable to make lengthy notes of this wide-ranging reading. Little can ever be reproduced in examinations or essays of the tortuous facts. You will not have occasion to refer to the multitude of almost analogous cases dredged up and cited in argument nor to recreate the winding thought processes of each learned judge. Keep your notes succinct so that you have on paper that which you can later find of practical use. The next and more difficult stage is rendering this chaos of information into your own semblance of order.

HINT ⇒

In legal research read widely, but note briefly.

Presentation of essays

Written English

Lawyers do not set a very good example to law students. Whether the reader is tackling the law reports or law books he will be oppressed by the amount of unexplained jargon and the unnecessary complexity of language and sentence structure. What follows is a short list of simple clues to good, clear essay writing.

(i) *Write in simple sentences.* Clear English consists of short sentences made up of short words. In legal writing, complex thoughts have sometimes to be arranged in lengthy sentences with dependent and sub-dependent clauses, colons, semicolons and parentheses. This should not be done unless it adds to the meaning of the pertinent passage. Avoid the temptation of drifting into complex sentence structure as an affectation of scholarship.

(ii) *Use simple words.* This may seem odd advice to a lawyer. It makes, though, for much clearer English if you can save your use of long technical words for occasions when they are precisely relevant. Especially, eschew the use of words the meaning of which is not absolutely clear to you. Comprehensible English uses sentences and words which are as simple as the context permits. The Plain English Campaign has trenchantly argued

HINT ⇒

Avoid complicated sentences and long words. Aim for simplicity, short sentences and simple words.

for this viewpoint. It may amuse you to use their Gobbledygook
Test (reproduced from the Plain English Teaching Kit and to be
found in the Online Resource Centre) to test the comprehensi-
bility of your own English style. Inevitably, a worthwhile
passage of legal prose will be more complex in structure
than an editorial in the *Sun* but it need not be entirely incompre-
hensible. Incidentally, note the spelling of judgment without a
middle 'e', when referring to the decision of a judge in a case.

(iii) In preparing short essays you do not need to use the same style
for references and footnotes as for a longer piece of work. The
following instructions may assist:

(a) *Case names.* Usually these should be given in full. If a party
has an unusually lengthy name, the abbreviation commonly
used in the textbooks should be followed. In short essays
there is no need or purpose in giving references to the law
reports. If the date of decision is important to your
argument it may be given in round brackets after the
case title or simply in the narrative.

✖ EXAMPLE

'In *Entores Ltd v Miles Far East Corp* decided in 1955, the Court showed
that it could adapt the rules of offer and acceptance to deal with new
technology . . .'.

When referring to a case name in an essay it is conventional to
underline the entire name. This reflects the practice in publishing of
printing the names of cases in italics. It also makes the completed
essay much easier to read and consequently to mark. The case
names should appear in the body of your answer and not in your
footnotes. The citation to a case should be included in a footnote.

(b) *Bibliography.* Students have often been encouraged at
school to include at the end of an essay a bibliographical list
showing the works they have read. In the case of a short law
essay, submitted for feedback purposes, this is quite
unnecessary. If you do refer to a case or published work
with which you suspect your lecturer will be unfamiliar
because of its exotic nature, then it will be helpful to give a
full reference to this either in the text or by a *brief*
footnote. Otherwise there is no need at all for references
or bibliography.

(iv) However brief the essay which you hand in it should have some structure. Students seem on arrival at law school to forget forthwith all they have been taught about the structure of essays. A piece of legal argument, like any other written work, benefits from having a discernible structure. At the very least it should have a beginning, a middle – divided into proper paragraphs – and an end. That much seems too mundane to require saying but the reader has not been subjected, as we have, to the reading of piles of essays which drift from a casual beginning to falter into an uncertain ending. Avoid a naïve ending, eg 'Therefore, I conclude that Frederick will win and win heavy damages'. Aim for an ending which leaves your reader with something to ponder, eg 'Thus, the political decision not to enforce anti-trade union legislation has created a power vacuum. Though endowed with seemingly enormous powers, the constitutional forces of law and order seem practically powerless. Does this herald some major realignment of constitutional forces in Britain?'*

HINT ⇒

Ensure that you consider the best way to structure your answer..

On a practical note you will find it helpful towards your examination performance if your essay writing bears a reasonable relation to the piece of work you can be expected to produce in the written papers. Undergraduates' routine essays are usually much too long. They are not intended to be encyclopaedic in content or style. They are essentially limited exercises in legal analysis and expression. Given that the topic or problem on which you are writing will, almost certainly, be one on which you will be restricted to forty minutes or so in the examination it seems sensible to restrict your written answer to an amount that can be written in that period of time. This will give you useful practice towards the exercise by which much of your undergraduate career will be formally assessed. Many students will find it a helpful practice to close their books, put away their notes and then allow themselves this more or less limited time to write out their essay.

Preparing substantial pieces of work

Many law courses give students the opportunity to prepare a long essay or dissertation. This represents a test of the many skills you have acquired during your legal education. In many ways it may be seen as the culmination of the process to produce a self-motivated, independent law

---

* This, the reader will note, was written in 1984. How different these issues appear by 2007!

student who is able to collect materials, interpret them and then produce a coherent account on a particular area of law. Sometimes the desired length is as little as four or five thousand words; sometimes as great as ten or twelve thousand words. Even for the second or third year student this can be a fairly daunting task and the chance is often missed of carrying out a work of both interest and quality.

The most important advice that can be given is to start early. Lawyers, perhaps all of us, have a culpable habit of leaving what must be done within a particular time right until the end of that available period. If you start early and work steadily towards a slightly early deadline you will enjoy the task more; you will suffer less from the temptation to 'get it over at all costs', and you will have time for the reflective thought and careful revision that will improve the finished quality of your work.

Finding a title

You will probably find, unless you have an unusual bent for legal writing, that beginning is the hardest part of all. In some universities you may be asked at the outset to find, or even simply be given, a title. Where students are asked to decide upon a title for themselves, many find this the most difficult part of producing a dissertation. The difficult step is clarifying in your own mind the content of your work. Before commencing the search for a title you would be well-advised to consider the areas of law you have particularly enjoyed and also to reflect on where your best marks thus far lie. A dissertation is a major undertaking that will occupy you for much of your final year, so it is important to select a topic that will retain your interest. Once you have decided upon a general area for your dissertation you must next look for a more specific topic within the area. It is often the case that students at this stage tend to aim for a work of too wide a scope. If your field of enquiry remains too broad and your consequent written work too general in approach, this will lead to an essay that is superficial and probably descriptive. Such an essay will not satisfy the criteria of assessment for a final year dissertation and your final grade may suffer very badly. This is a most common shortcoming in student project-work and an area in which students are prone to disregard their lecturer's advice. Therefore, it is important to read around your chosen area to look for an 'angle' for your essay. Consider the following possible 'angles':

- ► inconsistencies in an area of law;
- ► problems in the existing law and the consequent need for reform;
- ► uncertainties in a legal concept;

- the way in which a rule or concept may be further developed (this may involve a comparison with the law in other jurisdictions);

- how a reformed area of law is working in practice.

✖ EXAMPLE

A student may indicate an interest in the law of property. This is clearly too wide. The area may be narrowed to that of proprietary estoppel. Although narrower in scope the title gives no indication of an 'angle'; it is likely that any dissertation on this topic will be purely descriptive, resembling an explanation contained in a textbook. However, if an aspect of proprietary estoppel is identified, for example estoppel as a cause of action and then a comparison drawn with promissory estoppel, this gives an issue to explore. If the title is developed to encompass the question of why proprietary estoppel gives rise to a cause of action, whereas promissory estoppel does not, then an essay on such a subject will avoid being purely descriptive. The title could be further developed to consider whether promissory estoppel ought to give rise to a cause of action.

Literature search

A literature search has two purposes: first, it confirms the viability of your proposed area of research; and, second, it allows you to locate material relevant to your area of study.

In carrying out a literature search you must find sufficient material to enable you to produce a piece of work of the required length. Problems may be encountered if you are considering recently passed legislation where little or nothing has yet been written. Again caution should be exercised where an area of law is likely to be reformed imminently; getting to grips with an area that is changing rapidly can be overwhelming. Another problem often encountered is that of accessibility of source material. You need to consider whether the materials you need are available in your university library or are easily obtainable through inter-library loans. While availability of material on the Internet has lessened this problem, not all sources are yet in electronic form. You must check to ensure that material you have to order from another library will arrive in time for your purposes. On carrying out a literature search, should you find that there is a lack of information you will need to revise your dissertation title or possibly look for another title.

Once you have collected materials relevant to your dissertation you will need to assess the weight of the material. Have you too much, or too

HINT →

Ensure there is sufficient and available source material before finalising your dissertation title.

little, material? Is your subject area too wide? Perhaps your title needs to be refined.

Development of your dissertation and the role of the supervisor

Before you start work in earnest a little more detailed specification of your venture is required. You will doubtless begin with the germ of an idea from something that has stimulated your interest in a lecture or seminar. It is a good idea at an early stage to talk this over with a knowledgeable member of staff, who will be able to direct you towards the most recent sources in that particular area and suggest valuable lines of enquiry. These preliminary readings and discussions should be directed towards producing, before too much time has elapsed, a more precise title, a list of chapter headings and, if possible, a brief synopsis of what your essay will achieve. It is to be borne in mind that the title you have chosen is not written in stone and may develop with your research.

The development of a dissertation is not only a vehicle for assessment but is also an important part of your education. You will be allocated a supervisor who will guide you throughout the process of preparing and writing your dissertation. It is important that you maximise this opportunity. The supervisor will be able to give guidance on the formulation of your essay title, organisation of material, development of your answer, presentation of material and adherence to the university regulations, among other matters. However, this is not to say that the supervisor will do these things for you: the onus is upon you to identify an area of law, formulate a title, assemble a body of material, organise the material and so on. In an early meeting your supervisor may map out what is expected of you, for example when draft chapters are to be produced. You need to keep to such a schedule to allow the supervisor to give you feedback on your work. Being prepared for each meeting is essential to ensure that you make the most of your supervisor's experience.

> **KEY POINT** ●
>
> A dissertation is the product of a student's efforts; do not expect the guidance of a supervisor to mean that a supervisor will do those things for you that you should be doing.

Content of a dissertation

A dissertation must include:

- ▶ identification of clear objectives;
- ▶ accurate statement and explanation of law;
- ▶ evidence of research, drawing upon appropriate sources;
- ▶ analysis of the subject matter, including where relevant critical evaluation;

- appropriate presentation, including use of footnotes and inclusion of a bibliography;

- valid conclusions drawn from information and discussion contained in the body of the work.

Originality is not a requirement for success in an undergraduate dissertation, although if it is present it will ensure that the mark awarded to you will be a good one.

You will probably experience some difficulty in arriving at the 'chapter headings and synopsis' stage. To many this is the most difficult part of the entire task. If, by this stage, you are developing a clear 'thesis' or 'plan' and meaningful chapter headings, the detailed research and writing should prove much more straightforward than expected.

Much of the advice given in this book in relation to writing essays (see the next chapter) holds true for dissertations and longer essays.

■ CHECKLIST FOR PREPARATION OF A DISSERTATION

- Identify a general area.

- Narrow the scope of the area.

- Determine an 'angle'.

- Be aware of the university regulations for preparation of a dissertation.

- Carry out a literature search.

- Meet with your supervisor.

- Establish a working timetable for the development of your dissertation.

- Ensure that you produce timely draft chapters of your essay.

- Keep a record of the development of your dissertation.

Presentation of the finished work

Each university will doubtless have its own rules or guidelines as to presentation of the finished work. It is churlish to ignore these, as some students will each year. To do so will inescapably lead to the marking examiner looking less favourably at your work. Some detailed points as to presentation may be of assistance.

(i) The most acceptable form of presentation to the reader is to type the material with generous margins, double-spaced on A4 size paper. Leave time to correct the typescript and have the corrections neatly included in the finished work. If you are not, as most of us are not, able to spot all the errors or infelicities in your own writing, persuade a friend or relation to read it for you (if this is permitted by your college rules!). Should this be allowed, it is illuminating to give your legal answer to a reasonably intelligent layperson and ask if your answer is intelligible. If the answer is no, then you need to revise your explanations.

(ii) Do not clutter up your work with pointless footnotes. It is, for example, common for students to cite student textbooks for very basic propositions. This can be irritating to the reader. Save footnotes for statements and opinions that are sufficiently distinctive or controversial to merit reference to some authority therefor.

(iii) Footnotes are indicated in the text by a raised arabic numeral immediately following the pertinent word. The footnotes themselves are conventionally either printed at the foot of the page to which they belong or collected together at the end of the chapters or the entire work. For the reader there is no doubt as to the superiority of the first method cited. Special caution is needed in keeping the numbering of your footnotes synchronised with the footnotes themselves – where the text is revised or retyped this can very easily go astray and the numbering of footnotes should be carefully rechecked. Thankfully, Microsoft Word has a footnote facility which does this task for you.

(iv) For lengthy pieces of work, divide your work into clear chapters. Start each chapter on a fresh page. Within each chapter use a clear system of headings and sub-headings.

(v) In the citation of cases, statutes and other works it is important to keep to established conventions and to be consistent within your own work. American law students are greatly assisted by a small work published by the Harvard Law Review Association, *A Uniform System of Citation* (Gannett House, Cambridge, Massachusetts). This can be glanced at with profit by any would-be legal writer. There is no such work for English students though the *Oxford Manual* of *Style* and *New Hart's Rules* are a good stating part, and some advice has been given in the relevant chapters of this book. A useful list of conventional abbreviations is found in the opening pages of any volume of *Current Law Yearbook*. (Because there is no standard list of abbreviations in England you may need to search in other sources and the following may be useful – *Osborn's Concise Law Dictionary* (located at the rear of the book); Knowles and Thomas *Effective Legal Research* (Appendix II); any volume of *Halsbury's Laws of England* (the beginning).)

(vi) The chapter in this book on 'Citation of legal sources and plagiarism' contains a summary of the major conventions of legal citation. In using this remember that internal consistency is even more important than keeping to established conventions. Do not be tempted into a pompous or pedantic use of references. Not every single proposition needs to be justified by decided authority. In an examination it is wiser to err on the side of over-citation of authority. In a piece of written work, cite authority only for significant or problematical statements.

Above all, aim for a style which is direct and uncluttered. Do not wander into obfuscation simply because you have not undertaken enough preliminary work to be able to deal with the topic clearly. There follow two examples of essay-writing style. Which will a marking examiner prefer? How would you improve the other and still convey the same meaning?

✖ EXAMPLE 1

The principle of waiver is simply this:

> If one party, by his conduct, leads another to believe that the strict rights arising under the contract will not be insisted upon, intending that the other should act on that belief, and he does act on it, then the first party will not afterwards be allowed to insist on the strict legal rights when it would be inequitable for him to do so: see *Plasticmoda Societa per Azioni v Davidsons (Manchester) Ltd* [1952] 1 Lloyd's Rep 527 at 539.

There may be no consideration moving from him who benefits by the waiver. There may be no detriment to him by acting on it. There may be nothing in writing. Nevertheless, the one who waives his strict rights cannot afterwards insist on them. His strict rights are at any rate suspended so long as the waiver lasts. He may on occasion be able to revert to his strict legal rights for the future by giving reasonable notice in that behalf, or otherwise making it plain by his conduct that he will thereafter insist upon them: *Tool Metal Manufacturing Co Ltd v Tungsten Electric Co Ltd*. But there are cases where no withdrawal is possible. It may be too late to withdraw: or it cannot be done without injustice to the other party. In that event he is bound by his waiver. He will not then be allowed to revert to his strict legal rights. He can only enforce them subject to the waiver he has made.

(Lord Denning in *W J Alan & Co Ltd v E L Nasr Export and Import Co* [1972] 2 QB 189 – discussing promissory estoppel, of which you will hear much in contract law.)

✖ EXAMPLE 2

The second example is from a case brought against the Law Society by a solicitor trying to show that it had acted wrongly in imposing a compulsory insurance scheme upon its members, and then receiving a commission on each premium from the insurance brokers. Had the Law Society been in a position of trust for its members in so doing and thus rendered itself bound to account for the proceeds?

Lord Diplock explains:

'This left constructive trusteeship, and the Court of Appeal held that, although the Law Society did not act in the capacity of agent in entering into and maintaining the master policy, it nevertheless did so as trustee for the individual solicitors of the benefit of the promises by the insurers made in the master policy to insure those individual solicitors against professional liability. In this, for reasons given by Lord Brightman, I think they erred. This is one of those reasons which for my part I find conclusive in itself. The obligations imposed by the master policy and certificate of insurance on the insurers and each assured are mutual; they are not limited to promises by the insurers to indemnify the assured against professional liability conditional on the assured's acting in a particular way, as in a unilateral or "if" contract. To an "if" contract, since it involves no promise by the promisee to act in that way, it may be that the concept of constructive trusteeship of the benefit of a promise may properly be applied. But the master policy imposes on the assured as well as positive obligations to the insurers, as in synallagamatic contracts. The concept of constructive trusteeship of promises which confer a benefit on a cestui que trust is not, in my view, capable in private law of extension to promises which impose a burden on a cestui que trust; an agent acting within his authority can create burdensome obligations on the part of his principal, a constructive trustee cannot.'

(*Swain v Law Society* [1982] 2 All ER 827, 833.)

You will come across this case when you study the duties of a trustee; to give Lord Diplock a fair trial you may need to glance at the case, which is not too lengthy!

The morals of this rather mischievous comparison are these: use simple words if simple words will do. Do not conceal your reasoning behind a conceptual smoke-cloud. Try to make each step in your reasoning clear and consecutive. If what you are saying involves a conclusion that may be open to doubt do not conceal that by a verbal sleight-of-hand. What you write is intended to be understood. It is not lacking in depth, necessarily, simply because it can be understood readily. You will find in Lord Denning a model of clear English if not in all ways a strictly model judge!

■ CHECKLIST

■ PREPARING WRITTEN WORK

During preparation of an essay consider the following:

▶ Are you able to justify the inclusion of information in your draft answer? If you have not related the information to the question is the information relevant?

▶ Have you explained the relevant law fully and accurately?

▶ Are you clear as to the structure of your answer?

▶ In answering a problem question have you ensured that the law is applied directly to the facts?

▶ Is your answer reasoned or are you relying upon assertions?

▶ Do you include authorities in your answer?

▶ Is your answer clear to a reasonably intelligent layperson?

Chapter 9

Advice on completing coursework

Matters to be considered

Much of the advice that follows is universal in that it applies equally to writing coursework and to writing answers to examination questions. Basic points about structuring your answer, stating principles of law and using authority hold good for both. The obvious differences are that in preparing coursework you will be able to refer to source material and you will be expected to fully reference the sources used, in footnotes and in a bibliography. There will usually be no immediate time constraint on writing your essay, beyond a submission date, but there may be a word limit.

Preparation

Before you start researching the area of the coursework it is wise to look at the assessment regulations for your programme. This will ensure that you are aware of what is required of you, including how your work is to be presented.

Read the coursework instructions carefully. Check for any requirements, such as:

▶ what, if any, are the formal requirements. For example, do you have to submit your work in typed form or do you have to submit a disk copy or is a particular system of citation required;

▶ is the coursework subject to a word-limit and, if it is, does the word-limit include or exclude footnotes and bibliography;

▶ is the coursework to be submitted in an essay form or as a report or in the form of advice;

▶ what are the assessment criteria;

▶ when is the coursework to be submitted?

Criteria for assessment

The criteria for assessment indicate what a marker will be looking for in your answer. It is worth spending a few moments considering what you need to demonstrate in your answer. The following is a typical list of criteria:

The work will be assessed on normal academic criteria which will include:

- ▶ analysis, including appropriate legal content;

- ▶ relevance of subject-matter;

- ▶ awareness of sources, including the correct use of cases and statutes;

- ▶ clarity of expression;

- ▶ accuracy;

- ▶ presentation, including the correct citation of sources and use of a bibliography.

Form of the question

A question may be divided into two or more parts. A few words of advice are offered on this seemingly unimportant feature. First, if a question is in parts then answer it accordingly; do not be tempted to write a single answer to a multi-part question. The reason for this advice is that you need to show the examiner that you know the answers to each part of the question. By writing a continuous answer you leave an examiner in doubt as to your understanding of the individual parts of the question. So if a question is in two parts, for example (i) and (ii), then organise your answer in that way, identifying each answer by (i) and (ii). Second, in a multi-part question consider the marks breakdown. The marks allocated to a particular question usually give an indication of the amount of time and effort you should expend in producing an answer to that part. If a question has been divided into two parts and the marks allocation is 80% for one part and 20% for the other then, generally speaking, your answers should not be of equal length. On completion of your coursework consider the relative weighting of your answer.

What does the question instruct you to do?

Having understood what is expected of you in an answer, spend a little time reflecting on what the question is instructing you to do.

The instruction in a question needs to be carefully interpreted as this determines what it is you must do with the information you are asked to assemble. The following are the most common instructions found in law questions: discuss, evaluate, compare, contrast, critically assess, explain, justify or advise.

▶ *Discuss* – consider a subject area by, for example, the use of argument or debate;

▶ *Evaluate* – appraise the worth of an argument or topic;

▶ *Compare* – look for similarities between, for example, concepts or rules;

▶ *Contrast* – to set in opposition, to reveal differences;

▶ *Critically assess* – find fault with, for example, an area of law or legislative provision, and offer a justification for so doing by reference to evidence;

▶ *Explain* – to make clear or understandable;

▶ *Justify* – provide grounds or evidence for a position, or a concept, or an idea;

▶ *Advise* – give an opinion as to future action based upon a consideration of information or arguments.

Interpreting an essay title

Questions in essay form, rather than problem form, cause students particular difficulties. An answer to a problem question will usually have an inherent structure because the law to be applied has a structure. (For specific advice on approaching problem questions, see Chapter 12 on 'Answering degree-level examination questions'.) With an essay question there is no one correct structure, students are faced with a choice as to how material should be organised. An initial consideration is how to structure your answer. You may find that your organisation changes as your research develops.

Your first task must be to identify the main subject area of a question, as this will shape the direction of your research and reading. Research and understanding of the material will further aid you in deciding what the question requires by way of an answer. You must break the essay

HINT →
Ensure that you understand the instruction to the question.

HINT →
Break an essay title into its constituent parts.

title into its constituent parts. It is useful to list the issues or requirements of the question and to revise or supplement this list as your research progresses. Note the limits of the question, as they determine the relevance of the information you are to use. Do not go beyond them.

In analysing an essay question be prepared to challenge assumptions, if any, made by the question. You may be asked to explain concepts or to criticise how the law works or to make an assessment of why and how the law ought to be reformed. Whatever the question your starting point is the same, break the question into its constituent parts.

For example, consider the following question taken from the law of contract:

> The justification for the rule in *Pinnel's case*, as approved in *Foakes v Beer*, is no longer valid. English law has developed to such a point that agreement to accept part-payment of a debt ought to discharge the full debt.
>
> **Discuss.**

Students of contract will instantly recognise that this is a question concerning consideration. Your answer, in consequence, should contain an explanation of the doctrine of consideration. Further key issues arising from this question are:

▶ What is, and what is the justification for, the rule in *Pinnel's case*?

▶ Why was the rule approved in *Foakes v Beer*?

▶ What criticisms may be made of the rule in *Pinnel's case*?

▶ In what way has the English law of contract developed to make this rule unnecessary?

▶ Alternatively, have developments made the rule unnecessary? (The question assumes that the rule in *Pinnel's case* is no longer valid, but is this correct. Remember to challenge assumptions.)

This list will have to be developed as you read further.

For example,

▶ What are the criticisms? See the comments of Lord Blackburn in *Foakes v Beer*, of Jessel MR in *Couldery v Bartrum* (1881) 19 Ch D 394 and the Law Revision Committee (1937) Cmd. 5449. Note the harshness of the rule is mitigated by a number of exceptions.

HINT →
Don't be afraid to challenge assumptions made by a question.

HINT →
Make a list of the key issues raised by the question.

- English law of contract seems to have moved away from a concept of legal benefit or detriment to one of practical benefit or detriment, see *Williams v Roffey Bros & Nicholls (Contractors) Ltd* [1991] 1 QB 1.

- Is the rule in *Pinnel's case* consistent with the other rules of consideration?

- The real issue is that the rule does not allow a bargain freely agreed between the parties to be enforced. The development of a doctrine of economic duress perhaps allows a different approach to be adopted to the issue of consideration when an existing contract is varied.

- The question states that English law has developed to such a point that agreement to accept part-payment of a debt ought to discharge the full debt. While you may argue the law ought to recognise that part-payment of a debt should discharge the full debt, the question is does the law recognise this? The case of *Re Selectmove Ltd* [1995] 1 WLR 474 highlights inconsistencies in the law and illustrates the impact of the doctrine of judicial precedent.

Each of the above points needs to be explained and then related to the question.

It is essential that you avoid description and also avoid writing generally about the legal area raised. Quite often answers read too much like textbooks, stating the law in an explanatory form without any indication of how the law stated relates to the question asked. Sometimes the material stated does not even relate to the question. Choice of relevant material is essential as it demonstrates understanding. In attempting to answer the above question on *Pinnel's case* a student could write generally about consideration, looking at, amongst other matters, sufficiency, adequacy and past consideration. The use of such material would not answer the question asked and the student would be hard-pressed to explain the significance of its inclusion. Think carefully about the relevance of the material you select.

Above all else, make sure you are answering the question asked and not a question of your own devising. Constantly test the material you are explaining against the requirements you have identified in the question.

> **HINT** →
> Avoid description; at degree level what is expected of you is analysis.

Planning your answer

The structure is a very important indication of whether or not you have understood the question asked. So spending time creating a good structure for your essay is time well spent. There are two aspects to this process. First, developing an overall structure for your answer, that is ordering the issues you have identified and, second, structuring your consideration of each of the issues raised by the question.

First, many essays submitted by undergraduates have no clear overall structure. As has already been said, all essays should have a beginning, a middle section and an end, a conclusion, unless the question clearly does not require this approach. This is trite advice but, remarkably, quite often ignored. It is essential that your answer has such a structure.

Introduction

In an introduction you should identify the area of law raised by the question and outline the issues that will be discussed in the middle section of your answer.

Do not start your answer with a conclusion. For example, an answer to a criminal law question on homicide should not start with: 'X is liable for murder'. The purpose of your answer is to reason towards a conclusion. Your answer should introduce the topic raised by the question: 'This question concerns the crime of murder and whether or not X has committed such a crime'. You may want to identify the main issues raised under this general topic ie murder. Your essay should then develop towards a conclusion.

HINT ⇒
Never start your answer with a conclusion.

Middle

This is the main body of your answer where relevant material is presented and the issues outlined in the introduction are explored. Depending upon what you have been asked to consider, your answer may be critically of the law, or may balance the advantages and disadvantages of a particular concept or suggest why and how a particular area of the law might be reformed. All the information you want to present and comment upon should be included in this section of your answer.

Conclusion

A conclusion seeks to draw together the material explored in the middle section of your answer. It should relate the previous discussion directly to the question asked, demonstrating how this provides an answer. Your conclusion must not introduce new material.

HINT ⇒
A conclusion should draw on material explored in the middle section of your answer; it should not introduce new material.

The second aspect to planning your answer is structuring the exploration of the issues in the middle section. Again, a clear structure will impress the marker that you have understood the question. The middle section is the heart of your answer and the content of it will determine what is written in your introduction and also in your conclusion.

Look carefully at the question to establish the limits of the content. Only discuss those matters raised by the question. Decide upon the order of your discussion. Students often fall into the trap of relying on assertion, for example: 'The law relating to industrial disputes in the workplace favours employers over employees'. Such a statement will not attract marks unless it is explained and justified by supporting argument. In developing your arguments you must avoid unsubstantiated opinion. It is permissible to express an opinion only in so far as it is supportable by evidence. An essential part of your answer must be the citation of evidence or authority for the statements you make.

In attempting to formulate arguments the following description of critical thinking taken from Harry Maddox *How to Study* Pan, 1963 may be of use:

(i) definition of the problem or issue;

(ii) formulation of hypotheses and possible solutions;

(iii) the search for evidence or relevant facts;

(iv) drawing inferences from the facts; and

(v) drawing conclusions and verifying them from evidence already presented and considered.

> **HINT** →
> Before you start writing your essay, prepare an outline plan of its contents.

Remember that this process may include considering opposing arguments and then reaching a conclusion as to their relative weight.

Writing the coursework

Form of the coursework: an essay, report, advice or other

It is necessary to determine the form that your assignment is to take. It may be that the instructions, accompanying the essay, give some indication of what you are required to do. If the task does not indicate a form then it is likely that you are expected to produce an answer in essay form.

When writing an essay it is best to adopt a third person singular form. In adopting this approach write, for example, 'it is argued that . . .' or 'the position to be taken is', rather than 'I think that . . .' or 'I believe the position to be taken is . . .'. Of course, if you are writing a letter then your style will be different. Your style will be influenced by what you are asked to do.

Whatever style your answer is to take it is useful to consult examples of the style you are instructed to use. If you are asked to produce a report then finding a report, for example a Law Commission report, is a useful

> **HINT** →
> When you are asked to write in a particular style, eg a report, look for examples of the style as a guide when laying out your answer.

starting point for developing your answer. Look at the style of writing, its tone, the organisation of material and general points as to layout.

Using legal reasoning

In writing your coursework, make use of your understanding of legal reasoning. A good introduction to this may be found in Chapter 11 of Holland and Webb *Learning Legal Rules* 6th edn, Oxford. Many students embark on a law degree thinking the law is based wholly on logic and that diligent research will throw up the answer to any legal question asked. These myths are quickly disposed of in the first few weeks of legal study. While logic has an undoubted role to play, it does not always provide an answer. Often students will ask, what is the '*right*' answer to a question posed. Tutors may well explain that there is no one right answer, indeed there may be several possible answers. For example, the law may be unclear because the case law reveals judicial disagreement as to what is the law. Another illustration is where facts of a question are uncertain. Such uncertainty may give rise to several possible answers and an answer must reflect this. Also the question asked may not admit of only one answer.

An example of this would be a question which asks: 'Should the United Kingdom have a written constitution?'. There are arguments for and against a written constitution that you must present, but they will not lead you to a definitive conclusion. Your conclusion must seek to weigh the arguments so as to persuade the reader that the position you have adopted is to be preferred.

In the law of contract it has been decided that a display of goods in a self-service store is usually to be treated as an invitation to treat and not an offer to sell: see *Pharmaceutical Society of Great Britain v Boots Cash Chemists* [1953] 1 QB 401. The conclusion in this case is not based upon legal logic, but upon a choice made by the judges that this was a better answer for practical reasons. Lord Goddard CJ said, and the Court of Appeal agreed, that by analogy a self-service shop should be treated in the same way as a bookshop where customers also had access to books but this did not mean that the bookseller intended to offer the books for sale. Additionally it was argued that if a display of goods was an offer then as soon as a customer put an item in the basket provided a contract was made. This made no sense as a buyer would be prevented from returning an item to the shelves, as acceptance of the offer would take place upon the item being placed in the basket. This latter inconvenient consequence, in part, persuaded the judges that the display of goods was merely an invitation to treat and the consequence was thus avoided.

The above example illustrates that some legal reasoning is not based on logic but on the presentation of freestanding arguments that lead to a particular conclusion. One writer said that some legal reasoning was like a three-legged stool: the arguments do not depend upon one another in a sequence, but together they support a particular position. The weight of the arguments may persuade a court that the answer presented is the one to be adopted.

Relevance

To convince a marker that you understand the question asked you must present source material and comment upon its relevance. The yardstick of relevance is the terms of the question. Be prepared to constantly test the information you want to include against the requirements of the question.

To this end you must demonstrate not only that you can choose the material necessary to answer the question, but also that you can explain the importance of the material to the needs of the question. Students tend to lose marks because they expect the material to be self-explanatory in its relationship to the question. It is necessary to relate the material to the question and to explicitly spell out the link. In your answer link the law you state expressly to the specific terms of the question whenever appropriate. By tying together material and aspects of the question you are demonstrating another facet of your understanding of the task set.

Quotations

Only use quotations sparingly, and for a specific purpose, not as a substitute for your own summary of relevant law or a writer's arguments.

If you wish to quote directly from a book, case, legislation or article, and the quote is lengthy, indicate the extent of the quotation by indentation and state its source precisely in a footnote (ie refer not only to the case or book, but also to the page on which the quoted passage appears. This should also be done where you refer to a specific idea or comment that is contained in a book, article or case). For lengthy quotes there is no need to use quotation marks. If the quote is short include it in your sentence, placing it in quotation marks. As above you must refer to the source in a footnote. For examples, see the illustrative essay below. The subject of quotations is returned to in Chapter 10.

> **HINT** →
> Be selective in your use of quotations.

Footnotes and bibliographies

For the reasons to be explained in Chapter 10 it is an important to ensure that sources used in the text of your answer are fully acknowledged. Acknowledgement of sources should appear in footnotes and a bibliography. In Microsoft Word it is easy to create footnotes by use of the Insert function (followed by a click on Reference and then on Footnote). The footnotes are arranged in a numerical sequence automatically by the program; this applies to further footnotes inserted among existing footnotes.

In using footnotes the following terms may be of use:

▸ *Ibid.* (in the same place). Used instead of a full reference when the same work is being referred to as that in the immediately preceding footnote. Always add a page reference.

▸ *Op. cit.* (in the work cited previously). This is used when the source referred to has already been cited, but not in the immediately preceding footnote. The author's name should always be cited and also a page reference.

▸ *Loc. cit.* (in the place cited). Used when the reference is exactly the same, even in respect of the page, as in the immediately preceding footnote.

Your assignment should end with a bibliography directing the reader to the sources you have used in its preparation. Further advice on referencing is contained in Chapter 10, which deals with footnotes and bibliographies.

Use of authorities

An assignment in essay form should contain relevant authority as would a problem question. The authority may, however, have to be used differently. In a problem question authority is used to advise on a particular application of the law to a given set of facts. An essay question may expect an evaluation of the reason for certain rules. Thus, in a problem question you will be expected to show an understanding of how a rule applies, whereas in an essay question you may have to explain the justification for a rule or rules.

A frequently asked question is whether the facts of relevant cases should be included in an answer? As with many aspects of writing it is a question of judgement. Will such an explanation assist in answering the question? In general, there is no need to explain the facts of a case: a statement of the principle coming from the case will suffice. However, for example, if you are arguing that the case has been wrongly decided or that the case cannot be authority for a particular principle then you may need to explain the facts of the case in some detail.

Time management

Once you have been given an assignment and are aware of the submission date, the temptation might be to put the task in your file and leave it to another day. Many students operate on a 'just in time' basis. This does not maximise the learning opportunity attaching to the preparation and writing of an assignment. First, consider devising a timetable for the task, bearing in mind you will have, in all probability, other course commitments. Set aside time, to read the assignment and initially consider the issues raised. Next you may wish to read your textbook to get a general idea of the area of law involved. Then you will need to start your research in earnest by collecting references to source material and undertaking reading and note-taking. This may lead you to further references that need to be considered for inclusion in or exclusion from your assignment. Once you have completed reading you must give thought to the organisation of material. Upon completion of the above you will be ready to start the writing process. Create drafts of your answer and build in periods of time when you can reflect upon what you have written, possibly leaving your answer for a short period of time and then re-reading it to see if it achieves what is asked for. Finally, check your answer and make any necessary revisions. Plan when you are going to carry out each of the above steps. Draw up a timetable, setting aside appropriate time for each stage of this process. Remember, if a task is daunting then seek to break it into manageable sections. The sections then become aims which you should strive to achieve within an overall programme for completing the task. This approach requires organisation and discipline, but allows you to achieve your overall aim incrementally.

> **HINT →**
> A daunting task may be broken into manageable parts and the overall task achieved incrementally.

Checking your assignment – leaving nothing to chance

By the time you have completed your assignment you may be heartily sick of the area of law, but it is at this stage that you must steel yourself to check your assignment. Spelling or grammatical errors must be corrected; check the pagination of your essay and ensure that footnotes are sequential; revisit the assessment criteria to ensure compliance; and, finally, check that you have followed all instructions attaching to the assignment. On this last point, if there is a word-limit double check that your work is within the limit. Quite often it is required that you must state the number of words you have used and certify that you have not exceeded the limit. It is advisable to comply with the limit and not to trust to 'urban myths', such as you can exceed the word limit safely by 5%. A piece of work which exceeds the word-limit may be an automatic failure. Look to the assessment regulations for your programme to see what the rules are and what the consequences might be for infringement of them.

After submission – feedback making the most of the opportunity

As important as the experience of writing the essay is the feedback derived from having your written work corrected. There can be little doubt that the attention paid to learning and teaching in law schools has improved in recent years. Of importance also is the acceptance by students of a role as active consumers of legal education instead of one as passive recipients.

The law teacher likes nothing less than a class of students who receive his words of undoubted wisdom with mute acquiescence. Law schools derive their *raison d'etre* and law teachers their salaried position from the presence of law students pursuing legal education. Consequently, there is no need for students to be at all reluctant in coming forward to their lecturers to ask for advice or elucidation. This is especially important in respect of deriving benefit from written work.

It is all too easy for the law lecturer to write on student scripts remarks such as '!', 'how', 'why', 'what on earth do you mean by this', and so on. It goes without saying that written work will be marked promptly and returned to students but, even so, very often the mark and the comments will require careful explanation. Do not be reluctant in asking for this. The lecturers are engaged by the university full-time in order to teach you, and will be only too glad to go over the parts of your essay on which you are still confused or about which you are unhappy. Your lecturer will probably be willing to explain how he would have structured an answer to the particular question, which cases he would have included and which articles referred to. This provision of a 'model' answer is valuable and something for which it is well worth your while to press. However, such an answer can only ever be an example; there are many ways to express an answer. It is much more important to understand how to structure an answer and how to select the material that should be included.

So once your marked work is returned there are various things that you should do. Read the comments that the tutor has written on your assignment and ensure that you understand them. The comments may highlight concerns about your understanding of the law, or your ability to use and apply the law, or your technique in answering the question. Such comments need to be digested and acted upon, as feedback is an important learning experience. Additionally, you may be given a sheet of notes, which outlines the points that the question raised and the law relevant to the answer. Again ensure that you are able to comprehend where your answer succeeded and failed in addressing the question.

A tutor may also indicate in a lecture period some general points about the assignment.

Finally, you may wish to discuss with your tutor some further points concerning your assignment. As part of the teaching process tutors are available to discuss all aspects of assignment preparation and writing. Take this opportunity to talk through the strengths and weaknesses apparent from your work.

HINT →

Feedback is an important part of the learning process.

Time spent on your approach and writing technique early in your programme of legal studies can 'reap dividends' in later years.

Writing an assignment – an example

In the early stages of your legal studies you may be asked to write an essay. You have previously been introduced to assessment criteria which set out the expectations you are to meet in producing such an essay. By way of illustration, see below an essay of the form and substance that might be expected of you. Earlier we looked at an essay title from the law of contract:

> The justification for the rule in *Pinnel's case*, as approved in *Foakes v Beer*, is no longer valid. English law has developed to such a point that agreement to accept part-payment of a debt ought to discharge the full debt.
>
> **Discuss.**

Assuming that this is subject to a maximum word limit of 3,000 words, what should be included in an answer to this question?

An introduction to the question ought to include the following points.

> The rule in *Pinnel's case*[1] is a fundamental rule of the doctrine of consideration. In English law for a promise to be enforceable[2] it must be supported by consideration, that is the promise must be given in exchange for the consideration. The rule in *Pinnel's case* states that where a debtor merely pays part of a debt at the request of a creditor this does not discharge the entire debt, as the debtor has given no consideration for the creditor's promise to forgive the balance. The question asked seeks to explore the basis for the rule in Pinnel's case and why it was approved by the House of Lords in *Foakes v Beer*. The rule has been criticised as absurd. Moreover, it may be argued that in the light of the decision of the Court of Appeal in *Williams v Roffey Brothers & Nicholls (Contractors) Ltd*[3] it is no longer necessary, as the justification for the rule has been rendered largely redundant.

1 (1602) 5 Co Rep 117a.   2 Unless the promise is contained in a deed.   3 [1991] 1 QB 1.

NOTE ✳

The introduction to your answer should set out your understanding of the issues raised by the question and indicate, in general terms, what you are to discuss. You should not reach conclusions at this stage.

Having introduced what is to be considered in the answer, you must seek to develop the issues in the body of your answer.

> The classic definition of consideration was given by Lush J in *Currie v Misa*[4],
>
> > A valuable consideration, in the sense of law, may consist either in some right, interest, profit, or benefit accruing to the one part, or some forbearance, detriment, loss, or responsibility, given, suffered or undertaken by the other.
>
> For a promise to be enforceable a promisee must, either, confer on a promisor a benefit or suffer a detriment. The question is what may amount to such benefit or detriment? Is it for the parties to decide or, as Lush J seems to indicate by his use of the words "in the sense of law", for the courts to determine? The case law on this fundamental issue is not conclusive.[5] However, it would seem that the courts do reserve the right to decide that something requested as consideration does not have 'value in the eye of the law'[6] and, in consequence, is not sufficient consideration. Treitel[7] draws a distinction between factual benefit and detriment and legal benefit and detriment. Factual benefit or detriment is something of value which is in fact obtained or suffered. Whereas legal benefit or detriment, in the context of this question, refers to no consideration being given if a party is merely doing what he is legally obliged to do, even though this may in fact confer a benefit on the promisor or be a detriment to the promisee.

NOTE ✳

In this paragraph consideration is defined and the question is put into context, with an explanation of what the courts look for in establishing the existence of consideration.

---

4 (1875) LR 10 Ex 153 at 162.   **5** See, for example, *Chappell & Co Ltd v Nestle Co Ltd* [1960] AC 87 where the House of Lords disagreed as to whether or not chocolate bar wrappers, which were to be discarded by a promisor, could amount to consideration. The majority held that the wrappers were part of the consideration for a promise; as Lord Somervell said at p114, '[a] contracting party can stipulate for what consideration he chooses. A peppercorn does not cease to be good consideration if it is established that the promisee does not like pepper and will throw away the corn'.   **6** Per Patteson J in *Thomas v Thomas* (1842) 2 QB 851 at 859.   **7** G H Treitel *Law of Contract* 11th edn, Sweet & Maxwell, 2003.

The rule in *Pinnel's case* must be viewed in the light of what constitutes consideration. In that case a defendant was sued for the outstanding part of a debt owed to the plaintiff. His defence was that the plaintiff had agreed that he could pay a smaller sum in full satisfaction of the debt; the smaller sum being paid, at the creditor's request, at an earlier date than the debt had been due. The plaintiff succeeded due to failure of pleading on the part of the defendant. The Court of Common Pleas, however, said,

> that payment of a lesser sum on the day in satisfaction of a greater cannot be any satisfaction for the whole, because it appears to the judges that by no possibility a lesser sum can be a satisfaction to the plaintiff for a greater sum: but the gift of a horse, hawk or a robe, &c., in satisfaction is good, for it shall be intended that a horse, hawk or a robe, &c., might be more beneficial to the plaintiff than the money, in respect of some circumstance, or otherwise the plaintiff would not have accepted of it in satisfaction.[8]

Although the action was in debt, the case is authority for the rule that payment of a smaller sum on the day is not good satisfaction to discharge a debt, even though an obiter dictum.

The above case suggests that the court had taken the view that, as part-payment was no satisfaction to a promisor, therefore, there could be no consideration. But it could be argued that should a promisor promise to forgo the balance of a debt in return for immediate part-payment of a debt, the promisor is receiving the consideration requested and the promise should be enforceable. This view did not find favour with the House of Lords in *Foakes v Beer*.[9]

In that case Foakes owed Beer £2,090 on a judgment. Foakes asked for time to pay and it was agreed that if Foakes paid £500 immediately and the balance in instalments, Beer would not 'take any proceedings whatever on the judgment'. Foakes paid the sum as agreed, but Beer then sought to recover interest (a judgment debt attracts interest) of £360. Foakes argued that the agreement prevented further action. The House of Lords had to decide whether the agreement covered the matter of interest and had consideration been provided by Foakes for Beer's promise. Their Lordships were divided on the issue of did the agreement cover the interest but were unanimous in holding that part payment of a debt did not discharge the full debt. Beer was entitled to the interest.

---

8 Op. cit. It is to be noted that the court also said that where a promisor accepts part-payment of a debt before its due date or at a different place to that agreed this will provide sufficient consideration   **9** (1884) 9 App Cas 605.

The rule in *Pinnel's case* was approved in *Foakes v Beer*. The ostensible justification given for the rule is, however, less than convincing. Lord Selborne said,

> [t]he doctrine itself, as laid down by Sir Edward Coke, may have been criticised, as questionable in principle, by some persons whose opinions are entitled to respect, but it has never been judicially overruled; on the contrary I think it has always, since the sixteenth century, been accepted as law. If so, I cannot think that your Lordships would do right, if you were now to reverse, as erroneous, a judgment of the Court of Appeal, proceeding upon a doctrine which has been accepted as part of the law of England for 280 years.[10]

Thus on the basis of age, an obiter dictum was elevated to a ratio decidendi of the House of Lords and firmly established in English law.

NOTE ✱

These paragraphs explain the nature of the rule in *Pinnel's case* and the justification for the rule given by the House of Lords in *Foakes v* Beer. The rules of judicial precedent are also used to explain the bindingness of the rule. Note also the way that the lengthy quotations are presented, indented and without quotation marks.

The lack of a reasoned justification must be viewed alongside criticisms as to the absurdity of the rule. In *Couldery v Bartrum*[11], Sir George Jessel considered the rule to be absurd when placed alongside the rule that consideration must be sufficient but need not be adequate. He said,

> [a]ccording to English Common Law a creditor may accept anything in satisfaction of his debt except a less amount of money. He might take a horse, or a canary, or a tomtit if he chose, and that was accord and satisfaction; but by a most extraordinary peculiarity of the English Common Law, he could not take 19s.6d. in the pound.[12]

Significantly Lord Blackburn in *Foakes v Beer* had been minded to depart from the rule in *Pinnel's case* recognising that there could be benefit in part-payment. His Lordship said,

> . . . all men of business whether merchants or tradesmen, do every day recognise and act on the ground that prompt payment of a part of

---

10 Ibid at 612.   11 (1881) 19 Ch D 394.   12 Ibid at 399.

their demand may be more beneficial to them than it would be to insist upon their rights and enforce payment of the whole. Even when the debtor is perfectly solvent, and sure to pay at last, this is often so. Where the credit of the debtor is doubtful it must be more so.[13]

Thus it was recognised that there could be a benefit even though less was being paid than was due. The test would seem to be, did the creditor consider that part-payment was beneficial to him, if so there was consideration. So primacy here is given to the wishes of the contracting parties over what the law may recognise as consideration.

NOTE ✳

The above sections of the essay explain the criticisms that might be made of the rule and question its validity.

Lord Blackburn, however, did not persist in his view and agreed with the other Law Lords not to disturb the rule as to part-payment. Treitel offers a convincing view of what motivated the House of Lords to approve the rule in *Pinnel's case*.[14] The concern was that Mrs Beer had been tricked into entering the agreement. Had the House of Lords overruled the rule in *Pinnel's case*, and decided that part-payment was sufficient consideration, injustice may have resulted.[15] It can be seen that the rule has a protective function; shielding creditors from unscrupulous debtors. As a justification for the rule this has much merit, but fails to assist where the creditor behaves unscrupulously or where the parties have genuinely reached an agreement on a part-payment satisfying a debt. In *D & C Builders v Rees*[16] Lord Denning considered the lack of accord between the parties caused by the debtor's resort to intimidation (and it could be added, in the light of subsequent legal developments, economic duress) prevented the enforcement of the agreement reached. The focus of Lord Denning's point is to ask if the agreement has been freely concluded. Furmston says, 'the real criticism of *Foakes v Beer* is perhaps that it provides no means by which such cases [of debtors behaving badly] can be treated differently from genuine bargains.'[17]

NOTE ✳

The above paragraph seeks to explain the reasoning behind the rule in *Pinnel's case* and the possible concerns of the House of Lords in *Foakes v Beer* and then suggests the crux of the difficulty with the rule, that it is a blunt instrument treating all re-nego-

---

13 Op. cit at 622.   14 G H Treitel *Some Landmarks of Twentieth Century Contract Law* Oxford University Press, 2002.   15 Ibid 24–26.   16 [1966] 2 QB 617.   17 M Furmston *Cheshire, Fifoot and Furmston's, Law of Contract* 14th edn, Butterworths, 2001.

tiations in relation to debt in the same way. In the last three lines of the above paragraph is an example of another way to introduce a quotation into your essay as part of a sentence; see the quotation of the words of Professor Furmston.

The harshness of the operation of the rule in relation to debtors has been mitigated by the development of several exceptions. In *Pinnel's case* it was recognised that the introduction of fresh consideration at the creditor's request, such as a chattel, would be sufficient to support a promise to accept part-payment.[18] To these exceptions may be added, by way of example, that the rule does not apply to disputed claims[19], nor does it apply to unliquidated claims.[20] The development of the doctrine of promissory estoppel also provides a defence to a creditor going back on a promise to accept part-payment in full discharge of a debt.[21]

NOTE ✳

Here the student is indicating that the law does address situations where the rule might operate harshly by the development of exceptions.

The position adopted by the House of Lords in *Foakes v Beer* also ensured that there was consistency in the law as performance of an existing public or contractual duty owed to a promisor in return for a further promise was also seen as providing no consideration.[22] However, this position has changed following the decision of the Court of Appeal in *Williams v Roffey*.[23] In this case the claimant was engaged to carry out carpentry work on flats which were being refurbished by the defendant for a housing association. Work was to be completed by a certain date. The claimant, due to a combination of under-pricing the work and a failure to efficiently manage his workforce, was unlikely to complete the work by the contractual due date and indeed was in danger of going out of business. The defendant wished to avoid payment under a 'penalty clause' for late completion in their contract with the housing association and so offered a further sum of money to ensure that the claimant completed on time. Payment was to be made upon completion of the carpentry work on each flat. Such work was substantially completed in eight flats. The question for the Court of Appeal was, had the claimant given consideration for the promised additional sums of money?

The Court of Appeal decided that the defendant had received consideration for the promise of additional payment as the defendant, said

---

18 See note 7.   **19** *Cooper v Parker* (1885) 15 CB 822.   **20** *Wilkinson v Byers* (1834) 1 A & E 106.
21 See *Central London Property Trust Ltd v High Trees House Ltd* [1947] 1 KB 130.   **22** *Collins v Godefroy* (1831) 1 B & Ad 950 and *Stilk v Myrick* (1809) 2 Camp 318.   **23** [1991] 1 QB 1.

Glidewell LJ, had obtained in practice a benefit or obviated a disbenefit. It is arguable that as the defendant had wanted completion on time and this had been substantially done in relation to 8 flats, penalty payments were avoided and the claimant remained on site there was in practical terms consideration. This reasoning echoes that of Lord Blackburn in *Foakes v Beer*[24] concentrating as it does on what the promisor wanted in return for his promise, rather than the law determining that performance of an existing contractual duty cannot amount to consideration.

The obstacle of the case of *Stilk v Myrick*[25] had to be overcome as it was authority for the principle that performance of an existing contractual duty owed to a promisor could not be consideration for a further promise made by the promisor. While the case was not overruled, the judgments of the Court of Appeal in *Williams v Roffey* sought to explain it in terms of a concern that the masters and owners of ships might be held to ransom by disaffected crews.[26] With the advent of economic duress the protective role may be taken away from the doctrine of consideration and genuine agreements between the parties enforced.

NOTE ✳

The law has developed since *Foakes v Beer* was decided and there is now another way in which the concerns about the protection of creditors may be met. The outcome in *Williams v Roffey* allows for a different approach to part-payment of a debt. But an inconsistency in the law has been created by *Williams v Roffey* which is now explained.

If in the performance of an existing contractual duty a practical benefit can be said to amount to consideration, then in the context of part-payment of a debt can a practical benefit not also be found to constitute consideration? A creditor may see a benefit in receiving a part-payment of £1,000 from a debtor in full satisfaction of a debt of £1,500, in circumstances where a debtor may become bankrupt in the near future. In that situation the agreement reached is binding as the creditor is getting what he wants in return for his promise to discharge the remaining sum. Such an approach is now possible as the protective function of the rule in *Pinnel's case*, to avoid the imposition of 'agreements', is now performed by the concept of economic duress. Moreover using the approach of *Williams v Roffey* to part-payment of a debt would also restore some consistency to this area of law.

24 See note 11.   **25** (1809) 2 Camp 317.   **26** Op. cit 21, per Purchas LJ.

The protective function of the part-payment rule served a useful purpose while the law relating to economic duress remained undeveloped. It may now be argued that, with the growing sophistication of the law of contract in the regulation of agreement, the parties should be free to arrive at a bargain of their choosing, which should be enforced if the creditor receives a practical benefit. However, it may be countered that the law has no yet reached a position where it is ready to abandon the protective role of the rule in *Pinnel's case*. McKendrick comments that, '[t]he concerns surrounding the application of the practical benefit test to the part-payment of a debt are that the test is so easy to satisfy and that the defences, such as duress, may not provide sufficient protection for the creditor'.[27]

There is much to be said in favour of the re-alignment of *Williams v Roffey* and *Foakes v Beer*, but this can only be achieved by the House of Lords. This was explained in *Re Selectmove*.[28] In this case a defendant argued that the practical benefit as consideration principle from *Williams v Roffey* applied to part-payment of a debt. The Court of Appeal while finding the argument attractive refused to so find, saying that the instant court was bound by the House of Lords in *Foakes v Beer*. Moreover, *Foakes v Beer* had not been considered in *Williams v Roffey*. Therefore, for these reasons, it was not open to a Court of Appeal to extend the principle of *Willliams v Roffey* to circumstances governed by the rule in *Foakes v Beer*. Peter Gibson LJ correctly concluded that any extension would have to be made by the House of Lords or by Parliament. This leaves the law in this area in a state of uncertainty due to the inconsistency created by *Williams v Roffey*. It should be noted that not all academics take the view that *Foakes v Beer* should be overruled. Blair and Hird[29] argue that the approach in *Williams v Roffey* is undesirable because it distorts the nature of consideration, it creates inconsistency and is based upon incorrect reasoning. They suggest that a similar result could be achieved by expanding the concept of promissory estoppel to allow for enforcement of a positive promise. It may be counter-argued that by promoting estoppel this will also affect the role of consideration and, of course, the question of consistency cuts both ways, there is a choice of approach either that in *Williams v Roffey* or that in *Foakes v Beer*.

After the discussion in the body of your essay it is important to conclude by drawing together the points you have made and demonstrate how they relate to the question.

---

27 E McKendrick *Contract Law Text, Cases, and Materials* 2nd edn, Oxford University Press, 2005.   **28** [1995] 1 WLR 474; see also *Re C (a debtor)* (1994) The Times, 11 May.   **29** A Blair and NJ Hird 'Minding Your Own Business–Williams v Roffey Re-Visited: Consideration Re-considered' (1996) JBL 254.

The question set concerned the continued validity of the rule in *Pinnel's case*. It has been established that justification for the rule is not convincing and the rule is open to criticism. However, it must be acknowledged that the rule has served a protective function with regard to creditors, while the harshness of the operation of the rule in relation to debtors has been mitigated by the development of exceptions and defences. The main issue is that the rule does not allow a bargain freely agreed between the parties to be enforced. If a creditor wishes to discharge a full debt in return for a reduced payment why should the parties not be able to enter into an enforceable agreement upon this without the introduction of fresh consideration in the form of a legal benefit or legal detriment? The answer to this question lies in the development of the concept of consideration and the notion of the practical benefit and the introduction of the concept of economic duress which allows a court to distinguish between genuine bargains and bargains not entered into freely. Concerns remain that the meaning of practical benefit is too vague and too easy to satisfy, while economic duress is not yet ready for the protective role it has been assigned. Regardless of these arguments the current answer to the question is provided by the doctrine of precedent. The argument raised in *Re Selectmove*, that the rule in *Williams v Roffey* should be applied to instances of part-payment of a debt, was rejected as to accept such an argument would leave *Foakes v Beer* without any application. The Court of Appeal could not have taken this decision as it would be one which had the effect of overruling a precedent of the House of Lords. Whilst the justification for the rule in *Pinnel's case* is unconvincing the law is clear, part-payment of a debt does not discharge the full debt. The rule remains valid unless and until it is reconsidered by the House of Lords.

NOTE ✳

The conclusion draws on the material in the main body of the essay; no new information is introduced at this stage. Reference is made to the requirements set out in the question:

▶ the justification for the rule in *Pinnel's case*, as approved in *Foakes v Beer*, and whether it is still valid;

▶ how the harshness of the original rule has been mitigated by exceptions and defences;

▶ how English law has developed, the expanded concept of consideration and the development of economic duress; and

▶ whether or not an agreement to accept part-payment of a debt ought to discharge the full debt, in the light of the doctrine of judicial precedent.

Bibliography

Blair A and Hird N J 'Minding Your Own Business—Williams v Roffey Re-Visited: Consideration Re-considered' (1996) JBL 254.

Cheshire, Fifoot and Furmston *Law of Contract* 14th edn, Butterworths, 2001.

Treitel G H *Some Landmarks of Twentieth Century Contract Law* Oxford University Press, 2002.

McKendrick E *Contract Law Text, Cases, and Materials* 2nd edn, Oxford University Press, 2005.

Oral presentations

At some point during your degree programme you may be instructed to prepare a particular topic for oral presentation, for example, to your seminar group. The task set falls into two parts:

(i) preparation of the substantive area; and

(ii) presentation of the material to the group.

This is not a neat division as the substantive material you choose and how you organise it will have an impact on its presentation.

Nervousness is a natural part of oral presentations. The best way to suppress nerves is to ensure that you are confident of the material you are to present. Thorough preparation of a presentation is essential. It is certainly true that the more often you speak in front of other people, whether in seminars or in mooting or in making an oral presentation, the less nervous you feel.

Instructions

What is the task? Determine what the purpose of your presentation is and who it is for. This gives you an aim, and some initial help as to structure, and addresses the matter of the level of the presentation.

Structure in your presentation is important to demonstrate that you understand, but it is equally important to allow your audience to understand. The structure you employ should be clear, and reinforced, if appropriate, by points or diagrams on an overhead projector slide or by the use of Powerpoint. You may, additionally, want to give your audience a handout which includes the salient points you are to make in your presentation.

The nature of your explanation depends upon your audience. If you are presenting information to lawyers your approach will be different to the approach you would employ in giving a presentation to lay people. In these instances, the level of explanation would differ, as would the nature of language to be used.

✖ EXAMPLE

If you are presenting information to a lay audience you would have to explain legal terms. A presentation on a particular criminal offence would have to include a basic outline of the concepts of *actus reus* and *mens rea*. In relation to a presentation to lawyers you may assume in your audience knowledge of these concepts.

HINT →

Identify the purpose of a presentation and who is the audience at which it is aimed.

Is the presentation individual, joint or as part of a team?

Should your task be a shared one with other students then a preliminary meeting should be held to decide upon the nature and purpose of the presentation, allocation of the tasks to be performed, how the presentation is to be organised and a timetable for the completion of the work. A meeting to pull together the presentation ahead of the date of the seminar is also desirable.

The presentation

An issue you might like to consider is how you are to deliver your presentation. There are various types of delivery.

First, there is the impromptu delivery. No full consideration is given as to how to deliver the material, although work may have been done on understanding the substantive material. The danger with this approach is that no structure may be apparent and the presentation meanders rather than making the necessary points.

Second, the presentation may be prepared and then memorised. This places much pressure on the person delivering the material and may lead to 'stage fright'.

Third, a speech is prepared and then read. The major problem with this approach is that it is difficult to engage with an audience when reading. Presentational skills may be ignored in concentrating upon your prepared speech.

Fourth, while the content and structure of the presentation have been prepared, and notes made, the explanation has not been prepared word for word. This approach allows some emphasis to be placed on other presentational skills, for example maintaining eye contact, pace of delivery etc. One suggestion for notes is that they should consist of key-words, phrases and short sentences. These should be written clearly on postcards which may be held in your hand without being a distraction to the audience. Ensure that the information on the cards is structured and that the cards are clearly numbered, to avoid organisational problems.

You need to identify a method of delivery with which you are comfortable and to remember that this form of activity benefits from practice.

HINT ⇒

Identify a method of delivery with which you are comfortable.

Content

The yardsticks against which to measure the content of your presentation will be, first, the aim of the presentation and, second, the audience. In relation to the aim, matters to consider are: the relevance of the material; the organisation and logical development of arguments; ensuring that the information provided is related to the stated aim; and use of examples and quotations where appropriate.

It is important to retain the interest of your audience, so the content must not be too dense and must be sufficiently varied to demand attention. Techniques of delivery, outlined below, are also important in this respect.

Delivery

The following are matters to be borne in mind when delivering material.

▶ Speak clearly, but be prepared to vary the tone of your voice and to emphasise key points. A monotonous delivery is to be avoided.

▶ The pace of delivery of material must not be too fast or too slow. Some clues as to this may be gauged from the reaction of the audience. In consequence, you may need to alter your pace during your presentation.

▶ Seek to maintain eye-contact with your audience. This allows you to read the audience and their reaction: have they understood; are you going too fast, and so on.

▶ If you are not aware of the audience are you concentrating on your notes to the detriment of the presentation?

▶ Try to make your explanations lively and enthusiastic. Keeping the attention of your audience is vital to the success of your presentation.

▶ Use visual aids wherever possible as this also helps to retain the attention of your audience.

▶ Use rhetorical questions to engage with your audience. The questions stimulate thought and may be used as a vehicle for exploration of a particular point.

Presentational faults

You need to avoid the following common faults.

▶ Poor posture. Do not lean on or over the lectern or desk during your presentation. It is important to stand up straight, to ensure that you direct your voice at your audience and not the floor.

▶ Movement. Do not stand stock-still or pace continuously backwards and forwards. The former lacks interest and the latter is distracting.

▶ Gestures. Be aware of your gestures. The use of gestures is part of communication but overuse is to be avoided. Repetition of gestures is distracting and will detract from your presentation.

▶ Space-fillers. When speaking, avoid using 'er' and 'um' to fill in gaps during your presentation. A short silence is preferable.

▶ Rapid speech. The 'machine-gun' method of delivery is often the consequence of nerves, but must be suppressed. Concentrate on pausing at appropriate points, but do not make the pauses overlong.

Review

Once you have given your presentation, seek feedback. Learn from your mistakes. If your performance has been recorded seek to view this. Make up a checklist from the information above and make notes on the good and not so good features of your presentation.

Group work

You may encounter assessments that depend upon working as part of a group. The skills that are being examined are different to those expected in more traditional forms of assessment and a different approach to the task set is required. Look carefully at the learning outcomes of the group work.

Achieving the task is important, but so also is the process by which you complete the task. The assessment is seeking to test the group's ability to work as a team. In consequence, the group needs to reflect on how to establish a team that will successfully complete the assessment set. One of the outcomes of the project will be the development of inter-personal skills. Certainly successful group work depends upon the use of good communication skills. At the heart of this process is the creation of an effective working group. A first meeting will have to address this issue before the task set can be undertaken. Some thought will have to be given to how the group is to work and how potential problems are to be dealt with, for example a group member not meeting deadlines or missing meetings. If at the outset the expectations of the group are established, it may be easier to talk frankly later should the task not be going according to plan. A record of what the group agrees ought to be taken.

Spend some time getting to know each other and assessing the qual-ities and abilities of the group members, such assessment will be of importance when tasks are to be allocated. To avoid later difficulties every effort needs to be made collectively to ensure that all members of the group feel included.

Having considered the building of a team, the next meetings will have to be used to:

▶ discuss aims;

▶ agree deadlines;

▶ allocate work;

▶ review progress;

▶ complete the task.

A first point for the group is to be very clear of the aims of the task and for all members of the group to appreciate these. It is important that all members are involved in this process, everyone is able to contribute and that agreement to the plan is reached. So as to avoid misunderstandings and potential conflict the agreement should be reduced to writing and copies given to all members of the group. The plan may include the following:

▶ what aim is to be achieved;

▶ what are the tasks to be performed;

▶ allocation of the tasks – names should be attached to the tasks;

▶ a schedule of dates for the production of material;

▶ a timetable of meetings;

▶ if necessary, a specification of a common format for the production of material;

▶ a deadline for the completion of the assessment.

HINT →

Establish a framework for the assessment and also channels of communication.

As group work is an exercise in collaboration, effective organisation is essential. In the early meetings a schedule of work should be established, breaking the task into constituent parts, allocating tasks among the members of the group and agreeing deadlines. A system of communication must be created; the existence of e-mail and mobile phones makes this task easier than in the past.

A member of the group should be designated as the 'manager' of the project who will seek to ensure compliance with the schedule. Having a mechanism for reviewing the progress of the task is important so that should problems arise they may be addressed in a timely manner.

Aim to complete the project a few days in advance of the submission date; this allows for reflection by the group on the end-product and the possibility of changes being made.

■ CHECKLIST

■ ADVICE ON COMPLETING COURSE WORK

Consider whether you have done the following:

▶ Familiarised yourself with the Assessment Regulations?

▶ Read the assignment task carefully, noting what is expected of you?

▶ Understood the assessment criteria?

▶ Structured your assignment appropriately, including in your work an introduction and conclusion?

▶ Used appropriate sources?

▶ Used relevant sources and demonstrated how they relate to the question asked?

▶ Referenced your sources?

▶ Used a consistent system of citation?

▶ Included a bibliography?

▶ Not exceeded the word-limit?

▶ Checked your work?

▶ Complied with the assessment regulations?

▶ And afterwards . . . have you explored all feedback opportunities?

Chapter 10

Citation of legal sources and plagiarism

Authority of sources

In preparing assignments, reports or projects you will have recourse to source materials. As you have seen the primary sources of law are case law and legislation and secondary sources include textbooks, journals and other legally-related material, such as Law Commission reports and Parliamentary debates. The sources not only provide information, but give weight to your work by supplying authority for argument and discussion. Material you have relied upon must be correctly referenced so as to allow a marker to check your sources. Also ideas and arguments belonging to others must be attributed to their author if you are to avoid accusations of plagiarism.

The obvious location to access such legal source material is a library, but increasingly many sources are available on the Internet. Indeed the advent of the Internet has led to a proliferation of materials, which can often bewilder and beguile. It is important to use source materials correctly to avoid problems such as accessing material of dubious authenticity; anyone can set up a website and publish material. Libraries exercise a form of quality control, in that the materials stocked will come from official sources, or textbooks and journals coming from recognised publishers will have been reviewed or refereed. Some Internet sources will merely be electronic versions of hardcopy materials that may be found in a library and as such are reliable and citable. Other Internet sources may be solely produced in electronic form, but nonetheless have been reviewed or refereed. However, yet other materials might not have been subjected to any scrutiny or peer review. The latter materials are to be treated with caution and are not to be used in your assignment in preference to the sources outlined above.

> **HINT** →
> Be aware of the origin of materials and only use materials from an authoritative source.

Reliability of Internet resources

Materials obtained from a university library may be used with confidence as they will have been selected by a librarian, or after consultation with an academic member of staff. In using materials from the Internet you will have to evaluate the reliability of the source you are about to use. Your university may direct you to reliable websites and certainly governmental and commercial legal databases, such as Westlaw or LexisNexis, may be used with confidence. With other sites caution will need to be exercised. The following gives guidance as to what you should consider in assessing the value of Internet resources.

(i) The authority of the author. What authority has the website? Is the body or author an expert in a field? What qualifications does the author possess? Is the author associated with a recognised body, for example a university? Can you find the same information in your university library? If you can, use the information from the source in the library instead.

(ii) Look at the homepage to the site. How is the site created and managed? Is there any evidence of quality control? For example, some sites indicate that anyone can contribute information to the site. Obviously sites of this type should be avoided.

(iii) Currency of the site. Check to see when the website was last updated; is the information current?

HINT ➡

Always evaluate the reliability of Internet sites before use.

Citation

There are various systems of citation, for example, the Harvard system and the British Standard. Your department or school may have a preferred system of citation and it is essential that you identify what this is. Should no indication of system be given then you must choose which system to use; do not mix and match. The important point is that you choose a system and use it consistently.

Whichever system you use there will be certain information as to the reference you must collect. For example, in relation to a textbook it is necessary to note the author, date, title, edition, publisher and possibly page number. So when you consult a source immediately make a full note of the reference. Habitually making a full note can prevent much frustration and unnecessary work later searching for a reference.

The following information gives guidance as to how to reference legal source material.

HINT ➡

When you consult a source make a full note of the reference.

Cases

(1) Always cite the more prestigious series of reports. The
     hierarchy of law reports is the *Law Reports, Weekly Law Reports,
     All England Law Reports*, and then other series. In other series,
     generally, the fullest report is the most satisfactory. Indeed in a
     Practice Direction (Sup Ct: Form of Judgments: Form and
     Citation) [2001] 1 WLR 194 it was stated that both the High
     Court and the Court of Appeal required that where a case has
     been reported in the *Law Reports* published by the Incorporated
     Council of Law Reporting for England and Wales then citation
     before the court must be made from this source. Citation of
     other series of reports, for example the *All England Law Reports*,
     is only permitted if a case has not been reported in the *Law
     Reports*.

HINT →

When using cases always
cite the most authoritative
set of reports, *the Law
Reports*, published by the
Incorporated Council of
Law Reporting.

(2) In 2001 a Practice Direction (Sup Ct: Form of Judgments: Form
     and Citation) [2001] 1 WLR 194 was made to aid the publication
     of judgments of the Court of Appeal and High Court (the system
     adopted was extended to all judgments of the High Court by a
     further Practice Direction [2002] 1 WLR 346) on the World Wide
     Web. This related to the layout of cases which were not to have
     page numbers but would be broken into numbered sequential
     paragraphs. Additionally, there was to be a system of neutral
     citation introduced, whereby cases would be identified by year,
     court and a number. So the citation, *R v Kennedy* [2005] EWCA
     685 at [29] means that *R v Kennedy* was the 685th judgment
     of 2005 in the Court of Appeal, Criminal Division and reference
     is made to paragraph 29. The neutral citation appears before
     the more familiar citations from the *Law Reports* or other
     series.

     The practice of neutral citation has also been adopted by the
     House of Lords, the Privy Council and the Immigration Appeals
     Tribunal.

     This neutral method of citation has been incorporated into
     the *Law Reports*, the *Weekly Law Reports* and the *All England Law
     Reports*. The citation of [2004] 2 AC 457 is to the case of
     Campbell v MGN Ltd. In the law report the neutral citation
     appears beneath the case name at the beginning of the case
     as follows:

     Campbell v MGN Ltd
     [2004] UKHL 22

     The paragraph numbers used in the neutral citation also now
     appear in the above series of law reports.

In referencing cases, if there is a neutral citation it is cited before the citation to the law report: [2004] UKHL 22, [2004] 2 AC 457.

Where there is a neutral citation and you wish either to use a quotation or indicate where a point is made, then reference may be made to a paragraph number instead of to a page number.

HINT →

If there is a neutral citation to a case use this alongside a reference to hard copy case reports.

✖ EXAMPLE

Farley v Skinner [2001] UKHL 49; [2002] 2 AC 732, at [107].

(3) Note the proper use of round and square brackets for the date in citing law reports. The rule (with reports in this jurisdiction) is that square brackets are used if the date is an essential part of the reference and round brackets if the date is not. The correct mode of citation is given in each volume of the law reports.

✖ EXAMPLE

In *Hedley Byrne v Heller* [1964] AC 465, the date in square brackets is essential to locating the case. Whereas in *Redgrave v Hurd* (1881) 20 Ch D 1, the date is not essential to finding the case, the volume number 20 is sufficient.

(4) If referring to a particular page of a report, then cite it as follows:

R v Butterwasser [1948] 1 KB 4, 9

thus showing that you refer the reader to page 9 of the report. Obviously this advice applies to cases pre-dating the introduction of the system of neutral citation. Where a case has a neutral citation then reference may be made to a paragraph number, as seen above in the example of *Farley v Skinner*.

(5) To refer to a particular statement in a judgment place your quotation in the text, eg 'the evidence of a police officer who knows the prisoner and his habits, and has seen him in the streets, is, no doubt, very proper evidence' and in your reference cite *R v Butterwasser* [1948] 1 KB 4, 9 (per Lord Goddard LCJ). Alternatively, as follows: 'As Mr Justice Veale said in *Halsey v Esso Petroleum Co Ltd*, setting the tone for the rest of his

judgment, "This is a case, if ever there was one, of the little man asking for the protection of the law against the activities of a large and powerful neighbour" (see [1961] 2 All ER 145, 149).'

(6) If words are omitted from a quotation, this is indicated by a short row of dots. Words you insert to make sense of a quotation in your text are shown in square brackets.

Words in a quotation which may seem incorrect or ungrammatical or shocking to a reader may be followed by the word *sic* in brackets (ie the Latin for 'thus'). The following is an example of the modern usage to indicate an unacceptable or shocking train of thought: '. . . society can prevent those who are manifestly unfit from continuing their kind. The principle that sustains compulsory vaccination is broad enough to cover cutting the Fallopian tubes . . . Three generations of imbeciles are enough. '(sic) (per Holmes J in *Buck v Bell* 274 US 200 (1927)), a now discredited (?) decision of the United States Supreme Court.

(7) Once a case has been cited in the text, it may be referred to afterwards by an abbreviated name as follows: 'The sentiment expressed in *Butterwasser* is typical of the English judiciary. That expressed in *Halsey's* case is not. As for *Buck v Bell* decided before the holocaust we can now see with hindsight the danger of the eugenic beliefs it endorsed.'

Statutes

(1) There are two conventional methods of citation: by short titles and by regnal year, ie by the number of an Act of Parliament within a parliamentary session – the year of that parliamentary session being denoted by the year or years of the monarch's reign. So, 26, 7 Will 4 & 1 Vict, refers to the 26th Act of Parliament passed during the parliamentary session which straddled the seventh or last year of King William IV's reign and the first year of Queen Victoria's. This Act is now more commonly known as the Wills Act (1837).

Since 1962, Acts have not been arranged chronologically in regnal years but only in calendar years. Even in respect of older Acts of Parliament it is now a quaint anachronism to use regnal years. The short-title will invariably be used unless it is an Act for which there is none.

(2) It is important to learn the correct name for each division of an Act. (For examples see the sample Act of Parliament in

Appendix 2.) References to an Act should be as follows. A number of sections may be grouped in a *part*, eg Law of Property Act, Pt I (ss 1 – 39). A section may be divided into sub-sections and sub-sections into paragraphs. For example: 'An estate in fee simple absolute in possession may exist as a legal estate in land (see Law of Property Act 1925 (s 1(1)(a)).' This refers to paragraph (a) of sub-section (1) of section 1 of that well-known Act.

(3) Schedules to Acts of Parliament are divided into paragraphs and sub-paragraphs and cited as follows. The Theft Act 1968 (Sch 1, para 2) provides that unlawfully taking any fish in water which is private property is an arrestable offence.

(4) In an essay an Act referred to often may be referred to by a clear abbreviation, eg the LPA 1925. In a more formal work, abbreviations may still be used, eg referring for the second time to the 'Prevention of Fraud (Investments) Act 1958', you may say 'the 1958 Act' or 'the Prevention of Fraud etc Act' as appropriate to the context.

Statutory instruments

These are normally divided into *rules* and *paragraphs* and *sub-paragraphs*. Occasionally longer instruments are divided into *sections*, *paragraphs* and *sub- paragraphs* see, eg Land Registration Rules 1925. They are cited by their short title and the correct citation is now invariably given in rule 1 of each instrument. In more formal works it is customary to cite the number as well as the name, eg 'For this purpose the definition of "Qualifying Student" is found in rule 2 (2) (see Rent Rebates and Rent Allowances (Students) (England and Wales) Regulations 1976 (SI 1976 No 1242)).' Further on in your text, an abbreviated reference may be used, eg 'Part- time teacher training courses seem to be excluded (see the Rent Rebates etc Regulations 1976, r 2(2))'.

Textbooks

(1) Try to avoid references to textbooks unless the reference adds something of substance to your argument. A textbook is no substitute for a reference to a primary source. Only where a textbook, for example, offers an explanation of the law, not apparent from the case law, or an alternative interpretation of the law or seeks to resolve an uncertainty or suggests a way of reconciling case law developments should it be used. The view must be attributed to the author and not passed off as your opinion.

(2) Use the author's surname and cite the necessary bibliographic detail, as follows:

(a) Harvard system
Treitel G.H. (2003) *The Law of Contract* 11th edn, Sweet & Maxwell.

(b) British Standard
Treitel G.H. *The Law of Contract* 11th edn, Sweet & Maxwell, 2003.

Journals

(1) Frequently journals state, in each issue, the recommended form of citation. Use this. You should cite the year (this must be done where the year is essential to finding the article), volume number (if there is one), the name of the journal appropriately abbreviated and the page number. You will soon come to recognise the standard citations. When including a reference to an article in a bibliography, you should cite the number of the first page and end page of an article eg 54–62. The author and title of an article should also appear in a bibliography.

✖ EXAMPLE

The *Law Quarterly Review*	(2002) 118 LQR 4.
The *Modern Law Review*	(1967) 30 MLR 369.
Lloyds Maritime and Commercial law Quarterly	[2002] LMCLQ 231.
The *Criminal Law Review*	[2003] Crim LR 28.
New Law Journal	(2003) NLJ 252.
Solicitors Journal	(2004) SJ 844.

---

(2) In short essays an exact reference is not necessary, eg 'Wilkinson in his article (1984 Conveyancer) examined the case concerning the application of the Misrepresentation Act 1967 to sales of land . . . '.

(3) In a longer piece of work, place your reference in a footnote - the first citation should give the whole reference.

> **✖ EXAMPLE**
>
> 'Edelman J and McKendrick E *Employee's Liability for Statements* (2002) 118 LQR 4.'
>
> Future references may be, provided there is no ambiguity, much foreshortened, eg '*Edelman and McKendrick* (op cit) p 8.'

A note about citing references from Internet sources

If you access a law report or other legal source material on an electronic database, you should cite the primary reference, not the address of the database. Such information is irrelevant; it's akin to saying I found a law report in the library!

> **✖ EXAMPLE**
>
> For *R v Shivpuri*, cite [1987] AC 1, not the web address of, for example, Westlaw or LexisNexis.

Obviously, if the information you are using is only to be found on the Internet then it is appropriate to cite the Internet reference. Remember as with all references you must give sufficient information for the reader to locate the source.

If the source is not static, that is it is likely to be updated or changed, it is usual after stating the web address to include the date on which you accessed the site. For example, after the web address you would put, '(Accessed on 25 September 2006)'.

> **✖ EXAMPLE**
>
> Suppose you want to cite statistics as to the number of female judges in England and Wales in 2006 you may consult the website of the Judiciary of England and Wales. A footnoted reference to the site would be as follows:
>
> Judiciary of England and Wales (2006). Available at http://www.judiciary.gov.uk/keyfacts/statistics/women.htm. (Accessed: 25 September 2006.)

Members of the judiciary

A source of irritation to a marker is the failure of some students to refer to judges by their correct title. In making notes on a case ensure that you also correctly record the title of the judge or judges.

(1) Use their correct full titles before their name or the conventional abbreviation after their name.

(a) For judges in the House of Lords:
Lord Mustill; collectively the judges are termed the "Law Lords".

(b) For judges in the Court of Appeal:
The Lord Chief Justice, Lord Phillips
or
Lord Phillips CJ

(c) The Master of the Rolls, Sir Anthony Clark
or
Sir Anthony Clark MR

(d) The President of the Queen's Bench Division, Sir Igor Judge
or
Sir Igor Judge PQBD

(e) The President of the Family Division, Sir Mark Potter
or
Sir Mark Potter PFD

(f) The Chancellor of the High Court, Sir Andrew Morritt
or
Sir Andrew Morritt C (note that the prior to the Constitutional Reform Act 2005 there was an office of Vice Chancellor, which was abbreviated to VC).

(g) Lord Justice Pill or Lady Justice Arden
or
Pill LJ or Arden LJ
Collectively the judges are known as Lords Justices of Appeal or LJJ.

(h) For judges in the High Court:
Mr Justice Veale or Mrs Justice Baron
or
Veale J or Baron J. The plural for High Court judges is abbreviated to JJ.

(i) For a Crown Court judge:
His Honour Judge Cohen

> **HINT**
> Ensure you accurately record the names of the judges when making notes on a case.

or
Judge Cohen

(j) For a magistrate:
Dr S Marsh JP

(2) Do not use familiar names, first names or slovenly abbreviations. Even when referring to legal authors, avoid the use of first names unless this is the author's own usage – many still find this practice a vulgar Americanism. Finally, in your use of citation aim for unambiguity, neatness and consistency. If you achieve these three goals you will have achieved enough.

The correct use of quotations

The process of quoting from sources is one that is apt to be misused. Very often students will quote from a textbook or article at length for the purpose of explaining a particular point, rule or idea. As the purpose of an assignment is to demonstrate that a student understands, this rather defeats the purpose of the exercise. Quotation of this type is to be avoided and an explanation should be supplied in a student's own words. Failure to do this will at the very least lead to a much reduced mark and at worst, if unattributed, disciplinary proceedings for plagiarism. Quotation is not to be used as a substitute for an explanation in your own words.

HINT →

Do not quote from textbooks in place of giving an explanation yourself.

So when is it permissible to use quotations? Quotations should be confined to instances where, for example, an author expresses a viewpoint, or in a case a judge states a rule, or pithily sums up a development. They are to be used to add weight to an argument or as evidence supporting a viewpoint. It is permissible to quote a legislative provision if you wish to analyse the elements of it, but remember the quote in itself does not demonstrate that you understand it. Quite frequently, you will need to explain the significance of what is said in the quote and relate this to the requirements of the question.

The quotation must be reproduced as it appears in the original source.

The source of the quotations must be carefully referenced, including a page reference.

The correct use of footnotes

Footnotes will normally be used for referencing purposes, but may include additional information. They are not to be used to as vehicle for circumventing the word-limit; material that should be in the text of your answer should not appear in a footnote. Further detail on a particular point may be included in a footnote, if to include it in the body of the answer would detract from the point being made.

Creating a bibliography

The aim of a bibliography is to alert the reader to the sources you have used in the writing of your essay. It is also some protection, but not a complete defence, against an allegation of plagiarism. All sources referenced in your footnotes must appear in your bibliography; entries should start with the author's name and are to be arranged alphabetically. See earlier for the information to be included and the form of such references. There is no need to include page references to books, but in relation to articles you should indicate the pages at which an article may be found. A bibliography should appear after the end of the text of your answer.

HINT
A bibliography should include all referenced sources used in writing your essay.

Plagiarism

Nearly all degree courses now include an element of assessed coursework. This coursework has to be your own. Unfortunately, it is the experience of all universities that instances of plagiarism and copying occur from time to time. The result for an individual may be complete failure of the course and loss of the opportunity to become a lawyer. Work given for assessment cannot be copied or digested or reformulated from that of another student. If, as you must, you rely on other writers on the subject you must acknowledge their influence. If you quote directly from another author you must give an accurate reference for this quotation. Background reading in commonplace textbooks need not be referenced, but the borrowing of original ideas and the use of all direct quotations must be. It is not sufficient to refer by name to a work in your bibliography if you have taken an idea or quotation from it – this use of someone else's original work must be properly noted. Thus, in an essay on contract you will obviously in preparation look at *Anson*, *Treitel*, and *Cheshire, Fifoot and Furmston* – this scarcely needs stating. However, if an insight of *Treitel* informs your essay you should in a footnote to the relevant passage add an acknowledgment such as 'I am grateful to Treitel *Law of Contract* (11th edn) p Y for the suggestion that . . . '. If you use the words of Professor Treitel then those words *must* be placed in quotations or parenthesis and a footnote reference *must* enable the reader to discover the origin of your extract. You may be tempted to use copyright (or apparently uncopyright) extracts downloaded from the Internet. Subject to what was said at the beginning of the chapter, there is no reason if they *add* to your thesis why you should not do this. However, the source must be identified as clearly as possible in the same way as any other resource on which you have relied.

With the advent of the Internet there is a plethora of legal material available electronically, which is downloadable. The integrity of a degree award depends upon the standards applied to the assessment process. In consequence, universities treat very seriously the issues of plagiarism and collusion. Students must be very clear as to what constitutes plagiarism and collusion as even an unwitting misuse of material may lead to disciplinary proceedings. Sanctions vary from a downgrading of marks to expulsion from a programme of study.

Plagiarism is defined at Northumbria University as,

'The deliberate and substantial unacknowledged incorporation in a candidate's work of material derived from the work (published or unpublished) of another. Examples of plagiarism are:

(i) the inclusion in a candidate's work of more than a single phrase from another person's work without the use of quotation marks and acknowledgement of the sources;

(ii) the summarising of another person's work by simply changing a few words or altering the order of presentation, without acknowledgement;

(iii) the substantial and unauthorised use of ideas of another person without acknowledgement of the source;

(iv) copying the work of another candidate, with or without that candidate's knowledge or agreement'.

Collusion is a variation on the above with, for example, students working together to produce a piece of work or one student allowing another student to copy his or her work. Needless to say you should not lend your tape, disk, draft or copy of assessed coursework to any other student until you both have had your separate work assessed. Most universities treat the lender and the borrower as equally guilty.

It is clear that many students do not appreciate what constitutes plagiarism. It is important that you look at what is and what is not acceptable conduct in writing your assignment.

Once you have received an assignment the regulations applying to assessment might indicate that you are not allowed to discuss the subject matter of the assignment with anyone. In consequence, you must not discuss it with fellow students or even your tutor! This should not deter you from asking your tutor questions as to the formal requirements of the assessment or indeed discussing with a tutor your understanding

HINT ⇒
Be aware of what constitutes plagiarism.

of a legal area related to the assignment. But a tutor will not be willing to discuss with you how to answer the assignment or what material is relevant for inclusion in your answer. The onus is upon you to ask questions that do not contravene the regulations relating to plagiarism. Obviously, if a question is too closely related to an assignment a tutor may decline to give an answer.

It should be said that sometimes students are expected to work collaboratively in producing assessed work and, of course, there is much merit in students discussing legal issues with one another; after all this is part of the learning process. However, the point at issue is that you must follow the instructions given by your tutor and be aware of the pitfalls of plagiarism and collusion. It is not impressive for a law student to say, 'I wasn't aware of the rules' or 'I don't understand what is meant by plagiarism'!

It is tempting when you have read a textbook which explains a principle very clearly, to merely reproduce the relevant paragraph. Even if you acknowledge the source this is an unacceptable practice. As it is your understanding that is being assessed, you must explain the principle in your own words. Equally, quoting a passage from a textbook which gives a clear explanation is misusing the process of quotation. Allied to this is overuse of the process of quotation; an assignment then appears like a 'patchwork quilt' of the words of others. None of the above techniques is acceptable.

HINT →
Ensure that you understand how to use quotations.

A common technique used by some students is that of 'cut and paste'; taking sections from different texts and then arranging them into an essay form. Another well-practised approach is to change certain words, but to retain the sentence structure and style of the original author.

✖ EXAMPLE

The following is original text from K Malleson *The Legal System* 2nd edn, Oxford University Press, 2005.

'By adopting this literal approach the scope for the judges to apply their own preferred interpretation of the law and run the risk of undermining parliamentary sovereignty is reduced. Provided that the drafters are meticulous in their choice of words, supporters of the literal rule would argue that is the best hope for ensuring that judges do not interfere inappropriately with legislation. However, the assumption that laws can and will be drafted so clearly and coherently as to avoid all gaps or ambiguities is, arguably, an unrealistic one. Moreover, by definition those cases which have reached the higher courts to be interpreted are those where there is at least an arguable case for different interpretations.'

The following is an example of how not to use the above text.

By using the literal approach there is less chance of judges applying their own interpretation of the law and undermining parliamentary sovereignty. If the drafters are careful in the words they choose, the literal rule it may be argued is the best hope for ensuring that judges do not interfere inappropriately with statutes. However, is it realistic to assume that laws can and will be drafted so clearly and coherently as to avoid all gaps or ambiguities? Additionally, those cases which have gone to the higher courts to be interpreted are those where there is an argument as to the meaning of the legislation; there is a case for different interpretations.

There is no attribution by the student and the sentence structures and order remain largely those of Kate Malleson. An essay containing sections like this would fall within the definition of plagiarism. That is not to say that the information that Kate Malleson provides could not be used, just that it would have to be expressed in your own words and reference made to the text in your bibliography.

The following is an example of how to use Kate Malleson's text.

The literal rule was preferred by judges as it allowed them to appear to be objective; they were merely collecting Parliament's intention from the words used in a statute, not seeking to make a choice of interpretations. However, the literal rule has serious weaknesses; not least that legislation may be unclear, ambiguous or not clearly applicable to unforeseen situations. So judges, for example, in relation to ambiguities in legislation, are left with a choice to make between rival interpretations where a literal approach offers no assistance.

HINT

When making notes from a source always note the reference for the source.

The research process will bring to light articles and commentaries on particular legal topics which are relevant to coursework. Ideas and arguments obtained from these sources may be used in answering an assignment but must be acknowledged in footnotes and bibliography. Failure to attribute ideas and arguments constitutes plagiarism; to avoid this you must reference your sources. Always note the reference when making notes from a textbook, case, article etc so that you can immediately identify its source. This may help you when you come to write your assignment from inadvertently presenting materials, ideas or comments as your own.

Aside from the obvious lack of educational merit and worth in plagiarised work, the chances of being detected are these days much greater with the development of search engines designed to check assignments. The search engine may check for the use in a student's work of plagiarised sources accessed via the Internet. It can also be used to check for similarities among pieces of work submitted by students by loading student assignments into the system. There is a national Plagiarism Advisory Service which offers advice to students on how to avoid inadvertent plagiarism. This is available at www.jiscpas.ac.uk/ and includes practical advice on assignment preparation. A final point to note is that just as a student may use Google to find material to cut and paste into an essay, so may a tutor use Google to identify the source!

■ CHECKLIST

■ CITATION OF LEGAL SOURCES AND PLAGIARISM

▶ Ensure that you use appropriate materials. While the Internet allows ease of access, a law library may contain more authoritative sources. Be aware of the origin of materials and only use materials from an authoritative source.

▶ Always evaluate the reliability of Internet sites before use.

▶ When you consult a source make a full note of the reference; this will save time in the long term.

▶ When using cases always cite the most authoritative set of reports, *the Law Reports*, published by the Incorporated Council of Law Reporting.

▶ If there is a neutral citation to a case use this alongside a reference to hard copy case reports.

▶ There is no need when referring to a case or a piece of legislation to reference the website on which it was found, for example, Westlaw; you would not say in relation to a hard copy case that you located it in the library!

▶ Look to see if your department or school gives guidance as to the system of citation to use. If no guidance is given then whatever system of citation you choose, use it consistently.

▶ Ensure you accurately record the names of the judges when making notes on a case.

▶ Do not quote from textbooks in place of giving an explanation yourself.

▶ A bibliography should include all referenced sources used in writing your essay.

▶ Be aware of what constitutes plagiarism and collusion. On being given an assessed piece of work note what is, and what is not, acceptable behaviour, in producing your work.

▶ Ensure that you understand how to use quotations.

▶ When making notes from a source always note the reference for the source; this is a good way of avoiding inadvertent plagiarism.

Chapter 11
Undergraduate examinations

Law and law exams

This chapter deals primarily with the preparation for law examinations at degree level. The professional examinations in law present different challenges and are dealt with separately in the chapters on 'Becoming a solicitor' and 'Becoming a barrister'. The material in this chapter will also be found useful by students studying law at a degree level on mixed degrees and non-law degrees such as accountancy and surveying. It will also help students who are attempting the Common Professional Examination for would-be solicitors and barristers.

It is a fact that all students embarking on law degree examinations and the other courses mentioned are already proven successful examinees. How curious, then, that the approach of law examinations is faced with such dreadful anticipation! Yet, the greatest difficulty for students is that law examinations still depend to an enormous extent upon memory and recall. To be able to analyse the questions asked depends very much on an extensive knowledge of relevant law. Most undergraduate examinations and many of the professional examinations consist of unseen written examinations of two or three hours' duration.

> **KEY POINT**
>
> Success in unseen law examinations depends to a great extent upon memory and recall. However, memory and recall in themselves are not enough they must be allied to analytical ability.

This style of examining competence whether in academic ability or lawyerly skills does not commend itself to those able to contemplate the subject rationally. It does to a certain extent test knowledge and to a lesser extent skills of verbal expression and analysis. It is also a test of diligence – certainly a meritorious quality. The test takes place, though, in such artificial circumstances and under such an atypical form of stress as to leave one very dubious as to its overall suitability for the assessment of entrants to any profession. Nevertheless, it is time-honoured and it is indubitably there and the student must not shirk the challenges posed: there is no doubt that law examinations loom before law students as an all too terrifying prospect. Partly, no doubt, this is due to the nature of the subject matter being examined. At first there is the unfamiliarity of the material being studied. There is also the rather odd style of law examination questions of which more below.

Assessment of law examinations

In a law degree performance is generally assessed roughly as follows:

70%+ = First Class

60%+ = Second Class (First Division)

50%+ = Second Class (Second Division)

45%+ = Third Class

40%+ = Pass

Typically this performance will be distributed in something like the following way. Out of any hundred students, a handful will obtain first class honours. A few will obtain a pass degree and a few more, perhaps more than 10%, will obtain a third-class honours degree. The remainder will obtain second class honours with the greater number of these falling nowadays in the upper division.

The marking of examination scripts

This subject is worth some mention as some conclusions can be drawn that are helpful to the examinee. The process of arriving at student assessment is perhaps cloaked in more mystery than is necessary. Students have in the past found that the normal practice is that the raw marks obtained by them, at least in their final assessment, are not made known to them. The justification for this seems to have been to avoid arguments as to whether borderline decisions have been correctly made. Nowadays students will be given access to their actual marks. Unfortunately students still generally have no access to their worked and marked examination papers. This is something of a pity as it would prove a salutary experience.

Law examiners tend to be somewhat grudging in the allocation of marks, particularly high marks. There is a phenomenon that examiners call the *effective range* of marking. That is the fact that for each question the effective range of marks is between 6 and 14 with only exceptional cases falling above that range, and the overwhelming bulk of instances falling in the middle range. This tendency to mark so restrictively particularly at the top of a range is vividly captured in the French adage: '20 is given only to God, 19 to his saints, 18 to the professor's professor, 17 to the professor himself – so the student of French composition can't be expected to score more than 16.' (Quoted from Clignet 'Grades, Examinations and Other Checkpoints as Mechanisms of Social Control' in *Liberty and Equality in the Educational Process* Chapter 10.)

These facts, the reluctance of law teachers, particularly, to use the full range of marks, the tendency in law examinations to use an aggregate sum as the main indicator of class achievement and the tendency of such a sum to produce a drift towards the norm have important simple implications for law students.

(i)   Within any one examination paper, compensation for poor performance on or omission of a question is extremely difficult to come by. A student in a five-question paper managing 8, 8, 8 and deciding to go 'all out' on one further question is extremely unlikely to achieve the 16 necessary to pass. An excellent student managing 14, 14, 14 has little chance of achieving his aggregate of 70% by neglecting one question and going 'all out' for the others.

(ii) Within any diet of examinations the same message applies as between performance in each paper. A student 'on a first' virtually has to achieve a standard of 'almost a first' in every paper to achieve something close enough to the aggregate to win such an award.

(iii) The clear message is thus that the full number of questions must be attempted and *equal time and effort* allocated to each.

It is important to remember, too, that with anonymous marking you will be judged on what is contained in your examination script, not on the marker's knowledge of you as a diligent and able student. It is the written words only on which you will be assessed and only those which can be read by the examiner – perhaps someone rather impatient with the task – who will not pause to unravel the confused or obscure and cannot be expected to assume that the unintelligible or illegible was in truth correct or even profound.

The formal assessment process

In virtually all degree-giving institutions, the examination paper is set internally and moderated by an external examiner. Usually, before being sent to the external examiner, the paper is moderated internally in a committee drawn from those involved in teaching a particular course. This process of setting the examination paper and internal and external moderation will, for a June examination, normally be completed before March for the year in question.

The exact procedure of marking the examination scripts does not vary widely. In nearly every case of a degree examination, the scripts are marked internally, moderated internally and the marking standard and individual cases of difficulty are then moderated by an external examiner. The progress of a student or award of a degree concomitant on the examination result is formally determined by an Examinations Board of some or all of those involved in teaching the course and the external examiners.

The procedure in internal marking – whether scripts are double-marked, marked independently without knowing the mark of the other marker and so on – in practice varies so considerably that it would be profitless to attempt to describe a common practice.

The class of your degree – does it matter?

There cannot be much disagreement that for the workaday lawyer, outstanding academic achievement does not have the same importance as professional and personal virtues such as integrity, reliability and diligence. This conclusion and the difference in kind between much of the achievement in law examinations and the later achievements in practice can too easily lead a student to settle for a modicum of effort and a performance lacking in distinction. Nevertheless, there are a number of sound reasons why each student is urged to look carefully to the quality of his or her performance in early study, whether of the law or some other first discipline.

KEY POINT ●

Your performance throughout your law degree is important in securing legal employment.

In some forms of employment, the quality of your academic performance will in itself be important, certainly if you wish to pursue a career in law teaching or a higher qualification in law. Also, more than ever in the past, law firms recruiting to their strength are explicitly concerned with the measured academic performance of applicants. This would particularly be true if you sought a career away from provincial private practice in a large city firm or in the increasingly attractive careers in the public service.

More important still than these considerations is the fact that your performance in your law studies is a direct measure of your knowledge, understanding and application of legal rules. Obviously, throughout your career you will wish to draw on this knowledge and on the training you have given yourself in the comprehension and analysis of legal principles.

In particular this foundation of understanding and knowledge if gained in the pursuit of a first degree in law will be of direct assistance in your professional examinations. It is a fact that the better you perform in your degree studies the better you equip yourself to perform in your professional studies. Analysis of the results in the solicitor's professional examination has shown that there is a direct and very strong relationship between success in this examination and the class of a student's first degree. This is not at all surprising since the degree is the academic foundation on which the somewhat more practical course for the professional examination is based and a sound understanding gained in the former is a prerequisite of success in the latter. It is worth knowing from an early stage in the law degree that obtaining a second class honours degree is the general requirement for entry to the Bar Vocational Course for future barristers.

As competition for a training contract has increased, it has become very much harder to obtain one without an upper second class honours degree.

Different types of examination

Among their academic colleagues, law teachers have a reputation for conservatism in method and content. Very probably this reputation is deserved. Thus, it still remains true that in law schools the traditional three-hour examination paper, unseen closed book, combining problems and essay questions, remains the most widely used form of assessment.

Nevertheless, different types of law examinations are in use and some consideration is given to these and to the special problems associated with them.

Unseen open-book examinations

This is an examination paper not seen until the examination where the student is given the use of various materials ranging from Acts of Parliament through books of collected or annotated statutes to the student's own prepared materials. The two special problems of this kind of examination, in the authors' experience, might be given the watchwords *organisation* and *approach*.

Organisation

Suppose in a land law examination you are, as is now very common, permitted to use a property statutes book or, in a criminal law examination, copies of the Theft Acts. It is noticeable how many students, although fully aware that this text will be available to them in the examination, and having taken the trouble to attend lectures and read textbooks and even reported cases, will not familiarise themselves thoroughly with the form, layout and content of the given material. This is particularly important if, like the property statutes, the text is bulky and its layout not instantly comprehensible. If you are not thoroughly familiar with the text and able to turn rapidly and confidently to different parts of it, then you will find in the examination that you can make little use of the text. The watchword is – learn the organisation of the work that will be supplied or the material you are taking into the examination and be familiar with its content.

Approach

The reason lecturers favour this type of examination is to decrease the need for the student to rely on sheer memory and by doing this to enable the examination to test better the candidate's analysis and handling and application and manipulation of legal rules rather than mere reproduction of them. A student faced by such an examination needs to undertake certain preparatory tasks. Ensure that you know what you are permitted to take into the examination and that you have such materials with you on the day. At first sight the prospect of an open-book examination does not seem as daunting as that of a closed-book examination. However, you must still follow a structured revision programme if you are to make the most of this opportunity. Usually, an open-book examination will be subject to a time limit so you do not have time to spend reading extensively. The materials should be used as an aide memoire and not as a substitute for knowing the materials in the first place.

With closed-book examinations some credit will be given for knowing relevant law, but with open-book examinations such credit will not be given; thus more time must be spent upon analysis. A good illustration from one of the author's experience is with one candidate's answer to the following question:

> **Q.** Explain the significance of the Law of Property (Joint Tenants) Act 1964.

This Act, as the reader may be aware, is a short Act of only four sections passed to deal with a rather complex lacuna in the 1925 property legislation.

The question was set in a second year degree examination and the examiner when marking the papers handed the script of one student to the author with the query, 'What do you make of this?'. The script was duly read and found to set out the three important sections of the Act with fair accuracy and passable clarity and the reply was – 'Nothing exciting but a fair pass in the 45% range'. But, it was then pointed out that the students had had, in this examination, a copy of the Act in *Sweet & Maxwell's Property Statutes*. In this case, reproducing the contents of ss 1–3 was worth virtually no credit at all. In any examination, whether open-book or not, a good answer to this question would explain the mischief the Act was passed to deal with; how the 1925 legislation tried to deal with this problem and why it failed; the incumbent practical difficulties, if possible; how this Act tried to deal with them and what the reasons were for the way it was drafted, including the exception thereto; and, if possible, point out outstanding problems in this area. In an examination where the text of the Act is given to the student, an answer which does not attack the question in that pattern or something approaching it can gain no credit – although in a completely closed-book examination, the mere reproduction of the contents of the relevant Act may suffice for a pass mark.

Seen examinations

Not greatly used in law, but not unknown, is the examination paper that the candidate is allowed to see some time before he is required to answer it. In some varieties, the examination paper is 'taken home' and the student given a period of days or even weeks to produce an answer, frequently of a specified length. In other varieties, the candidate has to reappear in due course in an examination hall and write an answer to the paper. In an examination of this kind, the general advice given on form and content of examination answer remains valid. The crucial change of emphasis is a heightening of the need for analysis illustrated in the last paragraph on open-book examinations. No credit is given for the kinds of skill involving memory and facsimile reproduction of texts but exclusively for the other types of performance which a law examination tests.

Multiple choice examinations

Multiple choice questions (MCQs), or sometimes multiple choice tests, are now fairly commonplace in legal education. Should you not encounter them as an undergraduate, you will in pursuing the vocational courses to become a solicitor or barrister (see Chapters 13 and 14 on the Legal Practice Course and the Bar Vocational Course). Such questions may be used to assess knowledge or, in a more sophisticated form, to assess understanding. In attempting MCQs you must read the instructions given carefully and then follow them precisely when completing the test. As your answer sheet will most likely be computer-read, adherence to the instructions is essential. On a practical note a pencil and eraser should be used in answering MCQs, as an answer in ink cannot be altered and a written amendment will not be recognised should your answers be computer-read.

Study the instructions to each question, as what is required of you may differ from question to question. For example, you may have to select one right answer or, instead, one wrong answer.

Read carefully the possible answers as the examiner will be trying to produce statements that are very similar and choosing the correct answer may require a good understanding of an area or point of law.

✖ EXAMPLE

Which of the following statements accurately reflects the stated precedent practice in the House of Lords?

(a) The House of Lords must follow its own previous decisions.

(b) The House of Lords in any circumstances may depart from its own previous decisions.

(c) The House of Lords is strictly bound by its own previous decisions.

(d) The House of Lords may refuse to follow one of its previous precedents if it appears right to do so.

The answer depends upon a knowledge of the *Practice Statement* [1966] 1 WLR 1234 where Lord Gardiner LC speaking for the Law Lords announced a change to the precedent practice in the House of Lords allowing the House of Lords to depart from its own previous decisions. So (a) is inaccurate, reflecting the precedent practice before the *Practice Statement*, as is (c) which states the same practice in a different way. Answers (b) and (d) appear similar but indicate different circumstances as to when the House of Lords may depart from one of its own previous decisions. The *Practice Statement* provides that while former decisions of the House of Lords are treated as normally binding, their Lordships may 'depart from a previous decision when it appears right to do so'. The correct answer must therefore be (d). Answer (b) is too wide as the House of Lords will not depart from a previous decision in any circumstances; the Practice Statement indicates that their Lordships are to 'bear in mind the danger of disturbing retrospectively the basis on which contracts, settlements of property, and fiscal arrangements have been entered into and also the especial need for certainty as to the criminal law'.

You must not spend too long on each question. If you are uncertain of an answer, do not agonise over it, move on to the next question. You may come back to an unanswered question later in the examination. Finally, if a negative marking scheme is employed by an examiner, that is for each wrong answer marks are deducted, only answer questions where you are confident of the answer to be given. If there is no negative marking then answer all the questions asked; a guess will cost you nothing!

Viva voce examinations

An oral examination, although universal in assessing higher degrees, is otherwise rarely used. There are two principal uses – to assess project work and to assess candidates who after the written examinations are found to be on the borderline between two classes or between pass and fail.

In these situations, specific preparation would probably be of little use and in any event the summons generally comes too late for this to be practicable. However, some general pointers may help to give confidence if the day does dawn.

First, it is particularly important to have your mind clear and alert. Do not stuff yourself in the ante-room with cribs and mnemonics; simply relax or go for a walk. Even the day before, do not cram ceaselessly at your worn-out notes but find some unlawyerly activity – tennis, squash, snooker, cinema or what you will – something to 'stretch yourself in the other direction' and leave your mind fresh and uncluttered.

Equally important is to have a positive attitude to the experience. The examiners want merely to find out what you do know and do understand – they are not concerned to badger and trip you. Invariably they will be on your side and see the viva as a way of letting you add to your written performance.

Finally, in the viva, do not rush or be rushed. Take as much time as you like. Listen carefully. By all means ask for a question to be repeated or rephrased. Think about your answer slowly and at length and do not be hesitant to divert the discussion into areas in which you are familiar and confident.

Continuous assessment

If by this is meant assessment by sporadic or phased tests of any of the above types then no separate treatment of the topic is necessary. However, the term more usually refers to assessment by reference to coursework in the form of essays or projects undertaken during the course. Assessment of such work is dealt with in the preceding chapters dealing generally with the subjects of course essays and projects.

Very occasionally there is another form of continuous assessment based on the student's performance of other tasks of a lawyerly nature. Such assessment is associated with clinical legal education but incurs difficulties because of the subjective nature of the assessment.

Revision for examinations

Memory will play an important part in nearly all your law examinations. An able student can achieve a bare pass with moderate attention throughout the year and a modicum of revision. But even an able student pursuing this plan of campaign may miscalculate and fail.

It is important that you pace your effort throughout the year so as to avoid any temptation to overstretch yourself as the examinations approach. Ideally, you should have developed an even working week which will see you through the course and the examination period. When lectures and tutorials cease some weeks before the examination you should have ample time for revision without stepping up your working-hours at all, let alone to the absurd degree attempted by some students. A continuity of effort will prove more rewarding than periods of relative slackness followed by a fortnight of delirious cramming.

The mechanics of revision are not something on which it is valuable to be dogmatic. It is suggested that a clear timetable, not overdemanding in the hours allotted, is essential – but there is no doubt that some students appear to profit from a more haphazard approach.

HINT ➡
Create a revision timetable.

The essential advice on revision is that you must do as much as you can to render it unnecessary. There is a kind of student who will be very largely unprepared by Easter. He or she will have a scrappy set of lecture notes from some of the lectures and will have a random and indecipherable clutter of jottings resulting from tutorial or seminar work. Many of the key cases and journal articles will have been left unread. Revision for this student will be a nightmare. Other students' notes will be photocopied to fill in gaps. Cases will be read hurriedly and partially digested. As Spring rushes on towards Summer, the student's now frenetic work reaches a crescendo. He or she is up working till beyond midnight, meals are missed, panic grows. By the time of the examination the student is exhausted, half-prepared and thoroughly frightened. All this can easily be avoided.

Take on the other hand the model student. His or her lecture notes contain a succinct record of each lecture – for all of them have been attended – and are filed in order in ring folders. Each page is interleaved with the cases and supplementary material that have been produced as a result of his or her own reading. There are brief accounts of the important cases, summaries of journal articles and, spicing the whole, useful quotations, further references and explanatory notes. The prudent student will also seek assistance should his or her understanding of a particular area be incomplete. It is preferable to deal with problems as they arise during the course. When shortly after Easter the lecture course draws to its close, this student's preparatory work is complete. Already assembled in one place is all the material which is needed in the examination hall. All that needs to be done now is to peruse this material sufficiently thoroughly for it to be at his or her finger-tips during the examination. Revision can proceed in an orderly fashion and in the confidence that a workmanlike foundation has been laid. If the student keeps his or her head, the ideal revision programme can be achieved. That is one in which his hours do not increase during the weeks before the examination but if possible decrease. Remember there are more enjoyable things to do at college in the Spring than repair the damage caused by previous ill-attention to your studies!

HINT ➡
Ensure that you organise your notes and materials well in advance of the examinations to allow you, when the revision period arrives, to concentrate on reading your notes and materials without unnecessary distractions.

However carefully you prepare for the event, revision for examinations is a chore. The art of the successful examinee is to exercise foresight throughout the year and avoid the need for eleventh-hour excitement. The task can be made even easier by adding to your armoury of aide-memoires. It is a sad fact that much still depends upon memory. There will be large numbers of case names to commit to memory and a great deal of statutory material which many find even harder to recall in examinations. Although it is far from being a worthwhile academic venture, you will find a little effort put into practical organisation of this material very worthwhile. Cases can be arranged in suitable lists according to headings and other groupings. The same can be done with statutes in respect of which much memory work is required such as the sale of goods and unfair contract terms legislation and the enormously bulky property legislation. You will find that statutory material as presented by the draftsman is not a total jumble. Try to see how it is arranged in groups of sections according to subject matter, and how the arrangement has been arrived at. Try to produce an easily scanned 'revision scheme' of an Act which is likely to feature in the examination. It is likely that the work involved in this exercise will help to increase your understanding of the Act as well as assist in the drudgery of revision. It is too easy to study legislation piecemeal as a series of unrelated sections instead of building up an understanding of the whole.

Some of this advice may seem a far cry from the heady intellectual challenge expected by the beginner in legal studies. But, the examinations are there and have to be passed. The memory work is important and preparation for this trial a skill in itself. The comfort is that in order to make any worthwhile criticism of the law, it is necessary first to have both knowledge and understanding. The quantity of law is increasing at a rate that is sometimes alarming. The skills of digesting, organising and subsequently recalling a welter of detailed information will remain with you long after you graduate as will the solid acquaintanceship with law and legal reasoning which your methodical work has enabled you to acquire.

> **HINT →**
> It is necessary to commit large bodies of law to memory in order to succeed in a law examination. Without law an answer will appear to be merely based upon common sense and your mark will suffer accordingly.

Specific revision preparation

One of the most difficult pieces of advice is to give general advice on revision. But, knowing that students must tailor this to their own needs, here is one approach. First, enough has been said to indicate that it is one's approach to the whole course which indicates success in examinations – the last week or so's revision must not be seen as of the greatest importance.

Assimilation of large amounts of material is important for any law examination. This remains true even if the examination is totally open-book. One of the author's experience at Columbia University

HINT →

Set aside time throughout the academic year of study to revise your material. Repetition will help you remember.

HINT →

Look for a structure in your notes and highlight this.

HINT →

Revise throughout the year and be methodical in devising a revision plan for the period leading up the examinations.

many years ago was as follows. One examination was completely open-book. Any material that we liked could be taken into the examination. Yet, my own experience was that there was no time during the entire examination period to look at any of this.

Assimilation should be seen as a part of each stage of the course from the beginning. Try to set aside a little time each week or fortnight for this purpose. Do not use this time simply to re-read your notes – action-packed and exciting though they doubtless will be. Try to digest the material into a pattern – perhaps as follows: topics; sub-headings; and under each sub-heading a listing of the relevant cases, statutes and perhaps articles or other material. You may wish after each case to add a few words reminding you of its importance. This skeleton of each stage of your course will be the backbone of your final revision. Its key words and ordered pattern of presentation will 'bring it all flooding back'. The recall you need in the examination must be effortless. For this, an orderly scheme on which your assimilation of material is based is very useful. Repetition in the learning process *throughout* the year is also a crucial part of laying the foundation for effortless recall of relevant material.

This systematic structuring of subjects such as contract, tort and land law will lay the foundation for an understanding of the common law which will never leave you throughout your career.

Predetermine your pattern of revision at the commencement of each year and keep to this. Work out in a revision chart when you will cover each subject for the first, second, third (etc) time. Try to keep to the same number of hours, approximately, devoted to study when lectures finish and the examination approaches. There is no need for the good student to 'step-up' the number of hours devoted to revision. The same methodical working week is what is required. In the Summer term there is ample time for tennis, parties, country visits, weekends away and the countless more aimless forms of relaxation which are part of the richness of student life.

What to revise

Students constantly ask what they should revise – no lecturer can answer such specific questions. After all, the entire course of study is arranged as a whole. It is not arranged so that students can simply select enough to pass the examinations. Certainly students should participate in and benefit from the whole course. Nevertheless, as far as actual revision is concerned, it is possible to adopt a more ruthless approach. A typical examination will require four questions out of ten to be answered. Leaving out a simple discreet topic from final revision will simply reduce the choice to four out of nine. Such a small adjustment to the final stage of revision seems to be perfectly reasonable. Reducing by

10% overall the material to be re-revised in the final few weeks can give a welcome feeling of 'space' and a much needed psychological boost. It is unwise to go significantly further in omitting material from revision. You need to build into this approach a significant margin of error; paring revised areas to five in number when you have to attempt answers to four questions carry considerable risks.

Sitting the examination

The advice which follows is all obvious and all based upon common sense. You might at times feel it is wholly unnecessary. It is included because experience has shown that it is often ignored by students and always to their detriment. It seems probable that sitting examinations is one of those things that becomes a little harder with each fresh exposure to the experience. Consequently, simple steps must be taken to reduce the unnerving effect of examinations. What is said here is not novel. Try to let the novelty lie in the extent to which the advice given is noted and relied upon. It is most important to remember that the examination tests your performance once and for all on the day of the examination. It is self-evidently detrimental to your performance to be physically and mentally tired. A student who has been a lackadaisical drifter throughout the year and who winds himself up to a Herculean effort of round-the-clock revision will do himself no good. You need to think in law examinations and to do that you need to be awake. It might be salutary to produce two quotations from a book largely about examinations:

'Over 80 per cent said they had been extremely tired from lack of sleep, either because they were unable to sleep or because they had curtailed their normal number of hours through working late into the night or getting up very early in the morning to revise.'

'Fatigue effects particularly affected the exams coming near the end of the series. Those near the beginning were most likely to be affected by nervous tension.'

The extracts quoted speak for themselves (both are from Miller and Parlett *Up to the Mark* (1974) p 90). Plan your whole period of revision and your work during the examination period so that you remain physically and mentally fit. Take plenty of time off for recreation. On no account shut yourself off in a ceaseless whirl of revision and ever more frenetic glances at your huge accumulation of notes.

Examinations can be an ordeal and quite often students will feel that 'nerves have got the better of them'. In order to manage nervousness there are certain steps that may be taken. Foremost among these is careful planning and preparation. In planning and preparing for examinations it is also important to attempt to maximise the time available to you in the examination hall. Remember the key to this is to exercise control over the parts of the process where control is possible and to try to lessen the impact of the parts of the process where you have no control.

What is within your control

The following is a list of matters you should consider in preparation for the examination day.

(i) *The examination timetable.* A simple step to avoid last-minute panics is to locate the examination venue in advance of the day of the examination. Ensure you are familiar with the whereabouts of the examination room. Check the examination timetable. It is worth double-checking when the examination is to be held and also ensuring that it is the right examination. Write out your examination timetable noting the subject of the exam and the date and time. Arriving at an examination venue only to find that you have prepared for the wrong examination is not an ideal way to start an exam! Make sure you can arrive on time without being rushed and without having to spend too much time 'hanging about' with other candidates while the excitement mounts.

(ii) *Be prepared.* Be armed with plenty of writing materials.

(iii) *Open-book examinations.* If you are allowed materials in the examination, have these ready and in good order. Check to see that they conform with the examination rules. A silly oversight can lead to disaster.

(iv) *What are the instructions on the exam paper?* In consulting past papers note the following information from the rubric to the examination paper: how long is the examination; how many questions are to be attempted; are any of the questions compulsory; is the paper arranged in parts; are materials allowed in the examination? Check to ensure that there have been no changes to the instructions on the paper.

When you are in the examination hall and told to begin – do not. Your first thoughts, particularly in the first examination, will be incoherent. Set yourself a simple procedure as to how you will read and re-read the examination paper and select your answers. When the examination begins, follow this careful procedure. It will still your spinning mind. Calmed by the routine of a familiar process, the ability for rational thought will return. After selecting your questions begin to write slowly. The examination will be underway, and you will not look back until the final whistle.

As a last word on the subject, it is worth repeating advice you will have been given a hundred times in your school career but which is still forgotten in the dread panic of an examination. Check and double check the instructions on each paper. Answer the correct number of questions and the correct number of parts of each question. In law examinations it is equally important to remember to follow the instructions for each question. If it instructs you to advise Fred, advise Fred, and not some other party or the parties generally. More attention is given to this topic in the following chapter – here it is sufficient to stress the importance of paying careful and deliberate attention to these matters.

(v) *How long have I to answer each question?* A simple calculation may be made in advance of the examination to discover how much time you have to answer each question. You should adhere to this time constraint strictly. If you run out of the allotted time leave the answer unfinished and move onto the next question. Leave space between the answers, so that should you have any time towards the end of the examination you may return to complete the unfinished answer. The reason for this advice is that in answering questions a law of diminishing returns applies; it is easier to pick up marks when you start an answer than to attain the higher marks where greater sophistication is required in your answer.

It is essential that you attempt to answer all the questions that are required of you. Obviously, it is easier to get 40 out of 100, than 40 out of 75 (should you fail to attempt a fourth question as required).

(vi) *What if I run out time?* As has been previously indicated it is important to attempt the required number of questions. Should you find that you are running out of time then you should complete your answer in note form. While you will not gain full marks, you will be given credit for indicating that you appreciate what issues the question raises and for any mention of relevant legal principles.

(vii) *Avoid examination post-mortems* Once you have completed an examination try to forget about it and concentrate instead upon your next examination. There is little to be gained from discussing the content of your paper with your peers, and should you perceive that you have made a mistake this can be an unwelcome diversion in either preparing for or attempting to do an examination.

■ CHECKLIST

Those matters over which control is possible:

► Find the location of the exam hall in advance of the examination;

► Double check the dates and subjects of all of your exams;

► Be armed with plenty of writing materials;

► Ensure that you understand the instructions on the exam paper;

► Calculate how long you have to answer each question;

► If you are allowed materials in the examination, have these ready and in good order;

► Have strategies in place should you find that you are running out of time during an exam;

► Avoid examination post-mortems.

Those matters lying outside your control

What may appear on the paper? Look at the available past papers to get clues as to the form of the questions and possible subject areas. Be aware that the emphasis placed upon the subject syllabus may vary from year to year. A good indicator of the current emphasis is the subject seminar programme. Some students decide to indulge in selective revision; this is not recommended and should not be necessary if you have worked diligently and systematically throughout the year. Should you indulge in this practice then ensure that you leave a margin for error, as noted above; you may feel you have a good knowledge of the areas of law you have chosen, but the question you expect might not appear on the paper or might not be in the form you anticipate!

The main matter lying outside of your control is the content of the examination paper. You cannot predict with certainty what will feature in the examination paper. While you will not know what is contained in the examination paper until you turn the paper over and start reading in the examination hall, this does not mean that you cannot take steps to be ready for this moment.

Planning ahead

Examinations are subject to time constraints and so time is at a premium. The usual advice, as indicated above, is to read the examination paper thoroughly, noting the questions that you would prefer to answer and then to draft outline plans to each question before writing your answers. Certainly having a structure for your answers is to be encouraged for the reasons outlined earlier. But why leave the planning process until you are in the examination room? Clues as to the likely content of the examination will have been given throughout your year of study. The areas of law upon which you are likely to be examined will to some extent be apparent. So spend some time prior to the examination identifying the structure of the legal areas you have studied. The inherent structure of a legal area might provide a ready made plan. The structure of the topic might not 'fit' exactly the requirements of a question but it may give you a head start. Remember, problem questions are an amalgam of factual problems giving rise to legal issues. Each part of the question will have been created with a particular legal point in mind. If you have a thorough knowledge and understanding of a legal topic it is usually easy to spot the points. Usually there will be a structure to the area of law raised by a question and it is again a relatively easy task to impose such a structure on a problem question.

The following is another example of structure taken from criminal law.

> **HINT** →
>
> Plan your answers to questions using the inherent structure of legal areas.

✖ EXAMPLES

Unless you are directed by a question to the contrary, it is usual to seek to establish liability for the most serious offence that the facts will support. If, for example, a question raises issues of non-fatal offences against the person then the structure of the area can be expressed in the following points:

State the offences: Sections 18 and 20 Offences against the Person Act 1861. For the injury to amount to grevious bodily harm it must be 'really serious'.

Section 18

Actus reus – (i) grevious bodily harm caused; or (ii) wound.
Mens rea – A defendant must (i) intend to do grevious bodily harm or (ii) intend to resist or prevent the lawful apprehension or detainer of any person.

Section 20

Actus reus – (i) grevious bodily harm inflicted; or (ii) wound.
Mens rea – A defendant must act 'maliciously' ie intend harm or be subjectively reckless.

Section 47

Actus reus – (i) assault; (ii) occasioning (causing); and (iii) actual bodily harm.
Mens rea – A defendant must intend or be subjectively reckless as to the application of force.

Assault and battery

Two separate common law offences.

Assault

Actus reus – an act by a defendant which causes apprehension in a victim of immediate and unlawful personal violence.
Mens rea – intention to cause apprehension or subjective recklessness as to causing such apprehension.

Battery

Actus reus – an act by a defendant which inflicts unlawful personal violence on a victim.
Mens rea – intention to inflict violence or subjective recklessness as to such infliction.

Once liability has been established consider any relevant defences.

Another example concerns restraint of trade clauses in a contract. The structure of the area can be expressed in the following way:

What is the doctrine of restraint of trade?

Does the doctrine apply to all contracts?

The doctrine makes a contract in restraint of trade prima facie void.

However, a restraint clause may be enforceable if reasonable in interests of the parties and reasonable in the public interest.

A clause is reasonable in the interests of parties if

(a) there is a proprietary interest to protect – trade secret or customer connection;

(b) the clause is reasonable in protection of the interest, in terms of duration, geographical area, employment area and the clause must be certain; and

(c) the clause is also reasonable in the public interest.

Finding ways of saving the clause – construction and severance.

The structure of an area of law provides a plan for dealing with a problem question. By identifying such a structure in advance of your examinations, valuable time will be saved in the examination room as you have a ready-made plan for such a question.

Using the restraint of trade structure, see how this approach may be employed in the following question and sample answer.

HINT →
As you study various legal areas identify their underlying structure.

✖ EXAMPLE

Grantmore Bank plc has its head office in Newcastle and branches across the North East of England. Sid, a financial adviser with Grantmore Bank plc, has worked for the Bank for the past two years in several of its North East branches. During that time Sid has handled the affairs of more than a thousand customers, both private investors and corporate clients. Last month Sid attended a training course with Grantmore where advisers were introduced to various new financial products that the Bank was intending to launch on the market.

However, since attending that course Sid has been offered a position as Financial Accounts Manager with Northern Investment Bank plc. Northern Investment has its head office in Liverpool and branches across the whole of Northern England. On commencing employment with Grantmore Sid was asked to sign a document containing the following term:

'The adviser agrees that she/he will not within two years of termination of this employment, howsoever caused,

(i) carry on or be engaged, concerned or interested in any business which competes with the business of Grantmore Bank plc;

(ii) canvass or solicit in competition with Grantmore Bank plc orders or custom from any person, firm or company who shall have engaged the services of the Bank;

(iii) be employed in the financial services industry or any related industry.'

Sid has approached you for your advice on whether he is legally entitled to accept the new offer of employment.

Advise Sid.

Sample answer

The structure of the answer is in **bold** to illustrate how the above approach may be used.

The law may refuse to allow a contract to have legal effect on the grounds of illegality. Illegality includes contracts for the commission of a crime or a civil wrong and contracts contrary to public policy. This latter ground encompasses **contracts in restraint of trade**. Cheshire, Fifoot and Furmston describe a contract in restraint of trade as: 'one by which a party restricts his future liberty to carry on his trade, business or profession in such manner and with such persons as he chooses'. Such **contracts are prima facie void, but may be valid if reasonable in the interests of the parties and in the interests of the public**, Nordenfelt v Maxim Nordenfelt Guns and Ammunition Co. The doctrine does not apply to all contracts that potentially restrain, Esso Petroleum Co Ltd v Harper's Garage (Stourport) Ltd. In this case Lord Wilberforce said that there is no comprehensive test for deciding whether the doctrine applies to particular contracts, but that **the doctrine applies to certain contracts, such as those between employer and employee** as in this question.

In order for the clause in the contract between Grantmore Bank and Sid to be valid, Grantmore must establish that it has a **proprietary interest**, a trade secret or the customer connection, to protect and that the restraint is reasonable in the protection of that interest. Grantmore, as an employer, may not protect against competition from Sid after he leaves its employment, Herbert Morris Ltd v Saxelby. However, Grantmore may argue that Sid has information which is in the nature of a **trade secret**, which is a protectable interest. In Lansing Linde Ltd v Kerr, Staughton LJ said that a trade secret included confidential information which if given to a competitor would cause real harm to the owner of the secret. Sid knows of various new financial products that the Bank is intending to launch on the market which, as in Littlewoods Organisation Ltd v Harris where knowledge of an unpublished catalogue was considered to be in the nature of a trade secret, could also amount to a trade secret. Of course, Grantmore would have to show that details of the new products were indeed secret. Another possible interest is the **customer connection**, as Sid handles the affairs of more than a thousand customers. In Herbert Morris Ltd v Saxelby it was said that an employee must have some influence over the customers to establish this interest. Grantmore would have to show that Sid had acquired such influence. If Sid has no face-to face contact with the customers then, as in S W Strange Ltd v Mann, it is unlikely that a relationship of influence will be established.

If Grantmore is able to establish the existence of one or both interests then it must further show that the **restraint clause in the contract is reasonable in the protection of such interest or interests**. Consideration must be given to the **duration of the clause and to its geographical and employment area**. The operation of the clause is to last for 2 years. Each interest gives rise to different considerations. First, the information on new products; it may be argued that as soon as these are released to the public or within a short period thereafter the interest will end. This is similar to Littlewoods Organisation Ltd v Harris where a restraint of 1 year was reasonable, as the catalogue once published would only last for six months. On this basis 2 years may be too long. As to the customer connection, how strong is the influence? If Sid's position is relatively lowly, as in M&S Drapers v Reynolds, the influence may weaken before the end of 2 years. The restraint clause does not include a **geographical area** expressly, but seeks in paragraph (i) to prevent competition. As stated above competition cannot be prevented per se, Herbert Morris Ltd v Saxelby. Paragraph (ii) is an anti-solicitation clause and seeks to protect the customer connection, but it refers to "any person, firm or company who shall have engaged the services of the bank" rather than merely to those customers with whom Sid has had contact. As such paragraph (ii) seems to be wider than is reasonably necessary for the protection of the interest. Finally, in paragraph (iii), the reference to employment in 'the financial services industry or any related industry' seems again to be **too wide as it specifies forms of employment** in which Sid has not been engaged while in the employment of Grantmore. In Commercial Plastics v Vincent an employee, engaged in a small specialist section of the PVC calendering industry, was restrained from working in any part of the PVC calendering field. This restraint was too wide and unenforceable.

The use of "howsoever caused" in relation to termination is of no effect as the restraint clause would be unenforceable should Grantmore wrongfully dismiss Sid, General Billposting v Atkinson. Note however that the words "howsoever caused" are not subject to the restraint of trade doctrine and therefore, even though legally inaccurate do not make the clause unreasonable, Rock Refrigeration v Jones.

Even if the clause were to be reasonable in the interests of the parties **it could be unreasonable in the public interest**, Wyatt v Kreglinger v Fernau. In Sid's case there do not appear to be public interest considerations.

The restraint clause appears to be too wide and therefore unenforceable, but the courts have been willing to save such clauses by either a process of construction or by the use of severance. In **construing a clause** the courts will seek to narrow it so as to reflect the intention to protect an employer's interests. This was seen in Home Counties Dairies v Skilton and Littlewoods Organisation Ltd v Harris. In the latter case a restraint prevented Harris, who worked in a mail order business based solely in the UK, from being employed by a rival GUS. GUS were a world-wide organisation involved in various businesses. The clause was construed as only applying to employment for GUS in mail order in the UK. It could be argued the restraint clause seeks implicitly to cover Grantmore's area of operation in Newcastle and the North of England only. Can it be said with any certainty what is meant by the North East of England? The process of construction was criticised by Simon Brown LJ in Mont v Mills as weakening the incentive for employers to draft appropriately worded restaint clauses in the first place and so must be treated with some caution.

Grantmore could argue that the offending words may be **severed**. This may be done by using the 'blue pencil' test which means that words may be excised so long as what remains makes grammatical sense. This must be achieved without the addition or substitution of words, Goldsoll v Goldman and the nature of the clause must not be altered, Attwood v Lamont The only severable part of the restraint clause would seem to be in paragraph (iii), 'or any related business'. Paragraphs (i) and (ii) could be severed in their entirety but this appears to alter the nature of the clause.

In conclusion, the restraint clause while seeking to protect the proprietary interests of Grantmore, trade secrets and the customer connection, is too wide in terms of duration, geographical area and employment area. The processes of construction and severance do not seem capable of saving the clause and, in consequence, Sid is able to enter his new employment.

As you can see in the above example there is an underlying structure, within which discussion of relevant legal principles and their application may take place. Note how a number of legal issues have been identified and then considered with reference to relevant principles of law. After such identification and consideration, the impact on the facts of the problem is then explained. The process of answering questions under examination conditions is developed further in the next chapter and the above answer is analysed in further detail.

■ **CHECKLIST**

■ **UNDERGRADUATE EXAMINATIONS**

▶ The prerequisite to success in unseen law examinations is, to a great extent, memory and recall but this is not enough. These must be allied to a demonstration of analytical ability.

▶ Always remember it is only the written words in your examination script on which you will be assessed, so you must present your work in a clear and intelligible way.

▶ Examinations take a variety of forms. Be aware that different approaches may need to be adopted.

▶ If you are allowed to take materials into an examination be thoroughly acquainted with the layout and content of such materials.

▶ When revising you might find it helpful to create a revision timetable.

▶ Preparation for examinations should be undertaken throughout your year of study. Ensure that you organise your notes and materials well in advance of the examinations to allow you, when the revision period arrives, to concentrate on absorbing the information contained in your notes.

▶ Look for a structure in your notes and highlight this so that you can readily identify it.

▶ Exercise control over those parts of the examination process where control is possible.

▶ Try to lessen the impact of the parts of the process where you have no control. Plan ahead by identifying the underlying structures to the areas of law you study.

Chapter 12

Answering degree-level examination questions

. . . .

Answering law examination questions

In this chapter a close look is given to the answering of law examination questions. This is not, of course, the *raison d'etre* of legal education. Passing examinations is still, however, the main criterion of successful completion of your education. In the bulk of law examinations the unseen written question-paper is the norm. This is likely to remain so for the foreseeable future, especially because the professional bodies – the Law Society and the Bar Council – are insistent that this form of examination is a part of the essential test for would-be practitioners. Exams and examination technique must, therefore, be taken seriously. Much can be gained in the way both of enhanced performance and reduced anxiety by giving some rational and detailed thought as to how to approach the examinations.

Setting and marking questions for examinations is notoriously easier than answering them. If students had experience of being examiners they would be more successful in their role as examinees: the changes they need to make in style and content would be blindingly clear. It is necessary to return as a starting place to the question – what is special about the study of law? But, this time concentrating on a slightly different facet – what is special about answering law examination questions?

Types of questions

Law examination questions are readily divisible into two kinds: problem questions and essay questions. These two types of question will be dealt with separately and illustrations of how to produce a high quality answer and an analysis of the thought processes involved given. In reading these, it should be borne in mind that what is illustrated is how to answer examination questions during an examination *not* how to produce a complete account of each problem raised with no constraints as to time or space. Students who had the opportunity to scrutinise answers submitted by successful students would be surprised at their apparent simplicity and very often their brevity. There is no need either for a good answer to be packed with the names of countless cases. A good answer will reflect clarity of expression, clarity of analysis and a succinct and relevant use of cited authority.

There is not time in an examination, unless you know very little, for everything you know on a subject to be spelled out. For the knowledgeable student it is a paradox that a first class answer is as much a matter of omission or ellipsis as of inclusion. Equally it is an important truism that students most often fail not because they do not know enough to pass but because they are not able to deploy their hard-learned knowledge to good effect.

Problem questions

Students generally find problem questions more of a challenge than essay questions. But they should not be avoided – they provide plenty of opportunity for the well-prepared examinee to shine. Problem questions consist of a series of factual clues upon which to hang discussion of legal principles. The examiner has included the facts for a particular purpose and a clear understanding of the law allows the points to be readily identified. Questions asked vary from the coyly brief (for example, the notorious question: 'A lets down B's bicycle tyres. Discuss.') to questions apparently styled on classical opera with many characters and a diffuse but strong story-line. In each kind of problem, the essential key is the identification of the actual legal issues at which the examiner is aiming – though this is harder in a three-hour examination if the examiner has used a scatter-gun instead of a laser.

The punchline in problem questions

The punchline in problem questions is the rubric and it is frequently misunderstood or carelessly or cavalierly ignored. You will be asked to respond to the collection of strange events which make up a problem question in various ways. You may be asked to 'Advise Mr Smith' or 'Explain the defences available to D', or simply to 'Discuss', a command much like the instruction commonly added to Scottish problem questions: 'Quid Juris?' (meaning of course: 'What is the law applicable to these facts?'). Note that in being asked to give advice this is not an invitation to give unbalanced counsel; it is necessary in advising a party to explain the strengths as well as the weaknesses of their legal position.

It is important, as mentioned in the previous chapter, to follow this instruction to the letter. In cold print, this may seem rather trivial advice. In the examination hall it is all too often forgotten and the knowledgeable student comes to grief by answering the wrong question. It is especially easy if you are asked to advise multiple parties to overlook the different considerations which the examiner has skilfully made applicable to one or other of them. An addition to the rubric in the form of some slight twist to the facts is also often overlooked* and the proportion of the marks which the examiner has mentally reserved for this section of the answer jeopardised.

A method for answering problem questions

Faced with a body of facts and an instruction how should you set about imposing some order on the question. A device which has helped law students structure and write answers over the years at Northumbria University is the mnemonic IDEA. This stands for the following:

Identify the legal problems raised by the facts of the question;

Define any legal concepts or terms raised by the facts of the question;

Explain legal principles relevant to the issue raised by the facts, supported by authority; and then

Apply the stated law to the facts of the problem.

By using IDEA to address individually each issue raised by the facts of a question you build up an answer which demonstrates your abilities to successfully analyse the problem, select appropriate law, explain the legal principles and then advise on the impact of the law on the facts. It is not suggested that an answer should fall into four sections, that is identification, definition, explanation and application, rather that each issue is treated in this way. So if there are five issues in a question then IDEA will be used five times. This ensures that the law and its application to the facts are interwoven throughout the essay and avoids a common problem in student answers of pages of law followed by a half-page of application, which never quite connects back to the relevant principle. By way of an illustration of this process let us once more consider the answer discussed in the previous chapter, on p 204 et seq.

> **HINT** →
> The mnemonic IDEA (Identify, Define, Explain and Apply) is a useful template for answering problem questions.

---

* For example, in the question last noted, "Would it make any difference if A quite foolishly assumed the bicycle was his own?"

> **✖ EXAMPLE**
>
> The law may refuse to allow a contract to have legal effect on the grounds of illegality. Illegality includes contracts for the commission of a crime or a civil wrong and contracts contrary to public policy. This latter ground encompasses **contracts in restraint of trade**.
>
> > Identification The student has identified the overall legal issue raised by the question and sought to place it in its context.
>
> Cheshire, Fifoot and Furmston describe a contract in restraint of trade as: 'one by which a party restricts his future liberty to carry on his trade, business or profession in such manner and with such persons as he chooses'. Such **contracts are prima facie void, but may be valid if reasonable in the interests of the parties and in the interests of the public**, Nordenfelt v Maxim Nordenfelt Guns and Ammunition Co.
>
> > Definition The nature of restraint of trade and the doctrine of restraint of trade are defined.
>
> The doctrine does not apply to all contracts that potentially restrain, Esso Petroleum Co Ltd v Harper's Garage (Stourport) Ltd. In this case Lord Wilberforce said that there is no comprehensive test for deciding whether the doctrine applies to particular contracts, but that **the doctrine applies to certain contracts, such as those between employer and employee** as in this question.
>
> > Identification There is identification of a specific legal issue, some **explanation** (including use of authority) and **application**; the problem concerns an employer and employee.
>
> In order for the clause in the contract between Grantmore Bank and Sid to be valid, Grantmore must establish that it has a **proprietary interest**, a trade secret or the customer connection, to protect and that the restraint is reasonable in the protection of that interest. Grantmore, as an employer, may not protect against competition from Sid after he leaves its employment, Herbert Morris Ltd v Saxelby. However, Grantmore may argue that Sid has information which is in the nature of a **trade secret**, which is a protectable interest. In Lansing Linde Ltd v Kerr, Staughton LJ said that a trade secret included confidential information which if given to a competitor would cause real harm to the owner of the secret. Sid knows of various new financial products that the Bank is intending to launch on the market which, as in Littlewoods Organisation Ltd v Harris where knowledge of an unpublished catalogue was considered to be in the nature of a trade secret, could also amount to a trade secret. Of course, Grantmore would have to show that details of the new products were indeed secret.

Identification There is identifcation of a specific legal issue, that of a proprietary interest, the trade secret, and **definition** of what is, and what is not, a trade secret. There is an **explanation** (including use of authority) of the law relating to trade secrets and, finally, an **application** of the law to the facts, are the new financial products proprietary interests capable of protection?

Another possible interest is the **customer connection**, as Sid handles the affairs of more than a thousand customers. In Herbert Morris Ltd v Saxelby it was said that an employee must have some influence over the customers to establish this interest. Grantmore would have to show that Sid had acquired such influence. If Sid has no face-to face contact with the customers then, as in S W Strange Ltd v Mann, it is unlikely that a relationship of influence will be established.

Again there is **identification** of a specific legal issue, that of another proprietary interest, the customer connection, an **explanation** (including use of authority) of the law relating to the customer connection and, finally, an **application** of the law to the facts, Sid may have acquired influence over Grantmore's customers and so should Sid leave the customers may go with him.

If Grantmore is able to establish the existence of one or both interests then it must further show that the **restraint clause in the contract is reasonable in the protection of such interest or interests**.

This sentence **identifies** an issue that again may be subdivided into parts; IDEA may be used in relation to each and all of the parts.

Consideration must be given to the **duration of the clause and to its geographical and employment area**. The operation of the clause is to last for 2 years. Each interest gives rise to different considerations. First, the information on new products; it may be argued that as soon as these are released to the public or within a short period thereafter the interest will end. This is similar to Littlewoods Organisation Ltd v Harris where a restraint of 1 year was reasonable, as the catalogue once published would only last for six months. On this basis 2 years may be too long. As to the customer connection, how strong is the influence? If Sid's position is relatively lowly, as in M&S Drapers v Reynolds, the influence may weaken before the end of 2 years.

This paragraph **identifies** and deals with the issue of duration of the restraint clause. An **explanation** of the law, supported by authority, is given and it is **applied** to each of the interests identified. Note there may be no need to define terms in every application of IDEA.

The restraint clause does not include a **geographical area** expressly, but seeks in paragraph (i) to prevent competition. As stated above competition cannot be prevented per se, <u>Herbert Morris Ltd v Saxelby</u>. Paragraph (ii) is an anti-solicitation clause and seeks to protect the customer connection, but it refers to 'any person, firm or company who shall have engaged the services of the bank' rather than merely to those customers with whom Sid has had contact. As such paragraph (ii) seems to be wider than is reasonably necessary for the protection of the interest. Finally, in paragraph (iii), the reference to employment in 'the financial services industry or any related industry' seems again to be **too wide as it specifies forms of employment** in which Sid has not been engaged while in the employment of Grantmore. In <u>Commercial Plastics v Vincent</u> an employee, engaged in a small specialist section of the PVC calendering industry, was restrained from working in any part of the PVC calendering field. This restraint was too wide and unenforceable.

> In this paragraph there is **identification** of two further issues – the geographical and employment areas of the clause. Reference is made to the approach of the courts to these issues and supporting authority. An attempt is made to analyse the words of the clause and to establish if the clause goes further than is necessary in the protection of the interests.

The use of 'howsoever caused' in relation to termination is of no effect as the restraint clause would be unenforceable should Grantmore wrongfully dismiss Sid, <u>General Billposting v Atkinson</u>. Note however that the words 'howsoever caused' are not subject to the restraint of trade doctrine and therefore, even though legally inaccurate do not make the clause unreasonable, <u>Rock Refrigeration v Jones</u>.

> The clause is further analysed, with the significance of the words 'howsoever caused' being explored.

Even if the clause were to be reasonable in the interests of the parties **it could be unreasonable in the public interest**, <u>Wyatt v Kreglinger v Fernau</u>. In Sid's case there do not appear to be public interest considerations.

The legal issue is again **identified** but as the facts of the problem do not give rise to any difficulties the issue can be dealt with briefly.

The restraint clause appears to be too wide and therefore unenforceable, but the courts have been willing to save such clauses by either a process of construction or by the use of severance. In **construing a clause** the courts will seek to narrow it so as to reflect the intention to protect an employer's interests. This was seen in <u>Home Counties Dairies v Skilton</u> and <u>Littlewoods Organisation Ltd v Harris</u>. In the latter case a restraint prevented Harris, who worked in a mail order business based solely in the UK, from being employed by a rival GUS. GUS were a world-wide organisation involved in various businesses. The clause was construed as only applying to employment for GUS in mail order in the UK. It could be argued the restraint clause seeks implicitly to cover Grantmore's area of operation in Newcastle and the North of England only. Can it be said with any certainty what is meant by the North East of England? The process of construction was criticised by Simon Brown LJ in <u>Mont v Mills</u> as weakening the incentive for employers to draft appropriately worded restaint clauses in the first place and so must be treated with some caution.

> Even if the restraint clause is too wide it may be saved. So another issue is **identified**. The process is **defined** and then **explained** by reference to the relevant case law. There is an attempt to **apply** this process to the facts.

Grantmore could argue that the offending words may be **severed**. This may be done by using the 'blue pencil' test which means that words may be excised so long as what remains makes grammatical sense. This must be achieved without the addition or substitution of words, <u>Goldsoll v Goldman</u> and the nature of the clause must not be altered, <u>Attwood v Lamont</u>. The only severable part of the restraint clause would seem to be in paragraph (iii), 'or any related business'. Paragraphs (i) and (ii) could be severed in their entirety but this appears to alter the nature of the clause.

> Finally, the issue of severance is **identified, explained** and **applied**, albeit briefly. Obviously, an examination is time limited and it may be necessary to truncate an explanation even though you have more to say.

In conclusion, the restraint clause while seeking to protect the proprietary interests of Grantmore, trade secrets and the customer connection, is too wide in terms of duration, geographical area and employment area. The processes of construction and severance do not seem capable of saving the clause and, in consequence, Sid is able to enter his new employment.

> The student then sums up the potential advice to Sid noting that the clause does not prevent Sid from accepting new employment.

Note from the above example the pattern that emerges when using IDEA. It is a formula used over and over again. This allows an examiner to see that you have analysed the question by identifying an issue and have shown that you understand by choosing relevant law and then defining terms and explaining the principles. Finally, you complete the examiner's appreciation of your understanding by demonstrating how the law may be used, by connecting the principles of law to the facts of the problem. Application in this way shows another facet of your understanding. Note the integrated approach promoted by using IDEA the identification of the issue, the explanation of the relevant law and the application of the law to the facts occurs in a paragraph and then starts again with the next issue. In this way you avoid a descriptive account of the law at the beginning of your essay and a paragraph of application at the end of your essay, with no real connection being made between the two parts.

The above answer also illustrates the succinct approach you must adopt in answering examination questions. Each issue could be dealt with in much greater depth.

For example, the issue relating to the use of 'howsoever caused' in the restaint clause could give rise to a much longer answer. The case of *General Bill Posting v Atkinson* could be explained and the difficulties raised by the decision explored, for example, why do some contractual obligations survive a repudiatory breach of contract and yet a restraint clause does not survive such a breach by an employer? Indeed the validity of the rule in *General Billposting v Atkinson* was doubted in *Rock Refrigeration v Jones* by Phillips LJ.

Exploration of this point might mean that you do not cover all the issues raised by the question or that you spend too much time on answering this question to the detriment of the other answers you have to give in the examination. The time constraint in an examination only allows you to identify the issue raised, briefly state the law as it presently stands and then explain how this may apply to the circumstances in the question. There is an large element of judgement involved and you need to develop a technique for this type of assessment. Practice under examination conditions is essential as this will alert you to what it is possible to write in the time allowed and also provide useful feedback should you submit the answer to your tutor.

Structure of problem questions

As was explained in the previous chapter, areas of law have a structure that can be used to structure an answer to a problem question. The bulk of problem questions contain more than one issue and have other similarities in their structure which make it possible to describe a common method of approach. Having in mind a settled idea as to how you will attack the daunting set of facts presented to you is particularly important when you are faced with questions containing complex facts and many parties – a genre of question which seems to have become prevalent in recent years.

It is rare for a problem question to contain only one problem and it is important to remember that each problem raised must be dealt with. Where there are several problems, they will commonly require answering in a conditional sequence. This means that your answer to one stage of the question will depend on your answer to the previous stage. It can usually be assumed that the 'answer' to any stage in this sequence is problematical, that is it is a question of argument. This means that the following stage of the problem must be approached on the basis of more than one hypothetical answer to the first stage and so on. It is the ability of the student to analyse a problem into this sequence and answer the problem systematically according to that pattern that is to a large extent the determinant factor in success. By and large, students will carry with them into the examination the same knowledge of very much the same case law and in answering problem questions it is this method of using and applying that knowledge that is most important. It will help to proceed to an analysis of a typical examination problem question.

HINT →
Being aware of the structure of an area of law will help you correctly sequence your answer.

✖ EXAMPLE 1

Take as an example the following question which would be found in one guise or another on very many first year contract law papers. It concerns the problems of formation of contract and the legal approaches to one party's attempts to introduce a clause restricting his liability under the contract. (You will probably find it helpful to return to the detailed answers to the exam questions and reconsider them as you come to the pertinent subject in your course.)

'There is a notice in a launderette. It says 'NO LIABILITY TO USERS FOR LOSS OR DAMAGE AT ALL'. The notice is sellotaped to the inside of the door. A few yards from the door is a dry-cleaning machine; it requires two fifty-pence coins to operate it . . . Alfred enters the shop. He places two fifty-pence coins in the machine. He does not see the notice. He places his sleeping-bag in the machine. The cleaning-fluid is too strong and dissolves his sleeping-bag. When Alfred extricates the remnants of his sleeping-bag his fingers are badly burned by the cleaning-fluid.

Advise Alfred on the application of contract law to his predicament.

Would your advice differ if he had read the notice after inserting his coins and before pressing the 'START OPERATION' button on the machine?'

First consider the answer given by the student who does just enough to merit a pass mark.

Answer A

The notice on the door is an exclusion clause. It must be part of the contract. In *Chapelton v Barry UDC* a man hired a deck-chair but it collapsed and he was injured. He had been given a ticket by the deck-chair attendant and the ticket had a notice on the back saying that the Council was not liable but the court said that this was not part of the contract and so he could recover. In *Olley v Marlborough Court* in a hotel case they were liable for loss of luggage where the notice was not seen until after the person went into his room in the hotel and in *Thornton v Shoe Lane Parking* the result was the same when a man was injured in a car-park – he could sue although there was a notice he did not see till he was in the car-park. The case is like the ticket-cases *Parker v SE Railway* and *Thompson v* LM&S Rly and the notice must be brought to the attention of the person before the contract is made. The position might be different if Alfred has been in the habit of using the launderette and had seen the notice before. Interesting cases on this point are *Hollier v Rambler Motors* and *McCutcheon v David MacBrayne*. This means that a course of dealings might have the effect of incorporating the exclusion clause in the contract so that the user could not sue. I would advise Alf that the clause is probably not part of the contract. The Unfair Contract Terms Act might also apply and since this is not a Sale of Goods Act case then whether the clause applied would depend on whether it is reasonable or not. This clause is not reasonable because there is no reason why Arthur should know that the cleaning-fluid is too strong.

If he had seen the exclusion clause it would have been part of the contract and anyway the clause was not reasonable so Alfred could still sue.

Alongside this, for comparison, consider the following answer which might be produced to this question by a first class student:

Answer B

It seems correct to assume in this case that the launderette is liable prima facie for breach of contract. This seems to be a clear breach of the implied term that the supplier of a service acting in the course of a business will use reasonable care and skill.

This problem is concerned with the effect of the exclusion clause on the launderette's liability to Alfred. The first problem is whether the exclusion notice becomes incorporated in the contract to clean Alfred's goods. If it does then the next problem is whether the exclusion covers the breach and finally if the exclusion clause does not become part of the contract and apply to this breach, whether its effect is vitiated by the Unfair Contract Terms Act 1977 in respect of either loss of the bag or personal injury. Finally, a different question of incorporation requiring an analysis of when the contract is formed is posed by the situation where Alfred does read the notice after inserting his coins.

A clause contained in a notice of this kind will be incorporated in the contract if reasonable steps have been taken to draw it to the attention of the other party – a principle established in *Parker v SE Railway*. Whether reasonable steps have been taken to bring the clause to the attention of Alfred is a question of fact – although the burden of showing this will be greater if, as here, the exclusion clause is not contained in a contractual document (cf *Chapelton v Barry UDC*). Also where the clause has a very serious effect such as excluding liability for personal injury, as may be the case here, then it may need to be more clearly drawn to the other party's attention (see eg *Thornton v Shoe Lane Parking Ltd* and cf dicta of Denning LJ in *Spurling v Bradshaw* [1965]).

Where Alfred has read the exclusion clause as is indicated in the rider to the question it will be incorporated only if the above rule is satisfied or if he read the exclusion clause before the contract was made – see *Olley v Marlborough Court* where the exclusion clause was read by a hotel guest in the room after booking into the hotel. An analysis of a similar situation to the problem in terms of offer and acceptance is given by the Court of Appeal in *Thornton v Shoe Lane Parking*. The ticket machine there (the laundry machine here) is seen as accepting the offer by issuing a ticket. The notice in this case was read after the offer was accepted.

In this case the laundry machine may be making a symbolic offer which Alfred accepted by putting in his money – in that case the notice was read too late to be incorporated. Alternatively, Alfred made an offer which the machine accepted (by switching on or flashing a 'Ready' light perhaps). On the facts as given it is difficult to see which is this case and whether the notice was read before the acceptance or not.

Even if the notice becomes a term of the contract, the laundry may not be able to escape liability in reliance on it. The courts construe such clauses 'contra proferentem' this is against the person relying thereon (see eg *Houghton v Trafalgar Insurance*). An example of this approach is in a situation where, as here, there might be strict liability (for breach of an implied term to clean the goods or even an express warranty written on the machine to that effect) and also liability for doing so carelessly (that is, negligence). In such a case a clause would be interpreted to apply only to the strict liability as in *Rutter v Palmer* unless the contrary was clearly intended as in *Archdale v Conservices*. Here the clause 'loss or damage at all' is like the 'all loss or damage whatsoever' in *Smith v SW Switchgear* – where the courts upheld the narrow rule of construction.

If there were no liability for such an express or implied term but only for negligent inflicting of the loss and injury in this case, then the clause would apply to such liability only if clearly intended to do so. A possible comparison is *Hollier v Rambler Motors*. A clause excluding liability for fire damage in a garage did not exclude liability for such damage caused by the proprietor's negligence – the notice only gave a warning that they are not liable for such damage not caused by their negligence. Such a construction could well be placed on the clause in this case.

Finally the clause will be affected by the Unfair Contract Terms Act 1977. The launderette's liability is business liability within s 1. The effect of s 2 is that liability for the personal injury to Alfred is caused by the negligence of the launderette in using too strong a concentrate of cleaning-fluid and cannot be excluded at all. Similarly s 2 prevents exclusion for negligent damage to Alfred's sleeping-bag unless such clause is reasonable.

So far as strict liability for breach of an express or implied term of a contract is concerned, s 3 of the Act applies. Assuming as seems likely that Alfred is a consumer in this contract (s 12) as the launderette is in the business of cleaning and Alfred does not make the contract in the course of a business, then liability for breach of such a term can be excluded only if the exclusion is reasonable.

In each of these cases the test of reasonableness is contained in s 11 of the Act and is in terms of fairness and reasonableness given the circumstances in the hypothetical contemplation of the parties at the time the contract was made. Why should a user of a launderette be expected to contemplate that the owner will not only use a dangerously strong concentrate of fluid but also escape scot free – especially when this is a matter peculiarly within the owner's control?

Comparison of answers

A comparison of these two answers (A and B) is revealing as to what is required by a candidate in answering a problem question.

Introduction

The question of whether to write an introduction to an examination answer is a vexed one and regrettably one on which different examiners do differ rather markedly. The advice given here is if you are answering a problem question then a general introduction should be avoided.

For example, in answering this problem a student might write:

> This question is concerned with exclusion clauses. Such clauses have been the subject of much judicial and legislative concern. There has been a running battle between the interests of those who might be adversely affected by the operation of generously worded exclusion clauses and the interests of those seeking by skilful drafting of exclusion clauses to reduce the economic burden of liability for damage suffered by the users of their goods or services.

This is an attempt to set the problem against the background of the area of law involved.

There is no doubt that a discussion along these lines would be of great interest and even of value in understanding the forces at play. But, it is not an answer to the problem. It is not the job of work in hand – *advising Alfred*. Some examiners will not mind wading through such a prolix introduction but it can count for little or nothing as it does not answer the question – other examiners will be (perhaps only unconsciously) somewhat prejudiced by the gratuitous burden this placed upon their valuable time. In answering a problem question the candidate is consequently advised to address the question directly and at once to answer the problem in a brief manner. An introduction specific to the problem may, however, help the student to proceed to a systematic exposition of his or her answer.

The more specific introduction

Answer A contains no introduction and Answer B an introduction of a particular kind. The introduction given in Answer B is recommended for the following reasons: the task that very many students find really difficult in answering problem questions is to pose the problem which has to be answered. A problem question will commonly pose a number of questions which must be answered in some kind of pattern, and that pattern is a conditional sequence. The first step in seeing what this pattern is in respect of a particular problem question is to restate the problem, not in terms of the facts, *but in terms of the legal problems which they pose*. The students faced with the egregious factual situations beloved of law examiners must first do

HINT →

At the outset of your answer identify the overall legal area raised by the facts of the problem.

the same – *state the problem*. Remember restating the facts of the question is not analysis, attracts no marks and is in consequence a waste of your time.

Added to this is the very difficult dimension for the average student that the question will contain a number of *dependent problems* which fall to be analysed in the 'conditional' sequence outlined above. If the student can state what these problems are and the order in which he or she will take them two very important things will be achieved. First, it will be demonstrated to the examiner that the student has correctly and clearly placed the factual problem in its legal context. Second, there will be set out a clear and concise plan of the answer which is to follow – one which covers broadly all the areas to be dealt with in the answer and in a manner which will give a shape and logic to that answer.

✖ EXAMPLE

In Answer B the student first identifies a breach of contract and thus establishes liability. As the courts generally view an exclusion clause as a defence, if no liability is found then there is no need for a defence. The logic of this is clear. If there is liability, then as Answer B shows, the next issue is that of challenges to the operation and validity of the exclusion clause.

Before leaving the first note on the answers to this examination problem, it is worth examining another way of viewing the structure of the question in the form of an illustration which might make visualisation of this type of structure easier. That is in the form of a *decision tree* or *algorithm* (see p 223).

This type of flow chart or algorithm has also been suggested as a way of analysing complicated legal rules. A useful discussion of this is found in Twining and Miers *How to Do Things with Rules*.

Whether you choose to analyse the problem set in an algorithm or not, it is essential that one way or another you reach the stage of being able to analyse a lengthy problem question into a series of legal problems which your written answer will then dispose of. This can be achieved only by an exposure to a large number of such questions and practice at how to answer them. The crucial importance of this practice in the type of questions you are going to face in the examination cannot be overstated.

For the problem on p 217 a decision tree might appear as follows:

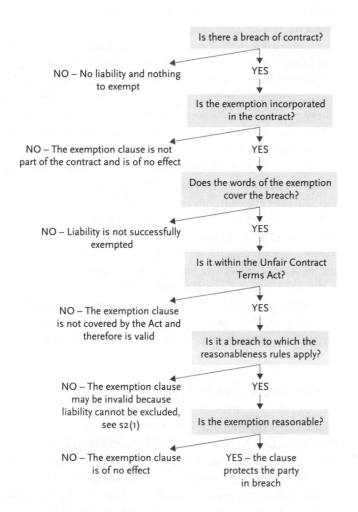

Is there a breach of contract?

NO – No liability and nothing
to exempt

YES

Is the exemption incorporated
in the contract?

NO – The exemption clause is not
part of the contract and is of no effect

YES

Does the words of the exemption
cover the breach?

NO – Liability is not successfully
exempted

YES

Is it within the Unfair Contract
Terms Act?

NO – The exemption clause
is not covered by the Act and
therefore is valid

YES

Is it a breach to which the
reasonableness rules apply?

NO – The exemption clause
may be invalid because
liability cannot be excluded,
see s2(1)

YES

Is the exemption reasonable?

NO – The exemption clause
is of no effect

YES – the clause
protects the party
in breach

Content of answers

After this digression, it is now useful to turn again to the two sample
student answers provided above and compare the different performances
of the two students.

The distinctive features of difference between Answer A and Answer
B are as follows.

(i) *Coverage.* Answer A does not cover all the different problems
     posed by the question. It is not bad on the problem of whether
     the clause is incorporated in the contract but it deals with this as

if it is the only issue of real importance and ignores the question of construction of the clause and hardly deals at all with the Unfair Contract Terms Act. In this last regard, the answer may reveal the working of a very dangerous psychological mechanism – *fear of difficulty leading to avoidance*. All students can follow the cases on incorporation – the facts are memorable and the principles simple. All lawyers find the structure of the Unfair Contract Terms Act difficult and its effect problematical. These two facts lead the weak student to concentrate on the former and to ignore the latter. But, the difficult problem does not go away. *Some areas of law are difficult to understand and hard to remember.* That is a proposition which all students can grasp. Harder to grasp is the corollary. These difficult areas are difficult for everybody. Because they are difficult they must not be evaded – neither must the student expect to reduce them to a state of simplicity which simply does not exist. These areas are difficult because they are complicated – often this is because the case or statute law is in a confused state – often, as in, say, the area of illegal contracts, an inextricably confused state.* The student must not sidestep the difficult areas of confusion and complexity to be found. Equally important neither must he or she feel inadequate because he or she cannot produce the ordered clarity which the law so often fails to present.

HINT →

Do not mentally arrive at conclusions: state explicitly your reasoning processes.

Associated with the problem of coverage is that of failing to explicitly state your reasoning processes. In Answer A the student does mention the Unfair Contract Terms Act 1977 and that the exclusion clause may be subject to a test of reasonableness, but, unlike Answer B, does not explain the circumstances in which the Act applies and the how reasonableness is to be established. In a similar way to the solution of a mathematical problem, it is the method in arriving at the solution that gains marks as this demonstrates understanding.

(ii) *Answering each part of the question.* The question, as is common, contains a rider: what if Alfred had read the notice, etc. In Answer A, the weaker student has dealt with this in a brief sentence and come to an extremely facile conclusion. In Answer B the candidate has tackled that part of the question fully, has tried to see the different legal problems raised in the altered circumstances and come up with a fair reasoned analysis of what this might be.

---

* A textbook writer tends to put this proposition more cautiously eg 'The law on this question is complex and not very satisfactory': G H Treitel *The Law of Contract* 5th edn at p 361.

(iii) *Source material.* Many points on how to introduce source material into an answer are dealt with separately (see below) – suffice it here to point out that:

Student A cites several cases on incorporation of exclusion clauses into contracts. He does not state clearly the principle illustrated by the case (see below). He cites facts that are irrelevant to the thrust of his argument, eg the thoroughly well-known story of the collapsing deck-chair. He also, and this is a particularly important point, becomes carried away on a crest of memory about the 'incorporation cases' and brings in the cases about habitual users (*Hollier v Rambler Motors*; *McCutcheon v David McBrayne*) that are not called for by the question. The student must produce authorities which are relevant to the facts given, and not deal with a factual situation which he hypothesises for himself. If the particular point as to habitual use of the launderette on incorporation is worth making on the question asked (which must be doubted) it must be made very succinctly, almost as an aside.

In contrast, student B categorises the legal problems succinctly by reference to the *principles* established in pertinent cases; eg he cites the well-known *Parker v SE Railway* case clearly as authority for a particular legal proposition which is briefly and accurately stated.

Also in contrast to student A, student B refers to the facts of the case only where necessary to make a clear comparison with the facts of the problem case and, thus, examine whether the principle in the decided case is applicable – a good example of this is the use of *Thornton v Shoe Lane Parking Ltd*, by using the facts of which student B is able to make a convincing attempt at legal analysis of the problem of incorporation in terms of the concepts of offer and acceptance and illustrate quite neatly how such reasoning might be used by the court.

Note that in an examination there is no need to state the reference to a case, eg [1964] AC 465 (such would be a great feat of memory, but would not gain you any extra marks) and usually no need to remember the date of the case. In relation to the latter point the date might be significant if there are a number of cases which conflict. It is well worth remembering the name of the deciding court as such information will help you argue the value of cases in precedent terms. For example, should a case decided by the House of Lords conflict with a Court of Appeal decision, then in precedent terms the opinion of the House of Lords has greater authority.

In an examination, should your memory fail you and a full case name not come to mind, then you may still get credit should you state one of the parties' names, eg in the *Hedley Byrne* case. Should you be unable to recall any name, then a diminished mark may still be obtained by the identification of the case by its factual content, for example 'in the case where a bank provided a carelessly compiled reference to the claimant, in respect of one of the bank's customers, which caused loss'.

A final useful comparison between Answer A and B is their different success in referring to statute sources. A is hopelessly vague and manages to refrain from penetrating the veils covering the Unfair Contract Terms Act 1977 in a way that leaves the examiner with considerable doubt not only as to whether he can apply the detailed and important distinctions within the Act skilfully but even whether he knows what they are. Student B, on the other hand, makes a good start of taking the reader (albeit quickly, as the question demands the covering of considerable ground) through the relevant distinctions showing clearly by reference to specific provisions that he understands the framework of the Act and can apply it in a situation such as this.

(iv) *Statement of applicable principles.* It is noticeable that Answer B exhibits a much clearer disposition and analysis of legal principles than Answer A. The important difference here is that in Answer A the relevant principles are hinted at, eg in the opening reference to the exclusion clause, the candidate says: 'It must be part of the contract.' Candidate B tries to state the relevant rule as a legal principle, viz 'A clause contained in a notice of this kind will be incorporated in the contract if reasonable steps have been taken to draw it to the attention of the other party'. The rule itself is obviously familiar to all law students. The credit, however, is given to student B for a clear, lawyerly statement of the rule in its relevant context clearly illustrated by pertinent case law.

> **HINT** ➡
> Each statement of principle must be supported by authority.

Essay questions

It is now helpful to look at an answer to an essay question. Essay questions are often deceptive. They appear easy but have hidden facets which deceive all but the very well prepared student. It is all too easy to produce a 'pat', straightforward answer which is simply a mundane account of the relevant area of law and can achieve only a mediocre grade. The difficulty is that some students are content to describe the law arising from a question, rather than analysing the essay question and then moulding relevant information to the identified requirements of the essay title. Often essay questions are seen by students as a 'soft' option to the more terrifying-seeming problem questions. On the other hand, it is probably harder to produce a really good answer to an essay question. Much more is required of the student in creating an answer – the shape of the answer is not, as is the case in problem questions, dictated by a sequence of facts presented in the question itself. A great danger, therefore, is producing an answer which is simply so much regurgitated and formless material more or less connected with the problems at which the essay was specifically directed.

✖ EXAMPLE 2

This question occurred in a first year contract paper.

> The statement that a claimant is to be compensated for his loss is not, in itself, particularly helpful. For a breach of contract may cause many different kinds of loss and we have to ask for which of these kinds of loss compensation will be given.

> Discuss.

A very ordinary pass answer provided by one student read as follows.

Answer

Breach of contract has taken a most interesting turn into the area of injury to feelings and it is the latter aspect that brings a question over when particularly damages can and cannot be recovered. Initially one must show that one has suffered loss as a result of a breach.

When a contract is broken the contract comes to an end and damages are recoverable for the loss sustained by the injured party. The damages received must be only the loss to the plaintiff and punitive damages over and above those suffered cannot be claimed. Although in some contracts eg the sale of land and contracts in which a trade secret is involved the plaintiff may finish with a profit being more than he could otherwise have made – *Maxim Nordenfeldt v Nordenfeldt*.

Furthermore, the injured party must prove that a duty was owed to him by the defendant, that the duty was breached and that as a result of that he received damage, in short he must prove some form of damages either to his person, personality or property. *Ruxley v Forsyth* provides an example of the law developing to compensate for non-financial loss.

The plaintiff is also able to claim for reliance loss, being the costs expended in expectancy of the contract being performed eg in *Anglia TV v Reed* the performer withdrew and they were able to recover this loss from him. Similarly loss of benefit of profits they could have made and restitution of damage caused is recoverable.

The damage caused must not be too remote and it must be calculable. *Hadley v Baxendale* set out the principle of recovery in contract, the case involves a mill shaft which was (unknown to the carrier) essential to the manufacturing process. It was sent for repair and the carrier was told to make the journey with all haste but he was not told why. The outcome was two rules. First, losses are claimable for losses which are a direct consequence of the act and secondly that losses were also recoverable if they were within the 'contemplation' of the parties. The test is thus different from tort. The basic ideas have remained as case law has developed. The *Victoria Laundries* case thus allowed a claim for losses of normal trade, but not an 'unexpected Government deal'. The *Heron II* allowed full recovery of lost sums because the ship carrying the sugar should reasonably have had it within its contemplation that the sugar was for the market at Basra and that it was unreasonable to extend the journey time from 12 to 29 days during which sugar prices slumped.

Parsons (Livestock) v Uttey Ingham tends to favour the tort principles and differs little from the similar tort case (the *Seale-Hayne* case). Nevertheless, it does point out that a difference exists. A similar case against a solicitor for incompetent conveyancing draws once more upon the *Hadley v Baxendale* principles.

The damages claimable must be calculated by the courts and the fact that it is a difficult task is no reason not to bother to sue eg *Chaplin v Hicks* in which a beauty contestant was awarded exemplary damages.

Finally the vexed question of whether or not a person can claim for loss to their happiness. Recent cases answer this question in the affirmative. *Bailey v Bullock* allowed a damage claim for a man whose mother-in-law had stopped with him, in *Cook v Spanish Holiday Tours* a honeymoon couple received damages for what is in effect loss of happiness. *Jackson v Horizon Holidays*, *Jarvis v Swan Tours* and *Farley v Skinner* are similar and reflect the modern trend.

Analysis of the above answer and lessons to be learned about answering essay questions

Among law examiners, it is axiomatic that the good student will be as likely to tend to answer problem questions as the bad to answer essay questions. It seems even a common creed among examiners that the essay questions are there to give the weak student a chance. Certainly it seems easy in practice to muddle through an essay without showing any distinction but hard to give an answer *demonstrating* real ability. There is no reason why this should be so, particularly since all law students have plenty of essay-writing experience in school examinations, and the advice given there as to form, directness and clarity is equally germane in answering law essays; but it is rarely, in the heat of the moment, put into practice. Let us examine the pertinent points a little further.

Form

Virtually all the points on answering an essay question can be subsumed under this head. An answer to an essay must follow a clear logical pattern.

The above essay is, in contract, typical of the average approach to answering this kind of question. The answer contains a fair amount of material but it pours onto the page straight from the student's turbulent brain. There is enough there to show the student has a fair smattering of knowledge about the topic under question but nothing to show that he or she can analyse, weigh the relative significance of different cases and provide a considered answer to the question asked.

When you are familiar with the topic covered by the essay you should try yourself to sketch out the form of answer that could be used to display your knowledge and understanding of the material. The following points should help you with this:

> **HINT** ⇒
> In writing an essay you must give thought to the form of your answer.

(i) How could you restate the question so as to provide an introduction which describes the legal problems you are going to discuss?

(ii) How would you state and illustrate the normal rules which apply in this area?

(iii) How would you state and illustrate the rules applying to more exceptional areas which illustrate deviation from the 'normal rules' which you have already outlined?

(iv) What particular areas of more recent development in the area would you single out for more lengthy treatment? How would you relate these to the theoretical background you have already set out?

(v) Try to round your essay off by opening up vistas of unsolved but important questions, or hinting at policy implications.

Other points to note

HINT ⇒
Principles of law must be explained clearly and fully.

(i) Note how badly principles of law are set out in the essay. A good example is the basic principle in *Hadley v Baxendale*. You must practise both in writing and orally in seminars the basic skill of formulating succinct clear statements of legal rules.

(ii) The essay does not provide a direct and straightforward answer to the question, instead leaving the examiner to speculate from the amorphous pile of evidence supplied by the student as to whether he understands the question or not.

(iii) Note the sloppiness of expression throughout the essay.

(iv) When you have examined the essay carefully, and considered the form that the author of this essay might have used you might find it helpful to write out sections of the essay to see how easy it would be to improve the woeful grade by taking notice of the above points.

✖ EXAMPLE 3

In this third example a further question will be taken and a method of producing an answer examined at greater length.

It will be helpful to work through one more problem question which is a salient example of a typical genre, that is, problem questions where there are a number of issues and parties to be sorted out. The following is an example of a typical first year tort question:

Adam, a surveyor, was sent by his company to inspect a ruined castle which it is thinking of buying. Ben owns the castle. Above the entrance gate was a sign 'No liability is accepted for any injury to any person entering this castle however caused'. Adam took his seven-year-old daughter, Catherine, with him to the castle because her mother was working. Adam fell into a dungeon through a rotten trapdoor and was trapped 50 feet below ground level. Catherine rushed off for help. She tripped over in the passageway as she hurried towards the exit. Adam died as a result of the incident and Catherine was severely injured. Ethel, Adam's widow, seeks advice on any tortious claims she has against Ben on behalf either of herself, Adam's estate or Catherine.

Advise her.

In dealing with questions which have numerous parties and facts your first task is working out some kind of structure for your answer. From the beginning you need to note the claims you are asked to deal with – these are *Ethel (on behalf of Adam's estate) v Ben*; *Ethel v Ben*; *Ethel (on behalf of Catherine) v Ben*. In your answer you must deal separately with each of these three possible actions. By doing so you avoid the potential for confusion in your answer. Also by 'jumping' from action to action the logic of your answer might be lost and you may also fail to consider all points raised by each action.

HINT ⇒
Where a question has multiple actions, deal with each action separately.

Secondly, you must proceed to analyse each 'action' into the 'points of law' involved and the result will be something similar to the following.

Ethel (on behalf of Adam's estate) v Ben

(a) Has she a right of action in respect of A's death?

(b) B's liability to Adam – is he a visitor? – standard of care owed?

(c) Exclusion notice – business use? – other defences? eg contributory negligence.

Ethel v Ben

Brief explanation of Fatal Accidents Act claim.

Ethel (on behalf of Catherine) v Ben

(a) Possible claim under Fatal Accidents Act (as above).

(b) Catherine a lawful visitor or a trespasser?

(c) If lawful visitor, standard of care owed.

(d) If trespasser, duty under Occupier's Liability Act 1984 – explain.

(e) Does B owe C a separate duty of care in her role as rescuer?

(f) Defences – possible contributory negligence? Causation.

HINT ⇒
Analyse each action in terms of the points of law raised.

You will see that even writing out the points to cover in note-form produces a lengthy answer. The difficulty in this kind of question is to give emphasis to the more difficult points, while still presenting your reasoning through the whole problem in a complete and coherent answer. The two difficult points are the exclusion of liability, dealing separately with the case of a lawful visitor and that of a trespasser, and the rather difficult conceptual problem of liability to a rescuer who is also a trespassing child. When you have analysed sufficient examination questions purposefully, you will not find it necessary to write out notes on the question. You will be able to analyse the question into its parts without putting pen to paper. When you are able to achieve this it will save you much time in the examination. Some students find it more helpful to continue to write in note-form to the answer – and it may, indeed, assist as an aide-memoire while you write your full answer. It may be concluded, however, that the need to write 'against the clock' still plays so large a part in law examinations that the counsel of perfection is to develop the facility of analysing questions mentally.

Having produced in your mind or on paper a scheme of your answer all that remains is to write your answer. To the present question, a first-class student's answer in examination conditions might be along the following lines.

Taking first Ethel's claim on behalf of herself or of Adam's estate: Ethel is enabled by the Law Reform (Miscellaneous Provisions) Act 1934 to bring an action against Ben providing she is Adam's personal representative. She can also bring an action under the Fatal Accidents Act 1976 on behalf of herself and Catherine. In the Law Reform Act action, Ethel recovers the damages due to Adam (but not in respect of loss of earnings after his death – see now Administration of Justice Act 1982, s 4) – and in the Fatal Accident claim, damages based on her and Catherine's financial dependency on Adam.

In each case, Ethel's claim depends first on establishing Ben's liability in negligence to Adam. It appears from the question most likely that Adam was a lawful visitor to Ben's castle. He was, thus, owed the common duty of care under s 2 of the Occupier's Liability Act 1957. This duty is one 'to take such care as in all the circumstances of the case is reasonable to see that the visitors will be reasonably safe in using the premises for the purposes for which he is invited or permitted by the occupier to be there', s 2(2). There may be a breach of this duty in leaving an unrepaired and dangerous trap-door.

It is relevant, however, that this was patently a ruined castle and Adam a surveyor. Section 2(3)(b) of the 1957 Act provides that an occupier may expect that a person in the exercise of his calling will appreciate and guard against special risks incidental thereto. Would a surveyor of a ruined castle not take care to avoid any inherent danger? If the breach of duty is established it must be proved that the breach caused the damage and that the damage was not too remote (although these issues are not problematic here and may be merely mentioned). The question also raises the possibility of Adam's contributory negligence or even the possibility (rather slight?) that he was *volenti* to the risk of such an accident.

Finally, if Ben's use of this castle was business use within s 1 of the Unfair Contract Terms Act 1977 (s 1(3)(a) or (b)) then his liability in negligence for injuring Adam is non-excludable (s 1(1)(c) and s 2(1)).

So far as liability to Catherine is concerned, assuming that she is a trespasser, the Occupier's Liability Act 1984, s 1(3) must be considered.

There is a duty of care if Ben is aware or has reasonable grounds to believe the danger exists or knows or has reasonable grounds to believe Catherine is in the vicinity of the danger and the risk is one against which in all the circumstances Ben could reasonably be expected to offer protection. If there is a duty, it is a duty to take such care as is reasonable in the circumstances of the case.

So far as the exclusion notice is concerned, Winfield argues that the statutory minimum duty to a trespasser might be non-excludable. No authority is given and *Herrington* (now no longer a direct authority) suggests if anything the contrary (Lord Pearson adverts to exclusion notices in a way that seems to accept their efficacy). The exclusion notice may anyway be relevant in showing that Ben has discharged his duty by providing adequate warning – but is such a notice adequate precaution if he knows of the presence of children?

Catherine is probably also owed a separate duty of care in her capacity as a rescuer of Adam. *Videan*'s case is authority that the rescuer is owed a separate duty of care. It seems not to matter in logic that the rescuer was first a trespasser. Some analogy is found in *Chadwick v BTC* where the plaintiff would have been a trespasser if he had not been a rescuer.

Liability here to Catherine will depend upon the reasonableness of her response to the peril Ben had created to Adam. Although her claim is not affected by Adam's contributory negligence (if any) it is affected by her own. Finally, of course, Ben might be able to show that the injury to her was caused not by his own breach of duty of care but by her carelessness.

Notes on the answer

(i) It is important to deal with issues on which the facts give no guidance one way or the other quite succinctly. Examples are: damages and the Law Reform and Fatal Accidents Acts; the possibility of a business user under the Unfair Contract Terms Act; and the issues of causation and remoteness of damage. On each of these points, the problem leaves you without the necessary facts to formulate a detailed answer. Consequently, do not make up a variety of hypothetical facts and produce a lengthy series of hypothetical answers to the problem. Simply state the alternative conclusion precisely and proceed with the next point.

(ii) The question covers too many issues for you to deal with any as fully as each might warrant in practice. The question is testing

HINT →

In an extensive question, deal with the main legal issues raised by the facts. Relevant issues where few or no facts are mentioned may be considered more briefly.

your skill at unravelling the legal framework where there are a
number of parties, fairly complex facts and some difficult
issues. In order to merit a good mark you must make a workmanlike attempt to answer the whole question in the form in
which it is asked. You may feel that you can demolish Winfield's
suggestion that the duty of care owed to a trespasser is non-
excludable. If you produce a well-argued case on this point alone
you will deserve credit – you may indeed succeed in devoting
your whole time to this point or to the conceptually more interesting point concerning liability to a child trespasser who
evolves into a rescuer. Such an approach may achieve a pass but
it cannot merit much more, however extensive your answer,
because it represents a contumacious refusal to tackle the
question on which the examiner has decided that your lawyerly
skills should be tested.

✖ EXAMPLE 4

To conclude this section on answering questions, the following answers
give illustrations of good, and not so good practice. The four answers
show, in turn, what is expected for a first-class answer, a second-class
(upper division) answer; a second-class (lower division) answer and a
third-class answer.

> Sarah, a painter, and Alan, a teacher, bought a house together in
> 1998. In the Form TR1* it is indicated that they each own all the land
> together. Alan contributed 80% of the purchase price and Sarah paid
> 20%. In 2000 their daughter was born.
> In 2004 their relationship deteriorated and they agreed that Alan
> would move out of the house temporarily while they tried to resolve
> their differences. Four months ago Alan wrote a letter to Sarah which
> read as follows: 'I think that the time is right to sell the house. We
> could each buy a smaller property of our own with our share of the
> sale proceeds'. He sent the letter to the house by first-class post and
> also sent a copy to his sister Margaret.

---

* **Explanatory note**, but not a part of the question. (The Form TR1 is the basic document
used to transfer ownership in registered land. It is, as with hosts of other valuable
information on land law, accessible through Her Majesty's Land Registry website
at www.landregistry.gov.uk. The TR1 form allows two or more persons buying
land together to state in box 11 (by a declaration of trust) whether they each own all the
land together: ie, as joint tenants beneficially, or whether they hold the land for themselves in notional shares in which each owns a stated proportion (that is, as tenants in
common)).

The next day Alan and Sarah met and they decided to really work at their relationship and Sarah agreed that he should move back into the house at the end of the week. While Sarah was in the garden Alan heard the postman and he rushed to the front door and recovered his letter as it was being pushed through the letterbox. He destroyed the letter immediately.

Since Alan moved back into the house their relationship has gone from strength to strength. However last week Alan was killed in a car accident. In his will he left his share in the house to his sister, Margaret. Margaret has contacted Sarah to say that she wants the house to be sold as soon as possible and that she is entitled to 80% of the sale proceeds.

Sarah seeks your advice on the following:

a) Whether Margaret is entitled to an 80% share in the house.

[70 marks]

b) Assuming Margaret is entitled to a share in the house, whether she can force a sale of the house against Sarah's wishes.

[30 marks]

Advise Sarah.

Answer One

(a) This question concerns co-ownership. This is where two or more people have a concurrent interest in the ownership of land. Co-ownership exists under a trust of land (s 34 LPA 1925). Two types of co-ownership exist: joint tenancies and tenancies in common. With reference to the TR1 form, Alan and Sarah are joint tenants at law. This means that together they own the whole of the property. It also means that the four unities of possession, interest, time and title are present. They are joint tenants in equity as there is an express declaration in the transfer deed. Even though they contributed unequal amounts, which does presume a tenancy in common in equity, the express declaration in the TR1 overrides this.

When Alan writes a letter to Sarah asking her to sell, we must consider severance in equity. Severance is where one joint tenant separates his share in equity. In *Harris v Goddard*, the effect of severance was said to be separating one's interest from a joint tenancy so that concurrent ownership will continue but the doctrine of survivorship no longer applies. This means that on the death of a joint tenant, the remaining joint tenants will not acquire the interest of the deceased. Instead it can be left to relatives in a will. The key effect of severance is that they become tenants in common in equity.

Severance cannot take place at law as s 36(2) LPA 1925 disallows a tenancy in common at law.

We need to consider statutory severance by notice in writing under s 36(2) LPA 1925. Firstly, the form of the notice isn't specified (*Re Drapers Conveyance*) so Alan's letter is acceptable. The contents of the letter must include an intention to sever, which must also be immediate, *Harris v Goddard* is authority for this. Alan's letter says 'the time is right' so immediacy is satisfied. By referring to the word 'share' Alan clearly had an intention to become a tenant in common in equity.

To see if Alan has successfully served notice he must have sent the notice in writing to all the joint tenants. This is satisfied as it has been sent to the only other joint tenant, Sarah. The letter has been sent in accordance with s 196(3) LPA 1925 regarding personal service. The notice has been "left at, or affixed to, the last known place of abode" of Sarah. Ordinary first class post is acceptable, as stated in *Kinch v Bullard*. Here a terminally ill woman sent notice in writing of severance to her husband. Before it could be read, the man went into hospital and so the wife wished to cancel severance by destroying the letter so that the doctrine of survivorship applied. However, the letter was served through the ordinary post when it was pushed through the letterbox and this amounted to severance. She couldn't claim the whole estate because the right of survivorship no longer applied.

Alan attempts to destroy the letter, as if to withdraw the severance. However, when the letter was pushed through the letterbox, notice was served whether or not Sarah saw it. Authority for this is *Re 88 Berkley Road*. Even though the letter was destroyed the joint tenancy had already been severed in equity. If Alan had spoken to Sarah or phoned her he may have been able to withdraw the severance but this must have been done before it was served. This was said obiter in *Kinch v Bullard*. Alan cannot rely on this. The mere fact that Alan has left his share in his will to his sister, Margaret, does not constitute severance.

When Alan is killed in a car accident there is a dispute over who owns Alan's interest in the property. In law Alan and Sarah were joint tenants and so by the doctrine of survivorship, Sarah acquires Alan's title and is the sole owner of the property at law. However, in equity, because severance has taken place Alan's share as a tenant in common is left to Margaret in his will. Margaret claims that she is entitled to 80% of the sale proceeds. She believes this because Alan initially contributed 80% of the purchase price. However, due to the effect of severance in equity, Margaret is only entitled to a 50% share. This is because in *Goodman v Gallant* it was held that equal shares are taken when there is severance in equity. Therefore Sarah is a trustee and holds the property on trust for herself and Margaret as beneficiaries with equal shares.

(b) Margaret is a beneficiary and therefore she may be able to force a sale of the property. When looking to resolve a dispute between the parties concerning a sale of the property, s 14 and s 15 of the Trusts of Land and Appointment of Trustees Act 1996 (TOLATA) are relevant. In order for there to be a sale of the property all the trustees must agree to sell. In this situation Sarah, as trustee, is not going to want to sell. Therefore Margaret may apply to the court under s 14 TOLATA for a court order for sale. The court will look at the s 15 factors. These include the intention of the parties who created the trust; the purpose for which the property is held; the welfare of any minor living there and the interests of any secured creditor. In this case the court will consider the fact that the property was bought as a matrimonial and then a family home for Alan and Sarah and their child. Sarah is a painter and if she does her paintings at home then it is possible to argue that the use of the property is for business purposes and this purpose is continuing even after Alan's death. Also Sarah has a daughter who occupies the trust property as her home and this will be a relevant factor. Section 15 gives no weighting to the four factors. Regarding *Bell and Bell*, the welfare of a child factor carried a little weight but was outweighed by the interests of a secured creditor of a beneficiary. There is no debt here and the welfare of a child seems the only relevant factor. Therefore it seems unlikely that Margaret can force a sale of the house but the court may allow Sarah to buy out Margaret's share or to require her to make compensation payments to Margaret under s 13 TOLATA if Margaret has a right of occupation under s 12 TOLATA but is excluded from occupation by the trustee.

This is a first-class answer.

Answer Two

(a) Sarah and Alan bought the house together as joint tenants in law and equity (see the express declaration in the TR1). This means that they both are entitled to the whole of the property and there are no specific shares. The four unities of possession, interest, time and title are present. Section 1(6) of the LPA 1925 states that in law there can only be a joint tenancy. Section 36(2) states that the joint tenancy in law cannot be severed to become a tenancy in common. The same section states that severance of the joint tenancy in equity can occur so that the tenants become tenants in common in equity. Severance of the joint tenancy in equity can occur by notice in writing constituting unilateral severance whereby one of the parties may sever without the agreement of the other party. Alan sent a letter to the house saying that he wanted his own share of the sale proceeds. To see if severance has been validly served by notice the court will look at three things. Firstly, the form of the notice, which is a letter. *Re Draper's Conveyance* applies and this stated that the notice can take any form. Secondly, the contents of the notice. *Harris v Goddard* set out the conditions that are needed. There must be the presence of an intention to sever and it must be immediate and the use of the word 'share' usually amounts to severance. Thirdly, the court will look at the service of the notice and apply the conditions of s 196(3) and (4) LPA 1925. *Re Berkley Road* applies where it was held that the notice didn't have to be read by the addressee. Sarah didn't get a chance to read the letter but that doesn't matter. Section 196(3) states that notice can be sent by ordinary post and Alan sent the letter by 1st class post to the house. Alan tore up the letter as soon as it was pushed through the letterbox. In *Kinch v Bullard* it was held that 'the notice was validly served as soon as it is pushed through the letterbox'. Therefore the joint tenancy in equity has been severed and Sarah and Alan are tenants in common in equity. In equity the doctrine of survivorship doesn't apply and Alan's share is left to whoever is mentioned in his will, which is his sister, Margaret. She is claiming that she is entitled to a 80% share in the house/sale proceeds. In *Goodman v Gallant* it was held that when severance occurs in equity the tenants are entitled to an equal share of the interests. Therefore Margaret is only entitled to a 50% share of the property. In law however the doctrine of survivorship still applies and Sarah becomes the sole owner of the legal estate.

(b) Because Sarah is the sole owner of the legal estate, she is holding it as a trustee for Margaret who is a beneficiary under a trust of land. Section 14 of TOLATA 1996 applies because any tenant or beneficiary under a trust is able to apply for a court order for a sale of the property.

The court will look at the s 15 factors of TOLATA 1996 in deciding whether to order a sale. The factors are 1) the purpose of the trust; 2) the reasons for which the property is held; 3) the welfare of any minor occupying the property and 4) the interests of any secured creditor of a beneficiary.

It is likely that the court will not order a sale because Sarah's daughter, who is aged 5 years, occupies the property. However, if Sarah could find somewhere to live with her 50% share then the court would probably exercise the power of sale.

This is a second-class (upper division) answer.

Answer Three

(a) We can identify here that Sarah and Alan were joint tenants of the property as this is indicated in the TR1 form. Also the four unities of time, title, possession and interest can be identified here. Usually upon the death of one of the joint tenants the share of the deceased will go to the surviving joint tenant by the doctrine of survivorship. However this will not be the case if severance has occurred. The letter Alan posted to Sarah showed an immediate intention to sever, which is necessary for this to be a valid notice of severance as in *Re Drapers Conveyance*. The case of *Kinch v Bullard* indicates that sending a notice by 1st class post is acceptable and the notice is served upon arrival. Therefore in the current case Alan's notice has been validly executed upon arrival. Severance can't be taken back once it is served. However it may be acceptable to revoke severance if steps are taken to do this before the notice is served. The fact that Sarah never acknowledged the letter is irrelevant as represented in the case of *Re 88 Berkley Road*. So for the reasons above I identify that severance has occurred.

Alan's will indicates that upon his death Margaret will acquire his 80% share of the property. Section 6 of the Trusts of Land and Appointment of Trustees Act gives the trustee (Margaret) all the powers of an absolute owner in relation to the land which is subject to the trust. Margaret has the majority share in the property and therefore under s 11 TOLATA her wishes take priority over Sarah's.

(b) Section 14 of TOLATA gives any trustee (or any person with an interest in the trust) the right to apply for a court order for sale. The courts will consider the s 15 guidelines in deciding whether to grant this order. The court will take into account the purpose of the property. In the case of *Jones v Challenger* the property was bought as a matrimonial home, therefore upon the dissolution of the marriage and divorce, the purpose of the trust and the intention of the creating parties was held to have expired. If Sarah is using the property for her business as a painter, it may be argued that the purpose is still continuing. The welfare of any minor must also be taken into account until the child is grown up. Sarah has a five-year-old daughter who occupies the house as her home. This will be a relevant factor for the court to consider.

This is a second-class (lower division) answer.

Answer Four

(a) Sarah and Alan are joint tenants of the house in Hill Street and as such they are regarded by law as an inseparable unit. In this regard there are no nominated proportions of ownership but both have equal rights over the property. This is very common in domestic situations and is regarded as the most perfect form of co-ownership. It is irrelevant as to how much of the purchase price either of them contributed.

Along with joint tenancy comes the doctrine of survivorship. This is why a joint tenancy is favoured at law because the number of people can only decrease. Whereas a tenancy in common lends itself more to equity where the number of beneficiaries has potential to increase. The right of survivorship is also a reason why most married couples adopt a joint tenancy arrangement. This means that when one of them dies, the survivor will inherit the sole ownership of the property and on his/her death may dispose of the property as they wish.

There are ways, however, in which the joint tenancy can be severed. A legal joint tenancy cannot be severed as this is prohibited in the Law of Property Act 1925. However, provisions were amended in TOLATA 1996 allowing for joint tenancies in equity to be able to be severed. Before even getting to this stage, it could be that words of severance were included in the deed which expressed that the property was actually divided and a list of suitable terms has developed through case law.

Once the joint tenancy has been severed it will become a tenancy in common. This is another, less perfect, form of co-ownership in which there are notional concepts of proportions of the division of the land.

In the case of Alan and Sarah, Alan had attempted severance by sending a letter with this information to Sarah. There are criteria that must be met in order for severance to be served. The first is that notice of the severance to the other party must be issued. This is done sufficiently by post either to the last known place of abode or business of this person. Also it is good practice to use recorded or registered delivery but it has been known to have been acceptable to use first class post.

Surprisingly, and quite relevant in this case, it has even been the case that the person who signed for the post had been the one who requested severance and this is still acceptable (*Re Berkley Road*). In *Kinch v Bullard* a very similar situation arose in which severance was attempted but the letter of notice was destroyed and later one of the parties died. It was held in this case that severance had been issued by notice of the letter.

In the case of Alan and Sarah, it is very unlikely that it could be regarded that severance had been served simply because Alan had tried his best to ensure that Sarah had not received the notice and it could be interpreted from the good will that the two had in improving their relationship that there was no real intention to sever the joint tenancy.

If it were decided that severance had been issued then there would have been a tenancy in common in which case Alan had specifically left his entitlement to his sister, Margaret. Therefore if Margaret can prove that the notice of severance is sufficient she will be entitled to Alan's interest in the property.

(b) If Margaret inherits Alan's share of the house she cannot force a sale of the house as she still only has an 80% share in the house. The only unity required for this is that of possession so it constitutes a tenancy in common. Margaret and Sarah now have proportional shares in the house of 80% and 20% respectively but in equity it is unlikely that Margaret would be able to force Sarah into a sale of the house because Sarah has a young daughter and her interests must be considered.

This is a third-class answer.

Exercise

Using the table of criteria below assess the answers above for yourself. Note for each answer how well the criteria below has been met.

Criteria	Excellent	Good	Satisfactory	Poor
Logical structure				
Coverage of issues				
Explanation of legal principles				
Use of authorities				
Accuracy				
Relevance to the question set				
Application of the law to the facts				
Clarity of answer				

Further preparation for examinations

Let it be said in conclusion that law examinations at degree level no more have right and wrong answers than they do one correct way in which to set out the answer. But, there is a distinctive identifiable style to both questions and answers. Some time is usefully spent in actually running through questions and working out the pattern of answers. So, you will find it most useful to acquire a stock of past examination questions and give to them systematic attention along the lines indicated. Many students probably begin this exercise by acquiring past papers but fail to carry it through usefully. It is very easy to peruse lightly a past paper, identify the topics dealt with and put the paper down with a sigh of relief. In order to develop the vital skill of analysing questions until a clear pattern is discerned and then tailoring your knowledge to this pattern, more is needed.

In your previous education you will have been deluged with suggestions on how to produce good answers to examination questions. You will have received extremely useful 'tips'. For some reason or other students uniformly discard all this accumulated wisdom on arrival at college – assuming, perhaps, that undergraduate studies are so totally different that it is now irrelevant. The simple advice you have already received on the construction and contents of examination essays remains valid. It is important to write in distinct paragraphs – yet, few students in exams seem to. It is very worthwhile to learn telling quotations and sprinkle these appropriately in your answer-book – yet an examiner may read a whole batch of scripts and find none. It gives an answer extra polish and bite if it contains carefully chosen reference to learned articles perhaps even with suitable critical comment – but, such references are usually strikingly absent from students' scripts . . .

■ **CHECKLIST**

■ **ANSWERING DEGREE-LEVEL EXAMINATION QUESTIONS**

- ▶ Do not write extensive rough notes, skeleton notes should suffice or better develop an ability to analyse questions mentally.

- ▶ Avoid description in your answer.

- ▶ Do not rewrite the facts of a question.

- ▶ Ensure that you answer has a clear structure as such shows understanding.

- ▶ Use the structure of an area of law as the basis for planning an answer to a problem.

- ▶ Write in paragraphs.

- ▶ State relevant principles of law explicitly and clearly.

- ▶ Where a question raises multiple claims deal with each action separately to avoid confusion.

- ▶ Analyse each action in terms of legal issues.

- ▶ IDEA may be used in discussing legal issues. Remember to use it in relation to each legal issue. You might use the approach several times in answering a question.

- ▶ Be relevant; only deal with issues raised directly by the question.

- ▶ Use authority: cases, legislation, opinions of writers of textbooks or legal journal articles.

- ▶ Quotations stating a viewpoint may be usefully employed.

- ▶ Read the question carefully and note any rider to the question, ensuring that you answer all parts of the question.

Chapter 13
Becoming a solicitor

. . . .

What is a solicitor?

Here is a description of a solicitor's office as you may possibly imagine it:

> 'Like most lawyers' offices. . . . the rooms – littered with files, the dust of ages upon them – looked dishevelled and untidy. The wall-papers were of the mock varnished and grained pine in favour a century before, though if you explored with a penknife you might light upon five or six other specimens, each more attractive than the one above. The windows were made to open; but a ponderous, legalistic atmosphere hung about the chambers: a curious conglomerate of parchment, ceiling wax, corroding ink, cuff bindings, stale tobacco, escaping gas, and myriad decaying matter . . . One's fancy was caught by the double doors of some of the principal rooms, an inner door of bays warranted to muffle the guiltiest of intimate confessions. The room I occupied possessed a secret chamber opened by a hidden spring in the wall large enough to conceal a confidential clerk if earshot evidence of a ticklish interview were needful.'

Thus is a description of a provincial solicitor's office in the not too distant past.* It is unlikely that it is this picture of a Dickensian solicitor's office which has attracted you to an interest in law. However, it does encapsulate the somewhat mysterious picture that many people have of what solicitors actually do. Alternatively you may have been attracted by the glamour of being involved in Old Bailey trials or the prospect of representing ageing rock musicians in their multi-million pound divorce actions. But what are the careers of solicitors really like?

It might be of help, before looking at how to qualify, to give some vignettes of typical roles.

....

* It is in fact by Reginald Hine in *Confessions of an Uncommon Attorney* (1945) about his early years in the law.

....

First, there is the solicitor in High Street practice. The work can be very similar to that of Reginald Hine, but not the working conditions! It may involve representing families in respect of their property in conveyancing, drawing up wills and administering estates, advising on divorce and the custody of children, helping in the establishment of small businesses, and dealing with the legal advice needed by local charities, clubs and so on.

Then there are the solicitors who work in large corporate firms which have as clients public companies, large public bodies such as housing associations, government departments, local authorities, hospital trusts and even foreign governments. Here the individual solicitor will be involved in a specialised and precise area of law, usually within a team of lawyers. The specialism may be as narrow as value added tax or stamp duty land tax on property transactions or it may be wider, dealing with agricultural estates or commercial property portfolios – where the clients are advised on issues ranging from a rent review in a lease to the root and branch redevelopment of a city centre.

Then there are more and more niche legal practices which specialise in one or a small number of areas. There are firms which act for the music business, or the publishing business, or in dealing with accident and compensation claims or with miners' claims against the government in respect of health compensation. There are firms which specialise in areas like mental health tribunal representation, or representation of parents in claims against education authorities in respect of their children's education. There are firms which specialise in publicly-funded claims, in immigration law, in dealing with trade union disputes, or literary and copyright issues. The range of work and the extent to which it depends on different kinds of skills is so enormously wide-spread that it is difficult to do it justice. Some areas involve high levels of personal involvement with clients, some areas involve a great deal of business acumen, and other areas the highest level of technical understanding of the most complex areas of law. There is thus, within the range of private practice, an almost bewildering array of choice as to the final area of work in which one may be involved.

Then, there are solicitors who work in local government and central government. This may be work of a largely administrative nature, involving advice on committees and the operation of public business. It may also involve in other areas, particularly in central government, a high degree of involvement, even influence on the development of legal policy and law reform. In other areas acting as a lawyer, for example Her Majesty's Land Registry or The Charity Commission, involves a degree of specialisation and technical expertise that is as great as can be found in any area of private practice.

The third main area in which lawyers will be found is as in-house lawyers in mostly the head offices of significant-sized commercial organisations. This again may vary from a role which involves

---

KEY POINT ●

The work of a solicitor may be broad or very specialist. Do not imagine that all solicitors are involved in all aspects of the law.

considerable involvement in the management and business side of the organisation or it may involve managing a team providing a particular legal service, for example, in a housebuilding company, providing the same kinds of property law services as private practice firms provide to the general public. In a newspaper or television company there will be specialised areas such as defamation, intellectual property and also the usual business-related issues.

Currently, so far as qualifying as a solicitor is concerned, the process of qualification is the same in respect of each of these different areas. It is possible that the choice of options on your law degree may be informed by the area in which you wish to practice, although generally, so far as the employer is concerned, it would be fair to say this has not been a crucial factor in selecting prospective employees. There are two ways of looking at this so far as the student is concerned. First of all, of course, the degree is an opportunity to study things in which you are interested and for which the chance will not come again. So an interest in studying legal anthropology, Roman law or Chinese law does not mean that your career as a lawyer will be restricted in any way or directed towards these areas. On the other hand, if you are tempted by the thought that being a tax lawyer, a trade union lawyer or a lawyer in the entertainment industry advising on copyright and licensing would be of interest, then it may very well be sensible to choose options in these areas. It will enable you to see if, in fact, you find the law in these areas interesting. It will also, when you attend firms for interview that specialise in such areas, give a strong indication of your interest and possibly – although this is a double-edged sword – give you something about which to talk in your interview!

HINT →

In considering option choices it is helpful to discuss this with your guidance tutor on your degree programme.

The routes to qualification as a solicitor

The role of the Law Society

The governing body for all solicitors in England and Wales is the Law Society, presently operating so far as regulation is concerned through the Solicitors Regulatory Authority. The Law Society of England and Wales was established by a series of royal charters in the nineteenth century and its position is now governed by the royal charters and by various Solicitors Acts. It maintains a very informative website www.lawsociety.org.uk

This contains access to historical information such as the royal charters and the legislation that applies to solicitors. More directly it also contains advice on qualification as a solicitor and electronic sources that will take you to the precise rules. Also, throughout England and Wales there are local law societies. You may find that these hold events to encourage interest in the profession. You may also find it helpful to

HINT →

Access the Law Society website for information on how to become a solicitor.

contact them with a view to obtaining work placements in your area. Local law societies for your area can be discovered from the Law Society's own website. The Law Society also publishes freely available information on how to qualify as a solicitor and this is available directly from the Law Society or by downloading from its website.

The different routes to qualification

Presently there are five clear routes to qualification and these will be described briefly before significant elements of them are described in detail.

The law degree route

The solicitor's profession has never been entirely a graduate profession. In its early years it was essentially a profession reached by apprenticeship followed by professional examinations. Since the 1960s the overwhelming preponderance of entrants have been graduates, although a very significant number of these are graduates in subjects other than law. Nevertheless, the most significant single route by numbers is that following a law degree. For this, the law degree has to be a qualifying law degree. A list of all universities offering qualifying law degrees which satisfy the Law Society standards is contained on the Law Society website referred to above.

The essence of a qualifying law degree is that it contains certain fundamental areas of knowledge and introduction to essential legal skills, particularly skills of researching legal materials which are the building blocks for entry into the profession. The course to be followed by somebody taking a law degree is shown in the diagram below.

A qualifying law degree may be either two, three, or four years in length. Two-year degrees are, at the time of writing, uncommon, although it is possible that financial pressures upon students may make them more attractive. There is nothing in the writers' experience which suggests that there is any benefit in a two-year degree, except a saving of time and money. This has to be very significant indeed in weighing up the decision as to where to study law if the benefits of attending university and participating for the more usual number of years in student life and the intellectual and social development that is part of that are to be foregone. There may be some people who look back upon school as the best times of their life, but there is no doubt that for the majority of those who go to university, it is the university years which are looked back upon as years of excitement and pleasure. Cramming studies into a smaller period of time is a very big sacrifice indeed to make.

Following the Law degree, it is essential to take a legal practice course (LPC). These courses are described in detail below.

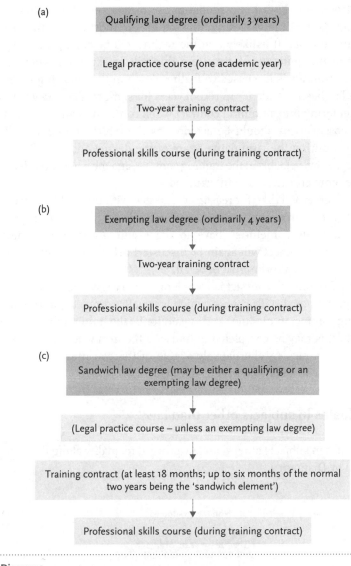

(a)
- Qualifying law degree (ordinarily 3 years)
- Legal practice course (one academic year)
- Two-year training contract
- Professional skills course (during training contract)

(b)
- Exempting law degree (ordinarily 4 years)
- Two-year training contract
- Professional skills course (during training contract)

(c)
- Sandwich law degree (may be either a qualifying or an exempting law degree)
- (Legal practice course – unless an exempting law degree)
- Training contract (at least 18 months; up to six months of the normal two years being the 'sandwich element')
- Professional skills course (during training contract)

Diagram 1
Qualifying as a solicitor by means of a law degree

The LPC can, however, be taken in full-time or part-time mode. It can be taken within five years of completing the law degree (after which time, subject to certain exceptions, the law degree is deemed to be 'stale'). There is nothing to be said for deferring the LPC once one has completed the law degree. The sooner it is undertaken the better. The writers have been involved with the provision of LPCs for very many years and would be hard pressed to say that the generality of the students find it to be as enjoyable a time as their undergraduate years. However, it does build upon the information and skills developed in the law degree and, following straight on from degree, it is easier to keep and develop the necessary study habits to obtain success on the LPC.

Following the LPC it is essential to complete a period of vocational training. At the time of writing, this requires in most cases a two-year training contract. It is likely that the regime will be changed to some extent in the quite near future, and this will be explained when the training contract is discussed in further depth in the following pages. There has been a tendency in recent years for some students to wish to defer entering into a training contract when completing an LPC, but if at all possible this should be avoided, as the information and skills obtained during the cumulative years of the degree and the LPC are developed very valuably in the training contract, and the whole experience will be more effective if not interrupted.

It is appreciated that, for reasons connected with the problems faced in obtaining a training contract, and possibly for financial reasons, many students sometimes have to defer entering into a training contract. This subject will again be discussed below when the topic of training contract is examined in detail.

After the training contract is complete, it is necessary to undertake a short professional skills course, which is usually completed during the training contract in modules and is paid for by the training firm. Some or all of this may be completed in-house in the firm where you have a training contract, or alternatively at one of the two universities that provide the course or a commercial provider.

Graduates in subjects other than law

Graduates in subjects other than law proceed to qualify along the route shown by Diagram 2.

Diagram 2
Qualifying as a solicitor – persons without a law degree

As this shows, after taking their degree, they need to take a graduate conversion course which is known as the common professional examination (CPE) or the postgraduate diploma in law. This is described in detail below. It is quite different from taking a law degree. It covers the same basic area of knowledge as is essential to the law degree but it does this in a very short period of time and without being able to develop the subject either over time or into specialist areas. The course may be taken in one academic year or by part time or distance learning provision spread over two years.

Why should any person choose the CPE course instead of the law degree route? In fact this is seldom chosen in terms of being pre-selected as a route. It is generally a later choice.

Our experience is that students come to this method of qualifying as a lawyer when their decision-making processes are sharpened by the need to find a career after university education. It is possible that a school leaver who wishes to study some particular subject at university out of interest may choose this route, although that makes the process of qualifying as a solicitor longer and more expensive. It is a more hazardous route than pursuing the law degree. This is because studying the entire academic stage in such a compressed period of time is a more difficult undertaking than reading for a law degree.

On the plus side, however, there is no doubt that those who have taken the CPE route are frequently very welcomed by solicitors seeking trainees and perform excellently in practice. All of the large and prestigious law firms have partners who have undertaken the CPE route and there is no reason why anybody who embarks upon it should regard it as an inferior qualification. The remaining part of qualification for somebody undertaking the CPE route that is the training contract, the LPC and the professional skills course, are exactly the same as for students taking a law degree route.

Other non-graduates

It is also possible to qualify as a solicitor, not only without a law degree, but also without another degree. The most usual method of doing this will be following a period in practice and the attainment of the legal executive qualification (see Diagram 3). The process of qualifying as a legal executive and how this leads to qualification as a solicitor is discussed in detail in the Chapter 15 on 'Alternative Legal Careers' and the pros and cons of this route to qualification are discussed there. Here it is sufficient to say that those who have qualified by this route are some of the most valuable members of the profession. Indeed one of the writers has often said that he learned more in his legal education from legal

> **HINT** →
> It is possible to study a non-law degree and still study the LPC after completing the CPE course. Some employers are attracted to students who have knowledge of another discipline.

Diagram 3
Qualifying as a solicitor – persons without a degree

executives when he was an articled clerk than from all the law profes-
sors that he heard put together.

Qualification by the exempting law degree route

It is possible to qualify as a solicitor by a route that involves a four-year
law degree that not only satisfies the academic stage of legal education,
but also exempts students from the need to take an LPC.

Currently, at the time of writing, there is only one such course,
although a number of universities are said to be planning such provision.
That course is at the Northumbria University at Newcastle, and it integrates
the legal and vocational stages of education from the commencement of
the course, so that by the fourth year of the course all students are
able to participate, through the student law office, in advising and representing clients. In this stage of the course, the students are divided
into firms supervised by practising solicitors, each of which has
an appropriate number of clients, which the students interview,
correspond with and represent throughout every stage of their legal
business. In addition, the university has provided a number of training
contracts itself, so that people have been able to complete their entire
legal education at the university. Of those who have done so, one is a
judge, many are partners in firms of solicitors, and some, the fortunate
or unfortunate, are university lecturers at Northumbria!

As the new training regime being mapped out by the Law Society
develops, it is anticipated that very many more students will complete
their vocational training at the university, in partnership with solicitors'

firms and other providers of legal services, such as the Crown Prosection Service and local authorities.

Foreign lawyers and barristers

The final route to qualification as a solicitor in England and Wales is for foreign lawyers. This is not dealt with in detail in this text. For most it will involve taking what is called the qualified lawyers transfer test, which enables lawyers from other jurisdictions to complete their qualifications when combined with a period of practice in this jurisdiction. Full details of this method of qualification are available on the Law Society's website. This method of qualification, through the qualified lawyer's transfer test, is also open to barristers, and the possibilities this opens up are discussed further in Chapter 14.

The legal practice course

Content

The legal practice course (LPC) is taken either as a one-year full-time course lasting a few weeks longer than the traditional undergraduate academic year or as a two-year part-time or distance learning course. Much of the content is prescribed by the Law Society and the areas covered by the course are as follows:

Contextual areas

Certain subject threads pervade the course and these are called 'Contexts for the Course'. They are:

▸ Ethical background for solicitors, including professional conduct, client care, solicitors' accounts rules and financial services including money laundering.

▸ The European background.

▸ Necessary tax background for the different areas including personal tax, corporate tax, capital gains tax and stamp duty land tax.

Compulsory subject areas

(i) Students are required to have a general overview of probate and administration of estates.

(ii) The main compulsory subject areas are:

- ▶ Business law and practice, which is a very large part of the course dealing with all areas of advising on, setting up, running and terminating business enterprises.

- ▶ Property law and practice, which is concerned essentially with conveyancing and may deal primarily with domestic or commercial property conveyancing.

- ▶ Litigation and advocacy. This should enable the student to understand both civil and criminal litigation.

Elective areas

In addition to the compulsory areas, students also choose three elective subjects, which last for about ten weeks of the full-time course. The choice of available electives varies very much from provider to provider and it may well be valuable to use this as an element in your choice of course. Some subject areas are much more suitable to high street practice, others to commercial practice and others to practice in government and local government service. If you are offered a training contract, the firm may give some advice on which electives it would prefer you to choose, although sensible firms are willing to take a much more liberal view of this area of student choice. There is no necessity to choose the electives until you have embarked upon the course, so there is ample time to examine the electives available in the college you are attending and discuss the content with relevant members of staff so you can make a fully-informed decision as to which will be better for your future career or for enhancing your performance on the course.

Skills

The LPC also contains training and assessment in essential skills. The most important of these is practical legal research. It is a curious fact that demonstration of this skill is the aspect of law graduates' performance that is most criticised by experienced lawyers. That does seem rather odd because if, during a three- or four-year law degree, students do not develop the ability to carry out effective legal research, it is difficult to see what the point of their law degree could be. Nevertheless, there has been in recent years a growing emphasis in the LPC on practical legal research and development of this. Particularly, the opportunity to use the increasing number of online databases is a very valuable part of the course.

The other skills developed are writing and drafting, interviewing and advising and advocacy. Each of these is an important part of the practising lawyer's range of skills, and the opportunity to develop these skills under the supervision of the LPC is a significant improvement on earlier forms of solicitors' vocational education. In many ways the skills part of the course – although it is a pity they are so heavily assessed – are the most valuable for students in preparing them for performance in practice. They should be approached with gusto, as the opportunity to practise these skills in a college environment, where your performance can be reviewed in an impartial and helpful way, will make attempting the same in the more harsh light of practice much less daunting.

A very full account of the standards expected to be achieved on the LPC is contained in a valuable document available on the Law Society website called 'Legal Practice Course Written Standards'. This is well worth reading carefully to give the student a very clear picture of what is expected of them on the course and what they have to achieve in each area. Having read it, you will then be able to read the prospectuses and course accounts of different providers with an intelligent interest to see how they have, in their different ways, approached the task set for them by the Law Society. This will assist in enabling you to choose between different providers.

HINT →

Familiarise yourself with the Law Society's 'Legal Practice Course Written Standards' before comparing the approaches of the different providers of the LPC.

The Common Professional Examination or Graduate Diploma in Law course

As with the LPC providers, these are all listed on the Law Society's website, as is the method for applying. There is a very wide range of different institutions providing the CPE, some of which do not also provide the LPC. In general, most students will find it convenient to take the CPE course at the same institution as they take the LPC.

So far as the content of the CPE course is concerned, it must include the following subjects:

► Law of contract

► Law of tort

► Land law

► Equity and trusts

► Criminal law

► Public law (encompassing constitutional law, administrative law and human rights)

► European Union law

► The opportunity to study for a brief period an additional or two additional subject areas.

Leaving aside the additional subject areas, the important thing for students to note is that each of the subjects listed normally takes up a quarter of an undergraduate year on a typical law degree course. This means that the CPE programme is at least equivalent in bulk to a year and a half of undergraduate study. Each subject is normally assessed by a three-hour written examination, although there may be an element of in-course assessment. The additional subject area is normally assessed by some form of coursework. The range of material covered and the form of assessment means that the CPE is a very challenging year. It involves the assimilation of a great deal of new material at a much faster rate than is normally required of university students. Additionally, students from many degree backgrounds these days will be unfamiliar with the rigid unseen written exams which are an essential part of the CPE assessment regime.

The heavy content of the course and the arduous assessment means that the CPE course is not one to be undertaken lightly. It is wise to ask yourself if you have enjoyed the 'study' side of being a university student. It is also wise to be honest with yourself about how successful you have been at this. It cannot be said that the CPE course can be recommended to students who have not performed well in their previous undergraduate course, or who have taken an undergraduate course which is not one which develops self study, reading and exam performance skills that are so important to success on the CPE. In selecting this course, it also has to be borne in mind that, although successful CPE candidates are much valued in practice, the same is not true of those who have scraped through the CPE course with difficulty. A good 60% level performance or above is the target to aim for, and it is wise to be ruthlessly honest with yourself about whether you are able to sustain this performance across the range of subjects demanded in the CPE. Those responsible for recruitment to training places will look very carefully at the level of performance reached, and a below par performance will not be accepted.

Many students do take the CPE by part-time or distance learning study, and many succeed and enter the profession with success. Our recommendation, however, would be that, if possible, it is advisable to take the CPE full time. There are strong advantages of being present at the university with all its available resources and accessibility of staff while undertaking this course. It will be much easier to understand the demands in each subject area and to ensure by contact with tutors that any difficulties are resolved as the course proceeds. Even more than on an undergraduate law degree, it is very important that the CPE should be approached with a constant effort throughout the year and this is much easier to achieve while attending a full-time course free from the distractions which are inevitable if you are studying in a part-time or distance learning mode.

List of topics of which knowledge is essential before embarking on the legal practice course

Contract law

A good general understanding of contract law is essential for conveyancing, consumer protection and to a lesser extent employment and company law. Especially important in conveyancing is a good understanding of 'formation of contract'.

Tort law

A reasonable basic general knowledge of this subject may occasionally inform your answers in the heads mentioned above.

Land law

Here a very thorough knowledge is required. The following topics may be especially noted:

▶ *Trusts of land and co-ownership*. This is of central importance. A very good grounding is necessary. Especially important is transfer by a sole surviving co-owner.

▶ *Registration*. Registered conveyancing figures very largely. It is a help if the student starts with a good grasp of the Land Registration Scheme, types of titles, methods of protecting incumbrances and overriding interests.

▶ *Leases*. A thorough knowledge of general principles is required.

▶ *Covenants, easements, mortgages*. A good understanding of the basic principles in each of these topics is desirable.

▶ *Equity and trusts*. It is important both in conveyancing and succession to have a fair grasp of these topics. Especial attention may be given to administration of trusts and the appointment, retirement, removal and duties of trustees.

European Union law

A knowledge of the principal EC institutions, sources of law and EC legal method is needed, as is an understanding of the relationship between national law and community law.

Human Rights

This area includes the European Convention on Human Rights, the Fundamental Freedoms and the Human Rights Act 1998.

An understanding of the structure of the civil and criminal courts is expected, together with an appreciation of the elements of common offences and causes of action.

It is also assumed that students embarking on the LPC will possess certain skills, such as an ability to conduct legal research.

HINT ➡

Before embarking on the LPC prepare by refreshing your memory of key legal concepts.

Given this preliminary understanding, the LPC will be found demanding but not especially intellectually taxing. There is a great deal to be learned, understood and digested and virtually all students find the weight of material and length of the course something of a trial. A sustained effort to work consistently is required over quite a long period. Consequently some thought must be given to management of your time.

The better approach is for an even effort over the whole of the course, rather than for a crescendo of effort towards the summer. There is no choice in the examination papers. Attention must, accordingly, be given to each part of the course – nothing can safely be omitted altogether. The parts of the course studied in November need to be understood as well as those completed in May. So, steady and consistent application is called for. Classes must be attended diligently from the beginning of the course to the end. A fortnight's lapse may lead you to gain no marks on a question which takes up a third of one paper. Failure will then be inevitable.

All this poses different demands for the student from the more dilettante days of the undergraduate past. A very deliberate programme of recreation is needed to avoid becoming jaded and to ease the tension which the course produces. Obviously every student must find their own route to this particular salvation. But, it is advisable to have regular, weekly days off – preferably the entire weekend. Equally large parts of the Christmas and Easter holidays should be kept *entirely* free of work. When the mind is absorbing vast sequences of material, periods of rest are vital otherwise you will feel murky and confined. Keep your nerve and take plenty of regular predetermined time off. Try to arrange a good long weekend break within your final revision period before the examination so that you will feel ready for the final push.

Assessment of the Legal Practice Course

Every course will contain an element of unseen written examinations. These will be set by the institution which is running the course and subject to external moderation on behalf of the Law Society in order to ensure that comparable standards are found at each institution. The examinations will normally be ones which permit students to use materials – such as notes and course materials – which they bring into the examination. The skills elements of the course will be assessed by students performing set exercises. For example, videos of advocacy exercises may be used as part of the assessment of this very important part of the course.

Legal Practice Course – part-time

It is now possible to take the LPC part-time. This can be done while in employment with a solicitor or not. The course will involve attendance at the university or college for a day or part of a day a week. Alternatively it may involve less frequent attendance but for several days or more at a time.

Part-time versions of the LPC have two substantial advantages. They are in effect more financially manageable because of the possibility of combining the course with paid work. In terms of the education achieved there is also considerable possibility of benefit – if the course is combined with useful practical training in a solicitor's office then there is a very real possibility of the overall value of the LPC being greater.

The negative side of part-time vocational education lies in two areas. Firstly, some of the larger solicitors' firms are very slow to see the advantage of this mode of education and may be reluctant to employ trainees on part-time training contracts. Secondly, combining work and study in this fashion may demand a greater overall commitment in both time and stamina. One of the writers, as someone who did the former Law Society Part II examinations by part-time study, can well see both its merits and demerits. In the end it comes down to either personal preference or economic necessity.

The part-time course may be taken over two or sometimes three years. The courses themselves differ very greatly in their arrangements although, of course, all have the same basic content as the full-time course.

Obtaining a training contract

Having completed the examination – successfully! – you will enter a training contract. In the post-1993 scheme of education for solicitors the traditional name of 'articles' has been abandoned and called instead a 'training contract'.

The first hurdle you have to cross is to discover a solicitor who is willing to take you as his or her trainee. This is a very difficult subject on which to advise students. Entry into the training contract is not an organised or streamlined business. There is a fairly useful guide (the *Roset Register of Solicitors Employing Trainees*, published by AG-CAS) as to which firms take trainees and a minimum of detail about each firm. It will almost certainly be available in your college's library or law school. If not, it is available from the Law Society. There are also formal lists of vacancies maintained by the Law Society and by secretaries of local law societies. It seems that these are only rarely of help in directing students to vacancies.

The *Gazette* does each week carry a few vacancies for trainees and also a smaller number of advertisements from persons advertising themselves as potential trainees. Given the large number of students placed every year this obviously caters for only a tiny fraction of the whole. It is possible, though, that a worthwhile offer may be found by responding to an advertisement. This has been particularly so in the autumn, when after the finals' results were published a number of firms found that their expected trainees had failed to pass.

Local authorities regularly circularise law schools with vacancies and also advertise in the national and local press. The salaries paid are competitive, perhaps £2,000 pa or more above salaries in provincial private practice. Until quite recently, it used to be widely said that local authority articles were not a good passport to private practice. It is doubted if this is still generally true. In a large local authority, you should encounter well-structured training, a high quality of supervision and an enticing variety of complex legal problems. Their vacancies are heavily over-subscribed. A good academic background – probably at least a better sort of second class honours – is needed to win a place and there will almost certainly be the need to perform well at a competitive interview.

The most common way of finding a training place remains the direct personal approach. The fortunate applicant will have the benefit of a personal introduction through a family friend or relative. Such has been the growth of the profession in recent decades that this avenue has been available only to a small minority. It is, however, possible for students to make their own contacts. Few students seem to attend the meetings of their local law students' societies. Solicitors are often met by prospective trainees in such surroundings as the Territorial Army or the rugby or cricket club. Solicitors, rather unsurprisingly, like to take on as trainees those who have interests and backgrounds quite like their own.

In our experience many students have obtained a satisfactory training contract as a consequence of finding themselves vacation employment in a solicitor's office. Sometimes this can be found through a relative or friend. Very often students find such an opportunity by direct approach. You can expect to be paid little, perhaps nothing. The experience will, however, be invaluable. First, you will discover for yourself what 'goes on' in a solicitor's office. This is a chance not to be passed

HINT ⇒

Seek vacation employment with solicitors' firms as this is useful experience in itself and may lead to employment opportunities.

over lightly when you are considering spending the best part of the next forty years in one. Second, it also allows you to demonstrate to a potential principal that you will make a worthwhile trainee solicitor, are willing to work and can adapt yourself to the office set-up.

The larger firms in London and the provinces now have application forms for prospective trainees to complete. They expect high academic achievement and demonstrably high personal qualities. Success in debating, student politics, competence at foreign languages, significant achievement in sport and so on can all be important. Outside these larger firms, by far the greater number of students find their training place by a direct written approach to solicitors in a given locality. They write to all solicitors listed in that area in the telephone directory or in the *Solicitors' and Barristers' Directory and Diary* (published annually by Waterlow and containing a list under town names of all firms of solicitors with some small details of their practice). Whether you are making an approach in this way or in reply to an advertisement, it is wise to give much thought to your letter of application. The writers would favour a handwritten letter of application accompanied by a typewritten curriculum vitae. In your letter of application, which should be brief, try to indicate both your strong interest in working for the firm in question and something special about your background that makes you a desirable candidate. In your curriculum vitae include full biographical details, education, examinations passed and standard reached. Solicitors will also be interested in other areas – have you held office in societies and clubs, played representative sport, taken office in the union at your college, etc? Try to demonstrate that you are a lively, sociable person who will be an asset to their firm. If there are features to your education that will assist, expand on them – have you represented your university in the national mooting competition, or written an extended essay on a complex aspect of commercial law?

> **KEY POINT**
> Use all the opportunities presented by degree education to develop and demonstrate your abilities and skills. These then must be presented effectively to prospective employers.

Choosing a firm

It may not be given to many to select the firm in which to be trained but it is still worth some consideration. At the top of the tree in terms of earnings and important or prestigious clients are the very large London firms whose names are familiar household words. The major commercial cities have two or three or possibly slightly more similar firms. These firms have many partners – twenty or more. Their work is for large commercial concerns or institutions and to only a small extent for the private client. (Solicitors use the expression 'private client' work in contrast to work for clients who are commercial or industrial concerns or public bodies.) Some of these firms visit colleges on the 'milk round'. They all have very competitive entry. A very good academic background is required. Such firms will also delve deeply into an applicant's background. Is she fluent in any foreign language? Has she excelled in student politics or societies? Is he widely read and highly cultured? Will his background endear him to the firm's clientele? Has she the drive and motivation to equip her for a highly competitive working environment? In such firms, at least in London, salaries and working conditions are good. It is not the life, though, for any but the very ambitious. A period of competition with other trainees for a limited number of vacancies will be followed by a long period of competition with other assistant solicitors at various grades of status and salary before success is finally achieved with a full partnership.

Beyond these heady reaches are a wide range of respectable hard-working solicitor's firms. By and large they 'specialise' in private client work – conveyancing, probate, trust and tax work, crime, divorce and family disputes and a wide range of litigious matters. The size of partnerships ranges from the large number of sole practitioners to very large firms indeed of more than fifty partners, with the most common being three to six partners. General advice on what to look for is extremely hard to give. On the whole it is best to avoid a training contract with a sole practitioner – he or she will probably be too busy to instruct you and there may well be little variety in the work. Beyond that, it is very much a matter of personal predilection. Some of the best and most independent-minded solicitors are found in small firms or as sole practitioners and may provide a wonderful introduction to a career in law. You must try to make a judgement in such a case as to whether the solicitor will set aside time for structured training.

If the type of work you desire and the locality in which you wish to practise is clear then choice may be straightforward. For the majority who are undecided here are a number of *flexible* pointers:

(i)   The salary offered is little indication of the quality of your training contract. A good firm may well feel it can afford to pay little if its ex-trainees are prized employees. The good firm is one that gives emphasis to the training it gives the trainee rather than the measure of work it expects for the high salary it pays.

(ii) Is there a clear scheme of training? Has there been a steady flow of trainee solicitors in the past? Have your conditions of work and supervision been carefully thought out by the firm or is it all 'hand to mouth'.

(iii) You cannot obtain references about your potential employer, though it is vital for you that the firm should be reputable, honest and professionally in good standing. If you are lucky, friends or relatives will be able to advise. If not, you must rely on your own judgement based on very little evidence. Think carefully about the attitudes your prospective principal exhibits in the interview you have. What do they indicate about his values and standards? If you are looking for a training contract near your former college, your tutor should be able to warn you against the odd rogue firm which exists in any area.

Many firms, particularly where the college trains solicitors as well as undergraduates, make a direct approach to a particular law school. These enquiries very often come in the vacation when there are few students about.

What to expect from a training contract

A good starting point in your search for a training contract is *The Training Contract and Pupillage Handbook*, which is published annually, and in association with The Trainee Solicitors' Group. The handbook includes information on firms and chambers offering training contracts and pupillages respectively. Helpfully the handbook contains chapters giving advice on the application process and interview technique. There is also a companion website at www.lawcareers.net.

HINT →

Consult *The Training Contract and Pupillage Handbook* when searching for a training contract.

The quality and style of training which you can expect is still very variable. Some trainees will be 'thrown straight in the deep end' and allocated in their early days a considerable number of files to deal with and expected to muddle their way through with little or no supervision. In the past there have at the other extreme been solicitors who have given to their articled clerks little or nothing to do but left them simply to spend their time in idle conversation. This last is now rather unlikely as solicitors have to pay at least a minimum salary to their trainees and, in any event, financial efficiency has become very much the leitmotif of contemporary solicitors' practice.

Nowadays, these extreme examples are not so likely to occur with any frequency. The Law Society's regulations governing training are stricter than in the past (see *Training trainee solicitors The Law Society Requirements* available on the Law Society's website). They now provide that trainees must receive experience in at least three different areas of English law. They must have the opportunity to learn principles of professional conduct and etiquette. They must also have the opportunity to practise the following basic skills: drafting; communication with clients and others; research; and office routines (procedures, costs and legal routines). An obligation to provide this experience is contractually binding upon each principal.

In order to make the monitoring of the quality of experience provided more realistic, there are more detailed regulations. New trainees are given a letter of offer from their principal and this sets out certain basic information. The offer letter and the contract itself entered into between the firm and the trainee must both be sent to the Law Society – where they are scrutinised and, if appropriate, the contract approved and registered with the Law Society. In addition each trainee is required during articles to maintain a 'training record'. This specifies the tasks that have been undertaken and the risks employed. It will be in the form either of a diary or checklist covering areas of work undertaken.

The subject of trainees' salaries has for long been a matter of concern to the Trainee Solicitors' Group. There are still many practising solicitors who themselves received no payment in articles or only a token wage. There are even some who paid a premium. There is, accordingly, quite a strong built-in reluctance to paying a 'proper' salary. The Law Society has, however, stepped in to ensure that at least a minimum salary is paid. Each local law society will publish a guide to salary levels. A training contract will not be registered by the Law Society unless they are at the minimum figure specified in the relevant local law society's guide except when there are very exceptional circumstances. The minimum salary specified originally tended to be based on a university student's grant grossed up for a full year. Nowadays even the minimum salary levels are enough to live on in passable comfort. The bigger firms pay salaries significantly above the minimum level. They also frequently help to support applicants during the earlier years of training by paying course fees and bursaries. A student of strong academic attainment willing to accept training in a good commercial firm of the larger size has every chance of receiving substantial financial support during the LPC or CPE.

Despite the somewhat frequent attacks levelled by the press upon the solicitor's profession, a would-be solicitor can expect high standards of personal and professional behaviour from his or her colleagues. The levels of competence of the profession are rising under the new training and education regulations. An increasingly competitive edge has entered the working life of solicitors. In the future this will become even more marked. The work is both challenging and satisfying and also of great social value and there is still a great deal of personal control over one's professional life together with an ever-increasing diversity of career opportunities.

The financial side of qualifying

At present those who are well off have a distinct advantage in qualifying in either branch of the profession. During the initial degree, the financial position is the same as for other degree students. During the further year at college, or the further two years for non-law graduates, the position is more complicated.

It is worth asking if a local authority grant is available for the LPC or even for the extra CPE year. It is quite unlikely that a grant will be available for both. It is probable that you will not obtain a grant for either. The award of a grant is in the discretion of your local authority and policies and practices vary from authority to authority and from year to year.

Once you become a trainee solicitor you will be paid enough to live on. But, there is still a period for many students – and for nearly all would-be barristers – when money has to be found from some source or other. The main banks may offer loan schemes on fairly generous terms for students qualifying in the professions. Loans for two or three years when no payments have to be made and interest accumulates below market rates are offered. The loan and the accumulated interest is then repaid in the early years of practice. In recent years, these loans have proved of value to numerous students.

The availability of training places

At the time of writing there are more would-be solicitors' trainees than there are places in training contracts. This illustrates very forcibly the way in which the profession is inexorably linked in its growth and prosperity to the financial state of the country as a whole. The 1980s were a time of unprecedented expansion and considerable financial success for solicitors in general. The 1990s commenced on a much more low key note. Some of the very large and successful firms were forced to make redundancies. The number of training places fell back. One effect of this has been to increase competition among students. Doing well on the degree and the vocational course is important. An element of vocation, even considerable willingness to accept relative hardship, may be necessary for someone struggling to enter the profession. Personally it is not doubted that the profession is set on a long-term path of growth and prosperity. But, experience has shown that those who leave the profession quite often do not return. It is probable that for some years there will remain an excess of persons qualified for training places over the number of training contracts firms feel they can make available. This will obviously colour your approach to your studies.

Preparation for a training place interview

Competition for a training place in a large successful firm of solicitors is very intense. Their selection processes have become very sophisticated. Your approach to this has to begin with filling in the form applying for a training place. The very first thing to do is to check with the firms to which you want to apply what the timescales are for the application, as these are surprisingly far in advance of the commencement of the training contract and the timescales tend to be rigid. With many such firms, there is a work experience programme and candidates who have attended this are favoured. If you do attend such a programme, you need to have in mind that it is a case of 'big brother is watching you'. Every person with whom you work during the work experience will report on your suitability as a trainee and your performance in any tasks that are set.

So far as completion of the application form is concerned, it is necessary to put your best foot forward. What you have to envisage is a partner or HR manager in the firm who is receiving many hundreds of applications. All of these will have excellent GCSEs and A levels, and all those who are considered seriously will have a high degree of success on their law degree or CPE programme. Many of the firms look for a second class (upper division) degree as the basic entry standard. You need to check carefully if the firm does set any such hurdle so that your application is not wasted. Because so many of the candidates will have excellent results, it is essential to stress in your application other achievements and performances that will lead to your application being considered favourably. Clearly attention needs to be drawn to particular academic successes and prizes. Firms also look for a high level of performance in other areas. Representation of school, county or university in sport is an important factor. Involvement in such activities as university debating, mooting and charitable activities should be fully described, especially where they show any suggestion of organisational and leadership abilities, as these will be looked upon very favourably by the firm to which you are applying. Distinctive skills, such as language skills, should also be firmly highlighted. It is very important to see the application as a showcase for your skills and achievements. This does not mean vainglorious boasting, but it does mean the clear setting forward of all those things that will make you stand out from other applicants. In doing this, it will be extremely advantageous if you can have some person who has been involved with such a process, perhaps in a similar profession or in education, who can provide helpful, critical comments on your form.

In many firms, the actual selection day or days is likely also to be quite a stressful experience. It may involve impromptu speaking, taking part in group tasks, small in-tray exercises, and will certainly involve a series of quite taxing interviews. Many firms also use personality, numeracy and literacy tests in order to assess the suitability of candidates. For people at the start of their career, all this can be very daunting. It should

HINT ➡
In preparing for an interview speak to your programme tutors for advice and use the careers service of your university.

HINT ➡
Your application for a training place must showcase your skills and achievements.

be approached with a realisation of what a valuable experience such a challenging process can be. It is very important to enter into all the activities fully. It is not possible to gain success in this process by standing back diffidently at the edge of a group. Equally important is a degree of preparation. Find out what you can about the firm. Find out what will happen on the selection day, so that you can be appropriately prepared. If it involves literacy, numeracy and personality tests, then it is possible to prepare for these. Such practice tests are freely available on the Internet and can be found with only a little effort. It may be a long time since you have attempted particular numeracy exercises, and a little practice will help you be confident enough on the day to pass with flying colours.

HINT ⇒
You must prepare thoroughly for a selection day or interview. Find out what you can about the firm. Look at the firm's website or search local newspapers' websites for items concerning the firm.

The other important thing to remember is not to be daunted by not being offered a training place at the first opportunity. Use the selection process to learn how to succeed in such a process. Bear in mind that there are sometimes many hundreds of applicants for each place. Also bear in mind that, whatever the firm might like you to think, selection is a two-way process. You want to make sure you choose them as much as you want to make sure that they choose you.

Alternatives to a training contract

In the section on qualifying as a barrister, it is explained how it is possible to qualify as a solicitor by choosing the Bar vocational course and a period of work experience in a solicitor's office. For some that may be a very good alternative. Also, at the time of writing, The Law Society is very sensibly looking at opening up this period of training to a wider range of possibilities. Periods of work which develop similar skills to those developed in a training contract are becoming increasingly accepted by The Law Society as a substitute for a part of the training contract. It is very likely that, in the near future, The Law Society will adopt a much more liberal approach to this phase of a solicitor's training. Then it may be possible to complete a large part of a training contract in commerce, industry or local government. The one word of caution that needs to be given in this area is that a period of work experience as a paralegal in a solicitor's office itself is a tempting way to approach an alternative to a training contract, but not necessarily a profitable one. This subject is developed at further length in the Chapter 15 on 'Alternative Legal Careers' and the pros and cons of the 'paralegal route' are looked at in detail.

■ **CHECKLIST**

■ **BECOMING A SOLICITOR**

► The work of solicitors may that of a generalist practitioner or that of a specialist. Currently, the process of qualification is the same irrespective of your career goal.

► There are a number of routes to qualification as a solicitor.

► To qualify as a solicitor a person must successfully complete both the academic and professional stages of legal education and satisfy the requirement of two years of vocational training.

► Non-law graduates may study the Legal Practice Course after completing a transfer course, the Common Professional Examination.

► From the outset of your legal studies you need to consider and develop what a prospective employer requires in a trainee if you are to secure a training contract.

► The training of trainee solicitors is now closely regulated.

► Having completed the Legal Practice Course there are alternatives to entering into a training contract with a solicitor or solicitor's firm.

Chapter 14

Becoming a barrister

The daily life of a barrister in chambers

Before committing yourself to training as a barrister it is important to have a good idea of what the work as a barrister is like. As with many things, there is no substitute for seeing things for yourself. Most chambers – and certainly any worthwhile one – have a system of 'mini pupillages' allowing prospective barristers to take some part for a small time in the life of chambers. This kind of experience is invaluable. Even so, it is hard to convey the life-style of a young barrister. There is no fixed working day and, as each barrister is self-employed, there is no 'line management'.

In the past, clerks exercised a tyranny over young barristers (as they could direct work in chambers their way or not) and might, for example, line them up to see if they were properly dressed. Nowadays, clerks, in this sense, play a more low key role.

The barrister's working day will be shaped by whether he or she has a brief to appear in court. If not, there may be an opinion to research and write. There may possibly be a conference, that is a meeting with lay client and solicitor client to advise on a particular case. There may be 'deviling' to do – that is research or draft writing for a more senior person. The times for conferences and even more for court appearances are imperative, but for the rest the working day is shaped by the barrister's appetite for work and commitment. It is likely to involve frequent and hurried travel – around London or outside London to distant and mysterious courts, often to meet and represent clients about whom until then nothing at all is known. For the young barrister there is often little time for preparation, and a willingness to work into the night if a brief needs mugging up is essential.

The young barrister is dependent for work and further work on the impression that is created, particularly to solicitors – who are, of course, used to seeing barrister's perform and will not wish to see their lay client's fortunes spoiled by an idle or inadequate advocate. Here by way of illustration is a story of how Norman Birkett (later Lord Birkett of Ulvaston) obtained an early brief and what it led to*:

'(a lawyer recalls)... And finally, after meeting a young man for the first time at the Bar Mess, whom I had never met before nor seen in robes, I decided to take the big risk of entrusting him with the brief solely upon the strength of his conversational powers. That was Norman Birkett... It was his first Poor Prisoner's defence... and a most ingenious and able defence it was. Mr Justice Shearman was the judge, and in the opening sentences of his summing-up to the jury paid the highest compliment I have ever heard paid to a young Counsel. I think I am right in saying that it was the flying start in his successful race.'

The Bar is a very small profession. There are approximately 12,000 practising barristers in self-employed practice. The following table produced by the Bar Council illustrates this:

Number of barristers in self-employed practice arranged by ethnic group and gender (excluding pupils). As at December 2005.

Ethnic Group	Male	Female	Total
White British	6,561	2,438	8,999
White Irish	77	46	123
Any Other White Background	123	77	200
White & Black Caribbean	4	10	14
White & Black African	9	5	14
White & Asian	24	18	42
Any Other Mixed Background	14	13	27
Caribbean	67	65	132
African	80	46	126
Any Other Black Background	14	22	36
Indian	154	95	249
Pakistani	86	38	124
Bangladeshi	28	16	44
Any Other Asian Background	43	31	74
Chinese	12	15	27
Other	96	54	150
TOTAL (excluding 'no ethnic group information held')	7,392	2,989	10,381
No ethnic group data held	883	554	1,437
TOTALS	8,275	3,543	11,818

Source of Information: The General Council of the Bar – Records Office.

* The Life of Lord Birkett by H Montgomery Hyde 1964.

There are also approximately 3,000 barristers in employed practice – as shown by the following table produced by the Bar Council.

Number of barristers in employed practice arranged by ethnic group and gender (excluding pupils). As at December 2005.

Ethnic Group	Male	Female	Total
White British	956	743	1,699
White Irish	28	30	58
Any Other White Background	37	39	76
White & Black Caribbean	4	3	7
White & Black African	3	5	8
White & Asian	12	7	19
Any Other Mixed Background	7	10	17
Caribbean	6	32	38
African	23	26	49
Any Other Black Background	1	9	10
Indian	35	39	74
Pakistani	10	10	20
Bangladeshi	5	4	9
Any Other Asian Background	15	12	27
Chinese	8	14	22
Other	8	12	20
TOTAL (excluding 'no ethnic group information held')	1,158	995	2,153
No ethnic group data held	376	276	652
TOTAL	1,534	1,271	2,805

Source of Information: The General Council of the Bar – Records Office.

Barristers in independent private practice work together in small groups called chambers. A set of barristers in chambers share an office and other administrative expenses. Their office and their business life is organised by their clerk with a number of clerical and secretarial assistants. Although the barristers share chambers, they do not work in partnership. Barristers work for themselves and must depend on themselves for work and income. This last is an essential distinction between life at the Bar and life in a solicitor's office. There is no holiday pay, no sick pay and no pension fund. Barristers are dependent from the beginning to the end of their careers, or until elevation to the bench, upon their own earning power and physical and mental resources.

The main clients a practising barrister has are solicitors. It is these he or she must impress if the practice is to become worthwhile. All contacts with solicitors in the way of arrangements of fees, collection of fees and the making of appointments and acceptance of briefs are conducted through the clerk – although the maintenance of punctilious ethics is no longer quite so absolute. The barrister's clerk is, thus, a pivotal part of the process by which a fledgling barrister will gain a reputation with potential client solicitors.

KEY POINT

The Bar is a very small profession and, in consequence, opportunities to become a practising barrister are limited.

HINT

In considering whether life as a barrister would suit your abilities consider not just the work but also the working arrangements of barristers.

The BVC as a qualification

It is presently the case that at least the majority of students who take the Bar Vocational Course (BVC) do not obtain a pupillage and hence do not have a career in prospect at the self-employed Bar. For those considering the Bar course, the prospect of not ever embarking upon the career to which it leads must be considered very carefully. It is possible to enter the solicitor's profession with the Bar qualification by obtaining employment with a firm of solicitors for a period of two years and taking the relevant parts of the qualified lawyers transfer test. For barristers, the relevant parts are professional conduct and accounts. This is curiously an alternative method of qualifying as a solicitor which does not take any longer than the LPC and training contract route. It means that the candidate does not have to find a traditional training contract, but instead can start work in a solicitors firm as a qualified advocate, which may well be both more remunerative and more interesting. Presently this route is available because of what is called 'automatic call'. That is, a person becomes a barrister by being called to the Bar when they complete the BVC. It is not necessary to undertake a pupillage first. This aspect of qualification as a barrister is under review by the Bar Council but is not likely to change before at the earliest 2010. Aside from this very obvious use of the Bar qualification, it does seem to be generally accepted that the qualification is valuable in employment terms and will assist in gaining employment in industry or government. Whether the cost of undertaking the course, and the moderately arduous nature of the course, is sufficient to justify this possible employment advantage is a difficult question to answer. There are undoubtedly valuable skills developed on the course. Particularly valuable are skills of personal presentation practised in the advocacy and conferencing aspects of the course. The skills developed in the drafting exercises are of general value too. Of course, in a career in industry and commerce and government, the specific and very detailed knowledge of evidence and the rules of civil and criminal practice, which are the meat of the course, may well turn out to have very little use.

On the whole, then, the advice would be that it is sensible only to embark upon the BVC if you envisage a reasonable opportunity for a career utilising the qualification in either of the legal professions. If you are certain that the area of the law in which you want to practise is litigation and advocacy, then whichever profession you wish to practise in, there is something to be said for taking the Bar qualification route to entry.

Because of its size, the Bar can be greatly affected by the incidental effect of legislative changes of procedural reform. In the late 1960s and early 1970s the Bar enjoyed a boom resulting from increases in legal aid work. From the mid-1970s on, the volume of work suffered considerably because of withdrawal of legal aid for various areas of divorce and other work. The picture in recent years has been a large number of qualifying barristers pursuing an apparently non-increasing amount of work. There have been suggestions that the Bar is over-crowded and attempts made to restrict the number qualifying, of which more below. There has also been an increase in the number of new chambers established or split off from existing sets. Overall it is probably correct to say that a newly-qualified barrister will find that these are not balmy days. But an advocate of outstanding quality, a person who is prompt and thorough in paperwork and in preparation will always make his or her mark. There is always work available for those with a demonstrable aptitude.

Qualifying as a barrister

Like the solicitor's profession, the barrister's scheme of education is divided into an academic and a vocational stage. Virtually all entrants will be graduates and most of these graduates with a law degree. Graduates in other subjects take the common professional examination (see Chapter 13). Whether the student is a graduate in law or another subject, generally speaking a lower second class honours degree must have been achieved.

The regulations dealing with the acceptance of non-degree students and those without a second class honours degree are not considered here. They are to be found together with other information of assistance to would-be barristers on the website of the Bar Council, www.barcouncil.org.uk.

> **HINT →**
> Much useful information concerning qualification as barrister may be found on the Bar Council website, www.barcouncil.org.uk.

Bar vocational courses

▶ The BVC is available in the following places:

▶ BPP – London and Leeds

▶ University of the West of England –Bristol

▶ College of Law – London

▶ Cardiff University

▶ Inns of Court School of Law – London

▶ Manchester Metropolitan University

▶ Northumbria University – Newcastle

▶ Nottingham Law School – Nottingham Trent University
For entry to the course students must apply online at www.
bvconline.co.uk.

All the above have available a one-year full-time course. In addition
there are the following:

(i) the Inns of Court School of Law, BPP, the College of Law and
University of the West of England have a two-year part-time
courses;

(ii) the University of Northumbria has a four-year LLB which
exempts its graduates from the BVC.

All the BVCs are approved by the Bar Council and cover broadly the
same law and skills areas. Applicants are allowed to list **three** choices
in order of preference; application to the four-year LLB at the
University of Northumbria is through the usual UCAS system.
Presently there are substantially more applicants than places on the
BVC. This means that some care must be taken in filling in the application form.

The form gives the applicant the opportunity to demonstrate their
suitability for the barrister's profession. Experience of activities such as
mooting, mock trials, work experience in the legal profession are
important. Experience of debating, activity in student societies are other
things that may be valuable. There is no doubt, despite the relevance of
these things, that the most weighty factor is academic experience,
primarily the class of degree obtained, although A levels and GCSEs are
also important.

Routes to qualification

The different routes to qualification are described in the following
paragraphs. It must be noted first that those intending to practise must
follow one of the routes set out in Diagram One below (prepared by the
Bar Council). Further information may be found on www.legaleducation.
org.uk, the Bar Council's education and training website.

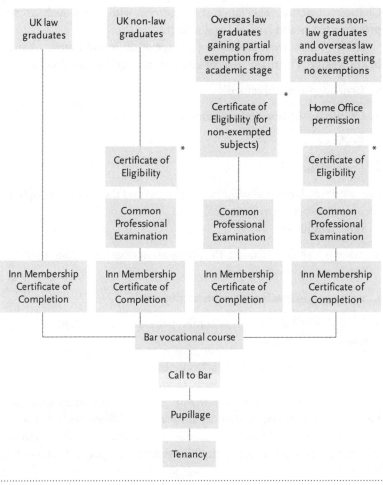

Diagram 1
Routes to qualifications for barristers who intend to practise at the Bar of England and Wales.

The vocational course for barristers

All persons intending to qualify to practise in England and Wales are required to attend the BVC at one of the universities or colleges providing this course. The course runs for one academic year from October to the end of June and is arranged in three ten-week terms.

The course is designed to give practical training in the skills required by barristers. It concentrates on court procedure, evidence and professional conduct. In the third term students elect to specialise in one of three areas of practice. These are general practice, commercial practice and

⁕ Certificates of Eligibility to sit the Common Professional Examination are issued by the Bar Council.

Chancery practice. The latter is concerned with areas such as real property, trusts and landlord and tenant.

The courses consist of teaching a range of skills and a range of areas of knowledge. The main areas of knowledge taught on the BVC are:

▶ Civil litigation and remedies

▶ Criminal litigation and sentencing

▶ Evidence

▶ Professional ethics

Two additional optional subjects are chosen and the number of options provided by each provider varies.

Skills taught are:

▶ casework skills, including the preparation of cases and the legal research necessary;

▶ written skills, such as opinion writing; and

▶ interpersonal skills such as conference skills, negotiation and especially advocacy.

The course is much more practically based than undergraduate law programmes. Assessment of areas of knowledge may be by multiple-choice tests. Much of the assessment centres on the skills learnt and includes assessing skills such as advocacy by videoed performance of practical exercises. Thus, the course is an extremely beneficial training experience for work which a pupil barrister and a young barrister will undertake.

During the course, tuition is both by large lectures and small group tutorial work. There are specific areas of knowledge to be covered during the course and these are dealt with as follows. First, great emphasis is given to the topics of *adjectival* law. This is the law concerned with the procedure in court cases. This is largely taught in the first half of the course in three topics – civil litigation, criminal litigation and evidence. Other material is covered by a series of short course modules and overview lectures at appropriate places during the course. A short-course module might last from, say, five to thirteen weeks and the following topics are covered:

▶ Basic accounts;

▶ Business associations;

▶ European Community law;

▶ Sentencing;

▶ Tax.

Overview lectures are used to provide a background of awareness to important areas of law which may arise in practice.

The topics to be covered in these lectures may, for example, be:

- Conflict of laws;
- Human rights;
- Legal aid;
- Social security law;
- Family law;
- Sale of goods;
- Landlord and tenant.

In addition to these topics, teaching based upon the Bar's code of conduct is intended to permeate the course.

Assessment on the vocational course

Multiple choice tests are used to assess memorised knowledge in civil litigation, criminal litigation and evidence. The skills programme is assessed by in-course assessments during the year. These are based on practical case studies. The third term ends with the final assessment. This is described by the Inns of Court School of Law as follows:

> 'It consists of a videoed advocacy presentation by each student, and four written papers, one of them on the module work of the third term and the other three testing the application of the remaining six skills.'

These final assessments are not a memory exercise. Candidates are entitled to use their course materials and expected to show a competent standard at the skills necessary for the early days of practice at the bar.

Entry to the vocational course

Formerly a person who was a member of an Inn of Court and intended to practise in any member state of the European Community and had the required standard of degree was entitled to entry onto the vocational course. The current position is that entry is competitive. An application, as explained above, must be made online. This must be submitted in accordance with the prescribed timetable in the year before entry.

Joining an Inn of Court

All barristers belong to one or other of the four Inns of Court – Gray's Inn, Lincoln's Inn, Middle Temple and Inner Temple. Before you register on the BVC, you must have joined, or be in the process of joining, an Inn. You will normally join an Inn as a student member before completing your degree. If you do so, as most students do, before the end of your law degree then you must satisfy certain rather complex requirements as to your 'A' level or equivalent examination passes.

It is not very material which Inn you select. It used to be said: Lincoln's Inn for Chancery work, Gray's for the provinces and overseas students, Middle Temple for the poor and Inner Temple for the rich. There is no more than the faintest glimmer of truth in this aphorism. Personal, family or college contacts may direct you towards one Inn or another. Otherwise, it does not greatly matter which you elect to join. Barristers from different Inns can and do practise in chambers together. It is said that Gray's Inn has the best in alcoholic refreshment and the quaintest dining customs involving the dining barristers in a variety of verbal practical jokes and rituals. Such considerations may sway you one way or the other.

HINT →
You must join an Inn before commencing the BVC. This may be done during your undergraduate studies.

Pupillage

After passing your Bar examination you must enter into pupillage if you intend to practice as a barrister in independent or employed practice. Pupillage is a period of twelve months spent as an assistant to a fairly senior barrister. During this period you will be expected to learn sufficient about the ways of the legal system to be able thereafter to practise as a barrister without any direct supervision.

Payments made during pupillage will vary. However, some chambers do make quite substantial pupillage awards to their pupils. During the second six months of your pupillage you will be able to receive briefs. It is not very likely, however, that solicitors will rush to instruct you – although you may be lucky in being given work other members of your chambers are too busy to handle.

Training during pupillage

Here is a description of the pupillage system as it operated up to the quite recent past:

'The traditional arrangement for pupillage was that a newly-qualified barrister, in return for a fee of 100 guineas, became the pupil of an established junior barrister, the master. Payment of the fee entitled the pupil to have accommodation in the chambers of his master, sometimes in the same room, to see his paperwork and to accompany him to court, receiving advice and instruction on what was done. At a later stage of his progress, the pupil might hope to be found a little work of his own. If he was judged to have done this well, and fitted by age, ability and disposition into his master's set of chambers, he might hope to be offered a seat in chambers when pupillage was completed . . . The system described above worked well in the first half of this century for those who had the connections and the money, and the recognised ability or good fortune, to enable them to find a conscientious pupil master in a good set of chambers.' (*Royal Commission on Legal Services* 1979, p 643)

This extract still captures the essential flavour of pupillage. The training given is still largely unstructured. In the first six months a pupil is not allowed to receive instructions on his or her own account or appear in court. At the end of that first six months the pupil master will sign a certificate saying that the pupil has completed six month's satisfactory pupillage. From that time for the remainder of the pupillage the pupil is entitled to appear in court and accept instructions on his or her behalf. At the end of the year of pupillage a certificate is given by the pupil master that the year's pupillage is completed.

During pupillage the content of training will in a large part depend upon the pupil master. Pupils are required to complete a formal checklist of the experience gained during pupillage. The checklist must be of a form approved by the Bar Council.

The financial side of pupillage

There is a book published by the Senate of the Inns of Court and the Bar giving details of awards to pupils offered by chambers in London and the provinces. This will be given to you when you register as a student on the vocational course. In addition, the various Inns each have their own booklets, giving details of the awards on offer to their students. In each case this is available directly from the Inn. Information is available on the websites of each Inn. There are scholarships awarded as a result of special examinations or other tests of scholastic merit, as a result of testimonial and interview or for success in the Bar examinations. If you are lucky, you may obtain enough for your subsistence from such a source.

You cannot count on earnings of any substance being received during the year you spend in pupillage. Neither is it wise to expect very much from part-time earnings. You will need to make a sound impression in your pupillage year and the period immediately following. Your earliest chances for work will come from briefs which your more established colleagues in chambers are too busy to take on. It is important to be

HINT →
Before embarking upon a qualification as a barrister assess the financial consequences and the risks should you not secure a pupillage.

available to pick up any similar opportunity. Equally, your reputation will be formed during these early months. You cannot afford to lose work because you are involved in some part-time activity.

Nevertheless, there are opportunities in legal journalism and quite a reasonable chance of finding some part-time law teaching work at one of the many colleges where law is taught. It is advisable for you to accept such a commitment only outside normal court hours otherwise, because of your prior commitment to honour your teaching obligation, you will have to forgo court work from time to time.

The Bar Council has, since 1988, recommended and now requires that sets of chambers make grants or payment to their pupils during the pupillage year. The more lucrative commercial sets of chambers are in a position to make substantial payments not dissimilar to the amount graduates can expect to earn in London. Other sets of chambers may find such payments out of the question. A 'safety net' can be provided by chambers providing that pupils will have guaranteed earnings up to a certain amount.

The financial position of newly-qualified barristers remains unsatisfactory for those who believe that professions should be open to all on a basis of fair competition rather than financial or social background. For the most able, there is the chance of attracting sufficient financial support and making a flying start at fee-earning. But it must be very few who qualify and continue into practice relying entirely upon their own resources. The topic of bank loans for students has been mentioned above in Chapter 13. A would-be solicitor feeling sure of future employment is perhaps safer relying on such a loan than a would-be barrister.

In an established chambers, the new barrister, rather than having to attract his own work, can cut his teeth on work which is sent to the chambers because of the standing of its other members or their long-standing harmonious relationship with instructing solicitors. Much of the work in a good chambers is in fact attracted to the chambers rather than the individual barrister. A well-inclined clerk, impressed by the start you have made, may well ensure that as a new entrant you receive a fair opportunity by being given a share of this work. You will have already realised that the quality of chambers in which you find yourself is a very important contribution to eventual success.

Obtaining pupillage and obtaining chambers

Traditionally pupillage was found in a haphazard fashion. In recent years the Bar Council has been driven to provide an organised system for obtaining pupillage. The present position is that from the 1 January 2003 all vacancies must be advertised on the designated website, www. pupillages.com. The vacancies are divided into: OLPAS (online pupillage application system) and non-OLPAS. OLPAS allows applications and communication to be effected online. Under the OLPAS system candidates will be able to apply for up to twelve sets of chambers in each application season starting in March. Applications have to be made by the end of April. There is also an Autumn season for applications. There is no limit to the number of non-OLPAS applications that may be made. As part of the new arrangements, pupils are to be funded at a current rate of at least £883.33p per month plus reasonable travelling expenses.

An important source of information is the *Pupillages Handbook*, which is produced annually. This is available directly from the Bar Council for a small price and a stamped, self-addressed envelope sent to the Bar Council. The National Pupillage Fair held in March is also an important source of contacts and information and details of this should be obtained from the Bar Council. Whether the new pupillage system will eradicate more pernicious practices in allocation of pupillage at the Bar remains to be seen. It is undoubtedly an improvement on past practice and students will find it much easier to see what is available and enter the competition. It has to be accepted that it is in the nature of the Bar as a small profession that some particular students will still find themselves more favoured than others but that does not mean that entry into the competition is not worthwhile. Students must however do so with their eyes open, realising that entry to the self-employed Bar is still currently a prize sought by many but obtainable by few. In 2002–03, 711 pupillages were available and many times this number applying. The very best may undoubtedly succeed. Some who should not will also still do so. Many good students who could practice perfectly successfully at the Bar complete the whole course of study and fall by the wayside. This is not an entirely defensible state of affairs and further change in this area must be expected. Presently the Bar is considering a system for providing much greater financial support to a proportion of students on the BVC. If implemented this will be a very significant development.

HINT
In seeking a pupillage consult www.pupillages.com and the *Pupillages Handbook*.

■ **CHECKLIST**

▓ **BECOMING A BARRISTER**

▶ The Bar is a small profession and opportunities are limited.

▶ Like the solicitor's profession, the barrister's scheme of education is divided into an academic and a vocational stage, the Bar Vocational Course.

▶ In order to commence on the BVC it is necessary to join an Inn of Court.

▶ The BVC is primarily practical in nature. A number of colleges and universities provide the course.

▶ At present, a person may be called to the Bar when they complete the BVC course and having satisfied certain matters, including dining requirements.

▶ Pupillage: to practise as a barrister twelve months pupillage must be completed.

▶ The Bar Council provides an organised system for obtaining pupillage. The present position is that all vacancies must be advertised on the designated website, www.pupillages.com.

Chapter 15
Alternative careers in law

What happens to law students?

There is no systematic survey which shows what careers most students intend when they embark upon a law degree. Curiously there is equally no total answer as to what careers they finally end up in. However, it is fairly certain that the overwhelming bulk of those who embark upon law degrees intend to become some kind of lawyer, maybe not at this stage having a clear idea about whether it will be as a solicitor or barrister, but in some area of legal practice. Equally, there is no doubt that eventually a very large proportion of law graduates do not become lawyers. From some law degree courses this may be as few as 10% where the course is quite vocational, from other courses it may be as high as 50% of those graduating. Part of this arises from the very competitive nature of the entry from a law degree into the vocational stage of training, whether into a training contract or pupillage.

It is now clear, as has been mentioned already, that a good second class (upper division) degree, (a 2(1)), is necessary to obtain a training contract in one of the well-known legal firms. It has for some time been the case that a second class honours degree is required to embark upon a Bar Vocational Course in order to train to become a barrister in independent practice. Certainly a high degree of attainment is necessary to succeed as a barrister. Thus, for one reason or another, very many embark upon different careers. The purpose of this chapter is to discuss what kind of careers those might be and how a law degree equips the student for them.

It is a universally held belief among law teachers that a law degree in itself is a valuable education, irrespective of whether the graduate becomes a practising lawyer or not. By now you will know enough about a law degree to decide for yourself whether this is true. Certainly, studying law tells you some valuable things about how society operates. It gives you some knowledge that is generally useful to anybody. It gives you experience in the reading, writing about and discussion of difficult concepts that is valuable in a large range of careers. It is generally regarded as a good graduate qualification, at least as much as any general arts or humanities degree.

What about non-graduate entry to the profession?

Suppose you decide that you do not necessarily want to spend your time at university. Is non-graduate entry to the legal profession a sensible approach? There are essentially two routes for this: what might be called the legal executive or the paralegal route. It may help to give some context to what these routes mean. Take a typical large law firm, such as that in which one of the authors is a consultant. This has 800 persons working in the firm. Of these, 60 or so are partners. Many of the remainder are not qualified lawyers. However, some hundreds of these carry out highly skilled law-related tasks. They manage the costs department for the firm. They manage groups of people providing conveyancing, debt collecting and housing repossession services. They manage areas giving tax advice and carrying out other related tax and financial services for clients. In the not so old days, when the same author was himself an articled clerk, such personnel in law firms were called clerks, and the more senior, managing clerks. It has to be said that in many firms the bulk of the client work was carried out by such persons. They were highly paid and still are highly paid. They were highly respected and still are highly respected. The difference now from those days is that they are no longer called clerks, and that there are clear career routes opening up for them with distinctive job titles. These will be looked at next.

Legal Executives

The first of these areas is that of the legal executive. The legal executive is the title of somebody who is a member of the Institute of Legal Executives and, as they become more senior, a Fellow of the Institute of Legal Executives. The diagram below shows the route by which legal executives qualify as such and may go on to qualify as solicitors.

The typical legal executive will have left school and found employment in a support role in a legal firm. This might be working in a team, say, who are carrying out a large volume of county court litigation. The legal executive will start with processing forms, maybe with delivering of and filing forms at the court, later with taking small applications in front of the district judge, and from there to handling their own caseload and eventually to being a manager of a team of persons involved in this area of work. A similar route might be followed by somebody entering a firm and being involved in their conveyancing work. Many conveyancing managers have teams of twenty or thirty staff under their control. They do work that is every bit as highly skilled as solicitors in smaller firms.

Diagram 1
Qualification route for legal executives

They are certainly as highly paid as solicitors in very many firms. Again, in the writers' experience, many such legal executives who choose not, for personal reasons, to qualify as solicitors, nevertheless have hugely rewarding and interesting careers. The work of legal executives and the means by which they qualify is well explained on the legal executives' own Internet site. The hardship of this route is that, instead of three or four pleasurable and fun-filled years at university, the school leaver begins life as a fairly lowly paid person carrying out fairly routine work in a large organisation. For those who are apt to learn and enjoy the work, it is a very steep learning curve. A lot in this will depend on the way the firm you enter is structured and the opportunities you make of it yourself. The other downside of this method of entry to the profession is that inevitably the exams side of things is something of a hardship compared to the acres of time which full-time university students have to deploy in preparation for their exams. The legal executive entrant will have a full-time job. Many firms will make some time available for study and the attendance of classes. Many will not. Many pursue the legal executive route entirely, or almost entirely, by correspondence course. This involves solitary study in the times when other young people are engaged in more amusing activities than reading *Megarry & Wade on Real Property* and *Winfield & Jolowicz on Tort*!

Many, however, do take the opportunity and are encouraged by their firm to go back to university at some stage, either to pursue a part-time law degree, to take the legal practice course either by part-time or full-time study, and eventually end up as fully qualified. In the writers' experience, these make lawyers of the highest quality.

Paralegals

This is quite a difficult area to describe accurately. There are now two organisations which claim to represent what are called paralegals employed in legal firms, and these are: The Institute of Paralegals; and The National Association of Licensed Paralegals. Contact details are to be found in the Online Resource Centre.

The term paralegal is not a term of precise definition. The Institute of Paralegals lists all the following as paralegals:

- ▶ contracts managers

- ▶ law clerks

- ▶ investigators

- ▶ health and safety officers

- ▶ probation staff

- ▶ enforcement officers

- ▶ regulatory body staff

- ▶ compliance officers

- ▶ company secretaries

- ▶ prosecution caseworkers

- ▶ claims assessors

- ▶ trading standards staff

- ▶ NHS claims advisors

- ▶ HR administrators

- ▶ insurance claims staff

- ▶ law tutors and trainers

This demonstrates an enormous range of possible occupations that can be described as paralegals. There is no doubt that, in recent years, the growth of numbers of people employed as paralegals in some areas of legal work has been enormous. This is in large part a result of the facilities available for processing some kinds of work electronically. Two examples might make this clear. There have been huge expansions of work in some firms in processing claims for industrial injuries such as asbestos-related cancers, and in other firms for processing certain areas of conveyancing work, particularly re-mortgaging of houses. These have been areas of work where very little legal expertise is needed and very little individual advice given to clients. There is essentially a process to be gone through, which can be driven by a software program. The paralegals employed, work in something not dissimilar to a call centre. Their work is carried out in front of a PC screen and largely in response to what is known as 'expert software'. A typical firm carrying out volume conveyancing might employ, say, a hundred persons in such an operation. They will be divided, say, into teams of fifteen to twenty or more persons, perhaps carrying out work related to particular mortgage lenders. The work is not highly paid. Many who do not obtain a training contract following their degree or legal practice course seek this form of work as a possible way of entering the legal profession. There is, however, an enormously important caveat. This work is what is known in current jargon as 'deskilled'. It is not similar to the process described in the paragraphs above on legal executives by which school leavers enter firms as clerks and become managing clerks or senior legal executives. In the jargon of another era, it might be possibly described as 'a dead-end job'. Therefore, this part of the paralegal route is one to be viewed with considerable caution. Such work may be very useful as vocation work to find more about 'life in a law firm'. If taken after graduation the question to ask is: where is this leading me?

HINT →
When applying for paralegal work, consider carefully the type of paralegal work that is being advertised.

Licensed conveyancers

Licensed conveyancers were established following the Administration of Justice Act 1985. They are a separate profession with their own examinations and rules of professional practice. They are run by the Council for Licensed Conveyancers, which has its own website at: www.conveyancer.org.uk.

Licensed conveyancers are specialist practitioners in property law but usually do not carry out a wider range of legal services. Many are employed within solicitors' firms, in areas such as managing volume conveyancing. Others are employed by building societies, banks and property solicitors. Licensed conveyancers are also able to practise on their own and there are a number of these. There are a small number of further education colleges that offer tuition for licensed conveyancers courses. However, most licensed conveyancers qualify through their distance learning course. It is a career choice generally made by persons who have worked as a paralegal or in a support role in a legal environment, usually a solicitors' office, for a number of years. The main result of the existence of this separate profession has been to provide competition to solicitors in the provision of legal services. It is, however, a very small profession. For somebody starting out on a legal career, there is no obvious reason why anyone would choose this instead of qualification as a solicitor with the wider range of career choices that opens up.

Other careers available

As has already been indicated, a law degree is generally regarded as a valuable degree level qualification for entry into work that requires or values degree level education. Given this, there are a range of occupations that are particularly suited to those with a legal background. Very many law graduates work in the civil service, in local authorities and other public sector employment. Opportunities exist in journalism and publishing. Another valuable opportunity also open to law graduates is to begin training as a chartered accountant. For general advice on training, the website of the Institute of Chartered Accountants, www.icaew.co.uk, provides an enormous amount of very valuable information that is surprisingly useful to anyone pursuing graduate entry to almost any career path. The remainder of this chapter is taken up with general guidance on how to approach an alternative career building on the law degree.

The first thing that seems to be inevitable is that looking for employment in any kind of large organisation these days will take a considerable amount of preparation. Large firms of surveyors, accountants, banks and financial organisations are typical kinds of commercial entities that will consider employing law students for their trainee programmes. However, obtaining employment and the prospects of a progressive career in one of these organisations is not simply a matter of filling in a simple application form. They are all very likely to have lengthy employment processes. The starting point is to prepare a full curriculum vitae (CV). This has to set out a detailed account of your educational attainments and other relevant skills and experience. It is important to see that this will be your first point of contact with the potential employer and is thus a crucial 'marketing' opportunity. If you simply set out your school and university record, this will not single you out from one of the many thousands of other applicants. Nevertheless, it should not be an enormously lengthy document. Your initial application may be looked at in an accountants firm, for example by a quite senior partner whose time is also taken up with many other important matters. Two, two and a half or three pages of typed A4 will be sufficient for this purpose. It goes without saying that this should be presented well so that a good impression is made. Within this space it is important to contain all your basic contact details, but you also need to take the opportunity to profile yourself, your skills and experiences in a way that indicates that you will be a valued employee in that kind of organisation. When submitting a CV, it should always these days be a word-processed document and, because it is word-processed, it should contain no errors whatsoever. Typographical and spelling errors, particularly in the days when it is so easy to correct them, create a dreadful impression and may well alone be sufficient to ensure rejection of your application. The properly prepared CV should always be accompanied by a covering letter. The Chartered Accountant's website suggests that this should be word processed. So far as the writers' experience is concerned, a neat business-like handwritten letter may make a better impression. One important tip on these communications with potential employers, particularly as you may well be sending out a significant number and varying the content to suit the kind of employer, is to ensure that you keep a careful and complete copy of each application. You will need, before any subsequent interview, to check this through: few things look worse at an interview than a discrepancy between your account of yourself and your aspirations at the interview and the account you have given in your written application! For the preponderance of these large organisations, the selection process will involve two further steps: participation in an assessment centre and an interview.

> **HINT** →
> Keep copies of all applications you submit to prospective employers.

Assessment centres

Assessment centres are a novelty that were not around when the writers were seeking employment themselves. Certainly so far as the older of these is concerned, he is certain that he would never have found employment if he had to surmount this hurdle. There is no doubt that an assessment centre is a challenging experience for a young person. The experience may include a variety of experiences. There may be a requirement for impromptu presentations. There may be a requirement to take part in group exercises to show teamwork. During the day in an assessment centre there may well be interviews with persons from HR or even with psychologists acting as assessors. There may well be paper (in-tray) exercises that have to be completed and will later be assessed. It is very likely that there will be some written tests to complete. These may involve numeracy, literacy and psychometric tests.

For successful performance in an assessment centre, a degree of preparation is advisable. There are texts readily available by looking at the Internet that will assist in preparation for the different tests involved. It is important on the day of such an event to arrive in plenty of time, to be well but not overly dressed, to be relaxed and, as it were, 'fit' for the exercise. Remember that in the whole of your life you will take part in only a small number of such events, so regard it as a valuable and, if possible,

> **HINT** →
> Research the firm to which you are applying. Many firms have websites which can be an important source of information.

fun experience. It is possible to enjoy nearly everything that you have to do of this kind if entered into with a positive spirit. Since you may have to participate in more than one of these exercises, although it is sometimes painful, it is well worth, after the exercise, perhaps with a sensible and trusted friend, going through the experience to see what you can learn and what you can change on future occasions.

Interviews

There is certainly likely to be at least one formal interview. Much that has been said about assessment centres generally is relevant to this. However, in addition, taken from the Institute of Chartered Accountants' website is an enormously helpful set of interview hints and tips:

Interview Hints & Tips

Interviews are notoriously stressful, but they don't have to be. With the right preparation and frame of mind, you'll have a chance to shine.

- Make sure you know the format of the interview.

- Decide what you're going to wear – try to find out how formal the interview will be, and dress accordingly.

- Make clear travel plans to allow you to turn up in good time.

- Re-read your application to remember what you said.

- Find out as much as you can about the organisation to help you add some detail to your answers.

- Prepare your answers. Interviews are built around three basic questions: Why should we employ you? What interests you about this job? Why are you applying to us? Think about broad answers to these questions beforehand.

- Prepare some questions to ask your interviewer – this shows an interest in the organisation and a keen attitude.

- Rehearse. However confident you are, it's always worth getting used to hearing yourself answer formal questions in as formal a setting as possible. If your careers service doesn't offer interview practice, you could always get a friend to do it.

- Be positive, enthusiastic and natural. You're there to sell yourself – so make sure the interviewers see the best of you.

- Steer clear of one-word answers. 'Yes' and 'no' don't tell the interviewer anything.

- ▶ Answer the question you've been asked – don't ramble on about everything you know.

- ▶ Don't be afraid of silence – take the time to form your responses. This is a sign of a steady, confident mind.

- ▶ Don't tell them what they already know, especially about the organisation. Don't just regurgitate the brochures you've read – if you've done your research, this is your chance to impress your interviewer with your keen interest in their organisation.

- ▶ Ask the interviewer to clarify anything you don't understand.

- ▶ Watch your body language – try to stay as 'open' and relaxed as possible. Don't cross everything and don't fidget.

- ▶ Speak clearly and concisely – keep a glass of water to hand for any dry mouth moments.

- ▶ Don't be too bashful; don't be too bold – aim to maintain 80% eye contact.

As is the case with assessment centres, it is important to learn what you can from interviews. Some of us are lucky enough to go through life having to be subjected to very few such experiences. No-one really looks forward to being tested in this way. However, it is inevitable that you will be, so enjoy it if you can!

■ CHECKLIST

■ ALTERNATIVE CAREERS IN LAW

- ▶ It is possible to have a career in law without qualifying as solicitor or barrister.

- ▶ The main alternatives to a career as a solicitor or barrister is one as a legal executive or a paralegal or a licensed conveyancer.

- ▶ It is possible for a legal executive to qualify as a solicitor.

- ▶ Other careers involving law include, working in the civil service, local government, accountancy, journalism or publishing.

- ▶ Non-law websites may contain valuable advice on creation of a CV, completing an application form and interview technique.

Chapter 16

The postgraduate study of law

Why engage in postgraduate study?

Over the last forty years there has been an expansion in postgraduate education, with numerous opportunities available. For example, in the writers' law school at Northumbria University, there are in excess of 1,000 postgraduate academic students taking LLMs, MPhils and PhDs. This growth is largely a result of two quite different things. The first is the intense competitiveness of careers in law. Many students take a post-graduate qualification to assist in their chances, either of obtaining a training contract or obtaining a place on a Bar Vocational Course with a view to practising as a barrister. The other reason is the immense growth in post-qualification education. There are now specialist postgraduate degrees in areas such as advanced commercial practice, professional negligence, medical law, mental health law and practice, information law and myriad other subjects. Then there are some who take further degrees in law with a view to an academic career. This topic is mentioned later in the chapter. It has to be said, so far as the first reason for taking a postgraduate degree in law is concerned, this has to be approached with caution. Before embarking on the programme, you have to decide whether it gives you a genuinely increased chance of pursuing your career objective. For example, many students take an LLM because they cannot enter upon the Bar Vocational Course unless they have at least a second class honours degree. This requirement is usually waived by the Bar Council if the students have an LLM. What has to be asked for a student pursuing this way of improving their curriculum vitae is whether they will, at the end of the day, have a realistic chance of practis-ing in their chosen profession. So far as students having difficulty finding training contracts is concerned, it is certainly true that specific further degrees in law, for example in tax law, may open up very advanta-geous career opportunities and this aspect of further qualifications has been looked at in more detail in the chapter on 'Alternative Careers in Law'. The remainder of this chapter is concerned with the use of postgraduate study of law in its more usual academic guise.

Research in law has very different meanings. Students may find it interesting to consider the varieties of research in which they find their own teachers are engaged and the importance of this to the development and improvement of the legal system. The range of law research undertaken at law schools has grown quite considerably over the past decade or so. It may, briefly, be described and divided into the following categories.

Empirical research

The last twenty years or so have seen a more or less general recognition that empirical (or socio-legal) research has a proper place in law schools. These two expressions refer to studying aspects of law in operation or aspects of the legal system using the methods developed by social science. This methodology involves, for example, survey research through questionnaires or interviews, the systematic analysis of official or other published statistics, or the use of techniques as varying as participant observation and content analysis.

If you have an opportunity on your undergraduate course to study the methodology of social enquiry you will find the exercise very valuable. The past few years have seen a sometimes vitriolic debate as to the worth and objectivity of the social science method. The debate has entered the political arena. Much of the criticism has been ignorant or bigoted. Unfortunately the debate has detracted in the public regard from the strength of the social sciences. The legal profession can all too easily learn to decry the profound insights that are to be gained from social scientific enquiry. An example of the areas of disagreement may be of interest and illustrate also the difficulties involved in producing social-scientific research of objective and lasting value.

✖ EXAMPLE

Suppose you wished to examine the behaviour of our county courts in actions brought by landlords against tenants in which the landlord seeks to have the tenant evicted from the premises. These actions are known to lawyers as 'possession actions' since the landlord's aim is almost invariably the eviction of the tenant. You could readily examine the frequency of such cases and the success of defendants. You could relate this statistically to whether defendants had legal representation. These are objective matters and an indisputably objective survey can be undertaken. But, you will also wish to obtain more qualitative data.

How do judges treat tenants? What is the quality of performance of lawyers assigned to these cases? Are they well-prepared in the complex law involved? Is the law properly applied in difficult cases? You will wish to obtain by your study of some county courts on certain days data that is of more universal validity.

Some of these questions are ones the investigator will have to use indirect measures to test. It might be relevant to consider the length of cases or the age or experience of the solicitors involved. It might be relevant to try to record what happens between the parties in the precincts of the court during periods of adjournment. What kind of bargains as to payment of arrears of rent are struck between the parties? What role does a tenant's legal adviser play in any such negotiation? Can an observer who might feel strongly as to the political and social issues involved produce a scientific record of what happens?

Developing techniques to study such difficult areas of social behaviour is one of the most exciting areas of research. You will readily see how interesting involvement in such work could prove, and how vital it is to the improvement of our legal system. You will also see how easily evidence produced in such investigations can be the source of political controversy and how important it is that the analysis of accumulated data, or even its very collection, is not distorted by the researcher's own strongly felt beliefs. During your professional life and the education that precedes it, you will often be presented with arguments based on conclusions from research of a similar nature. In order to assess for yourself whether the evidence produced is reliable it will be essential to have some understanding of the nature and techniques of social science research.

HINT →
A different approach may be adopted to the study of law by using the methods of another academic discipline.

Traditional legal scholarship

The bulk of academic lawyers, however, are involved in research of a very different nature. They engage in legal writing and the scholarship pertinent to this, having as their aim the production of a book or an article in a journal. The variety of works to which they contribute are described at some length in Chapters 6 and 7 of this book. There is no methodology of legal scholarship as there is of science and of social science. This sometimes leads research of this kind to be regarded in a different light from research that is more easily seen to be such.

Work of this kind is the province of the person who is interested in library work. It is not necessarily, though, work completed entirely on one's own, and working in a team on a writing project can prove very satisfying indeed. The work can also prove very exciting. Changes in the law, whether case law or statute law, can obviously stimulate great controversy. Commenting on the developments gives one a chance to contribute to or provoke constructive debate.

Other fields of research

Apart from traditional legal scholarship and the socio-legal field, there are other areas in which the law graduate may be able to pursue an interest in research. Mention has already been made of the growing role of computers in legal education. A few universities are undertaking research in this field and advertise occasionally for research students or research assistants. Lawyers interested in a research or teaching career could also consider taking a qualification in some related field and among the disciplines where there is research carried out with a strong legal flavour are: information (librarianship), economics, history and political science. A period of systematic exposure to ideas other than as presented by lawyers or academic lawyers is likely to benefit any aspiring researcher.

Becoming involved in legal research: taking a postgraduate degree in law

Further degrees in law will be by research, by further coursework or by a combination of both. There is considerable variety of one-year postgraduate courses in law and some opportunity for further study.

A taught master's course leading to LLM or equivalent qualification will not represent all that dramatic a change from your first degree course. It will consist of a variety of lectures and seminars and lead to examinations very similar to your previous law examinations.

What is to be gained by such a course? You may wish to study an area that you have studied previously only scantily or not at all. There are, for example, such programmes taught in Britain in sociology and law, criminology, comparative law, international law and welfare law.

Equally you may simply wish to study in a different or a particular college. There is much to be said for taking a postgraduate course in a different jurisdiction. It does seem sensible for anyone who can find the opportunity to do so to spend a year studying law in the United States of America. Both the legal system and the system of legal education experienced in another jurisdiction will prove good sources of constructive criticism of our own style of doing things.

HINT ➡️
A comparative approach to the study of law can provide an insight into how English law may develop.

Selecting a postgraduate course

A student embarking upon a postgraduate course should have good upper second class ability. It is not perhaps as necessary that you have actually achieved this standard on your degree as that you have the requisite ability and motivation. You will receive considerably less direct teaching and supervision on a postgraduate course. If you are not certain of your ability your tutor should readily provide a frank opinion.

You will at an early stage need to choose between a taught postgraduate course and one pursued primarily by research. Taught courses have been briefly described. An LLM by research will almost certainly take you more than one full-time year to complete, and although three years are allowed for a doctorate by research most students who complete do exceed this period.

Pursuing a degree by research will prove more taxing and ultimate completion of the degree is a good deal less certain. It is not a course to embark upon unless you have a good clear idea of the area in which you will carry out work. You will also need the backing and encouragement of a supervisor who is interested in your project and willing to devote a considerable slice of time to assisting you.

Law teachers have very different attitudes to the role to be adopted by a supervisor in a research project. Obviously the work must be that of the student and not of the supervisor. But attitudes to the proper amount of help and supervision to give vary very greatly. For the student, however, there can be no doubt that the greater the amount of assistance, advice and critical appraisal you receive, the more chance there is of achieving a successfully completed thesis.

For this reason, caution is advised before embarking upon a degree by research only. Seek to ensure that your supervisor has some real and abiding interest in the research you propose. Test his or her reactions carefully to ascertain that you are starting with reasonable horizons to your research. You cannot research into a subject as large and open-ended as 'the need for reform of property law' (though there may be a crying need!) nor can you pursue for a whole thesis the case law on frustration of a lease! You need from the beginning a specification of your project that is neither too ambitious nor too easily exhausted and you will almost certainly need the assistance of a committed supervisor in arriving at this specification.

The life of a research student or research assistant

If you pursue a further degree by a course of study and examination, then your working life will be very much the same as in your undergraduate

HINT →
Before approaching a university with a proposal for a degree by research you must have a very clear idea of the legal problem you wish to consider.

HINT →
In undertaking a degree by research consider at which universities there is strength in the subject area you wish to study.

days. If you enrol for a degree by research alone or obtain a post as a research assistant it will be different. As a research student or research worker you will be very much in control of your own pattern of work. There will be no, or virtually no, lectures or seminars for you to attend. Very often formal supervision is less than one session with your supervisor per week. You will require a capacity for independent work and the ability to organise yourself and meet deadlines that you have set yourself or, more satisfactorily, set in consultation with your supervisor. Many students who embark upon degrees by research fail to complete and obtain the desired qualification. The underlying cause is very often the failure to create a framework within which to stage completion of the various parts of their programme. There is a temptation to delay writing up any section of the final report. This is very risky. The longer you delay commencing to write, the more timorous you will become. The task will seem even greater. Your files of notes and boxes of findings will multiply around you. If you can, early on in your research, formulate a clear idea of the shape of your final report or thesis this will help you greatly. You will be able to begin writing early chapters on previous research in the area, background, design of your research programme and so on. Once your writing is well under way the mountain you have to climb will shrink into perspective. Final completion will seem assured.

HINT ➡
Discuss with your supervisor a timetable for the completion of various parts of your programme.

Part-time research

It is worth mentioning that even after you qualify as a lawyer or begin some different career there are still possibilities for research. A part-time further degree can be obtained either by a course of study or by research. Both routes are arduous. Obtaining a master's degree by evening study will take two or three years of attendance at college. Obtaining a research degree by part-time study is likely to take at least three years. Neither is a course to be embarked upon unless you are strongly motivated and can be reasonably hopeful that the domestic and work situation will leave you ample time to devote to study.

Other than a further degree as such, there are interesting professional qualifications which can be obtained by part-time study. Three examples that might interest lawyers as their careers develop are in accountancy, arbitration and taxation. The Association of Certified Accountants* offers a diploma in accounting and finance. This is available for non-accountants to gain a grasp of the subject and could be of great interest to lawyers operating in a commercial environment. The Chartered

---

* The addresses of the professional bodies mentioned here are to be found in the Online Resource Centre.

Institute of Arbitrators also has its own examination scheme. Although membership of the institute is not required in order to practise as an arbitrator it would undoubtedly assist in obtaining entry to this field of work. You should note that the minimum age for full membership is 35. The Institute of Taxation offers qualifications based on its own examinations which are fairly stringent.

Finance for a research degree

Grants are awarded in small numbers by the Research Council, the British Academy, or the Department of Education and Science. (For useful addresses see the Online Resource Centre.) Before making application for an award obtain careful advice from your tutor as to the appropriate body and procedure as this will depend on the particular course or programme which you have in mind. Competition is very great and a very good second class degree will normally be the minimum requirement. In order to obtain a current list of law schools in the Commonwealth and the degrees they offer, write to the Commonwealth Legal Education Association, c/o Legal Division, Commonwealth Secretariat, Marlborough House, Pall Mall, London SW1Y 5HY, and ask for the *Directory of Schools of Law in the Commonwealth*. Your law school will have a copy of this directory in any event.

If your interest lies in the United States of America, then there are suitable courses and funds available. Some persistence may be necessary in order to obtain financial support in the United States.

The prestigious Ivy League university law schools have postgraduate study programmes which are suitable or even tailor-made for overseas students. Columbia University in New York, Harvard in Boston and Yale in Connecticut are the leading law schools. Others might well have a programme that would interest you and your enquiries will reveal to you the enormous number of institutions offering law degrees in the United States. To obtain a place with financial support at one of the first flight American law schools, you will need an excellent academic record. You will probably need a first class honours degree or a reference from your tutor that you were near to that standard.

The value of further academic qualification?

Very few practising lawyers have higher degrees. It is also a perhaps surprising feature of law teaching that very many, perhaps the majority, of law teachers do not have higher degrees. What considerations, therefore, might propel you down this not overly well-trodden path?

It is certainly at present much harder to obtain a teaching post in law in higher education than it has been for several decades. If you wish to become a law teacher, a further qualification may be a help. It is another curious fact of life that very many law teachers have no professional qualification or experience of practice. Either further academic qualification or professional experience or both is to be desired.

It may be that a further degree of some kind may be a useful means of entry to specialised areas of practice. There are specialist commercial law degrees available and a performance of distinction on one of these may conceivably assist in finding a place in a large London firm. It has to be said, though, that the academic and practitioner's legal worlds remain undesirably far apart, and the effect of dazzling academic qualifications upon the hardened and successful practitioner can well be less than startling.

In reality, it will be interest in the thing itself that drives you on to further study in law and provides both the excuse and the justification. Even students not so motivated will find in the years ahead that they have to participate in compulsory continuing professional education. So the spectre of the classroom will remain even for the least enthusiastic! The immediate past has seen quite an improvement in the training and education of lawyers, particularly solicitors. The future, with its twin challenges of ever more complex and multivariate legislation and of an increasingly rugged climate of competition, makes it ever more important for lawyers to be fully equipped for their task. There will certainly be an ever-increasing need for specialists in many fields.

Lawyers now find themselves in an area of continuous and far-reaching law reform. Their working practices are being radically altered by new technology. Their professional codes are, quite rightly, under the continuous scrutiny of a much more consumerist society. You can have no doubt that even with all this background of change which will amount to a revolution in the lives of the legal professions lawyers will have an increasingly important role to play in our more complex society. The challenge that you have set yourself in embarking upon the study of law is, thus, as boundless as it is important.

Continuing professional education

The Law Society has recognised that solicitors' education will continue throughout their career. A scheme for compulsory continuing education for solicitors was first introduced in 1985. Initially the scheme applied only to those qualifying after that date but it has been extended to cover all practising solicitors. The scheme involves attending a small number of courses during each year and collecting the required number of continuing education points. Continuing education has, of course, as its prime purpose the updating of the solicitor's legal knowledge and skill. It is not intended to be an extension merely of academic study.

However, it is possible for solicitors to continue their compulsory continuing education with the acquisition of valuable vocational qualifications. London Guildhall University, for example, has an MA in business law from which the commercial practitioner can gain much. Northumbria University, for example, has an LLM (Advanced Legal Practice). This includes topics such as marketing, financial management and personnel management. It also permits development of a particular area of specialist practice such as commercial property or professional negligence litigation. Specialisation within the profession is undoubtedly a major force for the future and courses such as these will be important in assisting in such development. The Bar has also taken the first steps toward a system of compulsory continuing education.

■ CHECKLIST

▦ THE POSTGRADUATE STUDY OF LAW

▶ Research in law may take a variety of forms, being of a traditional legal type or informed by other disciplines.

▶ At postgraduate level degrees may be taught or by research and either full-time or part-time.

▶ Before approaching a university with a proposal for a degree by research you must have a very clear idea of the legal problem you wish to consider. Ensure that your subject is neither too broad nor too narrow.

▶ In undertaking a degree by research consider at which universities there is strength in the subject area you wish to study. Potentially there is much to be learned from a specialist supervisor.

▶ Some finance is available for postgraduate study but it is very limited.

▶ Continuing professional education is now an important part of life in legal employment.

Appendix 1

Sample law report: Mullin v Richards and Another [1998] 1 All ER 920

Mullin v Richards and another

Court of Appeal, Civil Division
Butler-Sloss, Hutchison LJJ and Sir John Vinelott
6 November 1997

b. *Negligence – Duty to take care – Foreseeable harm – Child – Test of foreseeability – 15-year-old plaintiff injured during game with defendant of same age at school – Game not considered dangerous or prohibited by school authorities – Whether accident foreseeable to 15-year-old child – Whether defendant negligent.*

c. M and R, two 15-year-old schoolgirls, were fencing with plastic rulers during a class when one of the rulers snapped and a fragment of plastic entered M's right eye, causing her to lose all useful sight in that eye. M brought proceedings for negligence against R and the local education authority. The judge, dismissed the claim against the education authority, but found that both M and R had been guilty of negligence of which M's injury was the foreseeable result and, accordingly, that M's claim against R succeeded subject to a reduction of 50% for contributory negligence. R appealed, contending, inter alia, that the judge had erred when considering

a. NAME AND INTRODUCTORY INFORMATION

It is important to note the name of the case, *Mullin v Richards and Another*, the citation for the case [1998] 1 All ER 920, and the deciding court, the Court of Appeal (Civil Division).

You should get into the habit of recording this information as a matter of course. The court deciding the dispute has an impact on the importance of the case as you will discover when you consider the principles underlying the doctrine of judicial precedent. As you can see the names of the judges deciding the dispute are also indicated.

b. CATCHWORDS

These are not part of the case, but give a brief indication of the subject-matter of the dispute and the law raised. The catchwords will help you decide whether the case is of any use to you.

c. HEADNOTE

Again this is not a part of a case and so should not be relied upon. It is useful in that it gives an indication of the facts of the dispute, the legal issues arising from the facts and, after the word **Held**, what the court decided. While you may find the headnote of use as a 'map' of the case, it should be treated with caution, as it is not created by the judges but by the barrister who reports the case. So it is a secondary source and is no substitute for reading the words of the judges themselves. When embarking on your legal studies you must establish good habits, one of which is to be able to interpret case law. It is important that you read the judgments and learn how to distil the information your task requires.

foreseeability by omitting to take account of the fact that R was not an adult.

Held – Although the test of foreseeability in negligence was an objective one, where the defendant was a child the question for the judge was not whether die actions of the defendant were such as an ordinarily prudent and reasonable adult in the defendant's situation would have realised gave rise to a risk of injury, but whether an ordinarily prudent and reasonable child of the same age as the defendant in the defendant's situation would have realised as much. Since the judge in his judgment had referred to M and R's age, it followed that he had in mind the correct principles and had approached the matter in the correct way. However, there was insufficient evidence to justify his finding that the accident was foreseeable, since there was no evidence as to the propensity or otherwise of such rufers to break or any history of their having done so, nor that the practice of playing with rulers was banned or even frowned on in the school, nor that either of the girls had used excessive or inappropriate violence. What had taken place was nothing more than a schoolgirl's game which was commonplace in the school and there no justification for attributing to the participants the foresight of any significant risk of the likelihood of injury. The appeal would therefore be allowed and judgment entered for R (see p 924 *e* to *j*, p 926 *c* to *ej*, p 927 *b* to *j* and p 928 *a* to *j*, post).

d. *McHale v Watson* (1966) 115 CLR 199 adopted.

e. Notes

For the standard of care required of children, see 33 *Halsbury's Laws* (4th edn) para 621.

f. Cases referred to in judgments

Bolton v *Stone* [1951] 1 All ER 1078, [1951] AC 850, HL.

Gough v *Thorne* [1966] 3 All ER 398, [1966] 1 WLR 1387, CA.

Hughes v *Lord Advocate* [1963] 1 All ER 705, [1963] AC 837, [1963] 2 WLR 779, HL.

McHale v *Watson* (1966) 115 CLR 199, Aust HC.

d. REFERENCE TO CASES

At the end of the headnote there may be a reference to cases reviewed by the court and what use the court has made of them. Reference is made to *McHale v Watson* (1966) 115 CLR 199 that is followed by the word 'adopted'. In this instance the court had considered an Australian case, *McHale v Watson*, and decided that the approach in that case had 'the advantage of obvious, indeed irrefutable, logic' and should be therefore be used in deciding the case of *Mullin v Richards and Another*. As an Australian case has no binding authority under the doctrine of judicial precedent, but is said to be of persuasive authority, the court has a choice of whether to use the case or not. In *Mullin v Richards and Another*, the Court of Appeal (Civil Division) decided to use the principle established in the Australian case and thus adopted it.

In other cases it might be indicated that judges have treated previous cases in the following ways: **follow**; **reverse**; **affirm**; **approve**; **overruled**; **distinguish**; **consider** (see Chapter 2 for meanings).

e. NOTES

In the *All England Reports* a helpful reference to *Halsbury's Laws* with regard to the area of law raised by the case is given.

f. CASES REFERRED TO IN JUDGMENTS

The cases used by the judges are listed for ease of reference. Additionally, the cases also cited by the lawyers in their skeleton arguments are listed.

Cases also cited or referred to in skeleton arguments

Carmarthenshire CC v *Lewis* [1955] 1 All ER 565, [1955] AC 549, HL.

Draper v *Hodder* [1972] 2 All ER 210, [1972] 2 QB 556, CA.

Latham v *Johnson & Nephew Ltd* [1913] 1 KB 398, [1911–1913] All ER Rep 117, CA.

Mahon v *Osborne* [1939] 1 All ER 535, [1939] 2 KB 14, CA.

Staley v *Suffolk CC* (26 November 1985, unreported), QBD at Norwich.

Vacwell Engineering Co Ltd v *BDH Chemicals Ltd* [1969] 3 All ER 1681, [1971] 1 QB 88.

Wieland v *Cyril Lord Carpets Ltd* [1969] 3 All ER 1006.

Williams v *Humphrey* (1975) Times, 20 February.

Wilson v *Pringle* [1986] 2 All ER 440, [1987] QB 237, CA.

g. Appeal

The first defendant, Heidi Richards, appealed from the decision of Judge Potter on 14 November 1995 in the Birmingham County Court whereby he awarded the plaintiff, Teresa Jane Mullin, damages of £27,500 for personal injury caused by the first defendant's negligence, but ordered that the damages should be reduced by 50% because of the plaintiff's contributory negligence. The judge dismissed the plaintiff's claim against the second defendant, Birmingham City Council, and the council took no part in the appeal. The facts are set out in the judgment of Hutchison LJ.

h. Richard Lee (instructed by *Cobbold & Gailey,* Lichfield) for the first defendant. Michael Stephens (instructed by *Sehdev & Co,* Birmingham) for the plaintiff.

i. **HUTCHISON LJ** (giving the first judgment at the invitation of Butler-Sloss LJ). On 29 February 1988 at Perry Beeches Secondary School in Birmingham two 15-year-old schoolgirls, Teresa Jane Mullin and Heidi Richards, who were friends and were sitting side by side at

g. APPEAL

This section gives information on how the case has arrived before the instant court. It may alternatively be headed 'Introduction'.

h. COUNSEL

This indicates the names of the barristers appearing for each side.

i. JUDGMENTS

The judgments are the most important parts of a case. It is from these that you must seek to establish the principle of law upon which the decision in the case is based. Depending upon which is the deciding court you might read a single judgment (eg the High Court at first instance), or three judgments (the usual number of judges in the Court of Appeal) or five opinions (the usual number of judges in the House of Lords). Before reading the judgments check to see if the judges are in agreement as to outcome; see the beginning and the end of the judgments or look at the headnote. If a judge disagrees with the majority in a case that judge is said to dissent. But be careful: even if the judges say they agree this may be as to outcome but not, necessarily, as to the reasoning for reaching the outcome.

It is important to read the judgments in full. This will help you get to grips with the legal method process.

their desk, were engaged in playing around, hitting each other's white plastic 30 cm rulers as though in a play sword fight, when one or other of the rulers snapped and a fragment of plastic entered Teresa's right eye with the very unhappy result that she lost all useful sight in that eye, something that must be a source, I am sure, of great distress to her and her family.

Teresa brought proceedings against Heidi and the Birmingham City Council, who were the education authority, alleging negligence. It is worth noting that her pleaded case involved facts quite different from those that I summarised a moment ago. My summary reflects the learned judge's unchallenged findings of fact as well as the case pleaded by Heidi in her defence. The judge dismissed the claim against the authority, holding that the mathematics teacher, Miss Osborne, whose class was coming to an end when the mishap occurred, had not been guilty of negligence and the plaintiff does not appeal against that decision. The case against the local authority was based only on lack of proper supervision in the classroom on the day in question. However, the judge having rejected Teresa's and accepted Heidi's version of how the accident occurred, concluded (that each had been guilty of negligence, that Teresa's injury was the foreseeable result and that, accordingly, her claim against Heidi succeeded subject to a reduction of 50% for contributory negligence.

From that decision Heidi now appeals to this court. I have referred already to the fact that it was not the plaintiff's case that the accident happened in the way the judge found and it is worth just taking a moment to see how things stood on the pleadings.

The plaintiff in her particulars of claim had alleged facts which involved that the first defendant, her friend Heidi, had tapped her from behind on the arm on a number of occasions with her ruler. She alleged that she had at some stage stood up and had been minded to go and speak to the class teacher to have this conduct stopped but had refrained from doing that, and there came a time when Heidi hit her again and she put up her arm to shield herself and the ruler broke against her arm, that she turned to the front and then, turning back again, felt some pain or discomfort in her eye, the inference being that at that moment it was that she was injured. The important feature of her account was that she was not doing anything or participating in anything with Heidi and that her accident resulted from the unwelcome attentions of Heidi and her use of the ruler.

In answer to that case, the first defendant by her pleading had denied the account given by the plaintiff and she had said in the particulars of contributory negligence:

'(i) The Plaintiff was a willing participant in a game in which the Plaintiff was fencing with the First Defendant, with rulers, during the course of which one of the rulers broke, (ii) If, which is denied, the Plaintiff suffered any injury, the First Defendant will aver that it was caused by a piece of plastic, detaching itself from the broken ruler and hitting the Plaintiff in the eye.'

It would have been open to the plaintiff, had she wished to do so, to amend her particulars of claim and allege an alternative case based upon the possibility that the judge might accept the case being advanced by the first defendant, but her advisers chose not to do that, probably for tactical reasons because they thought it would weaken her primary case about which she was resolute and maybe also because they thought that it was a case that was unlikely to be successful, one knows not. But the important thing is that there was no amendment and therefore those two versions were before the judge. No one was advancing a case of negligence based upon Heidi's version of what occurred.

Most of the judgment of the learned judge was devoted to resolving the dispute as to whether Teresa's or Heidi's account of what happened was the correct one, a task which the judge made clear, and I have to say I understand why he said this, and I sympathise with him, was made much more difficult by the fact that the trial was in November 1995, many years after the accident which occurred.

Having rejected Teresa's account the judge also held that Mrs Osborne, the class teacher, did not really see what had happened. She had said in evidence: 'Heidi and Teresa were playing with rulers, playing at a sword fight.' Heidi's account was that contained in her pleadings and the judge said of that:

'I was not willing to accept the evidence of the twins on the matter [the twins being a reference to Heidi and her twin sister, who gave evidence to the same effect] simple though it was, merely because they repeated it so many times with such enthusiasm. I have had to examine the notes they both wrote close to the event . . . I think these . . . are far more valuable . . . The first defendant's note is very interesting: "Me and Teresa were playing around, hitting each other. I hit her with the ruler. It snapped out, went in her eye. It was a pure accident." Her sister wrote a similar note: "Heidi and Teresa were messing around, hitting each other. Heidi['s] ruler snapped and accidentally went into Teresa['s] eye. It was a complete accident." '

When he came to make his findings as to what happened, the judge, who plainly gave the matter very careful consideration, said:

'. . . I conclude on the balance of probabilities that die plaintiff has not correctly stated . . . what occurred and that in the concluding stages of the rough play between these two girls it is probable that what was going on was more like what is described by the first defendant and her sister than what is described by the plaintiff.'

Neither defendant argued volenti non fit injuria, though the particulars of contributory negligence, as will be recalled from my citation, referred to the plaintiff being a willing participant in the game. The judge adverted to the absence of any such contention in terms which suggest that he thought it would not have been a possible defence, something as to which I express no opinion. I simply note that it does not arise because it was never raised. The judge therefore had to determine whether negligence had been proved against either defendant; if so, whether the plaintiffs injury was foreseeable; and whether there was contributory negligence on the part of the plaintiff. What he said on these matters in so far as it relates to the position between Teresa and Heidi was:

> '. . . I do not think any doubt was raised as to this, that if on the balance of probabilities the two girls were participating on equal terms, or both as free agents participating in an event of horseplay which, as they must both have appreciated became in its concluding stage dangerous because it involved rulers being used with some violence, if those are the findings I make, and they are the findings which, as I say, on the balance of probabilities I feel driven to, then however surprising it may be to the lay mind, the result must be that both were negligent. One cannot describe it as a lawful assault so one could also say that they were mutually engaging in assault, although that does not matter to my mind, and their joint mischievous efforts produced a particular total of unintended damage which happened to fall entirely on one participant rather than both.'

The judge went on to refer to defence counsel's argument on foreseeability, saying:

> 'The point was raised by Mr Lee in his helpful argument as to whether what happened was foreseeable or whether I should put it down to something that leads to no liability as between them because it was a totally uncovenanted and unforeseeable event. Having considered that, I do not think that it is the view that I take. In fact it is not, because as the matter ended, these girls were playing with a degree of misdirected and dangerous force sufficient to produce the physical and mechanical result that it did, and at 15 I am satisfied they must both have appreciated that to play like that was dangerous and although the precise injury would not have been foreseen, the danger of physical injury,

including injury of this type, must have been readily foreseeable. So on that part of the case the plaintiff succeeds but only as to half.'

By her notice of appeal the first defendant contends, first, that there was no or no sufficient evidence for the judge's finding that she must have appreciated that what she was doing was dangerous; second, that there was no or no sufficient evidence for the judge's finding that it was readily foreseeable that her conduct might cause injury of the type that the plaintiff sustained; thirdly, that the judge erred when considering foreseeability by omitting to take account of the fact that the first defendant was not an adult but a 15-year-old schoolgirl. What he should have done, it is contended, was to consider objectively what a normal and reasonable 15-year-old schoolgirl would have foreseen. Fourthly, it is asserted that the judge's finding that Heidi must have appreciated that this sort of conduct was dangerous was inconsistent with his finding that it was common in the school and with his conclusion that it was comparatively innocent and the absence of any evidence of prohibition or previous injuries. Finally, it is said that there was no evidence on which the judge could find that the shattering of the ruler was foreseeable.

So far as negligence is concerned, the relevant principles are well settled and I do not understand there to be any real difference between the views of counsel for the parties to this appeal. I would summarise the principles that govern liability in negligence in a case such as the present as follows. In order to succeed the plaintiff must show that the defendant did an act which it was reasonably foreseeable would cause injury to the plaintiff, that the relationship between the plaintiff and the defendant was such as to give rise to a duty of care, and that the act was one which caused injury to the plaintiff. In the present case, as it seems to me, no difficulty arose as to the second and third requirements because Teresa and Heidi were plainly in a sufficiently proximate relationship to give rise to a duty of care and the causation of the injury is not in issue. The argument centres on foreseeability.

The test of foreseeability is an objective one; but the fact that the first defendant was at the time a 15-year-old schoolgirl is not irrelevant. The question for the judge is not whether the actions of the defendant were such as an ordinarily prudent and reasonable adult in the defendant's situation would have realised gave rise to a risk of injury, it is whether an ordinarily prudent and reasonable 15-year-old schoolgirl in the defendant's situation would have realised as much. In that connection both counsel referred us to, and relied upon, the Australian decision in *McHale v Watson* (1966) 115 CLR 199 esp at 213-214 in the judgment of Kitto J. I cite a portion of the passage I have referred to, all of which was cited to us by Mr Lee on behalf of the appellant, and which Mr Stephens has adopted as epitomising the correct approach:

> 'The standard of care being objective, it is no answer for him [that is a child], any more than it is for an adult, to say that the harm he caused was due to his being abnormally slow-witted, quick-tempered, absent-minded or inexperienced. But it does not follow that he cannot rely in his defence upon a limitation upon the capacity for foresight or prudence, not as being personal to himself, but as being characteristic of humanity at his stage of development and in that sense normal. By doing so he appeals to a standard of ordinariness, to an objective and not a subjective standard.'

Mr Stephens also cited to us a passage in the judgment of Owen J (at 234):

> '. . . the standard by which his conduct is to be measured is not that to be expected of a reasonable adult but that reasonably to be expected of a child of the same age, intelligence and experience.'

I venture to question the word 'intelligence' in that sentence, but I understand Owen J to be making the same point essentially as was made by Kitto J. It is perhaps also material to have in mind the words of Salmon LJ in *Gough v Thorne* [1966] 3 All ER 398 at 400, [1966] 1 WLR 1387 at

1391, which is cited also by Mr Stephens, where he said:

> 'The question as to whether the plaintiff can be said to have been guilty of contributory negligence depends on whether any ordinary child of 13 can be expected to have done any more than this child did. I say "any ordinary child". I do not mean a paragon of prudence; nor do I mean a scatter-brained child; but the ordinary girl of 13.'

I need say no more about that principle as to the way in which age affects the assessment of negligence because counsel are agreed upon it and, despite the fact that we have been told that there has been a good deal of controversy in other jurisdictions and that there is no direct authority in this jurisdiction, the approach in *McHale v Watson* seems to me to have the advantage of obvious, indeed irrefutable, logic. Then, even if the requirements that I have so far summarised are satisfied with the consequence that negligence has been proved, the defendant will not be liable if the injury actually sustained is not foreseeable, that is to say is of a different kind from that which the defendant ought to have foreseen as the likely outcome of his want of care (see in that regard *Hughes v Lord Advocate* [1963] 1 All ER 705, [1963] AC 837).

Applying those principles to the facts of the present case the central question to which this appeal gives rise is whether on the facts found by the judge and in the light of the evidence before him he was entitled to conclude that an ordinary, reasonable 15-year-old schoolgirl in the first defendant's position would have appreciated that by participating to the extent that she did in a play fight, involving the use of plastic rulers as though they were swords, gave rise to a risk of injury to the plaintiff of the same general kind as she sustained. In that connection I emphasise that a mere possibility is not enough as passages in the well-known case of *Bolton v Stone* [1951] 1 All ER 1078, [1951] AC 850, to which Mr Lee helpfully referred us, make clear. I cite some of the passages on which he relied.

Lord Porter said ([1951] 1 All ER 1078 at 1080, 1081, [1951] AC 850 at 857, 858):

'The question however remains: Is it enough to make an action negligent to say that its performance may possibly cause injury or must some greater probability exist of that result ensuing in order to make those responsible for its occurrence guilty of negligence? . . . It is not enough that the event should be such as can reasonably be foreseen. The further result that injury is likely to follow must also be such as a reasonable man would contemplate before he can be convicted of actionable negligence. Nor is the remote possibility of injury occurring enough. There must be sufficient probability to lead a reasonable man to anticipate it. The existence of some risk is an ordinary incident of life, even when all due care has been, as it must be, taken.'

Lord Reid said ([1951] 1 All ER 1078 at 1084, [1951] AC 850 at 864):

'My Lords, it was readily foreseeable that an accident such as befell the respondent might possibly occur during one of the appellants' cricket matches. Balls had been driven into the public road from time to time and it was obvious that if a person happened to be where a ball fell that person would receive injuries which might or might not be serious. On the other hand, it was plain that the chance of that happening was small.'

Lord Radcliffe made this observation ([1951] 1 All ER 1078 at 1087, [1951] AC 850 at 868):

'I can see nothing unfair in the appellants being required to compensate the respondent for the serious injury that she has received as a result of the sport that they have organized on their cricket ground at Cheetham Hill, but the law of negligence is concerned less with what is fair than with what is culpable, and I cannot persuade

myself that the appellants have been guilty of
any culpable act or omission in this case.'

I have omitted to cite two further passages
which were referred to in the speeches of Lord
Normand and Lord Oaksey which are to the same
effect (see [1951] 1 All ER 1078 at 1082–1083 and
1083–1084, [1951] AC 850 at 860–861 and 863).

I do not propose, in the light of the conclusion
to which I have come without hesitation in this
case, to deal individually with all the grounds of
appeal, though I should mention in relation to the
third ground, which asserts that the judge treated
the first defendant as an adult and not as a 15-year-
old child, that I reject that contention. It seems to
me that his reference to the age of the two girls in
the passage which I have cited from his judgment
shows that he had in mind the correct principles.
Accordingly I would hold that he approached the
matter in that respect in the correct way.

However the question of actual foreseeability
(that is to say the application of that correct
approach in law to the facts) raises, in my judgment, great difficulties. First, there certainly was
no evidence as to the propensity or otherwise of
such rulers to break or any history of their having
done so. There was evidence which the judge
does not say he rejects and which he may, since it
was an admission against interest, be taken to
have accepted, that ruler fencing was commonplace. That is to be found in the evidence of Heidi
herself, who said when she was asked:

> '*Q*. As far as this business of fencing with
> rulers is concerned, was this the only time
> you had ever done that? *A*. No, it was a popu-
> lar game at school.'

Miss Osborne, the teacher, was asked questions
to the same effect:

> '*Q*. . . . Had you seen this game going on
> around the school? *A*. Yes, I knew it was a
> common game with pupils.'

While I am dealing with her evidence I should
mention an answer on which Mr Stephens
places particular reliance. The judge asked her:

'*Q*. . . . . did you think perhaps it was a thing
to stop because it might be dangerous? *A*. Yes,
and it was also unacceptable behaviour in the
classroom.'

It seems me that though she assented to the
judge's proposition that she would stop it
because it was dangerous, the point she was
really making was she would stop it because it
was unacceptable conduct in the classroom.
There was no evidence at all that the practice
was banned or even frowned on. There was no
evidence that it was discouraged in any way. The
question of foreseeability therefore has to be
judged against that background, the prevalence
of the practice, the absence of prohibition, the
absence of warning against it or of its dangers
and the absence of any evidence of there having
been any previous injury as a result of it. The
further point can be made, which is that the
judge's finding, if that is the right description of
it, that excessive violence was used by either girl
is not supported by any evidence so far as I can
see. It has to be remembered that he had
rejected Teresa's account which did involve a relatively heavy blow on her forearm and there is
no reason to think that in rejecting it he had, as
it were, preserved and resurrected that one part
of it: and the passages in which Heidi gives her
account of the mock fencing do not bear the
construction that any degree of violence was
being used. Indeed there are passages in the evidence elsewhere that indicate that the two girls
were not even trying to knock the rulers out of
each other's hands but merely to touch rulers, as
it were, in mock fencing.

There was, therefore, as it seems to me, no evidence to support the finding that these two girls
were guilty of using misdirected and dangerous
force, which is one of the judge's phrases, or that
there had been a violent clash of rulers or that the
rulers had been used with some violence, which
are other phrases that he used. This had not been
said by the first defendant in her evidence. It had
not been suggested to her at any stage. I pause to
interpolate that not only was that case never put,
but it is at least doubtful whether it was urged in
argument as an alternative basis for a finding of

negligence, though for present purposes I shall assume that it may have been. Mr Stephens was not present at the trial and has no instructions on the matter.

The judge, it seems to me, found negligence without there being material on which he could properly do so. He seems indeed from the language he used to have regarded it as axiomatic that if there was a fight going on, such as he found there was, a play fight, that imported that injury was reasonably foreseeable and from his finding that the ruler broke that there was necessarily dangerous or excessive violence. For my part, I would say that in the absence of evidence one simply does not know why the ruler broke, whether because it was unusually weak, unlike other rulers; whether because it had been damaged in some way; or whether because rulers of this sort are particularly prone to break; one does not know. What certainly one cannot infer, and the judge was, I consider, not entitled to infer, was that there was here excessive violence or inappropriate violence over and above that which was inherent in the play fencing in which these two girls were indulging. This was in truth nothing more than a schoolgirls' game such as on the evidence was commonplace in this school and there was, I would hold, no justification for attributing to the participants the foresight of any significant risk of the likelihood of injury. They had seen it done elsewhere with some frequency. They had not heard it prohibited or received any warning about it. They had not been told of any injuries occasioned by it. They were not in any sense behaving culpably. So far as foresight goes, had they paused to think they might, I suppose, have said: 'It is conceivable that some unlucky injury might happen', but if asked if there was any likelihood of it or any real possibility of it, they would, I am sure, have said that they did not foresee any such possibility. Taking the view therefore that the learned judge – who, as I have said, readily and almost without question accepted that on his findings of fact there was negligence on the part of both these young ladies – was wrong in his view and there was no evidence on which he could come to it, I would allow the appeal and direct that judgment be entered for the first defendant. I have to say that I appreciate that this result will be disappointing to the plaintiff for whom one can have nothing but sympathy, because she has suffered a grave injury through no fault of her own. But unfortunately she has failed to establish in my view that anyone was legally responsible for that injury and, accordingly, her claim should have failed.

SIR JOHN VINELOTT I agree. It seems to me that, in the passage which Hutchison LJ has cited at length, the learned judge at the very end of his judgment comes very close to saying: 'This accident happened. It must therefore be the case that these young ladies were playing with these rulers with a degree of misdirected and dangerous force sufficient to cause a ruler to break or splinter as a result of which injury was caused; it was and must have been an injury which was reasonably foreseeable.' That is an inappropriate approach. There was in fact no evidence that the ruler broke because the mock fight was carried on with dangerous force and, equally, there was no evidence that physical damage would be likely to result if a ruler broke or splintered in the course of that activity. In the absence of any sufficient evidence on those two points, it seems to me that the conclusion that the learned judge reached was unfounded.

BUTLER-SLOSS LJ I agree with both judgments and since there has been little earlier authority on the proper approach to the standard of care to be applied to a child, I would like to underline the observations of Hutchison LJ and rely upon two further passages in the persuasive judgment of Kitto J in the High Court of Australia in *McHale v Watson* (1966) 115 CLR 199 at 213):

'In regard to the things which pertain to foresight and prudence, experience, understanding of causes and effects, balance of judgment thoughtfulness – it is absurd, indeed it is a misuse of language, to speak of normality in relation to persons of all ages taken together. In those things normality is, for children, something different from what normality is for adults; the very concept of normality is a concept of rising levels until "years of discretion" are attained. The law does not arbitrarily fix upon any particular age for this purpose, and tribunals offset may well give effect to different views as to the age at which normal adult foresight and prudence are reasonably to be expected in relation to particular sets of circumstances. But up to that stage the normal capacity to exercise those two qualities necessarily means the capacity which is normal for a child of the relevant age; and it seems to me that it would be contrary to the fundamental principle that a person is liable for harm that he causes by falling short of an objective criterion of "propriety" in his conduct – propriety, that is to say, as determined by a comparison with the standard of care reasonably to be expected in the circumstances from the normal person to hold that where a child's liability is in question the normal person – to be considered is someone other than a child of corresponding age.'

I would respectfully indorse those observations as entirely appropriate to English law and I would like to conclude with another passage of Kitto J (at 216) particularly relevant to today –

'. . . in the absence of relevant statutory provision, children, like everyone else, must accept as they go about in society the risks from which ordinary care on the part of others will not suffice to save them. One such risk is that boys of twelve may behave as boys of twelve . . .'

– and I would say that girls of 15 playing together may play as somewhat irresponsible girls of 15. I too would allow this appeal.

j. ▌ *Appeal allowed.*

Dilys Tausz Barrister.

j. APPEAL ALLOWED
This indicates the overall decision of the court.

Appendix 2

Sample Act of Parliament: Compensation Act 2006

- -

a. ▌ **Compensation Act 2006**

b. ▌ ### CHAPTER 29

c. ▌ ### CONTENTS

Part 1

Standard of Care

Part 2

Claims Management Services

a. SHORT TITLE

See section 18 below.

b. CHAPTER NUMBER

The chapter number is part of the citation to the Act; it enables us to locate the Act. The Compensation Act 2006 was the 29th Act passed in 2006, hence 2006 chapter 29.

c. CONTENTS

This gives an overview of the contents of an Act.

Part 3

General

16 Commencement
17 Extent
18 Short title

d.

An Act to specify certain factors that may be taken into account by a court determining a claim in negligence or breach of statutory duty; to make, provision about damages for mesothelioma; and to make provision for the regulation of claims management services.

e.

[25th July 2006]

BE IT ENACTED by the Queen's most Excellent Majesty, by and with the advice and consent of the Lords Spiritual and Temporal, and Commons, in this present Parliament assembled, and by the authority of the same, as follows: –

Part 1

f.

Standard of Care

1 Deterrent effect of potential liability

A court considering a claim in negligence or breach of statutory duty may, in determining whether the defendant should have taken particular steps to meet a standard of care (whether by taking precautions against a risk or otherwise), have regard to whether a requirement to take those steps might –

(a) prevent a desirable activity from being undertaken at all, to a particular extent or in a particular way, or

(b) discourage persons from undertaking functions in connection with a desirable activity.

2 Apologies, offers of treatment or other redress

An apology, an offer of treatment or other redress, shall not of itself amount to an admission of negligence or breach of statutory duty.

g.

3 Mesothelioma: damages

h.

(1) This section applies where –

i.

(a) a person ("the responsible person") has negligently or in breach of statutory duty

d. LONG TITLE

The long title gives a general indication of the scope and purpose of an Act of Parliament.

e. DATE OF ROYAL ASSENT

This is the date when a bill completes the legislative process and becomes an Act. The Act may come into force on this day, but not necessarily. This depends upon whether or not there is a commencement section at the end of the Act. If there is a commencement section then this governs when the Act comes into force, if not the Act is in force from the start of the day in which the Royal Assent was given.

f. CROSS-HEADINGS

A cross-heading indicates the scope of the following sections, for example see before section 1, 'Standard of Care'. Note that an Act may have several cross-headings grouping sections together.

g. SECTION

Acts of Parliament are arranged in sections. When using an Act of Parliament reference should be made for example to section 3 of the Compensation Act 2006.

h. SUB-SECTION

A section of an Act of Parliament may be further divided into sub-sections. So reference may be made to section 3 sub-section (1) of the Compensation Act 2006.

i. PARAGRAPH

A sub-section may be further divided into paragraphs. So reference may be made to section 3 sub-section (1) paragraph (a) of the Compensation Act 2006. Note while orally you will say section 3 sub-section (1) paragraph (a) of the Compensation Act 2006 when you refer to such in a written form it should appear as follows: s 3(1)(a).

caused or permitted another person ('the victim') to be exposed to asbestos,

(b) the victim has contracted mesothelioma as a result of exposure to asbestos,

(c) because of the nature of mesothelioma and the state of medical science, it is not possible to determine with certainty whether it was the exposure mentioned in paragraph (a) or another exposure which caused the victim to become ill, and

(d) the responsible person is liable in tort, by virtue of the exposure mentioned in paragraph (a), in connection with damage caused to the victim by the disease (whether by reason of having materially increased a risk or for any other reason).

(2) The responsible person shall be liable –

(a) in respect of the whole of the damage caused to the victim by the disease (irrespective of whether the victim was also exposed to asbestos –

(i) other than by the responsible person, whether or not in circumstances in which another person has liability in tort, or

(ii) by the responsible person in circumstances in which he has no liability in tort), and

(b) jointly and severally with any other responsible person.

(3) Subsection (2) does not prevent –

(a) one responsible person from claiming a contribution from another, or

(b) a finding of contributory negligence.

(4) In determining the extent of contributions of different responsible persons in accordance with subsection (3)(a), a court shall have regard to the relative lengths, of the periods of exposure for which each was responsible; but this subsection shall not apply –

(a) if or to the extent that responsible persons agree to apportion responsibility amongst themselves on some other basis, or

(b) if or to the extent that the court thinks that another basis for determining contributions is more appropriate in the circumstances of a particular case.

(5) In subsection (1) the reference to causing or permitting a person to be exposed to asbestos includes a reference to failing to protect a person from exposure to asbestos.

(6) In the application of this section to Scotland –

(a) a reference to tort shall be taken as a reference to delict, and

(b) a reference to a court shall be taken to include a reference to a jury.

(7) The Treasury may make regulations about the provision of compensation to a responsible person where –

(a) he claims, or would claim, a contribution from another responsible person in accordance with subsection (3)(a), but

(b) he is unable or likely to be unable to obtain the contribution, because an insurer of the other responsible person is unable or likely to be unable to satisfy the claim for a contribution.

(8) The regulations may, in particular –

(a) replicate or apply (with or without modification] a provision of the Financial Services Compensation Scheme;

(b) replicate or apply (with or without modification) a transitional compensation provision;

(c) provide for a specified person to assess and pay compensation;

(d) provide for expenses incurred (including the payment of compensation) to be met out of levies collected in accordance with section 213(3)(b) of the Financial Services and Markets Act 2000 (c. 8) (the Financial Services Compensation Scheme);

(e) modify the effect of a transitional compensation provision;

(f) enable the Financial Services Authority to amend the Financial Services Compensation Scheme;

(g) modify the Financial Services and Markets Act 2000 in its application to an amendment pursuant to paragraph (f);

(h) make, or require the making of, provision for the making of a claim by a responsible person for compensation whether or not he has already satisfied claims in tort against him;

(i) make, or require the making of, provision which has effect in relation to claims for contributions made on or after the date on which this Act is passed.

(9) Provision made by virtue of subsection (8)(a) shall cease to have effect when the Financial Services Compensation Scheme is amended by the Financial Services Authority by virtue of subsection (8)(f).

(10) In subsections (7) and (8) –

(a) a reference to a responsible person includes a reference to an insurer of a responsible person, and

(b) "transitional compensation provision" means a provision of an enactment which is made under the Financial Services and Markets Act 2000 and –

(i) preserves the effect of the Policyholders Production Act 1975 (c. 75), or

(ii) applies the Financial Services Compensation Schemes in relation to matters arising before its establishment.

(11) Regulations under subsection (7) –

(a) may include consequential or incidental provision,

(b) may make provision which has effect generally or only in relation to specified cases or circumstances,

(c) may make different provision for different cases or circumstances,

(d) shall be made by statutory instrument, and

(e) may not be made unless a draft has been laid before and approved by resolution of each House of Parliament.

j.

Part 2

Claims Management Services

4 Provision of regulated claims management services

(1) A person may not provide regulated claims management services unless –

    (a) he is an authorised person,

    (b) he is an exempt person,

    (c) the requirement for authorisation has been waived in relation to him in accordance with regulations under section 9, or

    (d) he is an individual acting otherwise than in the coarse of a business.

(2) In this Part –

    (a) "authorised person" means a person authorised by the Regulator under section 5(1)(a),

    (b) "claims management services" means advices or other services in relation to the making of the claim,

    (c) "claim" means a claim for compensation, restitution, repayment or any other remedy or relief in respect of loss or damage or in respect of an obligation, whether the claim is made or could be made –

        (i) by way of legal proceedings,

        (ii) in accordance with a scheme of regulation (whether voluntary or compulsory), or

        (iii) in pursuance of a voluntary undertaking,

    (d) "exempt person" has the meaning given by section 6(5), and

    (e) services are regulated If they are –

        (i) of a kind prescribed by order of the Secretary of State, or

        (ii) provided in cases or circumstances of a kind prescribed by order of the Secretary of State.

(3) For the purposes of this section –

    (a) a reference to the provision of services includes, in particular, a reference to –

        (i) the provision of financial services or assistance,

j. **PART**

For ease of reference an Act may be arranged in Parts. The Compensation Act 2006 is arranged in three parts.

> (ii) the provision of services by way of or in relation to legal representation,
>
> (iii) referring or introducing one person to another, and
>
> (iv) making inquiries, and
>
> (b) a person does not provide claims management services by reason only of giving, or preparing to give, evidence (whether or not expert evidence).

(4) For the purposes of subsection (1)(d) an individual acts in the course of a business if, in particular –

(a) he acts in the course of an employment, or

(b) he otherwise receives or hopes to receive money or money's worth as a result of his action.

(5) The Secretary of State may by order provide that a claim for a specified benefit shall be treated as a claim for the purposes of this Part.

(6) The Secretary of State may specify a benefit under subsection (5) only if it appears to him to be a United Kingdom social security benefit designed to provide compensation for industrial injury.

k. | **5 The Regulator**

(1) The Secretary of State may by order designate a person ("the Regulator") –

(a) to authorise persons to provide regulated claims management services,

(b) to regulate the conduct of authorised persons, and

(c) to exercise such other functions as are conferred on the Regulator by or under this Part.

(2) The Secretary of State may designate a person only if satisfied that the person –

(a) is competent to perform the functions of the Regulator,

(b) will make arrangements to avoid any conflict of interest between the person's functions as Regulator and any other functions, and

k. MARGINAL NOTE OR SIDE NOTE

Marginal notes are included for ease of reference. A marginal note gives a general indication of the scope of a section and where the section is not clear the courts have been willing to use it as an aid to interpretation. Since 2001 the note is placed in bold above the section to which it relates. Prior to 2001 the note, as the name suggests, appeared in the margin to an Act.

(c) will promote the interests of persons
using regulated claims management services (including, in particular, by –

   (i) setting and monitoring standards of
   competence and professional conduct
   for persons providing regulated claims
   management services,

   (ii) promoting good practice by persons
   providing regulated claims management services, in particular in relation
   to the provision of infonnation about
   charges and other matters to persons
   using or considering using the services,

   (iii) promoting practices likely to facilitate
   competition   between   different
   providers of regulated claims management services, and

   (iv) ensuring that arrangements are made
   for the protection of persons using
   regulated claims management services (including arrangements for the handling of complaints about the conduct
   of authorised persons)).

(3) If the Secretary of State thinks that no existing person (whether an individual or a body
corporate or unincorporate) is suitable for
designation under subsection (1), he may by
order establish a person for the purpose of
being designated.

(4) The Regulator shall –

   (a) comply with any directions given to him
   by the Secretary of State;

   (b) have regard to any guidance given to him
   by the Secretary of State;

   (c) have regard to any code of practice issued
   to him by the Secretary of State;

   (d) try to meet any targets set for him by the
   Secretary of State;

   (e) provide the Secretary of State with any
   report or information requested (but this
   paragraph does not require or permit dis-
   closure of information in contravention
   of any other enactment).

(5) The Secretary of State shall lay before Parliament any code of practice issued by him to the Regulator.

(6) The Secretary of State may pay grants to the Regulator (which may be on terms or conditions, including terms and conditions as to repayment with or without interest).

(7) A reference in this Part to the Regulator includes a reference to a person acting on behalf of the Regulator or with his authority.

(8) The Secretary of State may by order revoke a person's designation under subsection (1).

(9) While no person is designated under subsection (1) the Secretary of State shall exercise functions of the Regulator.

(10) The Secretary of State may by order transfer (whether for a period of time specified in the order or otherwise) a function of the Regulator to the Secretary of State.

I. ┃ **6 Exemptions**

(1) The Secretary of State may by order provide that section 4(1) shall not prevent the provision of regulated claims management services by a person who is a member of a specified body.

(2) The Secretary of State may by order provide that section 4(1) shall not prevent the provision of regulated claims management services –

(a) by a specified person or class of person,

(b) in specified circumstances, or

(c) by a specified person or class of person in specified circumstances.

(3) Provision by virtue of subsection (1) or (2) may be expressed to have effect subject to compliance with specified conditions.

(4) Section 4(1) shall not prevent the provision of regulated claims management services by a person who is established or appointed by virtue of an enactment.

I. **DELEGATION OF LAW-MAKING POWER**

This section gives authority to a secretary of state to make further legislation on behalf of Parliament. The legislation is referred to as delegated legislation and the form in this instance is that of a statutory instrument.

(5) For the purposes of this Part a person is "exempt" if, or in so far as, section 4(1) does not, by virtue of this section, prevent him from providing regulated claims management services.

7 Enforcement; offence

(1) A person commits an offence if he contravenes section 4(1).

(2) A person who is guilty of an offence under subsection (1) shall be liable –

(a) on conviction on indictment –

(i) to imprisonment for a term not exceeding two years,

(ii) to a fine, or

(iii) to both, or

(b) on summary conviction –

(i) to imprisonment for a term not exceeding 51 weeks,

(ii) to a fine not exceeding level 5 on the standard scale, or

(iii) to both.

(3) Until the commencement of section 281(4) and (5) of the Criminal Justice Act 2003 (c. 44) (51 week maximum term of sentences) the reference in subsection (3)(b)(i) above to 51 weeks shall have effect as if it were a reference to six months.

8 Enforcement: the Regulator

(1) The Regulator may apply to the court for an injunction restraining a person from providing regulated claims management services if he is not –

(a) an authorised person,

(b) an exempt person, or`

(c) the subject of a waiver in accordance with regulations under section 9.

(2) In subsection (1) "the court" means the High Court or a county court.

(3) The Regulator may –

(a) investigate whether an offence has been committed under this Part;

(b) institute criminal proceedings in respect of an offence under this Part.

(4) For the purpose of investigating whether an offence has been committed under this Part the Regulator may require the provision of information or documents.

(5) On an application by the Regulator a judge of the High Court, Circuit judge or justice of the peace may issue a warrant authorising the Regulator to enter and search premises on which a person conducts or is alleged to conduct regulated claims management business, for the purposes of investigating whether an offence has been committed under this Part.

(6) The Regulator may take copies of written or electronic records found on a search by virtue of subsection (5) for a purpose specified in subsection (3)(a) or (b).

(7) In subsections (4) to (6) a reference to the Regulator includes a reference to a person authorised by him in writing.

(8) The Secretary of State shall make regulations –

(a) specifying matters of which a judge or justice of the peace must be satisfied, or to which he must have regard, before issuing a warrant under subsection (5), and

(b) regulating the exercise of a power under or by virtue of subsection (4) or (5) (whether by restricting the circumstances in which a power may be exercised, by specifying conditions to be complied with in the exercise of a power, or otherwise).

m.   9 Regulations

(1) The Secretary of State shall make regulations about –

(a) authorisations under section 5(1);

(b) the functions of the regulator.

(2) The Schedule specifies particular provision that may be made by the regulations.

(3) Transitional provision of regulations under this section may, in particular, make provision about the extent to which functions under

m. DELEGATION OF LAW-MAKING POWER

This is a further example of a section which gives authority to a secretary of state to make legislation on behalf of Parliament. Once again the legislation made is in the form of a statutory instrument. See section 15(2).

this Part or under the regulations may be exercised in respect of matters arising before the commencement of a provision made by or by virtue of this Part.

10 Obstructing the Regulator

(1) A person commits an offence if without reasonable excuse he obstructs the Regulator in the exercise of a power –

(a) under section 8(4) to (6), or

(b) by virtue of paragraph 14 of the Schedule.

(2) A person who is guilty of an offence under subsection (1) shall be liable on summary conviction to a fine not exceeding level 5 on the standard scale.

11 Pretending to be authorised, &c.

(1) A person commits an offence if he falsely holds himself out as being –

(a) an authorised person,

(b) an exempt person, or

(c) the subject of a waiver in accordance with regulations under section 9.

(2) A person commits an offence if –

(a) he offers to provide regulated claims management services, and

(b) provision by him of those services would constitute an offence under this Part.

(3) For the purposes of subsection (2) a person offers to provide services if he –

(a) makes an offer to a particular person or class of person,

(b) makes arrangements for an advertisement in which he offers to provide services, or

(c) makes arrangements for an advertisement in which he is described or presented as competent to provide services.

(4) A person who is guilty of an offence under sub section (1) or (2) shall be liable –

(a) on conviction on indictment – to imprisonment for a term not exceeding two years, to a fine, or to both, or

(i) to imprisonment for a term not exceeding two years,

    (ii) to a fine not exceeding level 5 on the
       standard scale, or

    (iii) to both.

  (b) on summary conviction – to imprison-
     ment for a term exceeding 51 weeks, to a
     fine not exceeding level 5 on the standard
     scale, or to both.

    (i) to imprisonment for a term not exceed-
      ing 51 weeks,

    (ii) to a fine, or

    (iii) to both, or

(5) Where a person commits an offence under
this section by causing material to be displayed or made accessible, he shall be treated
as committing the offence on each day during any part of which the material is displayed or made accessible.

(6) Until the commencement of section 281(4)
and (5) of the Criminal Justice Act 2003
(c. 44) (51 week maximum term of sentences)
the reference in subsection (4)(b)(i) above to
51 weeks shall have effect as if it were a reference to six months.

12 The Claims Management Services Tribunal

(1) There shall be a tribunal to be known as the
Claims Management Services Tribunal.

(2) The Tribunal shall be constituted as follows –

  (a) members of the Financial Services and
    Markets Tribunal shall also be members
    of the Claims Management Services
    Tribunal,

  (b) the President of the Financial Services
    and Markets Tribunal shall also act as
    President of the Claims Management
    Services Tribunal,

  (c) the Deputy President of the Financial
    Services and Markets Tribunal shall also
    act as Deputy President of the Claims
    Management Services Tribunal, and

  (d) the panel of chairmen of the Financial
    Services and Markets Tribunal shall also
    be the panel of chairmen of the Claims
    Management Services Tribunal.

(3) An appeal or reference to the Tribunal shall be heard by a member of the panel of chairmen –

(a) selected in accordance with arrangements made by the President, and

(b) sitting alone or, in accordance with those arrangements, with one or two members of the lay panel;

and a chairman who sits with one other member shall have a casting vote.

(4) The Lord Chancellor may make rules about the proceedings of the Tribunal; and the rules –

(a) shall include provision about timing of references and appeals,

(b) shall include provision for the suspension of decisions of the Regulator while an appeal could be brought or is pending,

(c) shall include provision about the making of interim orders,

(d) shall enable the Tribunal to suspend or further suspend (wholly or partly) the effect of a decision of the Regulator,

(e) shall permit the Regulator to apply for the termination of the suspension of a decision of his,

(f) may include provision about evidence,

(g) may include provision about any other matter of a kind for which rules under section 132 of the Financial Services and Markets Act 2000 (c. 8) (the Financial Services and Markets Tribunal) may make provision,

(h) may include transitional, consequential or incidental provision,

(i) may make provision generally or only for specified cases or circumstances,

(j) may make different provision for different cases or circumstances,

(k) shall be made by statutory instrument, and

(l) shall be subject to annulment in pursuance of a resolution of either House of Parliament.

(5) The following provisions of Schedule 13 to the Financial Services and Markets Act 2000 shall have effect, with my necessary modifications, in relation to the Claims Management Services Tribunal –

(a) paragraph 5 (remuneration and allowances),

(b) paragraph 6 (staff),

(c) paragraph 7(3) and (4) (composition),

(d) paragraph 8 (sittings),

(e) paragraph 10 (practice directions),

(f) paragraph 11 (evidence), and

(g) paragraph 12(1) to (3) (decisions).

(6) In Part 1 of Schedule 1 to the Tribunals and Inquiries Act 1992 (c. 53) (tribunals under supervision of Council) insert at the appropriate place –

"Claims management services	The Claims Management Services Tribunal established by the Compensation Act 2006."

13 Appeals and references to tribunal

(1) A person may appeal to the Claims Management Services Tribunal if the Regulator –

(a) refuses the person's application for authorisation,

(b) grants the person authorisation on terms or subject to conditions,

(c) imposes conditions on the person's authorisation,

(d) suspends the person's authorisation, or

(e) cancels the person's authorisation.

(2) The Regulator may refer to the Tribunal (with or without findings of fact or recommendations)

(a) a complaint about the professional conduct of an authorised person, or

(b) the question whether an authorised person has complied with a rule of professional conduct.

(3) On a reference or appeal under this section the Tribunal –

(a) may take any decision on an application for authorisation that the Regulator could have taken;

(b) may impose or remove conditions on a person's authorisation;

(c) may suspend a person's authorisation;

(d) may cancel a person's authorisation;

(e) may remit a matter to the Regulator;

(f) may not award costs.

(4) An authorised person may appeal to the Court of Appeal against a decision of the Tribunal.

n.

14 Interpretation

In this Part –

"action" includes omission,

"authorised person" has the meaning given by section 4,

"claim" has the meaning given by section 4,

"claims management services" has the meaning given by section 4,

"exempt person" has the meaning given by section 6(5),

"regulated claims management services" shall be construed in accordance with section 4(2)(e),

"specified", in relation to an order or regulations, means specified in the order or regulations, and

"the Regulator" means (subject to section 5(7)) the person designated under section 5(1) or, where no person is designated or in so far as is necessary having regard to any order under section 5(10), the Secretary of State.

o.

15 Orders and regulations

(1) An order or regulations under this Part –

(a) may make provision that applies generally or only in specified cases or circumstances,

(b) may make different provision for different cases or circumstance, and

(c) may include transitional, incidental or consequential provision,

(2) An order or regulations under this Part shall be made by statutory instrument.

n. INTERPRETATION SECTION

An interpretation section will be found usually at the end of a Part, or towards the end of an Act. Its function is to provide definitions or partial definitions of words used in the Act. For example, see the meaning of 'action'. The use of the word 'includes' shows that the meaning is not exhaustive.

o. PROCEDURE FOR MAKING DELEGATED LEGISLATION

This section indicates the procedure for the making of orders and regulations under the Act. Note that the orders and regulations are to be made by statutory instrument. Also note the different ways in which the delegated legislation is laid before Parliament, eg compare the wording of section 15(8) and 15(9).

(3) An order under section 4(2)(e) –

   (a) may not be made unless the Secretary of State has consulted –

      (i) the Office of Fair Trading, and

      (ii) such other persons as he thinks appropriate, and

   (b) may not be made unless a draft has been laid before and approved by resolution of each House of Parliament.

(4) An order under section 4(5) may not be made unless a draft has been laid before, and approved by resolution of, each House of Parliament.

(5) An order under section 5 may not be made unless a draft has been laid before, and approved by resolution of, each House of Parliament.

(6) An order under section 5(3) may include provision –

   (a) for the appointment of members;

   (b) for funding;

   (c) for dissolution (which may include provision enabling the Secretary of State to make provision for the transfer of property, rights and liabilities).

(7) The first order made under section 6 may not be made unless a draft has been laid before, and approved by resolution of, each House of Parliament.

(8) An order under section 6 which has the effect of removing or restricting an exemption from section 4(1) may not be made unless a draft has been laid before, and approved by resolution of, each House of Parliament.

(9) Any other order under section 6 shall be subject to annulment in pursuance of a resolution of either House of Parliament.

(10) Regulations under section 8 or 9 may not be made unless a draft has been laid before, and approved by resolution of, each House of Parliament.

Part 3

General

16 Commencement

(1) The preceding provisions of this Act, other than sections 1, 2 and 3, shall come into force in accordance with provision made by order of the Secretary of State.

(2) An order under subsection (1) –

    (a) may make provision generally or only for specified purposes,

    (b) may make different provision for different purposes,

    (c) may make transitional, consequential or incidental provision, and

    (d) shall be made by statutory instrument.

(3) Section 3 shall be treated as having always had effect.

(4) But the section shall have no effect in relation to –

    (a) a claim which is settled before 3rd May 2006 (whether or not legal proceedings in relation to the claim have been instituted), or

    (b) legal proceedings which are determined before that date.

(5) Where a claim is settled on or after that date and before the date on which this Act is passed, a party to the settlement may apply to a relevant court to have the settlement varied; and –

    (a) a court is a relevant court for that purpose if it had, or would have had, jurisdiction to determine the claim by way of legal proceedings,

    (b) an application shall be brought as an application in, or by way of, proceedings on the claim, and

    (c) a court to which an application is made shall vary the settlement to such extent (if any) as appears appropriate to reflect the effect of section 3.

(6) Where legal proceedings are determined on or after that date and before the date on which

p. COMMENCEMENT SECTION

Such a section indicates when an Act is to come into force. Unless the Act indicates otherwise in a commencement section, an Act will come into operation on the date of the Royal Assent, which means that a Bill has completed all stages of the legislative process.

The Compensation Act 2006 has a relatively complex commencement section.

Section 16 provides that sections 4–15 will come into operation when the secretary of state by statutory instrument so orders (a commencement order). By omission, therefore, sections 1, 2 and 3 came into effect on the date of the Royal Assent, that is, 25 July 2006. See the Explanatory Notes for the unusual operation of section 3 which has retrospective effect, that is, applies to some cases before the Act came into force.

this Act is passed, a party to the proceedings may apply to the court to vary the determination; and –

    (a) "the court" means the court which determined the proceedings,

    (b) the application shall be treated as an application in the proceedings, and

    (c) the court shall vary the determination to such extent (if any) as appears appropriate to reflect the effect of section 3.

q. **17 Extent**

(1) This Act shall extend to England and Wales only.

(2) But section 3 (and section 16(3) to (6)) shall extend to –

    (a) England and Wales,

    (b) Scotland, and

    (c) Northern Ireland.

r. **18 Short title**

This Act may be cited as the Compensation Act 2006.

s. # Schedule   Section 9

CLAIMS MANAGEMENT REGULATIONS

Introduction

1   In this Schedule "regulations" means regulations under section 9.

2   Regulations made by virtue of a provision of this Schedule may confer a discretion on the Regulator.

Waiver of requirement for authorisation

3   (1) Regulations may permit the Regulator to waive the requirement for authorisation, as mentioned in section 4(1)(c), in specified cases or circumstances.

q. TERRITORIAL EXTENT

This section indicates where in a geographical sense the Act applies.

r. SHORT TITLE

This a brief label for the Act. It may be misleading. For example, the Unfair Contract Terms Act 1977 is not about all unfair terms (it concerns exemption clauses and indemnity clauses) and it is not restricted to contract terms (it also applies to non-contractual notices).

s. SCHEDULE

Schedules will appear at the end of an Act and contain detail. The function of a schedule is to prevent the main body of the Act becoming unnecessarily complex by the inclusion of detail.

(2) Regulations by virtue of this sub-paragraph may permit waiver in relation to a
person only –

(a) if the Secretary of State intends to
exempt the person under section 6,
and

(b) for a single period not exceeding six
months.

(3) The regulations may, in particular, permit or require the Regulator to provide
for waiver to be subject to a condition of a
kind specified in the regulations.

Grant of authorisations

4   (1) Regulations shall prescribe the procedure for applying to the Regulator for
authorisation.

(2) Regulations may, in particular, require
the provision of information or documents relating to the applicant or to any
person who appears to the Regulator to
be connected with the applicant.

5   (1) Regulations shall require the Regulator
not to grant an application for authorisation unless satisfied of the applicant's
competence and suitability to provide regulated claims management services of
the kind to which the application relates.

(2) For that purpose the Regulator shall apply
such criteria, and have regard to such
matters, as the regulations shall specify.

(3) Regulations by virtue of sub-paragraph
(2) may, in particular –

(a) refer to a provision of directions,
guidance or a code given or issued
under section 5(4);

(b) relate to persons who are or are
expected to be employed or engaged
by, or otherwise connected with, the
applicant;

(c) relate to –

(i) criminal records;

(ii) proceedings in any court or
tribunal;

      (iii) proceedings of a body exercising functions in relation to a trade or profession;

      (iv) financial circumstances;

      (v) management structure;

      (vi) actual or proposed connections or arrangements with other persons;

      (vii) qualifications;

      (viii) actual or proposed arrangements for training;

      (ix) arrangements for accounting;

      (x) practice or proposed practice in relation to the provision of information about fees;

      (xi) arrangements or proposed arrangements for holding clients' money;

      (xii) arrangements or proposed arrangements for insurance.

6   Regulations may –

    (a) provide for authorisation to be on specified terms or subject to compliance with specified conditions;

    (b) permit the Regulator to grant authorisation on terms or subject to conditions;

    (c) permit the Regulator to grant an application for authorisation only to a specified extent or only in relation to specified matters, cases or circumstances.

7   Regulations may –

    (a) enable the Regulator to charge –

      (i) fees in connection with applications for, or the grant of, authorisation;

      (ii) periodic fees for authorised persons;

    (b) specify the consequences of failure to pay fees;

    (c) permit the charging of different fees for different cases or circumstances (which may, in particular, be defined wholly or partly by reference to turnover or other criteria relating to an authorised person's business);

(d) permit the waiver, reduction or repayment of fees in specified circumstances;

(e) provide for the amount of fees to be prescribed or controlled by the Secretary of State;

(f) make provision for the manner in which fees are to be accounted for;

(g) make provision for the application of income from fees (which may, in respect of a time when the Secretary of State is exercising functions of the Regulator under section 5(9) or (10), include provision permitting or requiring payment into the Consolidated Fund).

Conduct of authorised persons

8 (1) Regulations shall require the Regulator to prescribe rules for the professional conduct of authorised persons.

(2) Regulations under sub-paragraph (1) shall include provision –

(a) about the manner in which rules are to be prepared and published (which may, in particular, include provision requiring –

(i) consultation;

(ii) the submission of a draft to the Secretary of State for approval);

(b) about the consequences of failure to comply with the rules (which may, in particular, include –

(i) provision for rules to be treated as conditions of authorisations;

(ii) provision enabling the Regulator to impose conditions on, suspend or cancel authorisations).

9 (1) Regulations shall enable the Regulator to
        issue one or more codes of practice about
        the professional conduct of authorised
        persons.

   (2) Regulations under sub-paragraph (1)
        shall include provision –

        (a) about the manner in which a code is
             to be prepared and published (which
             may, in particular, include provision
             requiring –

             (i)   consultation;

             (ii) the submission of a draft to the
                   Secretary of State for approval);

        (b) about the consequences of failure to
             comply with a code (which may, in
             particular –)

             (i)   provide for compliance with a
                   code to be treated as a condi-
                   tion of authorisations.

             (ii) enable the Regulator to impose
                   conditions on, suspend or can-
                   cel authorisations).

10 (1) Regulations shall provide for the
        Regulator to investigate complains
        about the professional conduct of an
        authorised person.

   (2) Regulations under sub-paragraph (1)
        shall enable the Regulator to –

        (a) impose conditions on a person's
             authorisation;

        (b) suspend a person's authorisation;

        (c) cancel a person's authorisation.

11 (1) Regulations may require, or permit the
        Regulator to require, an authorised per-
        son to take out a policy of professional
        indemnity insurance in respect of his
        actions in the course of providing or pur-
        porting to provide regulated claims
        management services.

   (2) Regulations under sub-paragraph (1)
        may, in particular –

        (a) make provision about the level or
             nature of insurance cover to be pro-
             vided by the policy;

(b) include provision about failure to comply (which may, in particular, provide for compliance to be treated as a condition of authorisations or enable the Regulator to impose conditions on, suspend or cancel authorisations).

12 (1) Regulations may require the Regulator to establish a scheme to compensate a client of an authorised person where –

(a) money is paid to the authorised person in complete or partial satisfication of the client's claim, and

(b) the client is unable to obtain all or part of the money because the authorised person becomes insolvent or is otherwise unable or unwilling to pay.

(2) In particular, regulations may make provision –

(a) about the purchase of bonds or other forms of insurance or indemnity;

(b) about the funding of the scheme (which may include the application of part of fees charged in accordance with paragraph 7 and may not include payments, or other financial assistance, by a Minister of the Crown);

(c) about procedure in connection with compensation (including criteria to be applied);

(d) about the amount of compensation.

Enforcement

13 Regulations may permit or require the Regulator to take action of a specified Kind for the purpose of assessing compliance with terms or conditions of authorizations.

14 (1) Regulations may enable the Regulator, for the purpose of investigating a complaint about the activities of an authorised person or for the purpose of assessing compliance with terms and con-

ditions of an authorisaton, to require the
provision of information or documents.

(2) The Regulations may provide that on
an application by the Regulator a judge
of the High Court, Circuit judge or justice of the peace may issue a warrant
authorising the Regulator to enter and
search premises on which a person
conducts or is alleged to conduct regulated claims management business, for
the purpose of –

   (a) investigating a complaint about the
      activities of an authorised person, or

   (b) assessing compliance with terms
      and conditions of an authorisation.

(3) Regulations may enable the Regulator
to take copies of written or electronic
records found on a search by virtue of
sub-paragraph (2) for a purpose specified in that subsection.

(4) Regulations may enable the Regulator
to impose conditions on, suspend or
cancel a person's authorisation if –

   (a) a requirement imposed by virtue of
      sub-paragraph (1) is not complied
      with, or

   (b) an attempt to exercise a power by
      virtue (of sub-paragraph (2) or (3) is)
      obstructed.

(5) In this paragraph, a reference to the
Regulator includes a reference to a person authorised by him in writing.

(6) Regulations shall –

   (a) specify matters of which a judge or
      justice of the peace must be satis-
      fied, or to which he must have
      regard, before issuing a warrant
      under sub-paragraph (2),

   (b) regulate the exercise of a power
      under or by virtue of sub-paragraph
      (1), (2) or (3) (whether by restricting
      the circumstances in which a
      power may be exercised, by speci-
      fying conditions to be complied

with in the exercise of a power, or otherwise).

15   Regulations may make provision about the exercise by the Regulator of a power under section 8.

t. **EXPLANATORY NOTES**

The notes are designed to aid a reader in understanding an Act of Parliament. They are not part of the Act and have not been approved by Parliament. See Chapter 7 above.

EXPLANATORY NOTES

INTRODUCTION

t.

1.   These explanatory notes relate to the Compensation Act 2006 which received Royal Assent on 25 July 2006. They have been prepared by the Department for Constitutional Affairs in order to assist the reader in understanding the Act. They do not form part of the Act and have not been endorsed by Parliament.

2.   The notes need to be read in conjunction with the Act. They are not, and are not meant to be, a comprehensive description of the Act. So where a section or part of a section does not seem to require any explanation or comment, none is given.

OVERVIEW

3.   The Compensation Act contains provisions in relation to the law on negligence and breach of statutory duty, damages for mesothelioma, and the regulation of claims management services.

4.   The explanatory notes are divided into parts reflecting the structure of the Act. In relation to each Part, there is a summary and background section. Commentary on particular sections is then set out in number order, with the commentary on the various schedules included with the section to which they relate.

5.   The Act is divided into 3 parts:

Part 1: Standard of Care

▶ Part 1 contains provisions relating to the law of negligence, breach of statutory duty and damages for mesothelioma.

Part 2: Claims Management Services

▶ Part 2 contains provisions relating to the regulation of Claims Management Services.

Part 3: General

▶ Part 3 contains technical provisions including provisions about commencement and extent.

PART 1: STANDARD OF CARE SUMMARY

6. Part 1 of the Act contains provisions relating to the law on negligence, breach of statutory duty and damages for mesothelioma.

BACKGROUND

Negligence and Breach of Statutory Duty

7. The purpose of this provision is to address what was suggested by the Better Regulation Task Force (BRTF) report of May 2004 (*Better Routes to Redress*) to be a common misperception, that can lead to a disproportionate fear of litigation and consequent risk-averse behaviour.

8. Under the current law, for a claim in negligence or for breach of a statutory duty involving a standard of care to succeed there must be a duty of care owed by the defendant to the claimant; a breach of that duty by the defendant; and loss or injury suffered by the claimant which is causally connected with the breach. Section 1 concerns a particular aspect of the current law, relating to the second component: whether there is a breach of the duty of care.

9. The question whether there has been a breach of the duty of care involves two elements: how much care is required to be taken (the standard of care) and whether that care has been taken. The ordinary standard of care is "reasonable care"; and the question whether or not that standard has been met – whether reasonable care has been taken – is a question of fact for the court to decide, having regard to all the

circumstances of the case. What amounts to reasonable care in any particular case will vary according to the circumstances. In some cases, what would be required to prevent injury of the kind suffered may be such that to demand it of the defendant would be to demand more than is reasonable.

10.   This provision is intended to contribute to improving awareness of this aspect of the law; providing reassurance to the people and organisations who are concerned about possible litigation; and to ensuring that normal activities are not prevented because of the fear of litigation and excessively risk-averse behaviour.

11.   This provision is not concerned with and does not alter the standard of care, nor the circumstances in which a duty to take that care will be owed. It is solely concerned with the court's assessment of what constitutes reasonable care in the case before it. It only affects statutory duties which involve a standard of care, such as those owed under the Occupiers' Liability Acts of 1957 and 1984. It does not extend to other forms of statutory duty, such as cases where there is an absolute statutory duty involving strict liability in the event of failure; cases which concern what is reasonable in a context other than carelessness; or cases where infringement of a right is actionable as a breach of statutory duty which does not depend on carelessness.

12.   Part 1 also contains a provision to the effect that in claims in negligence or breach of statutory duty, an apology, offer of treatment or other redress shall not of itself amount to an admission of liability.

Damages for Mesothclioma

13   In the 2002 case of *Fairchild v Glenhaven Funeral Services Ltd and others* [2002] UKHL 22, the House of Lords decided that a person who had contracted mesothelioma after wrongful exposure to asbestos at different times by more than one negligent

person could sue any of them, notwith-standing that he could not prove which exposure had actually caused the disease – because all had materially contributed to the risk of him contracting the disease. *Fairchild* did not resolve whether liability should be joint and several, although it was presumed by the parties that this would be the rule and this was the approach taken in practice. However, in *Barker v Corus UK Ltd (and conjoined cases)* [2006] UKHL 20, the House of Lords decided that the damages were instead to be apportioned among those responsible for the wrongful expo-sure according to their relative degree of contribution to the chance of the person contracting the disease.

14. That decision did not impose a limit on the damages which could be recovered from those responsible for the exposure to asbestos. But it did mean that the risk of any of them being insolvent and unable to pay the appropriate share would fall on the claimant, and that in practice the claimant would have to trace all relevant defen-dants, as far as this was possible, before liability could be apportioned and full compensation paid, or alternatively to issue multiple claims to recover damages on a piecemeal basis. The practical effects of this decision (which their Lordships were not asked to consider) were that claims could take much longer to be con-cluded, and would be much more difficult and time-consuming for claimants in cir-cumstances where they and their families are already under considerable pain and stress, The Act reverses the effects of the *Barker* judgment to enable claimants, or their estate or dependants, to recover full compensation from any liable person. It will then be open to the person who has paid the compensation to seek a constrib-ution from other negligent persons.

15. The Act also confers a power for HM Treasury to make provisions that would facilitate the speeding up of payment of claims to mesothelioma victims. These provisions would enable responsible persons to claim money back from the Financial Services Compensation Scheme in specified circumstances (thai is, in circumstances in which previously only the claimant would have had such a right), when another responsible person and their insurer are both insolvent and thus unable to pay their own share of compensation payments.

COMMENTARY ON SECTIONS: PART 1

Provisions relating to the law of negligence and breach of statutory duty

Section 1: Considering a claim in negligence or breach of statutory duty

16. Section 1 provides that in considering a claim in negligence or breach of statutory duty, a court may, in determining whether the defendant should have taken particular steps to meet a standard of care (whether by taking precautions or otherwise), have regard to whether a requirement to take those steps might prevent an activity which is desirable from taking place (either at all, to a particular extent, or in a particular way), or might discourage persons from undertaking functions in connection with the activity.

17. This provision reflects the existing law and approach of the courts as expressed in recent judgements of the higher courts.

Section 2: Apologies, offers of treatment or other redress

18. Section 2 provides that an apology, an offer of treatment or other redress shall

not of itself amount to an admission of negligence or breach of statutory duty. This provision is intended to reflect the existing law.

Section 3: Mesothelioma: Damages

19. Section 3 contains provisions establishing joint and several liability in cases where a person has contracted mesothelioma as a result of being negligently exposed to asbestos.

20. Subsection (1) sets out the conditions that must be satisfied before the substantive provisions of the section will apply. The conditions are that someone contracts mesothelioma from exposure to asbestos, that they were exposed to asbestos as a result of negligence by a person (defined as the 'responsible person') and that it is not possible to prove whose negligent act caused them to become ill. Paragraph (d) indicates that the final condition is that the responsible person must be liable in tort.

21. Subsection (2) provides that where the conditions in subsection (1) are met, the responsible person is liable for all of the damage caused by the mesothelioma. The provision establishes that it makes no difference whether or not someone else also could have caused the disease; whether the person could have contracted the disease from environmental exposure; or whether the responsible person would not be liable in tort for some of the periods of exposure. Paragraph (b) indicates that, if there is more than one responsible person, the liability is joint and several. That means that the victim (or any dependants if the victim is dead) may proceed against any of the responsible persons and that any person proceeded against is responsible for paying the full amount of compensation, and for recovering contributions from the others.

22. Subsection (3) confirms that contributions from other responsible persons may

subsequently be sought by the responsible person who has paid the compensation (or by any who have jointly done so). The subsection also makes clear that if the victim is found to have negligently exposed himself to asbestos then the damages may be reduced accordingly under the principle of contributory negligence (as is currently the case).

23. Subsection (4) provides that a court shall, when deciding the level of contributions, have regard to the relative lengths of exposure, unless the responsible persons agree to approach the apportionment differently or the court thinks another approach is more appropriate. This will assist parties in agreeing the basis on which contributions are to be made without going to court.

24. Subsection (5) makes it clear that the provision covers failure to protect someone from exposure to asbestos.

25. Subsection (6) makes provision in relation to the application of the section in Scotland.

26. Subsections (7) to (11) confer power on Her Majesty's Treasury to make regulations about the provision of compensation to a responsible person or an insurer of a responsible person in specified circumstances. These provisions would enable responsible persons to claim money back from the Financial Services Compensation Scheme when a liable employer and insurer are both insolvent. The power includes the ability to deal with situations arising prior to the establishment of the Financial Services Compensation Scheme that were settled under the Policyholders Protection Act 1975, The provisions would only come into effect once Treasury has laid the necessary regulations and the FSA has made the relevant rules. However, the power provides that rules could permit the liable party to claim contributions in respect of claims dealt with from the date of Royal Assent.

NOTE

The Explanatory Notes to the Compensation Act 2006 continue with commentaries on Parts 2 and 3 and give information on the Parliamentary stages of the legislation. To view this material go to www.opsi.gov.uk/acts.htm

Index